JOHN LYDGATE

POETS OF THE LATER MIDDLE AGES

General Editors

John Norton-Smith
Roger Fowler

Frontispiece Lydgate (third from left) with pilgrims leaving Canterbury (see p. 47): Prologue to *The Siege of Thebes*.

(see p. 47)

British Museum MS. Royal *18.D.ii.*

John Lydgate

DEREK PEARSALL

*Senior Lecturer in English
in the University of York*

THE UNIVERSITY PRESS OF VIRGINIA

CHARLOTTESVILLE

The University Press of Virginia
Copyright © 1970 D. Pearsall

First Published 1970

Standard Book Number: 8139-0293-2
Library of Congress Catalog Card Number: 70-103411

Printed in Great Britain

CONTENTS

310668

LIST OF ILLUSTRATIONS

GENERAL PREFACE

The Medieval Authors Series is intended (without dilution of scholarly high standards) to fulfil two aims: first, to produce a detailed critical evaluation of the literary achievements of the most important English and Scots authors of the later Middle Ages; second, to contribute towards a generous and systematic account of the literature of the 'high' and 'late' Middle Ages—supplementing the existing and (in some cases) continuing work of the Early English Text Society, the Scottish Text Society, the Clarendon Medieval and Tudor Series, Nelson's Medieval and Renaissance Library, and The Oxford History of English Literature.

The concentration on 'authors' is a deliberate attempt to remind a rapidly growing criticism of the worth of an humane medievalism—of the continuity and originality of an individual, personal contribution to our literature, of the extent to which the individuality of renaissance authors is anticipated and largely made possible by that of Middle English and Middle Scots writers. Most of the volumes in the series will appear over the decade 1969–79. The order of appearance does not represent an historical chronology or grouping.

University of East Anglia   ROGER FOWLER
University of Reading   JOHN NORTON-SMITH

AUTHOR'S NOTE

I should like to thank John Norton-Smith and the Clarendon Press, publishers of his edition of selections from Lydgate, for permission to quote from his texts; and Dr. Beryl Smalley and Sir Basil Blackwell for permission to quote at length from Dr. Smalley's *English Friars and Antiquity*. The general editors of the present series read the typescript of this book in its final stages, and made many useful suggestions. I should like to acknowledge help on particular points from Dr. Peter Newton, Mellon Lecturer in British Medieval Art at the University of York; Bernard Barr, librarian at York Minster; Mr. Neil Ker, of Oxford; and Anthony Edwards, whose work on the bibliography of Lydgate has proved invaluable. Finally, I should like to record my debt to Elizabeth Salter, for many helpful conversations; and to Geoffrey Shepherd and Derek Brewer, my earlier teachers, who first introduced me to the study of medieval literature. I hope they will approve the consequences.

York   D.P.

CHAPTER ONE

John Lydgate: The Critical Approach

John Lydgate achieved an extraordinary pre-eminence in his own day. His origins were comparatively humble, and his life as a monk may seem to some an unlikely training-ground for a secular poet, yet by 1412 he was being commissioned by the Prince of Wales, later Henry V, to translate the story of Troy into English. In 1431 Humphrey, duke of Gloucester, commissioned the translation of Boccaccio's *De Casibus Illustrium Virorum* which was completed eight years later as the *Fall of Princes*. These were tasks of magnitude and high seriousness, and were regarded as such by the poet, his patron and his public, and though we may have our reservations about Henry's literary tastes, those of Humphrey are not usually held in question. Among his other noble patrons, Lydgate could count Henry VI, Queen Katherine, the earl of Salisbury, the earl of Warwick and the countess of Shrewsbury. He was, in fact if not in name, official court-poet, and a request for a poem to exalt the pedigree of Henry VI as king of France came to him as naturally as a request for a poem on his coronation. Sumptuous presentation copies of the major works were prepared, many of them splendidly illuminated, and more modest versions found their way into the homes of the gentry, where they were treasured as prize possessions and passed on as bequests and dowries.

This might seem of less significance were it not also true that his works were widely read, universally admired and assiduously imitated. The history of English poetry, and of much Scottish poetry too,[1] in the fifteenth century is as much the record of Lydgate's influence as of Chaucer's.[2] His contemporaries and successors—Benedict Burgh, George Ashby, Osbern Bokenham, John Metham, Henry Bradshaw, Stephen Hawes, as well as the Scots, Dunbar, Douglas and Lyndsay[3]— all acknowledge their debt in a series of fulsome tributes, and his name is linked with those of Gower and Chaucer in a conventional triad of praise. English poetry may have needed such a pantheon, and some of the eulogy seems automatic and conventional, but the persistence of the tradition is remarkable. By some, it is clear, Lydgate was actually considered superior to Chaucer, by Hawes, for instance, who, in his remembrance of English poets at the end of his account of Rhetoric in the *Pastime of Pleasure*, devotes 2 lines to Gower, 19 to Chaucer and 63 to Lydgate.[4] We are told, what is more, that Hawes knew much of Lydgate by heart, and would recite long extracts from his work to Henry VII.[5]

The invention of printing gives us further evidence of the high regard in which Lydgate was held. Caxton printed *Horse, Goose and Sheep* three times, the *Churl and the Bird* twice, and the *Temple of Glass* and the *Life of Our Lady* once each, while Wynkyn de Worde printed the *Temple of Glass* three times, and the *Churl and the Bird*, *Horse, Goose and Sheep*, the *Complaint of the Black Knight* and the *Siege of Thebes* once each. These are not Lydgate's longest poems, but later Pynson undertook the *Troy Book* and two prints of the *Fall of Princes*, as well as shorter poems. In the middle of the sixteenth century, Lydgate seems to have been much in demand: the *Fall* was reprinted in 1554 and 1558, and the *Troy Book* in 1555. The *Siege of Thebes*, of course, because of its 'Canterbury prologue', continued to be printed, as Lydgate's, in the collected editions of Chaucer until 1687. Poets of the sixteenth century (George Cavendish and Alexander Barclay amongst others) were still acknowledging and demonstrating their debt to Lydgate, and a work as popular and influential as the *Mirror for Magistrates* was frankly conceived as a continuation of the *Fall of Princes*. Shakespeare's history-plays, through the *Mirror* and the chronicle-plays, thus bear the imprint of Lydgate's medievalism, as *Troilus and Cressida* does of the *Troy Book*.

Few discordant voices were raised among this chorus of acclaim, though Skelton, in a context of general approbation, has his doubts about Lydgate's style:

> Chaucer, that famus clerke,
> His termes were not darke,
> But plesaunt, easy, and playne;
> No worde he wrote in vayne.
> Also Johnn Lydgate
> Wryteth after an hyer rate;
> It is dyffuse to fynde
> The sentence of his mynde,
> Yet wryteth he in his kynd,

> No man that can amend
> Those maters that he hath pende;
> Yet some men fynde a faute,
> And say he wryteth to haute.[6]

It is interesting, in the light of later censure, that Skelton should single
out for criticism two obvious defects in Lydgate's style—the diffuseness
of his syntax and the ostentation of his vocabulary—and yet still have
room to admire his achievement as a whole. His attitude in the *Garland
of Laurel* is similar. There he meets Gower, Chaucer and Lydgate arm-
in-arm at the end of a procession of famous poets. Each addresses a
tribute to him, Lydgate speaking in a shrewd parody of his own style,
using words like *regraciatory* and *prothonatory*.[7] There might be another
dig later on, when Occupacion has a whole stanza in reply to Skelton's
'Tell me one thing', and the content of the whole stanza is 'Yes?'[8]

But Lydgate's journey down the stream of reputation continued
smooth until the late sixteenth century, when the difficulty of his
language caused him to fall into obscurity. Chaucer suffered a similar
fate: the list of 'hard words' in Speght's collected edition of 1602 sounds
a kind of knell, and classicising commentators of the seventeenth and
eighteenth centuries speak with patronising disdain of the roughness of
his language and versification, parroting the cry of 'Matter, but no art'
or, as one writer puts it, 'solid sense' but 'mouldy words'.[9] Similar
comments had already been made about Lydgate in 1586, as we may
gather from some lines appended on the fly-leaf of a late fifteenth
century manuscript of the *Troy Book*, MS. Rawlinson poet. 144:

> Owld Inglishe bookes, wher they be Ryme, or prose,
> Shew littell artte, and matter suett disclose,
> For Ignorance did knowlege then obscure
> And wilye witts, mad darknes long Indure,
> For proffe, but mark the substance of this book
> In wiche this mownk such paynes hath undertook.[10]

Unlike Chaucer, Lydgate never recovered from this fall into obscurity.
Gray had some kind and thoughtful things to say about him in the
eighteenth century, but Ritson's outburst of dyspeptic anti-clericalism
in his *Bibliographia poetica* of 1802 ('this voluminous, prosaick and
driveling monk') seems to have put paid to the possibility of any cool
and discriminating consideration of Lydgate's work, and in modern
times strings of literary historians have vied with each other to heap

ridicule upon his head. Various salvage operations have been mounted
in recent years, but the discrepancy between Lydgate's general reputation in his own day, and his general reputation now, remains as startling
as ever. The student of literature senses a challenge to his understanding
here, the need to find some explanation of this strange state of affairs
which will not be the product simply of five hundred years of accumulated ignorance.

Certain things should be admitted straightaway. One is that Lydgate
is unusually prolific. Something like 145,000 lines of verse are attributed
to him, twice as much as Shakespeare, three times as much as Chaucer,
and there can be no sense in which this works to his advantage. No one
who wrote so much can be anything but a hack, we may think, and
protect ourselves from what looks like an unrewarding task by simply
dismissing the man and his work as unworthy of our attention. This is
a defensive reaction, and an easy one, offering plentiful opportunity for
witty gibes at the poet's expense. Behind it, however, lie a whole series
of unreasoned assumptions about the nature of poetry. Poetry, it is
assumed, is the distillation of experience, the precious record of moments of heightened perception, moments which can, possibly, be
induced in the act of poetic creation, but which are bound to be rare.
There is only so much heightened perception to go round, and a handful of exquisite lyrics or a slim volume of verse are the best guarantee
that a poet has had some share in it. This fastidious notion of poetry,
which partially accounts for its valetudinarian state now, may be
sharply contrasted with the rude health of the medieval, indeed pre-
Romantic view that poetry is different only in form and style, not in
kind, from other forms of discourse. Poetry must therefore be much
more comprehensively defined for the Middle Ages, and for Lydgate,
whom I shall take in this book to be himself a comprehensive definition
of the Middle Ages. Lydgate's work includes very little that would
nowadays be accommodated in poetic form, perhaps only 'a handful
of lyrics'. For the modern equivalents of other poems, we should have
to look in history-books, encyclopaedias, the Complete Family Doctor,
devotional manuals, books of etiquette, souvenir programmes, collections of maxims. Above all—and this is the significant point—we should
have to look in the novel, the modern 'hold-all'. The immense bulk of
Lydgate's work, therefore, is in itself significant, apart from its physically deterrent quality, only as a mark of changing fashions and attitudes
to poetry.

Having said this, one is of course aware of the limitations of this kind of historical relativism. The historical approach, in this case the attempt to understand a much wider concept of poetry in the fifteenth century, is no more than an approach. It offers an explanation of literature in the light of history, but not as history; and the explanation only serves to prepare the mind for understanding. Lydgate's vast output is a historically explicable phenomenon, but it remains true that, although all of his poems engage our interest (as the ways of a man with words in poetry always command interest), some of them are more interesting than others, not because they are more 'poetic', but because they deal with subjects that are intrinsically more important. That Lydgate should have written a 'Treatise for Laundresses'[11] is a salutary and salubrious reminder of the comprehensiveness of his range in poetry, but to give it more weight than that would be quaint antiquarianism. What one would like to establish is a picture of Lydgate as a highly professional and skilful craftsman in a wide range of related literary arts, capable of turning his hand to an epithalamion as well as an epic, an exposition of the Mass as well as a satire on women's fashions in headgear, working like a mason or a sculptor or a mural-painter, not like a *poeta vates*. For him, poetry is a public art, its existence conditioned and determined by outer needs and pressures, not by inner ones. In this sense, all his poetry is occasional poetry. Writing of a Romantic poet, one would be tempted to create, even if there were no extant chronological evidence, a chronological structure in which each poem was so placed as to illustrate the growth of the poet's mind, or some mythical prototype of it. The pressures would be recognised as inward, a struggle towards self-expression. Problems (such as Byron's) of which self to express, might need more sophisticated handling, but would still tend to be evaluated in terms of the accuracy and intensity of the response to inward pressures. It is not profitable to study a medieval poet like Lydgate in this way—fortunately so, for we lack much of the chronological evidence we should need. There is development in his writing, but it is a development of style, or rather the development of new styles, not of poetic personality. Lydgate's personality is a matter for curiosity only, for it is of the supremest irrelevance to the understanding of his poetry. Every mask he puts on is a well-worn medieval one, and it is well to recognise these masks for what they are, otherwise we may find ourselves interpreting poems like the *Testament* as personal documents. The coherence of his work as a whole is to be found, not in terms of its relation to his inner self or to any concept of the self-realising individual consciousness, but in terms of its relation to the total structure of the medieval world, that is, the world of universally received values, traditions, attitudes, as well as, and more significantly than, the world of 'real life'.

These generalisations about Lydgate are aimed at medieval poetry in general, ill-advisedly, it may seem, in view of the many qualifications one would need to make in connection with Chaucer. Chaucer's personality is obviously interesting to us, and in a significant literary way, not out of mere curiosity. His playing off of real against assumed attitudes constitutes one of his characteristic signatures, and he talks about himself and provokes interest in himself far more than other medieval poets. Chaucer, in fact, as this study will make plain more than once, is not a very representative medieval poet—any more than Shakespeare is a representative Elizabethan dramatist. However, he remains a medieval poet, and the above reservations are over-scrupulous if they suggest any regard for the romantic-biographical interpretation of Chaucer's work, in which his poetry, dated or undated, may be stretched on a Procrustean bed of the 'three periods', and made to fit some fashionable theory as to the growth of realism or the emancipation from rhetoric. So tenacious is the hold of this literary biography that works like the *Clerk's Tale*, for which there is little evidence as to precise date, are assigned, because of their 'non-realistic' qualities, to an early period, thus completing and strengthening the circle of hypotheses.

There is one further point to make about Lydgate's prolific output. I have suggested that this needs understanding as a historical phenomenon, as a mark of the wider scope of poetry in his time, and qualified this suggestion by drawing attention to the fact that some poems will be intrinsically more interesting, by virtue of their subject-matter, than others. It is also true, obviously, that sometimes he will write less well than at others, when his attention and interest is not fully engaged. Every craftsman has his off-days, when his mind is not on his job— perhaps because he did not fancy the job in the first place. The historical approach is not intended to blanket discrimination between the better and the worse, though it should try to ensure that the discrimination is properly based. The bad poems are bad, not because of their subject, but because of what Lydgate does, or fails to do with them. The *Pilgrimage of the Life of Man* stretches to 26,000 lines, but fails because at no time does Lydgate attempt to shape, control or master his material; he merely goes through the motions of versifying in the most mechanical manner possible. Clearing the ground of rubbish like this

will help us to see and examine what is truly representative and intrinsically worthwhile. It is on these poems that judgment must be based.
The first task is to understand what Lydgate is trying to do, and for
this every discipline, every kind of historical information, is relevant.
Understanding can then inform judgment on the good and the less
good.

Two further charges against Lydgate, apart from that of having
written so much, can be considered in their wider implications in order
to establish this historical reorientation. They are the two most deadly
weapons in the critical armoury—that he is prolix, and that he is dull.
Prolixity is certainly a characteristic feature of Lydgate's style. No poet
can mark time with such profuse demonstrations of energy, can so
readily make twenty words do the work of one. Sometimes it is difficult
to slow down the processes of the mind to the breathless snail's pace of
his verse. Yet it would be fair to recognise that prolixity (sometimes
due to diffuseness of syntax) is deliberately cultivated by Lydgate.
Translating the Prologue to the *Fall of Princes*, he says, following
Laurent de Premierfait:

> For a story which is nat pleynli told,
> But constreynyd undir woordes fewe
> For lak of trouthe, wher thei be newe or old,
> Men bi report kan nat the mater shewe;
> These ookis grete be nat doun ihewe
> First at a stroke, but bi long processe,
> Nor longe stories a woord may not expresse.[12]

Of course, like most of Lydgate's comments on style and the art of
poetry, this is a formula, and one could set beside it numerous equally
stereotyped formulae in which he asserts that his main design is to
'eschewe prolixite'.[13] Both attitudes may be traced back to the rhetoricians of the twelfth century, who set side by side their recommendations
for 'amplification' and 'abbreviation'.[14] But in them, as in Lydgate,
abbreviation is of little more than formal interest, and is totally
swamped in amplification, the governing principle in medieval stylis-
tics. In academic theory, a poem essentially provides a theme for
amplification, and the prize goes to the man who can go on saying the
same thing longest without repeating himself—*varius sit et tamen idem*.[15]
Academic theory is one thing, of course, and poetic practice is another.
Obviously poems leap the confines of the rhetorical exercise, but the

school-training in amplification which Lydgate and every other educated medieval poet would have received must have exerted a powerful and lasting influence on their style. It would not be unprofitable,
for instance, to make a study of Chaucer's *Troilus* as an *amplificatio* of
Boccaccio's *Filostrato*, paying particular attention to the use of devices
such as exclamation, apostrophe and description, all listed by Geoffrey
among the forms of amplification. In these and other ways Chaucer
gives the story its rich and full-bodied quality, its wholeness or *inte-
gritas*.[16] Amplification is still the basis of sixteenth century poetic, under
the name of *copie* or copiousness,[17] and Shakespeare, though he mocks
copie in Touchstone,[18] still uses its machinery to construct long speeches.

In Lydgate, we may assume, rhetorical precept coincided happily
with a natural tendency to prolixity, and no doubt reinforced it. It is
not difficult to recognise his natural verbosity in this stanza:

> The rounde dropis of the smothe reyn,
> Which that discende and falle from aloffte
> On stonys harde, at eye as it is seyn,
> Perceth ther hardnesse with ther fallyng offte,
> Al-be in touchyng, water is but soffte;
> The percyng causid be force nor puissaunce
> But of fallyng be long contynuaunce.   (*Fall*, II,106–12)

But we must recognise, too, that Lydgate is consciously writing according to accepted canons of taste, and that his deliberate unfolding of
'Constant dripping wears away a stone' is as skilful in its own way as
the aphorism itself in another way. And though Lydgate is by nature
long-winded, he knows when this kind of elaborate tautology is not
appropriate, and can write in a comparatively abbreviated, aphoristic
style, as in the series of short moralistic poems with gnomic refrains,[19]
or in the fable of the *Churl and the Bird*. Lydgate's expansiveness clearly
forms part of a deliberate poetic style.

It looks perverse to us, though, and again, if we are not to assume
some gigantic aberration on the part of the Middle Ages, it is necessary
to reshape our minds to the major change of taste which has taken
place in attitudes to poetry. Poetry is now admired for its economy of
expression, its compression, compactness and intensity. Every line must
be packed with significant imagery, every rift loaded with ore. Eliot's
dedication of (*The Waste Land* to Ezra Pound, *il miglior fabbro*, records
his debt to the better craftsman, whose skill enabled him to unburden
the poem of the conventional paraphernalia of linguistic communication,

and to boil it down to its essence. Syntax itself is something of a handicap, in this view of poetry. Small wonder, then, that medieval poetry, Chaucer included, is found to be diffuse,[20] and that the search for fine lines is unrewarding. Any that one prises out of Chaucer— 'Singest with vois memorial in the shade'[21]—are fortuitous and un-characteristic, and Eleanor Hammond's attempt at a *florilegium* of fine lines in Lydgate[22] is a strange lapse of understanding and taste in a great scholar. Medieval poetry characteristically produces its effects over longer stretches, the stanza or the verse-paragraph, and the compara-tively free metrical systems of alliterative verse, even Chaucer's verse, are designed to operate over longer passages, not in single lines. Associated with this tendency, are a relaxed kind of syntax and a wide use of free-running paratactic constructions which make translation of medieval verse into modern logical units so difficult.

All these features, of course, have to do with something else, as well as being the general consequences of a particular poetic theory. They are the features of verse composed for oral delivery. Amplification, tautology, diffuseness of sense and looseness of syntax, are not only acceptable but desirable to the listening audience, which has no oppor-tunity to linger over close-packed lines, and which will welcome as well as recognise the familiar phrase.[23] Every medieval poet has a store of tags and formulae which he will use to establish this pattern of communication. Some have nothing else, perhaps, while others, like Chaucer, have such leisured control over the medium that they can afford to uncoil the formulae into new and ambiguous contexts. But for the most part the stereotyped nature of medieval poetic expression is better referred to conditions of delivery than to lack of 'originality', in its prevailing form a largely modern concept. It is not necessary to suggest that Lydgate's poems were habitually read aloud to a listening audience, though there is evidence in plenty in the fifteenth century for the persistence of this method of publication, alongside even more evi-dence for the growth of the habit of private reading.[24] The argument need only assume that the stylistic traditions of orally delivered verse were more tenacious than the conditions which produced them.

The revolution in reading habits produced by the invention of print-ing is one clue to the shift in attitude we have been discussing, and to the growth of a non-rhetorical poetic which finds Lydgate's prolixity excessively burdensome. I talked a moment ago of the difficulty of accommodating the mind to the leisurely processes of Lydgate's verse, but the mind referred to was of course an exceptional mind, the modern mind, trained to incredibly specialised kinds of short-cutting and short-circuiting of perception by generations of print-culture.[25] It may seem ridiculous to suggest that there might be value in training the mind to move more slowly, but a flexible attitude to the possibility is probably better than the assumption that things have never been better. Intensity is one standard of judgment for poetry, but not the only one.

Comparisons of medieval with modern poetic theory can help us with some of our problems of recovery, by illustrating to us the limited and relative application of such theories, and the inadequacy of assuming that any one of them is right, absolutely. Sometimes, though, the comparisons reveal such totally opposed points of view that one seems to be comparing not different manifestations of the same thing but different things. As has been said, poetry occupied the central literary position in the Middle Ages; it could be regarded as the highest form of discourse, but it existed also as the workaday form, the tool to which the professional craftsman naturally stretched his hand for a story, a treatise, a political pamphlet. Literary prose remained the specialised medium, though one sees its range being extended in the later fifteenth century, in the work of Malory, and Caxton's ambitious translations. The situation was already changing, and it is now changed completely. Poetry is now highly specialised, the property of an élite; the central literary position is occupied by the novel. The growth of the novel to accommodate virtually every kind of literary experience provides the major literary development of the last two centuries. Many of these kinds of experience have been taken over from poetry—historical and didactic interests, for instance—and it might be said therefore that we should be prepared to transfer to earlier poetry some of the appetites now satisfied by the novel, and in particular appetite itself. Novels are so much the staple of our literary diet that we hardly notice we are reading them, and we certainly do not find it necessary as we begin to read always to summon our faculties for a major literary experience. Some novels are more important than others, of course, but so are some medieval poems. The point is that the natural literary element in which we move is the novel, whereas in the fifteenth century it was verse. Lydgate's diffuseness and prolixity should therefore be referred, for a standard of comparison, to the diffuseness and prolixity of eighteenth and nineteenth century prose fiction, of Richardson, Scott, Dickens and Thackeray. Voluminousness is their natural condition, and to ask for them to be briefer would be to ask for them not to be. There is, admittedly, an exacting modern taste which makes precisely this demand, and which is quite prepared to leave *Clarissa* unread for the sake of it, but the limiting nature of this taste is so apparent that one would be quite content to allow Lydgate to profit by the analogy, and leave it at that.

The charge of dullness is more difficult to deal with, because it is mainly the product of a response, or of a failure of response, not of objective analysis. It can also cover many things, some of which can be historically argued, others of which are indefensible. The *Churl and the Bird* has been referred to as an example of Lydgate's more abbreviated style, but the opening seems designed to deter the casual reader:

> Problemys, liknessis and figures
> Which previd been fructuous of sentence,
> And han auctoritees groundid on scriptures
> Bi resemblaunces of notable apparence,
> With moralites concludyng in prudence. . . .

The quotation looks unfinished, but to continue would not help, for the sentence never reaches its verb. It is a conscientious opening, but it reveals the unselectivity of Lydgate's mind, the reluctance to leave anything out, which often causes his sentences to run into the sands. The lack of selection, combined with the relentless insistence and the essentially uncurious nature of Lydgate's mind, are the ingredients of dullness here. But beginnings are Lydgate's special problem; there are so many possible things to say, the furniture of his mind is so cluttered before the removal has begun, that neither he nor the reader can force any interest, or indeed any sense out of the material. What we see is the machinery working very badly, on the verge of breakdown, and the sight is not uncommon in Lydgate.

However, even working at the height of his powers, Lydgate is liable to incur this charge of dullness, not because he is working badly but because he is doing things that we may regard as intrinsically boring. He is, above all, incurably didactic. The stories of Troy and Thebes are for him not vehicles for the display of passion and human tragedy but storehouses of moral exempla. His whole theory of poetry is based on the idea that poets should teach by offering examples of behaviour:

> Their cheeff labour is vicis to repreve
> With a maner covert symylitude.   (*Fall*, III,3830–1)

In this, as in everything else, Lydgate was in perfect accord with the tastes of his age. If we are to judge by the marginal comments and signs added in manuscripts, what his readers valued above all in his long poems were the passages of moralising, passages which to modern taste are gratuitous and irrelevant.[26] We may think that the *Fall of Princes* carries already a heavy enough burden of moralisation, but to the fifteenth century this was the work's very reason for existence. Many MSS. contain extracts from the *Fall* in which the moralising envoys are written out as separate poems, as if it were the historical and human and dramatic interest that fifteenth century readers found to be otiose.[27] The first parts of the *Fall* to be printed were a series of such extracts, put out by Wynkyn de Worde under the title of 'Proverbs of Lydgate'.[28] The appetite for moral instruction seems to have been insatiable. Quotation from the classics, for instance, is most often of *auctoritees*, scraps of moral or practical wisdom culled from *florilegia*, not of 'fine lines'.[29] Lydgate's own praise of Chaucer clearly singles out his sententiousness as the basis of his memorableness as a poet. In the Prologue to the *Thebes* he speaks with admiration of his 'many proverbe divers and unkouth' (51), and when he has occasion to speak of specific Canterbury Tales, in the Prologue to the *Fall of Princes*, it is, unbeliev- ably, to the *Clerk's Tale*, the *Monk's Tale* and the *Melibeus* that he refers (337–50). A twentieth-century critic like Kittredge would regard the *Melibeus* as a joke, and the *Monk's Tale* as little better, but, think what we like of the *Melibeus*, there is no doubt that Kittredge is wrong about it, wrong in thinking that a work of such obvious dullness needs to be explained away as part of a dramatic joke on the part of Chaucer the pilgrim. Chaucer, on the contrary, is writing, in the *Melibeus* and in the tales of the Clerk and the Monk, to a perfectly serious and straight- forward taste. For once, he is being typical of the Middle Ages, and this is where Lydgate responds to him. It was where the fifteenth and sixteenth centuries responded to him, too. The second (1602) edition of Thomas Speght's collected Chaucer has a title page which draws attention to its more sophisticated apparatus, one feature of which ('Sentences and Proverbs noted') is the marginal indication of memor- able lines by means of a hand with a pointing finger. A modern reader doing this in the Prologue to the *Canterbury Tales* would tend to under- line perhaps some of Chaucer's more pithy ironies, like the Prioress's 'gretteste ooth', or some particularly significant bit of descriptive detail, like the Pardoner's voice 'as smal as hath a goot'. But in 1602 the taste was still for the wholesomely didactic, and these are the sort of lines signalled in the Prologue:

> And shame it is, if a prest take keep,
> A shiten shepherde and a clene sheep.
> Wel oghte a preest ensample for to yive,
> By his clennesse, how that his sheep sholde lyve.[30]

Sometimes it is less the content of the 'sentence' that is picked out for attention than the very formality of its introduction — 'For this ye knowen al so wel as I' or 'Eek Plato seith, whoso that kan hym rede'. The taste for doctrine is thus strengthened by the elevation of the *sententia* in medieval rhetoric as a recognised ornament of style.

The modern reader, however, whilst admitting the existence of this taste for 'sentence', may still consider it an unsophisticated taste. He may recall his early contacts with literature, and the commonplace-books that he filled, like Mary Bennet in *Pride and Prejudice*, with laboriously copied extracts, some of them purple passages and fine lines, but most of them aphoristic or formally identifiable statements of general moral truths. Such experiences perhaps reflect an unsophisti-cated attitude to literature in that they suggest that that is all there is to it, but they reflect also a very basic and enduring assumption, namely, that literature exists to endorse the values of the society in which it is produced, and provides not merely pleasure and profit but also reassur-ance, namely that the values according to which we try to live are the best available. Romantic and post-Romantic literature of revolt and disturbance is opposed to these attitudes, but does not deny that they are powerful. Literature, in its traditional social role, is bound to em-body statements of general moral truth, and nowhere would Mary Bennet have reaped a richer harvest than in Shakespeare. In Shakes-peare, such statements have always a dramatic context and therefore an extra layer of significance, but they have in the first place their own significance as part of his total meaning. Polonius's advice to Laertes is rich in 'character' but it is not nonsense.

It would be possible to speculate further on other changes of taste that have made us see Lydgate as 'dull', but perhaps enough has been said to make it at least arguable that dullness is a state of mind more than anything. Our ambition should be to create in ourselves a state of mind in which we find it possible to see the literature as it appealed to

its author and its audience, to regard the *Cursor Mundi*, for instance, as
a lively, even racy rewriting of Biblical history. After all, this has been
the historical process in the rediscovery of Chaucer. It is less than fifty
years ago that a critic was writing of the *Troilus*: 'There is no other of
the world's long poems not dependent on temporary reference that is
so completely wearisome.'[31] A statement like this looks absurd now,
and should be a warning of the inadequacy of critical judgment unin-
formed by historical understanding, for it is only the emancipation of
the poem from modern expectations that has revealed it as it really is.

It will be apparent by now that it is no part of the argument of this
book to suggest that Lydgate is an exciting writer. There are no thrills
of recognition, no stabs of pathos or passionate self-identification, but
rather good sense in its own sober garb, and the modest pleasures of
conventional expectations conventionally fulfilled. It has not been
denied that Lydgate is prolific, prolix and dull, but it has been argued
that such judgments need such a degree of historical qualification that
they are ultimately useless as judgments, and that paying too much
attention to them will obscure Lydgate's real virtues from us. Lydgate
is worthy of our attention because he is so useful to us, because he is so
perfectly representative of the Middle Ages. In him we can see, at great
length, and in slow motion, the medieval mind at its characteristic
work. To understand in precise detail the mechanics of a bird's flight,
biologists used film slowed down to record, frame by frame, the exact
process at each stage. Lydgate provides us with something like the same
sort of opportunity to understand the precise configurations and convolutions of a type of mind and of an intellectual and artistic tradition.
To see the bird in flight, we can look again at Chaucer. Reading Lydgate
is in fact the best possible introduction to Chaucer, for here is the soil
from which Chaucer grew, and the soil to which he returned. Lydgate
profited in a multitude of ways from Chaucer's example, but nevertheless in all his writing he reasserts medieval traditions and habits of
mind against Chaucer's free-ranging innovations. He throws into sharp
relief not only Chaucer's greatness but also his differentness.

It is for these reasons that one would question the effectiveness of the
approach made in the two existing book-length studies of Lydgate,
those of Schirmer and Renoir.[32] The two studies differ in scope and
method. Schirmer aims to give a definitive, full-length picture of
Lydgate against a detailed background of his times, to deal with every
aspect of his career and to mention and describe every poem. Renoir's

method is more general and discursive, and he groups his material around a series of themes. But both make the same sort of case for Lydgate, that he is interesting because he reveals new and important directions in English literary tradition, towards a more distinct political consciousness, for instance, and above all, towards humanism. It would not be good policy to deny any claims that can be made on Lydgate's behalf, but it must be said that there is poor basis for these claims. Lydgate has a good many things to say about politics, about kingship, government, war and peace, but they are the platitudes of his age, of the Middle Ages, in fact, no more than was being said by a dozen anonymous pamphleteers of the time,[33] and a good deal less apt and perceptive than the political comments being made by genuinely original minor writers like George Ashby or the author of the *Libel of English Policy*.[34] As for his 'humanism', it is true that he does sometimes mention classical deities without disapproval, and that he does show some knowledge of classical writers. But this can hardly be called 'humanism', except in a sense of the term which destroys its reference and its usefulness, for there is nothing that is not typically medieval. His knowledge of classical writers is in fact a good deal narrower than it looks. He has read Ovid, and has a smattering of Virgil and Cicero, but the rest are mere names, known to him at second-hand from his immediate source-text, from anthologies or from Latin grammars.[35] It is true also that his attitude to antiquity is more generous in the *Fall of Princes* than in the *Troy Book*, but this is not a sign of 'development' in Lydgate, but a reflection of the difference between Boccaccio and Guido della Colonna. And even here it is obvious that Lydgate is happier with Guido, whose tastes and attitudes he reproduces with emphatic approval, than with Boccaccio, whose outspokenness on history and politics he tends to tone down. Looking for signs of humanism in Lydgate is an unrewarding task, because the whole direction of his mind is medieval. One of the remarkable things about fifteenth-century literary tradition, in fact, is its resistance to the new humanism, which in the end had to make its way into England through writers in Latin, not in English.

The attempt to give Lydgate a spurious respectability by associating him with a forward-looking movement, with something that we regard as new and desirable in literature, is as unhistorical and misinformed as the other attitudes we have been discussing. It is of a piece with Kittredge's well-intentioned attempt to rehabilitate the *Troilus* by calling it 'the first novel, in the modern sense, that ever was written . . .

an elaborate psychological novel'.[36] Psychological novels may have been all the rage when Kittredge wrote, and perhaps some of their fashionable prestige would rub off on this old poem, but even if it was good propaganda, it was bad criticism. There are no terms on which Lydgate can, in the first place, be understood, but his own terms.

Sometimes the task of undermining the assumptions on which judgment of Lydgate has been based seems a heavy one. Much of our knowledge, for instance, of fifteenth-century life and literature, its tastes and interests, its books, its culture and sub-culture, is derived from the writings of H. S. Bennett. Yet in his account of Lydgate in the standard *Oxford History of English Literature*,[37] his penetrating knowledge of the age is not permitted to inform critical judgment. Indeed, any association between the two seems to be regarded as improper, and there is an implicit but systematic distinction between the interests of the 'student of literary history' and those of the 'lover of poetry'.[38] But it is difficult to see how the two can be divorced, how the lover of poetry can know what he is supposed to love until he understands what it is, unless he relies upon the mindless spine-chilling and skin-thrilling that Housman speaks of. Poetry cannot afford to have mind and understanding laid to sleep.

Again, Bennett speaks disapprovingly of fifteenth-century non-popular poetry as lacking 'a lively contact with life' (p. 124). Lydgate, being a monk, was worse off than anyone: 'Life passed him by while he spent endless hours in the scriptorium turning out verses on very many subjects' (p. 138). This represents, however, a limited view of life in the fifteenth-century monastery, and an even more limited view of poetry. In the first place, it would be a great mistake, as we shall see, to think of monasteries like Bury as being cut off from 'real life', even without going into the question of what is 'real'. In the second place, poetry does not necessarily depend for its existence or its value upon the material of experience, the accumulation of 'real' data, except in the most obvious and uncritical sense. The demand for the concrete and the personal is the mark of a strictly local preference, to be associated with the growth of naturalism, and one strange result of it is the present status of Hoccleve. Literary history assigns to him a place more or less as an equal of Lydgate, yet on all counts he is a much less important writer. His range is narrower, his style much less sophisticated, and though he claims some of the same patrons as Lydgate— Prince Henry, for instance, and Humphrey of Gloucester[39]—his relationship with them is clearly that of a man very much on the fringes of the world of literary patronage. One of his poems, the *Regement of Princes*, was frequently copied, or copied in part, in the fifteenth century, but the rest exist in only a few MSS., most of them Hoccleve's own autograph.[40] He exerted no influence on the fifteenth century, and there are very few references to him. However, he has something which endears him to modern taste, a vividly disreputable personality which he puts over with racy colloquial vigour. He enjoys nothing so much as talking about himself, about his life as a clerk in the office of the Privy Seal, and the way he would take the afternoons off to go boating on the river; elsewhere, in a more serious vein, he talks of the nervous breakdown which destroyed his health and his prospects, of his marriage, of the tedious drudgery of his job,[41] all with a wry self-mockery (perhaps caught from Chaucer). But he never disguises the directness and honesty of his record of his own life and personality. It is a kind of poetry to which we respond with immediate warmth, and against which the totally different nature of Lydgate's poetry is thrown in sharp and, to us, unflattering relief. Lydgate has no personality to put over, and any mention he makes of his life is as likely to be part of a rhetorical convention as anything. Literature is closer to him than life, and the material of his poetry is experience strained through literary convention, or sometimes literary convention alone. Unlike the Wife of Bath, he prefers 'auctoritee' to 'experience', and the Middle Ages on the whole shared his preference. So the taste for the concrete and the personal is faced with poetry which is systematically abstract and impersonal; it is hard to see how the one can be judged in terms of the other.

There are other assumptions in Bennett's treatment of Lydgate—and I quote this account only because it is representative and authoritative—which are equally open to question. It is taken for granted that pace and economy are the basic requirements of narrative, yet these, as we have seen, are criteria which are irrelevant to Lydgate's narrative technique. And perhaps we may conclude with a statement Bennett makes about Lydgate's religious verse: 'His religious lyrics have more to be said for them—especially the *Testament of Dan John Lydgate*—for in these his real religious fervour gives some excitement to his verse' (p. 141). It has already been suggested that an autobiographical interpretation of the *Testament* as self-expression is likely to be wide of the mark, but one could add to this, accepting that some of Lydgate's religious poems are more fervent than others, that it is a matter of genre, not of poetic quality. Some of his religious writing is expository, some of it historical, some propagandist, some celebratory, and some of it, certainly, lyrical.

To assess it all on the basis of the emotional expressiveness appropriate to the last-named misses this point. One could as well assess Lydgate's love-poetry in terms of its effectiveness in expressing erotic sentiment. To do so would clearly be improper as well as inappropriate. It would be salutary to remind ourselves, without necessarily committing ourselves to the same standards of judgment, of what some fifteenth century readers saw in a poem like the *Temple of Glass*. It was, it seems, a poem to be *used*, used, for instance, as a quarry by lesser rhymesters, such as the 'Lucas' who signs his name in MS. Sloane 1212 of Hoccleve's *Regement*, and adds some verses on the outer leaves:

> These vellum leaves contain two passages from *The Temple of Glas*, ll.98–132, and ll. 736–754 with 762–3, also two poems, one of which is a cento of lines from the *Temple* ingeniously fitted together, the other at first sight original, but actually a mosaic of small borrowings.[42]

Even more practical was the use it was put to by another fifteenth century reader:

> Sir John Paston demanded his copy in a hurry in 1461–2, when he was wooing Anne Haute; he probably wanted it, just as Slender wanted his 'Book of Songs and Sonnets', to woo another Mistress Anne.[43]

This is not quite the kind of 'usefulness' I was speaking of earlier, but at least it may serve to give our attitudes a jolt in the right direction.

Without too many concessions, therefore, to historical relativism, it is possible to see that Lydgate's reputation among his contemporaries and immediate successors was not a sign of some gross perversion of taste. What he was praised for, and what he has suffered for more recently, was his total acquiescence in the conventions and demands of his age. Like any competent professional, he did what was asked of him, and, working within an established literary tradition, he had neither the desire, nor the incentive, nor the creative power to make things new.[44] His claim on us, his usefulness to us, is precisely this, that he is perfectly typical of medieval literary tradition, and provides us with a series of paradigms for our reading of medieval poetry. Prince Hal no doubt enjoyed Falstaff's company more, as we enjoy Chaucer's, but he saw the value of cultivating Poins:

> Thou art a blessed fellow to think as every man thinks: never a man's thought in the world keeps the roadway better than thine.[45]

Notes to Chapter One

1 See, e.g. P. H. Nichols, 'William Dunbar as a Scottish Lydgatian', *PMLA*, XLVI(1931),214–24.

2 See my essay on 'The English Chaucerians' in *Chaucer and Chaucerians*, ed. D. S. Brewer (London 1966), pp. 210–39.

3 For accounts of Lydgate's reputation, and lists of allusions, see *The Temple of Glas*, ed. J. Schick (EETS, ES60,1891), pp. cxlii–cxliv; *English Verse between Chaucer and Surrey*, ed. Eleanor P. Hammond (Duke Univ. Press, Durham, N. Carolina, 1927), pp. 96–8; W. F. Schirmer, *John Lydgate: a Study in the Culture of the XVth century* (originally published in German, 1952; English translation by Ann E. Keep, 1961), pp. 255–9.

4 *Pastime of Pleasure* (ed. W. E. Mead, EETS,OS 173,1928), 1317–1407.

5 Hammond, *op. cit.*, p. 96.

6 *Philip Sparrow*, 800–12 (in Dyce's edition, 1843, i, 75).

7 *Garland of Laurell*, 428–34 (ed. in Hammond, *op. cit.*).

8 *Garland*, 715–21.

9 Samuel Cobb, in his *Poetae Britannici*, 1700: quoted in Caroline F. E. Spurgeon, *500 Years of Chaucer Criticism and Allusion* (3 vols., Cambridge 1925), I,271.

10 Lydgate's *Troy Book*, ed. H. Bergen, Part IV (EETS,ES 126,1935), Bibliographical Introduction, p. 52.

11 *Minor Poems*, ed. H. N. MacCracken, Part II (EETS,OS 192,1934), p. 723.

12 *Fall of Princes*, I,92–8. Lydgate is quoted, with some modification of spelling (e.g. *u/v*, *i/j*), from the standard texts cited in the Bibliography, except where otherwise stated.

13 E.g. *Fall*, II,2565.

14 For instance, Geoffrey of Vinsauf, in his *Poetria Nova*; Evrard the German, *Laborintus*; John of Garland, *Poetria*. See E. Faral, *Les Arts Poétiques du XIIe et du XIIIe siècle* (Paris, 1923), pp. 218, 348, 380.

15 Geoffrey of Vinsauf, *Poetria Nova*, 225: in Faral, *op. cit.*, p. 204.

16 See G. T. Shepherd, 'Troilus and Criseyde' (in *Chaucer and Chaucerians*, ed. D. S. Brewer, pp. 65–87), pp. 77–81.

17 One of the most widely used text-books in the sixteenth century was Erasmus's *De duplici copia verborum ac rerum*, of which there were sixty editions between 1512 and 1536: see T. W. Baldwin, *William Shakespere's Small Latine and Lesse Greeke* (2 vols., Urbana, Ill., 1944), I,99, II,176.

18 *As You Like It*, V.i.52.

19 *Minor Poems*, ed. MacCracken, Part II, pp. 744–847.

20 See A. C. Spearing, *Criticism and Medieval Poetry* (London, 1964), pp. 16–18.

21 *Anelida*, 18, quoted by C. S. Lewis, *The Allegory of Love* (Oxford, 1936), p. 201. Matthew Arnold's choice (in 'The Study of Poetry', *Essays in*

Criticism, second series) is 'O martyr souded in virginitee', from the *Prioress's Tale*, *CT*,VII,579.

22 *English Verse between Chaucer and Surrey*, pp. 81–2.

23 *Fourteenth Century Verse and Prose*, ed. K. Sisam (Oxford, 1921), p. xxxix. The standard works on this subject are H. J. Chaytor, *From Script to Print* (Cambridge, 1945); Ruth Crosby, 'Oral Delivery in the Middle Ages', *Speculum*, XI(1936),88–110, and 'Chaucer and the Custom of Oral Delivery', *Speculum*, XIII(1938),413–32.

24 See H. S. Bennett, 'The Author and his Public in the 14th and 15th Centuries', *Essays and Studies*, XXIII(1937),7–24.

25 There is much on this subject, and on a great many other subjects, in M. McLuhan, *The Gutenberg Galaxy* (Toronto, 1962).

26 See the Helmingham MS. and MS.Digby 230 of the *Troy*, as described by Bergen in Part IV of his edition, pp. 24, 29.

27 *Fall*, ed. Bergen, Part IV, Bibliographical Introduction, p. 105.

28 Bergen, *op. cit.*, p. 123; *Temple of Glas*, ed. Schick, p. clii.

29 Hammond, *Chaucer to Surrey*, p. 416.

30 *CT* Prologue 503–6. The others are 443, 500, 563, 652, 731, 741 and 830. All quotations from Chaucer are from F. N. Robinson's second edition (Cambridge, Mass., 1957).

31 A. A. Jack, *A Commentary on the Poetry of Chaucer and Spenser* (Glasgow, 1920), p. 47.

32 W. F. Schirmer, *John Lydgate* (1952, trans. 1961); A. Renoir, *The Poetry of John Lydgate* (London, 1967).

33 See C. L. Kingsford, *English Historical Literature in the 15th Century* (Oxford 1913), chap. IX; T. Wright, *Political Poems and Songs*, vol. II (Rolls series, 1861).

34 Kingsford, *op. cit.*, pp. 232–6; A. B. Ferguson, *The Indian Summer of English Chivalry* (Durham, N. Carolina 1960), chap. V.

35 Hammond, *Chaucer to Surrey*, pp. 92–3.

36 G. L. Kittredge, *Chaucer and his Poetry* (Harvard U.P. 1915), pp. 109, 112.

37 *Chaucer and the Fifteenth Century* (Oxford 1947), pp. 137–46.

38 It is made explicit on p. 155, referring to Hawes.

39 *The Regement of Princes* (ed. Furnivall, EETS,ES 72,1897) is dedicated and addressed to Prince Henry (see especially 2017–2163, 5440–63), and the *Tale of Jereslaus's Wife*, part of the *Complaint* 'Series' (in *Minor Poems*, ed. Furnivall, EETS,ES 71,1892), was written for Gloucester (see 554–623).

40 H. C. Schulz, 'Thomas Hoccleve, Scribe', *Speculum*, XII(1937),71–81; Jerome Mitchell, *Thomas Hoccleve* (Urbana, Ill. 1968), p. 14.

41 See the *Male Regle*; the *Complaint* and *Dialogue*, the first two parts of the 'Series'; and the Prologue to the *Regement*, the Dialogue with a Beggar.

42 Ethel Seaton, *Sir Richard Roos: Lancastrian Poet* (London 1961), p. 376. This book aims to establish Roos as the major poet of fifteenth-century

England by assigning to him much of its anonymous poetry, as well as poems by Chaucer, Lydgate, Wyatt, and others. The ascriptions are based on the 'discovery' of double acrostic anagrams of unprecedented complexity, and are wholly preposterous. However, the book is full of incidental good things, and shows a wide knowledge of fifteenth-century literature and MSS. See also, for this MS., H. N. MacCracken, 'Additional Light on the *Temple of Glas*', *PMLA*, XXIII(1908),128–40. But cf. J. Norton-Smith, *Lydgate: Poems* (Oxford 1966), p. 143.

43 Seaton, *loc. cit.*; see *The Paston Letters*, ed. J. Gairdner, no. 690 (ed. 1910, III,37).

44 His place in English poetry is very much like that of Gray, and it is interesting that Gray should have been one of the few to try to understand him.

45 *Henry IV Part 2*, II.ii.63.

CHAPTER TWO

The Monastic Background

In the Prologue to the *Siege of Thebes*, which is known, on strong evidence, to have been written about 1420, Lydgate portrays himself meeting up with Chaucer's pilgrims at their lodgings in Canterbury. The host, with some rude chaffing about the monk's pallor and his 'wonder thred-bar hood', asks him his name and where he comes from:

> I answerde my name was Lydgate,
> Monk of Bery, ny3 fyfty 3ere of age. (92–3)

One does not expect strict autobiographical accuracy in this sort of fictitious context, but neither does one expect deliberately misleading statements, and it has been deduced, therefore, that Lydgate was born about 1370, and this date fits in well with other events of his life of which we have definite evidence. He was born, as he tells us, in Lydgate (or Lidgate), a village in Suffolk, on the Cambridgeshire border, six miles south-west of Bury St. Edmunds:

> Born in a vyllage which callyd is Lydgate,
> Be olde tyme a famous castel toun;
> In Danys tyme it was bete doun,
> Tyme when Seynt Edmond, martir, mayde and kyng,
> Was slayn at Oxne, be recoord of wrytyng.[1]

From this village he took his surname, as was the common practice in the Middle Ages, and the regular practice in the case of monks, even where there was a family surname. For by about 1382 at the latest, Lydgate had been recruited to the great neighbouring abbey of St. Edmund's at Bury, and there, with intervals, he spent the remainder of his life till his death in 1449. The abbey held lands and jurisdiction in the village of Lydgate,[2] and it was most probably on a tour of the estates there that one of the monastic officials heard of the promising young scholar and recommended him to the master of the almonry school at

St. Edmund's. There he would spend some years receiving instruction in Latin grammar, the Scriptures and the liturgy, before taking the habit as a novice, a year after which he made his profession.

> Entryng this tyme into relygioun,
> Onto the plowe I put forth myne hond,
> A yere complete made my professioun.[3]

For the novice there would be further instruction in grammar, with some logic and rhetoric, and also training in the techniques of formal writing and illumination, as well as further study of the Scriptures, the psalmody and liturgy. Lydgate's progress through the novitiate must have been unusually rapid, for by 1389, according to records which offer the first documentary evidence of his existence, we find him being ordained. First, on March 13th, according to the register of Robert Braybrook, bishop of London from 1381 to 1404, he was ordained 'ad omnes ordines' in the church of Hadham, near Bishop's Stortford.[4] This must refer to all *minor* orders, and thus in effect records his admission to the office of acolyte, the highest of the four minor orders. It may be taken as clearing the way for his ordination later in the year, on December 17th, 1389,[5] as sub-deacon, the first of the three major or sacred orders. Sub-deacons were allowed to participate in the service of the Mass, and to prepare the sacred vessels and the bread and wine. Four years later, on May 28th, 1393, Lydgate was admitted to the office of deacon, to which were attached further privileges in the celebration of Mass, and in 1397, after receiving letters dimissory from his abbot on April 4th, he was ordained priest by John Fordham, bishop of Ely, on Saturday, April 7th, in the chapel of the manor at Downham.[6] Bury was actually in the diocese of Norwich, but there was a permanent feud between the abbey and the bishop of Norwich, and successive abbots made full use of their privilege of calling on other bishops to ordain their candidates.

The abbey of St. Edmund's at Bury, in which Lydgate had now taken the full orders of priesthood, was one of the great Benedictine abbeys of England.[7] It had been founded in 1020, to house the relics of St. Edmund, king of East Anglia, martyred by the Danes at Hoxne in the ninth century, and the great abbey church was laid out and partly built in the abbacy of Baldwin (1065–97), and completed by his successors in the twelfth century. The most famous of these is abbot Samson (1135–1212), who took over in 1182 at a time when the monastery was in debt and disarray, and by his energetic and capable management

3

restored its finances, enlarged its estates, and established its prosperity for the future. The record of his personality and achievement is in the well-known chronicle of Jocelin de Brakelond, as also in Carlyle's *Past and Present*. Later in the thirteenth century the Lady Chapel was rebuilt, and John of Lavenham (sacrist, 1358–81) built the great campanile central tower to replace the one burnt down in the fire of 1210. There was also extensive conventual building at this time, after the depredations of the townsfolk in 1327. The trouble dated from as early as 1264, and centred round the question of abbatial privileges. The town of Bury was in the abbey's 'liberty' or jurisdiction, where the abbot had full authority over gates and tolls, and over the appointment of town officials. In 1327 the townspeople, taking advantage of the unsettled state of the country at the death of Edward II, invaded the abbey, plundered and burnt down the domestic buildings, kidnapped the abbot, Richard of Draughton, and extorted from him a charter of privileges for the town. Its clauses do not look to us unreasonable, but it was rescinded in 1331, as soon as order had been restored by Edward III. This was not the end of fourteenth century discontent, for in 1381, the year of the Peasants' Revolt, John Wrawe and his followers murdered the prior of Bury, John of Cambridge, and then led a rabble of rioters on the abbey, which they plundered. The town of Bury subsequently bore a fine for this outrage.

With the fifteenth century, St. Edmund's moved into calmer and more prosperous times, though there were still natural calamities like the fall of the western tower in 1430–1, attributed to over-zealous bell-ringing, and the disastrous fire of 1465. But generally, the first half of the fifteenth century was an Indian summer for the great black abbeys, a time of consolidation. St. Edmund's, with vast estates in Suffolk and surrounding counties, was one of the half-dozen richest, along with St. Alban's, Westminster, Glastonbury, and Christ Church, Canterbury. Its annual income for 1291 is computed at about £1,000, and by 1535 this had risen to £2,336 (gross).[8] It is impossible to say what this means in modern terms, but it would be useful to think of Bury in Lydgate's time as a powerful business corporation with assets running into millions and an annual income of about a quarter of a million pounds. As for numbers, there were in the late thirteenth century 80 monks, 21 chaplains, and 111 servants; in 1381, after the ravages of the Black Death there were 47 monks, and in 1535, before the king's commissioners arrived, there were 62, which had fallen to 44 at the dissolution in 1539.[9] We may estimate that there were between 60 and 80 monks at Bury in Lydgate's time.

It was not a time of great spiritual activity. In common with many large organisations, the Benedictine abbeys in these late days seemed to exist for the sake of their own aggrandisement. Wealth, security, and independence were the objectives, though many devout lives may have been hidden from us by the very nature of the extant records, with their detailed accounts of legal and financial operations. William Curteys, abbot of Bury 1429–46,[10] was in many ways typical of the monastic administrator of his day. He was above all a great defender of abbatial privilege, in particular of the privilege of exemption from episcopal jurisdiction and visitation. This was granted to a number of the oldest abbeys, and to a few others which had special relationships with Rome. Bury was one of the latter, and guarded its freedom jealously. In 1348, for instance, the energetic bishop Bateman of Norwich levied a tax on his diocese, including Bury, partly to pay for the expenses of his trip to Avignon to be consecrated in 1344. Bury claimed exemption, and a long wrangle ensued, with frequent appeals to both royal and papal authority. On Bateman's part it was an episode in a long campaign to bring ill-regulated houses in the diocese under his control, and no doubt it was his agents who painted such a black picture of conditions at Bury in 1345 under the lax rule of William de Bernham (1335–61). Monks, it was said, were living in villages outside the abbey, wearing the dress of laymen, drinking, fighting, consorting with women, and scattering the countryside with their illegitimate progeny.[11] The account is certainly exaggerated, and the bishop lost his case, but the abbey was very much on its guard. When Thomas Arundel, the powerful archbishop of Canterbury, descended upon Bury in 1400, the abbey received him with scrupulous courtesy but the manner of the reception made it quite clear that it was a visit and not a visitation. Abbot Curteys was equally watchful. He asserts Bury's status as an exempt abbey at every opportunity, whether it is relevant or not,[12] and would be quick to respond to the appeal of John Fornset, a monk of Norwich, who wrote from the council of Basle (c. 1440), where monastic rights of tithe and exemption were being questioned, to advise Curteys to send an authoritative emissary to state the monks' case.[13] Curteys himself wrote a life of St. Edmund, not simply out of piety, but partly to prove the abbey's exemption as a pre-Conquest house. He also commissioned Lydgate to write his English Life of St. Edmund, and it would be surprising if there were not a propagandist motive in this too. Charters played an important part in the battle for independence, and Bury had a clear case, with authentic charters from Cnut and the Conqueror as well as their successors. These too were handed to Lydgate for versification, and he did his usual conscientious job, even to versifying the signatures.[14]

Curteys had particularly close links with the royal court, and Henry VI wrote to him frequently, as if to a generous uncle, asking him for advice, help and, always, money. He writes in 1441, for instance, asking for help in financing York's expedition to Normandy, in 1444 for Suffolk's embassy to fetch Margaret of Anjou, and again in 1444 for the relief of Bordeaux. In 1446 he writes asking Curteys to be present at the foundation-laying of King's College, Cambridge. The origins of this close personal tie between Curteys and Henry VI are to be found somewhat earlier, in the king's extended stay at Bury from Christmas 1433 to Easter 1434. This was a great event in the history of the monastery. It was usual for the court, in its progresses about the country, to use the monasteries as first-class free hotels, and monastic accounts record the colossal expenditure on such entertainments with evident mixed feelings. St. Alban's was a favourite stopping-place, standing as it did one day's journey from London on the way north, and duke Humphrey of Gloucester frequently celebrated Christmas and other festivals there. But the length of Henry VI's stay at Bury was an exceptional mark of favour and esteem, and was recognised as such by the abbey.

> Abbot Curreys made great preparations for the visit, and put the abbatial palace, which was at the time much out of repair, into complete readiness for the reception of his royal geust. The alderman and burgesses of Bury, dressed in scarlet, accompanied by the commons of the town, who also wore red livery, met the king, to the number of five hundred, upon Newmarket heath: the royal retinue, before this extended a mile. They brought the king within the precinct of the monastery by the south gate. Here he was received by the whole convent: the bishop of Norwich and the abbot appearing in full pontificals: the abbot sprinkling the king with holy water, and presenting a cross to his lips. Procession, with music, was next made to the high altar of the church, when the antiphon used in the service of St. Edmund, 'Ave rex gentis Anglorum', was sung: after this, the king paid his devotions at St. Edmund's shrine, and then passed to the abbot's palace.[15]

The king remained with the abbot till Epiphany, moving then to the prior's lodging, and after to the abbot's manor at Elmswell. He returned to the prior's lodging for Lent and stayed till Easter, when he was received into the fraternity of the abbey. It was during the king's visit that Curteys asked Lydgate to write his *Life of St. Edmund* to present to the king. A miniature in the presentation copy, MS. Harley 2278, one of the most richly illustrated of all fifteenth century English books, shows Lydgate delivering the work to the king (f.6a). It would not be extravagant to suppose that Lydgate's presence at Bury was one of the reasons for the king's visit, for the monk had already displayed his loyalty in poems on the king's coronation (1429) and on his return from France (1432).

The picture of the abbey and its life that we build up from the historical records is important to our understanding of Lydgate, for it shows quite clearly that the great monasteries stood in the main stream of English public life, that a monk's career was not necessarily limited to the cloister, that he could exercise his talents like other men—and from a secure base of wealth and privilege. There was opportunity of close contact with all kinds of men, including those who were rich and powerful in the realm; Dugdale's mention of Henry VI's admission to confraternity should remind us that it was considered a high honour in the fifteenth century to be made an associate of this great abbey. Humphrey of Gloucester was admitted at the same time as Henry VI, and other admissions during the abbacy of Curteys include William Paston, Richard Beauchamp, earl of Warwick, Eleanor, duchess of Gloucester, Elizabeth Vere, countess of Oxford, and the earl of Suffolk and his wife Alice.[16] It is no accident that many of these are to be counted amongst Lydgate's patrons. The monastic life was still a career of total spiritual dedication to those who wished it to be so, though probably those who did would now be making their way into other orders such as that of the Carthusians; but, roughly speaking, it may be helpful to think of an abbey in the fifteenth century as something like Oxford or Cambridge colleges in the eighteenth century—wealthy, privileged, celibate, rich in books and heavy with tradition, learned and scholarly, though often in an antiquarian way, close in the counsels of the great yet devoted to their own self-justifying interests and their own intricate manoeuvring: a rich soil, but fat with weeds.

Nor need we assume that the monk's life was physically much confined. The very existence of the large abbeys as great landed proprietors gave to many of their inmates a wide degree of freedom to move about the country, and the traditional communal life was much broken up by the obedientiary system (devolution of administrative office and responsibility) as well as by the practice, growing in the fourteenth century, of paying allowances for clothes and other extras. Many monasteries had rest-houses, where monks could retire temporarily to a less rigorous routine, such as St. Alban's 'holiday villa' at Redbourn. Some had houses in London, where monastic officials could stay when in London on business. Lydgate must often have been at 'Buries Markes', the town house of the abbot of Bury; it was probably there that he wrote the translation of *Gaude virgo mater Christi*, made, John Shirley tells us, 'by Daun Johan the Munke Lydegate by night as he lay in his bedde at London'.[17] Visits to friends and relations were common. In 1327, when the citizens of Bury attacked the abbey, no less than thirty-two of the monks, we are told, were away on visits or on holiday.[18] This may be a piece of scandal-mongering, and in any case reflects an exceptional laxity in the history of the abbey, but the fourteenth century was certainly a time of general relaxation of the rules as to enclosure and stability. The Great Schism contributed to this loosening of discipline by dissipating the Papal authority, making it much easier to obtain Papal dispensations and privileges. Conditions in the early fifteenth century are well illustrated by the ordinances of John Whethamstede, abbot of St. Alban's, which he issued on his departure for Rome in 1423 (on a mission to secure, amongst other things, limitation of fasting in Lent and permission to use portable altars in London and Oxford). The brethren are warned not to gossip with women, not to resort to places for nuns near the monastery, not to extend their walks in the neighbourhood of Redbourn, not to loiter on the high road, not to play practical jokes on one another, and so on.[19] Visitation could do little to halt the general erosion of discipline, especially in exempt houses; it is noteworthy that the complaint which most commonly appears in visitation records is of neglect to observe monastic enclosure.[20] Henry V made a determined effort at reform and summoned a great Chapter of the black monks in 1421 at London, and delivered to them a series of articles, prominent amongst which is the call for a curtailment of visits in society. But the Chapter demurred and delayed, broke up into sub-committees which reported on each article in detail,[21] and eventually produced watered-down proposals to be submitted to the Chapter of 1423, by which time Henry V was dead.

Monastic life thus gave to Lydgate not only a wide range of possible contacts but also a physical freedom of which he seems to have made good use. We know for certain that in the 1420's he was closely connected with the royal court, and spent time in Paris as well as London on its business. For the early years of the century we have less evidence, but we are fortunate in possessing one definite record of his where-abouts in 1406-8. From a note by John Shirley to *Isopes Fabules*, Fable VII, in which he tells us that the poem was 'made in Oxenford',[22] it had long been assumed that Lydgate was at one time a student at Oxford. The black monks had their own college, Gloucester college, and the more promising scholars were often sent there to work for the degree of master of arts (though this could also be taken in the larger monastic schools) or for their doctorate in theology, or even for short courses in preaching. Elaborate regulations concerning such students in the statutes of the provincial Chapter of 1363[23] show that the intention was to preserve the monastic atmosphere as much as possible at Gloucester college, but the nature of some of the regulations—prohibitions against incontinence, against hunting, fishing and poaching, against frequent-ing taverns and holding suppers in chambers—suggest that the rule was not easy to implement. Even at its strictest, life at Oxford would have implanted certain tastes, such as the use of one's own room and books, the ability to dispose one's own work and time, and to meet and make friends, which would have influenced the student's subsequent career. It is to his sojourn at Oxford that we may attribute some of the breadth of Lydgate's secular reference.

Bury had particularly close connections with Gloucester college. Abbot Curteys paid for a new range of buildings, and the abbey regu-larly had three or more students in residence there.[24] About 1406-8 one of these was John Lydgate, as we learn from a letter of the Prince of Wales, later Henry V, addressed to the abbot and chapter of Bury, in which he asks them to give further leave to Lydgate to continue his studies at Oxford, because of the good reports he has heard of him from Richard Courtney, chancellor of Oxford, and others.

Et pour ce que nous sumes par nostre treschier cousin et clerc, M[estre] R[ichard] C[ourteney], Chanceller d'Oxenford, et diverses aultres noz treschiers serviteurs continuelment entour nous esteantz enforméz sibien de les scen, vertue et bonne con-versacion de nostre treschier en Dieu Dan J[ohn] L[ydgate], vostre commoigne, come del grand desir qu'il ad a continuer a les Escoles, et mesmes noz cousin et serviteurs nous ont suppliéz de vous escrire et prier pour vostre comun assent ottroier que le dit J[ohn] pourra continuer a les Escoles susdites, si vous prions enterement et de cuer que a le dit J[ohn] par vostre comun assent vuilléz granter continuance as dites Escoles a tielle pension

comme ses aultres confreres y preignent illoeques pour leur sus-
tenance, tanque il pourra resonablement venir a perfeccion de
science, par ensi que mesme celui J[ohn] soit de bonne conversa-
cion et diligent pour apprendre, luy donantz aussi congié et elec-
cion d'estudier en divinitee ou en loy canoun a son plesir, et ce le
plus favorablement a cause de nous, si que il pourra sentir mesmes
cestes noz prieres lui valoir devers vous.[25]

Richard Courtney was close to the Prince, being subsequently a chap-
lain of his household and attendant upon him on the French expedition
of 1415, where he died at the siege of Harfleur.[26] His principal term of
office as chancellor was from 1406–8, which gives us dates for Lydgate's
residence at Oxford, though no information as to how long he spent
there. The document in fact, in answering one question, rouses a whole
series of further speculations. That the Prince knew Lydgate personally
at this stage is unlikely, and is not suggested by the letter, though we
have to remember that not long afterwards, in 1412, he commissioned
Lydgate's translation of the *Troy Book* and at some time may have
suggested the *Life of Our Lady*. One of the things that may have stirred
the Prince to intercede on Lydgate's behalf, apart from the desire to do
Courtney a favour, may have been the appeal made to his own strict
piety by Lydgate's undeviating orthodoxy, or what he had heard of it,
especially welcome in a place which twenty years before had been a
hot-bed of heresy. The vagueness as to what Lydgate is actually studying ('divinity or canon law') may reflect simply the general terms in
which Courtney had briefed him on the matter, but it may indicate
that Lydgate had embarked on no definite programme of study such
as a doctorate of theology but was simply at Oxford 'studying'.
Nothing in Lydgate's writing would make us think of him as a highly-
trained professional academic, though he has a smattering of everything
and it could be further argued that there would be no question of
Lydgate going back to Bury if he were a fully-registered student for the
eight-year master's or the nine-year doctor's course.

  More specific and more significant are the suggestions made by J.
Norton-Smith, in his excellent edition of selections from Lydgate's
poetry,[27] about Lydgate's connection at Oxford with Edmund Lacy,
who went on to a distinguished ecclesiastical career as dean of the
Royal Chapel at Windsor 1414–17, and, from 1420, bishop of Exeter.
Norton-Smith assumes that Lydgate spent a long time at Oxford,
c. 1397–1408, and that he made the acquaintance there of the Prince of

Wales, who was in residence at Queen's about 1398, and of Lacy, who was bursar and master of University college 1396–9 and later became a king's clerk. There are rubrics by Shirley to three of Lydgate's religious poems which testify to a link, and which suggest, as Norton-Smith says, 'a common interest in liturgical composition'. The rubrics are as follows:

1. 'And folowing begynnethe a devoute salme of þe sautier which Lydegate daun Johan translated in þe Chapell at Wyndesore at þe request of þe dean whyles þe kyng was at evensonge' (*Benedic anima mea domino*, MS. Trinity R.3.20, f. 165).
2. 'Here begyneth verses of þe sauter whiche þat kynge Herry the V. whom god assoyle by gret devocion usyd in his chappell at his hyȝe masses by-twene þe levacion and þe concecracion of þe sacrament, translatid by þe Monke Lydegat dan John' (*Eight Verses of St. Bernard*, MS. Add.27929, f. 126).
3. 'Loo my freendes here beginneþe þe translacyoune out of Latyne in-to Englisshe of Gloriosa dicta sunt de te, &c. translated by Lidegate daun John þe Munk of Bury at þinstaunce of þe Busschop of Excestre in wyse of Balade' (*Gloriosa dicta sunt de te*, MS. Trinity R.3.20, f. 1).[28]

Lacy's interest in the liturgy is evidenced by his efforts to gain Papal acceptance for a new office in honour of St. Raphael which he had composed himself. Henry V's piety is well-known. Norton-Smith concludes: 'Henry V and Lacy may well have been the main forces in shaping the direction and style of Lydgate's religious verse.'

The little that we know of Lydgate's career at Oxford leaves room for such speculation. The important thing is that it should help to broaden the rather narrow picture we may have of monastic claustrality ('What was a monk doing writing love-poetry?'), and strengthen our impression of Lydgate as a man who was exposed to the same kind of formative influences and experiences as those of other educated men of his day. There were still differences, of course; his life, however much we may stress its 'normality', especially during what must have been long absences from Bury, was still remote from that of, say, Hoccleve, and his contemporaries refer to him very often as 'the monk' or 'the monk of Bury', as if to them too it were worthy of remark that a monk should have gained acceptance as a professional man of letters. But it is clear that his profession, though it may have distinguished him, did not debar him from the literary world.

There is one respect, hardly touched on yet, in which a monk, especially a monk of Bury, possessed a definite advantage over non-monastic writers. Chaucer's clerk would have been glad to lay his hands on 'twenty bookes, clad in blak or reed', a large library for those days, and so would Chaucer too, probably, but Lydgate had access to a magnificent library of over 2,000 volumes, one of the largest in the country.[29] Like other fifteenth century abbots, Curteys had a special building erected (*c.* 1430) to house the collection, probably over the south walk of the cloister. In this new library the books were catalogued and shelved in accordance with a carefully worked-out system, the design of which can be discerned in press-marks on manuscripts still identifiable. The credit for this innovation goes to John Boston, a famous bibliophile, librarian of Bury at this time, who also compiled a catalogue of ecclesiastical authors in monastic libraries, arranged in alphabetical order of author, with list of works and reference to location. For this he visited some 195 libraries in England and Scotland, and his work is an invaluable record of the range of books available in monastic libraries.

The overwhelming emphasis in such libraries as Bury, if we ignore missals and psalters and other service-books, which were not properly part of the library and were not usually kept there, would be on devotional reading, the scriptures and patristic commentaries. Usually the Bible appears as a series of separate books or groups of books (such as the Pentateuch or the 12 Minor Prophets), heavily glossed, with the accretions of centuries of interpretation and commentary, but the integral Bible (Old Testament) is known, and the great treasure of the Bury library is the Bury bible, now Corpus Christi Cambridge MS. 2, produced at the abbey 1121–48, the masterpiece of twelfth century English manuscript illumination. Among patristic writers, Augustine is most heavily represented, followed by Gregory, Jerome, Bede, and Ambrose, down to later commentators like Hugh of St. Victor and scholastic theologians such as Peter Lombard and Aquinas. There are also *summae* (treatises on the vices and virtues), encyclopaedias (like Isidore's *Etymologiae*), numerous collections of sermons, chronicles, and technical works on medicine, astronomy, and mathematics. More interesting to us is the availability of classical and post-classical writings, and here Bury appears to have been particularly rich. Not only did it possess standard writers: Cicero, Virgil, Horace, Ovid, Juvenal, Persius, Sallust, Suetonius, Seneca, Martianus Capella, and Prudentius, but also others whose names appear only rarely in monastic catalogues or in

Boston, such as Caesar, Plautus, Statius, Quintilian, and Valerius Maximus.[30] Many familiar medieval Latin writers are also present: Bartholomeus *De Proprietatibus Rerum*, the standard medieval encyclopaedia of natural history; William of Malmesbury; John of Salisbury; Giraldus Cambrensis; and two copies of the *Bellum Troianum* of Guido della Colonna, interesting in connection with Lydgate's translation of the work in the *Troy Book*. Such are the Latin treasures. In addition, two Old English manuscripts are known to have been at Bury, a collection of Ælfric's homilies and a copy of the rule of St. Benedict. There may have been more. Most monasteries had some books in French, mostly of a didactic nature, though romances sometimes appear, as at St. Augustine's, Canterbury, and at the tiny Premonstratensian house of Titchfield in Hampshire.[31] There are only a handful of French books recorded for Bury, a grammar, some sermons, a book of Cato's proverbs, and *Le Livre de Sydrac* (an *imago mundi* encyclopaedia of the natural sciences of the late thirteenth century). English books seem to have been comparatively rare in monastic libraries, or at least they go unmentioned in the catalogues, apart from exceptional collections like those of the English mystics in the Carthusian houses.[32] Richard Rolle was in the Bury library, but only his Latin works. It may be that English books passed through the hands of the monastery, but were regarded as ephemera, perhaps like the copy of Gower's *Confessio Amantis* now in Glasgow, which may have been at one time at Bury.[33]

The library continued to grow in the fifteenth century, and the work of book-production went on unabated in the monastery's scriptorium. Formal writing and illumination were still major professional activities for monks. Many of the books in the library must have been produced in the abbey itself, and in addition to this there was the constant need to replace worn-out service-books. The practice of illumination flourished at Bury, and noble manuscripts of the *Troy Book* such as Cotton Augustus A.iv, Digby 232, and Rawlinson c. 446 may well have been written and decorated at Bury about 1420–40. Any one of them is sumptuous enough for a presentation copy. One book which was certainly made at Bury is the presentation copy of Lydgate's *St. Edmund*, MS. Harley 2278, of which mention has already been made. The miniatures are in a traditional style, but precise, richly coloured and highly professional, and their 'interest in rich and fantastic costumes' and 'soft modelled style' have been related by one writer to miniatures in MS. Cotton Faustina B.vi (of the *Desert of Religion*) and to the famous picture in MS. Harley 4826 of Lydgate with a pilgrim presenting the book to the earl of Salisbury.[34] Rickert refers to the style of the latter as the tinted outline style, and considers that it originated in Bury. She relates it further to the work of the famous fifteenth century illuminator Thomas Chaundler (e.g. MS. Trinity R.14.5), who was perhaps trained in the same atelier.

Lydgate must have had a working knowledge of the Bury library, even if he had conscientiously read few of the books in it. Reading played an important part in the Benedictine routine, being allotted two to four hours, sometimes more, per day, and careful arrangements were made to encourage and organise borrowing.[35] Naturally, the best-laid plans of librarians could not completely frustrate the magpie-like instincts of the inveterate book-hoarder, and there are two letters from Curteys,[36] the first of which complains that books borrowed by the monks have been lent out, used as pledges, and even sold by the brethren, and warns of the dire consequences of this in the future; special sanctions are imposed on students at the universities who are guilty in this matter, which shows that they were allowed to take books away from the abbey for their studies. The second letter demands the return of all books on loan within fifteen days. It is clear, too, that monks as well as students were allowed to own books, one of many ways in which the old rules against individual property had been relaxed. One of the articles drawn up by Henry V for consideration by the Chapter of 1421 concerns the widespread practice of private owner-ship, and books are mentioned, amongst other things.[37] Lydgate, as a well-known author, would have been in a specially privileged position, and no doubt possessed a collection of the books which he found most useful in his work, including some Chaucer. Another privilege of which he availed himself was the opportunity to work in his own private study, or scriptoriolum. Provision for such rooms becomes increasingly common in the fifteenth century,[38] and Pynson's picture of Lydgate at his writing-desk, in his print of the *Testament*, shows him at work in a scriptoriolum.

It would be interesting to trace in detail the connection between the Bury library and the characteristic configuration of Lydgate's thought and work, to see how his mind was formed and influenced by the books with which he was in such familiar contact. The value of such an investigation would extend far beyond its immediate relevance to Lydgate, but it is one which could be undertaken only by a scholar of exceptional powers. However, one or two points can perhaps be made. We have seen, for instance, that the Bury library offered, to anyone who wanted it, a fairly comprehensive range of reading in the Latin classics. It is clear, though, that it was an offer which meant little to Lydgate, for his knowledge of classical Latin writers is, apart from Ovid, very limited, far more limited than his own frequent allusions would suggest, and it is very often second-hand. Lydgate shared the general medieval attitude to the classics: they were useful for illustrations of grammatical and rhetorical points, and as history, but above all, and overwhelmingly, they were valuable as repositories of moral examples. This is one reason why Ovid was so popular in the Middle Ages—because his work was so rich in historical and mythological allusion, all of which could be used, either directly or allegorically. The literary nature or historcial provenance of the work is unimportant in this view; what is important is its content, and the opportunity that Christian revelation gives to revive this material in a doctrinally significant context. It is quite possible that medieval readers sometimes read classical authors for other reasons, for pleasure even, but such reading would rarely rise to the threshold of recognition, for there was no language in which its concepts could be handled. It would be a great mistake to think that the Middle Ages allegorised works like Ovid's *Metamorphoses* because they wanted an excuse to read them, some way of making them respectable. Allegorisation is simply an example of the selective manner of operation of the medieval mind (or any mind, for that matter), which draws from alien forms the 'truth' which it is preconditioned to find. Christian doctrine provided a universal framework in which all knowledge, including classical literature, history, and mythology, as well as the natural sciences, had its allotted place. Pre-existent patterns in such systems of knowledge were considered to be mistaken or irrelevant, even when the pattern was demonstrably 'real', for reality was of no account beside truth. The world of experience and reality in itself exists as a series of demonstrations, more or less transparent, of what is already known to be true, and the newness of any new discovery or experience can be valued only in terms of its effectiveness as such a demonstration.

This statement of the medieval position needs qualifying, of course, and its attitudes were already being qualified in the Middle Ages. Humanism, for instance, properly speaking, implies a recognition of the independent aud organic existence of classical literature. Bible scholarship, from the time of Andrew of St. Victor on,[39] was groping towards the idea that the words of the Old Testament might have a meaning of their own, might even refer to non-Christian historical fact, and that part of its 'truth' might therefore not be revealed in elaborate allegorical demonstrations of its total consonance with the doctrine of charity. On another level, it might be argued that Chaucer's willingness to see an artistic problem through, as in the *Troilus* or the *Knight's Tale*, suggests a degree of independence from the system, however isolated or precarious. But on the whole, the medieval attitude to experience in general, and to classical literature in particular, is encyclopaedic and syncretistic. The characteristic product of the medieval intellectual system is the *Summa*, the attempt to encompass all human knowledge and experience within a rationally organised framework, the whole structure resting upon the pinpoint of faith. It is the characteristic work of Aquinas as well as of the other friar who wrote the *Somme le Roi*, and the same ambition, to say everything that there is to be said, can be seen in literary 'anatomies'[40] like Dante's *Divine Comedy*, Jean de Meung's *Roman de la Rose*, Langland's *Piers Plowman*, and Gower's *Confessio Amantis*.

It can be seen too in persistent, perhaps obsessive form, in Lydgate, for whom the world seems to exist as a vast moral encyclopaedia, and classical literature as a dictionary of edifying fable and apophthegm. This is the reason that he can afford to pay the classics such scant personal, attention for their wealth is available to him in a much more easily assimilable form, in dictionaries, concordances, *florilegia*, collections of 'sentences', and collections of fables and anecdotes, such as those of Hygeia and Valerius Maximus, and bastardised versions like the *Gesta Romanorum*. This was Lydgate's classical reading, or at least this was the kind of filter through which the classics had to be passed before they were available to his understanding. He may have 'read' others. The only book in the Bury library in which he has left the undoubted mark of his physical presence is Bodley MS. Laud misc.233, in which, on the verso of the end fly-leaf, he has written 'Sciant presentes et futuri quod ego Johannis Lydgate'.[41] The book is a composite one, devoted chiefly to the *Synonyma* of Isidore and to the sermons of Hildebert, bishop of Le Mans in the early twelfth century, but I suspect that what interested Lydgate more were two subsidiary items, 'Versus circiter cxiv proverbiales' and 'Versus lxxiv heroici proverbiales'.[42] *Heroici* means 'drawn from the classics', and it is from this sort of compilation that Lydgate derived his knowledge of writers like Virgil and Horace and, in so doing, fortified the moralistic, encyclopaedic bent of his mind.

There are many other books in the Bury library which help us to understand the climate in which a medieval mind like Lydgate's grew and flourished. A volume of the writings of William de Conches, a French scholar of the school of Chartres, now MS. Gonville and Caius 225, would have been unremarkable in itself, but the book also contains or contained items of more significant and abiding interest to Lydgate, collections of sententiae culled from Plautus and Seneca, proverbial extracts and sayings from various writers, especially Ovid, and the *Valerius ad Rufinum*, a famous anti-feminist pamphlet.[43] The *Reductorium morale* of Pierre Bersuire (Petrus Berchorius), a Bury book of the fifteenth century, now MS. Pembroke (Cambridge) 31, is almost the typical medieval book, a moralised interpretation of Bartholomeus, *De proprietatibus rerum*, combined, for good measure, with an allegorical moralisation of Ovid's *Metamorphoses*.[44] Such evidence is general; but there are three books mentioned by Leland, in his examination of the Bury library just before dissolution, which are particularly important as representatives of a school of classicising commentators whose attitudes bear the closest resemblance to Lydgate's, and may have been instrumental in forming them. These are the books:

> Trivet super libros Boetii de consolatione philosophiae
> Waleys super Psalterium
> Ryngsted super Proverbia Salomonis.[45]

All three writers are English Dominican friars of the early fourteenth century, members of a group who employed a wide, if often superficial knowledge of the classics in commentary on the scriptures,[46] and whose techniques of encyclopaedic accumulation typify and dominate late medieval scholarship and culture. The movement goes back to the thirteenth century Franciscan John of Wales, who compiled various encylopaedias of edifying material, with titles like *Summa collationum* and *Breviloquium de Virtutbius*, in which the good deeds and wise sayings of ancient writers and philosophers are incorporated into moralistic schemes. The primary incentive is to provide illustrative material for professional sermon-writers and lecturers, using the classics as a great bran-tub of exempla, but the wave of interest soon moved out on a broader front. Nicholas Trivet is an example of the versatility of the movement; he wrote a chronicle in Anglo-Norman (a source of the *Man of Law's Tale*), an exposition of the Mass, and commentaries on various works, both classical and patristic, one of the best-known being his commentary on Boethius, which became a standard text-book. Trivet is a collector of data, an antiquarian rather than a historian or philosopher. For him Augustine's *De Civitate Dei* is a quarry of classical lore to be explained, and his commentary is primarily historical and grammatical, ploughing through, discussing authorship, provenance, subject-matter, explaining and amplifying allusions. There is no attempt to examine the nature of the work, or demonstrate its doctrinal or historical value, for this is taken for granted. The whole technique—accumulative, systematic, inorganic, non-creative—is typical, strongly reminiscent of Lydgate's methods in his long translations, and reminiscent too of nineteenth century editions of Shakespeare or of the attitudes of great nineteenth century medieval scholars like Skeat. There, too, we find the same unspoken assumptions about value and function, which leave the scholar free to indulge his bent for amplification, explanation and illustration.

Thomas Waleys goes further than Trivet, and uses the ancients as illustrations of Christian truth in the freest possible way. His *Moralitates* on various books of the Old Testament, which include a long commentary on the Psalter, are really a series of exempla, many of them of pagan origin, disguised as biblical commentary, 'using the text as a thread on which to string non-biblical stories'.

> His systematic procedure opened up new possibilities. The lecturer on Scripture from now onwards could indulge his secular interests and perform his statutory duties at one and the same time. A friar doctor who enjoyed reading the classics or indeed any other kind of secular literature no longer needed any special grace from his superiors. . . .[47]

This handling of classical and secular material, with its characteristic preoccupations, is the exact analogue for Lydgate's methods of procedure, and it would sometimes be helpful to think of Lydgate as a kind of vernacular Trivet or Waleys rather than as a cloistered Chaucer. Thomas Ringstead is somewhat later and less important, but his classicising commentary on *Proverbs* became widely known, and twenty manuscripts have survived, one of which, interestingly enough, was in the possession of Edmund Lacy, bishop of Exeter, and was left by him to his cathedral church, where it was chained in the library next to the most famous of these friars' commentaries, Robert Holcot on the book of Wisdom.[48] No copy of Holcot is recorded for the Bury library, but it is unthinkable that it did not possess one. Holcot is the classicizing commentator *par excellence*, ranging widely and freely over classical history and mythology, inventing and improving as he goes, touching the text only lightly before springing off after new game, so that his work can be seen, in its true light, as 'a vast *florilegium* of verse and prose'.[49]

Holcot provides an opportunity to be more specific about some of the resemblances that have been suggested between the fourteenth-century friars and the fifteenth-century monk. Here is an example of Holcot at work, manipulating his sources and assembling detail for his praise of good women in a moralisation of the word 'water' (*Wisdom*, 16:19).

> He begins with good Christian women. Our Lord found greater constancy and devotion in his women disciples than in Peter, John or James, and may well say in the words of Boethius that no fright could stay them at least from sharing his journey; he showed himself first to women after his resurrection. Holcot goes on to good pagan women. The *locus classicus* for his theme was St. Jerome's defence of chastity against Jovinian. Jerome listed Penelope, Portia, Lucretia and Dido as examples of faithful wives. He deliberately chose the older version of the Dido story, according to which she killed herself to avoid marrying again. Holcot takes over the list and embroiders by quoting Ovid's letter from Penelope to Ulysses. Anxious to call as many witnesses as possible, he ruins the effect, when he comes to Dido, by adding a reference to the *Aeneid*. Virgil's Dido was only too anxious for a second marriage; but Holcot does not notice what he has done. The Sabine women join his company, because he has found them coupled with Lucretia in the *Letter of Valerius to Rufinus*. Martial supplies him with lines on Portia, and on another faithful Roman, Arria, wife of Paetus. He also takes from Martial the name of Caesar's daughter, Julia, and of Sulpicia. He ends with 'Alcyone, Calyce and countless other women'. Alcyone and Calyce belong to Ovid's *Epistle* from Hero to Leander; Hero mentions them as women who were loved by the sea-god. They have no relevance as examples of faithful wives. Holcot perhaps liked their names and hoped that no one would investigate the context.
>
> (Smalley, *op. cit.*, pp. 155–6)

It is difficult not to be reminded of Lydgate's *Temple of Glass*, and of the catalogue of famous lovers whose pictures the dreamer finds painted on the walls inside the temple. In this long catalogue (42–142), various traditions merge and combine. There is the familiar list of good women who were unfortunate in love (Dido, Medea, Phillis),

4

along with other good women who were just unfortunate (Philomena, Lucrece); famous lovers like Paris and Helen, Tristram and Ysaude, mingle with faithful wives (Penelope, Griselda, Alceste); Venus appears twice, once with Adonis, once with Mars and Vulcan, as well as being the goddess to whom all are making supplication. Jove's rape of Europa and the story of Amphitryon and Alcmena are included, and the story of the *Knight's Tale* told in passing. By a strange quirk of association, the story of Theseus deceiving the Minotaur is told, without any mention of the love-affair which would make it relevant. Even the nuptials of Mercury and Philology find a place, and the list of names ends with the Canacee of the *Squire's Tale*, and how she had a magic ring which enabled her to understand the language of birds,

> And hou hir broþir so oft holpen was
> In his myschefe bi þe stede of bras. (141–2)

In the end, it is only necessary that people should have been of different sexes to be enrolled in this catalogue, which ends not because Lydgate has exhausted a category but because he has, for the moment, exhausted his memory. This compulsive accumulation is often spoken of as if it were peculiar to Lydgate; in degree it may be, but in kind it is clearly related to the medieval passion for a certain kind of encyclo-paedism.

Of course, the passage from Holcot reminds us of a famous virtuoso piece in Chaucer too, the long series of exempla in the *Franklin's Tale* (*CT*, V, 1364–1456), where Dorigen laments the impending loss of her wifely chastity with allusion to scores of other good women in history who were similarly threatened. Again, sheer accumulation gradually undermines the relevance, even the seriousness of the exempla, and Dorigen ends with three ladies of whom a critic has written: 'Valeria's glory had consisted in refusing to remarry, Rhodogune's, in killing her nurse, and Bilia's, in never remarking on the smell of her husband's breath'.[50] But Chaucer, as one might expect, does not do this sort of thing without a purpose. Like all medieval poets, he has a predilection for lists, but in him the passion for encyclopaedic comprehensiveness is, as Muscatine puts it, 'curved toward functional literary use'.[51] The very conventionality of Dorigen's complaint, and the slightly ludicrous note on which it ends, are designed to release the dramatic pressure on the narrative, so that it can end on its right romantic note, all-gratulant. It is a superb piece of manipulation on Chaucer's part.

There will be more to say on Lydgate's accumulative technique later, but it may be useful to establish one more connection with the classici-sing friars. Beryl Smalley has some harsh comments on John Lathbury, one of the later followers of the movement. In his commentary on Lamentations, she says, he 'seems to be working a mincing-machine', and illustrates this from his comment on 'How doth the city sit solitary' (*Lam.*, 1:1), where he compares the mourning city to the *mater dolorosa* and then collects all the instances he can find from biblical or profane history or myth, where anyone sat anywhere, either rejoicing or grieving, and pairs or contrasts them with Mary:

> Quomodo igitur sedet?
> Non sedet cum sublimato Salomone in throno dignitatis,
> sed sedet cum excecato Samsone in carcere dedecoris et
>   deformitatis.
> Non sedet cum Midride in solio regalis otii,
> sed sedet cum Appollone in pulvere servilis opprobrii.
> Non sedet cum Tantalo in cathedra studii perfamosi,
> sed sedet cum Ovidio in terra aliena exilii lacrimosi.
> Non sedet cum Sardanapallo in camera virginis delicate, languens
>   ex amore,
> sed sedet cum Appollonio in provincia mortis elongata (*sic*),
>   lugens ex dolore.   (Smalley, pp. 226–7)

And so on. Lydgate uses the same scholastic technique of amplification by accumulated comparison, usually to better effect, partly because his repertoire is sooner exhausted. He uses it not only in obvious exercises like *Misericordias domini in etenum cantabo* and *Gloriosa dicta sunt de te*,[52] but also in passages of greater literary significance, like the lament for Troilus, where he can, at times, tap a powerful sense of the world's grief and decay:

> And for his deth swiche a wo þer was,
> þat I trowe þer is no man a-lyve
> Whiche koude ariȝt halvendel discryve
> Her pitous wo nor lamentacioun:
> Certis not Boys, þat hadde swiche renoun,
> With drery wordis to be-wepe and crye
> In compleynynge to philosophie,
> þoruȝ his boke accusynge ay Fortune,
> þat seld or nouȝt can in oon contune—
> She is so ful of transmutacioun.

O Stace of Thebes make no bost nor soun
Of drerinesse for to write at al,
Nouþer of deth nor festis funeral,
Of makyng sorwe nor adversite;
Late be þi wepynge, O þou Nyobe,
ȝe suster also of Melleager,
þat custom han for to fle so fer,
From ȝer to ȝere ȝoure broþer to compleyne;
And þou þat weptist oute þin eyen tweyne,
Edippus, kyng of Thebeisþe cyte,
þou woful Mirre, and Calxtone,
þat so wel can in rage ȝou be-mene,
And Dido eke, of Cartage quene,—
Lat be ȝoure dool and contricioun
And Philis eke, for þi Demephoun,
And Echcho eke, þat now dost be-gynne
To crie and waille, and also þou Corrynne,
þat whilom were in so gret affray
For deth only of þi popyngay,
As in his boke telleþ us Ovyde,—
Late al þis wo now be leide a-side,
And make of hit no comparisoun
Un-to þe wo þat was in Troye toun
For deth only of þis worþi knyȝt. . . .
Allas! who koude al her sorwes telle?
I trowe, certis, Pluto depe in helle,
For al his torment and his peynes kene,
Nouþer she, Proserpina his quene,
Nouþer þe wery wode Tycyus,
Ixioun, nor hungri Tantalus
Ne coude nat, for al her bitter peyne,
So furiously wepen and compleyne
As don Troyens, Troylus, for þi sake.

(*Troy*, IV,3004–53)

Even here, it will be seen, he could not resist Corinna and her parrot, hardly appropriate in the circumstances.[53]

These comparisons are not intended to prove direct influence. That is not possible, though some ways have been suggested in which it might have come about; nor is it necessary, for the object is simply to build up some sense of the bookish atmosphere in which Lydgate was fostered. He wrote as a monk might be expected to write, but it is important that we should know about the sort of expectations we are entitled to, and I have tried to gauge these in writing about his monastic background. If at times the impression may have been that his total achievement is the product of a well-stocked library and a naïve encyclopaedic habit of mind, then one can leave the impression, not wholly false in itself, to be modified by examination of individual works. It is interesting to notice how close this impression is to what Chaucer expected of his Monk, who says in his Prologue:

> And if yow list to herkne hyderward,
> I wol yow seyn the lyf of Seint Edward;
> Or ellis, first, tragedies wol I telle,
> Of whiche I have an hundred in my celle.
>
> (CT, VII,1969–72)

Nothing could be more appropriate to the monk, with his library full of patchwork encyclopaedias and collections of exempla, than the catalogue of the falls of Princes which follows. It is almost like a premonition of Lydgate, whose longest work is a gigantic amplification of just this same theme. Chaucer is not making fun of the Monk here; he portrays the Monk standing on his dignity, partly to confound the Host, partly to balance the picture of the Monk's worldliness in the General Prologue. But he does manage to suggest the limitations of the Monk's Tale by having it interrupted by the Knight when only 17 of the proposed 100 tragedies have been recounted. Thus, dramatically, he expresses dissatisfaction with the formlessness of the encyclopaedic approach, and, by the very fact that it is the Knight who interrupts, draws attention to the more sophisticated handling of potential human tragedy in the *Knight's Tale*.[54] But all this should not make us assume, in our modern way, that Chaucer found the *Monk's Tale* ridiculous; and Lydgate certainly didn't.

Setting Lydgate against his background is useful in teaching us what to expect, but it is obvious that Lydgate surpasses expectations, partly because he acquired a facility in the writing of English verse, above all because he was exposed early to the influence of Chaucer. It is Chaucer who introduces the element of the unexpected into Lydgate, who raises his ambitions and extends his horizons and leads him out to and beyond the frontiers of his ability. To see the truth of this, we need only look at the work of his monastic contemporaries, all of them

writing in Latin, in entirely traditional fields of commentary and
chronicle: Thomas Walsingham, for instance, whose *Historia Anglicana*
is a typical late product of the St. Alban's school of historiography,[55]
and whose *Archana Deorum*, a commentary on Ovid's *Metamorphoses*,
reflects the fashionable interest in classical mythology and deities.[56]
Similar interests are incidentally displayed in the two chronicles of
Henry V by Thomas Elmham, a monk of St. Augustine's, Canterbury,
the *Gesta Henrici Quinti* and the *Liber Metricus de Henrico Quinto*, and
the verse of the latter, with its florid language, contorted syntax, and
elaborate apparatus of acrostics, anagrams and chronograms, shows
the growing taste for 'florida verborum venustas'[57] with which Lydgate's cultivation of aureate language is perhaps to be associated. The
most noteworthy of these monastic contemporaries, however, is John
Whethamstede, abbot of St. Alban's (d. 1465), a great book-collector
and book-lover.[58] He had some eighty-seven books transcribed in the
monastic scriptorium during his abbacy, a good many of them of his
own composition, and he was always advising Humphrey of Gloucester
about books, and sometimes supplying him with them. His own works,
such as the *Granarium* and the *Palearium Poetarum*, are all encyclopaedic
compilations of one kind or another, in which classical history and
mythology are ransacked for edifying *exempla* of Christian truth.
Part II of the *Granarium*, for instance,[59] treats in succession of Giges,
Graecus, Gratituda, Gula, Hannibal, and Hermes Trimegistus, of
Senectus (examples of old men), Silla, Socrates, Sol, Solon, Sompnum
(the significance of dreams and visions, such as Calpurnia's). A highly
coloured and exclamatory account of Lucrecia stands conveniently
next to the article on Luxuria, and Pudicicia offers the sort of list of
women we have already seen to be so popular. The longest article is
on Tullius. The *Palearium Poetarum*[60] is a dictionary of classical mythology, based on Boccaccio's *De genealogia deorum*, and here we find, in
sequence, Sepulcrum, Serapis, Serpens, Seston (the Greek island),
Sibilla, Sicanus (eponymous founder of Sicily), Sicilides Musae
('Theocritus), Sicoris (a river in Spain), Signum (as of the zodiac) and
Silvanus. Nowhere could the monastic habit of pillaging antiquity be
better displayed. To call it 'humanism' is grossly mistaken, except in so
far as we assume that this kind of indiscriminate spade-work prepared
the ground for humanistic reading of classical literature. Whethamstede's style, both in his prose and in his verse, examples of which can
be seen in his metrical additions to Amundsham's *Annals*,[61] is heavy
with classical allusion, ornate, highly coloured:

O me miserum! O me privatum gratia, et sinistra fortunae, non dextra, novercaliter consignatum! qui stellam sub nube latentem non agnoveram, nec dum mecum lucens fuerat, gratiam habui agnoscendi eam[62]

he says, in a letter from Italy to the brethren at St. Alban's, regretting his failure to get better acquainted with a fellow-traveller on the road to Florence.

Whethamstede's predilections for anecdotal encyclopaedism and for an ornate style are Lydgate's took. We can recognise the lineaments and habits of mind, at the same time that we recognise the wider range of Lydgate's secular reference, and something else too that we can only attribute to Chaucer. Better-born, and better-educated, Lydgate might have been a Whethamstede. Thanks to Chaucer, he has a place in English literature.

Notes to Chapter Two

1 *Fall of Princes*, IX,3431–51. Lydgate makes further reference to his birth-place in *Fall*, VIII,194, and in *Isopes Fabules*, Prologue, 32 (*Minor Poems*, II,567).

2 In MS.Harley 743, the Register of John Lakynghethe (Lakenheath), a fourteenth-century monk of St. Edmund's, Lidgate is mentioned in a list of charters granted to the monastery at different times (Dugdale, *Monasticon*, ed. 1846, 6 vols., III,121). In MS.Harley 1005, the *Liber Albus*, a collection of Bury documents of different date, the list of villages 'infra libertatem Sancti Eadmundi' includes Lidgate (Dugdale, III,165).

3 *Testament*, 670–2 (*Minor Poems*, I,354). Objective data of this sort in the *Testament* are to be distinguished from the confessional formula according to which it is framed, and can be used cautiously in a reconstruction of Lydgate's early life such as is suggested above. For the general patterns of recruitment, schooling and novitiate, see D. Knowles, *The Religious Orders in England*, vol. II (Cambridge 1955), pp, 229–33, 294–7.

4 See Schick, *Temple of Glas*, p. lxxvi. There are collections of the Lydgate life-records in Schick, pp. lxxxv–xcix; Schirmer, *John Lydgate*, esp. pp. 21, 246–7; Lydgate and Burgh's *Secrees of old Philisoffres*, ed. R. Steele (EETS, ES 66,1894), pp. xxiii–xxx; A. B. Emden, *A Biographical Register of the University of Oxford* (3 vols., Oxford 1957–9), II,1185–6.

5 This reference and the two following are actually to the date of issue of 'letters dimissory' (recommendation for ordination) not ordination itself, and are from MS.Cotton Tiberius B.ix, the register of William Cratfield, abbot of Bury 1389–1414 (ff. 35b, 69b, 85b).

6 Fordham's Register, ff. 234, 238 (Emden, II,1186).

7 For accounts of the abbey and its history, see the *Victoria County History of Suffolk*, ed. W. Page, vol. II (1907), pp. 56–72; Dugdale, *Monasticon* (ed. cit.), III,98–176; M. R. James, *On the Abbey of St. Edmund at Bury* (Cambridge Antiquarian Society, Octavo publications no. 28, 1895)—for the library and the abbey church; *Memorials of St. Edmund's Abbey*, ed. T. Arnold, 3 vols. (Rolls series, 1890–6).

8 *VCH*, pp. 67–9; D. Knowles and R. N. Hadcock, *Medieval Religious Houses in England and Wales* (London 1953), p. 61.

9 *VCH*, p. 69; Knowles and Hadcock, p. 61.

10 Other abbots during Lydgate's working life were William of Cratfield 1389–1414, William of Exeter 1414–29, and William Babington 1446–53. For a complete list of abbots see *VCH*, p. 72.

11 *VCH*, p. 71; *Memorials*, ed. Arnold, III,xiii,65.

12 E.g. *Memorials*, III,249.

13 *Memorials*, III,254.

14 Lydgate's versions of Cnut's charter (*Memorials*, III,217) and of the Conqueror's (III,233) can be compared with the originals in *Memorials* I,342, 348. Bury was better off than its great neighbour, St. Alban's, which in a dispute with the bishop of Norwich was constrained to produce copies of charters which are manifest forgeries (Amundsham's *Annals of St. Alban's*, ed. H. T. Riley, 2 vols., Rolls series, 1870–1, II,xlvii).

15 Dugdale, III,113 (translated from the Register Curteys, f. 110).

16 *VCH*, p. 71.

17 *Minor Poems*, I,288.

18 *Memorials*, II,xlvii; III,39.

19 Amundsham's *Annals*, I,112; II,xxiii.

20 Knowles, *Religious Orders in England*, II,209.

21 *Chapters of the English Black Monks 1215–1540*, ed. W. A. Pantin (3 vols., Camden Third series, 45, 47, 54, 1931–7), II,109–34; Knowles, *op. cit.*, II,184.

22 MS.Ashmole 59. See *Minor Poems*, II,598.

23 Pantin, *op. cit.*, II,64–82.

24 Pantin, *op. cit.*, III,221–2,229.

25 *Anglo-Norman Letters and Petitions from All Souls MS.182*, ed. M. Dominica Legge (Oxford 1941), pp. 411–12.

26 Emden, *Biographical Register* I,500–2.

27 *John Lydgate: Poems* (Clarendon Medieval and Tudor Series, Oxford 1966), p. 195.

28 See *Minor Poems*, I,1,209,315.

29 Probably second only to that of Christ Church, Canterbury. For Bury library, see James, *On the Abbey of St. Edmund at Bury*; also, for lists of Bury MSS. still extant, James, 'Bury St. Edmunds manuscripts', *English Historical Review*, XLI(1926),251–60; *Medieval Libraries of Great Britain*, ed. N. R. Ker

(2nd ed., 1964), pp. 16–22. There are about 260 Bury MSS. still extant, including 110 in the library of Pembroke college, Cambridge, which acquired them in 1599 by the bequest of alderman William Smart of Ipswich.

30 See R. A. Mynors, 'The Latin Classics known to Boston of Bury', in *Fritz Saxl: a Volume of Memorial Essays*, ed. D. J. Gordon (London 1957), pp. 199–217.

31 Knowles, *op. cit.*, II,340–2; see R. M. Wilson, 'The Medieval Library of Titchfield Abbey', *Proc. Leeds Philos. and Lit. Soc.*, V(1940), 150–77, 252–76.

32 Knowles, p. 343.

33 *English Works of John Gower*, ed. G. C. Macaulay (2 vols., Oxford 1901), I,cxlv.

34 Margaret Rickert, *Painting in Britain: the Middle Ages* (Pelican History of Art, London 1954), p. 173. But see below, p. 173. There are other Lydgate-portraits in MS.Harley 2278 (a presentation-picture, and also one of Lydgate praying for inspiration at the tomb of St. Edmund), in MS.Cotton Aug.A.iv and the Crawford-Rylands MS. of the *Troy Book*, and the Pynson *Troy Book* (all presentation-pictures, the last a woodcut), in MS.Royal 18.D.ii of *Thebes* (Lydgate? and other pilgrims), in MS.Harley 1766 of the *Fall* (Lydgate and his abbot before the king), and in Pynson's *Testament* (a little woodcut of Lydgate at his desk). Most of these are reproduced in Schirmer's book (he confuses two of them in his ascriptions, pp. 63, 146, and is surely wrong in identifying Lydgate as 'second from left' in the *Thebes* picture?).

35 See E. A. Savage, *Old English Libraries* (London 1911), pp. 23, 101; *The English Library before 1700*, ed. F. Wormald and C. E. Wright (London 1958), esp. pp. 15, 33.

36 James, *On the Abbey of St. Edmund*, pp. 108–111.

37 Pantin, *op. cit.*, II,114.

38 Savage, *op. cit.*, p. 73.

39 Beryl Smalley, *The Study of the Bible in the Middle Ages* (Oxford 1952), esp. chap. IV.

40 Frye's term, as derived from Burton's *Anatomy of Melancholy*.

41 'Let all, present and future, know that I . . .' etc., a legal formula used in letters patent. See Hammond, *Chaucer to Surrey*, p. 94; Emden, *Biographical Register*, II,1186. Mr. Neil Ker assures me that it is not a mark of ownership. The fly-leaf also has other writings, including repeated references to an abbot William of Bury (all four in Lydgate's time were called William).

42 The latter are on f. 123a. The last two verses, for instance, are 'Felix qui potuit rerum cognoscere causas' (*Georgics*, II,490) and 'Aut doluit miseras inopem, aut invidit habenti' (*ibid.* 499). Preceding this are three lines from Ovid, *Met.* I,84–6, 'Pronaque cum spectent . . .' and 'None bene conveniunt nec in una sede morantur Maiestas et amor' from *Met.*II,846. All are proverbial 'sentences' and appear in *Lateinische Sprichwörter und Sentenzen des Mittelalters*, ed. H. Walther (5 vols., Göttingen, 1963–7): nos. 8967, 22635, 17277.

43 Mynors, *op. cit.*, pp. 210, 208; M. R. James, *A Descriptive Catalogue of the Manuscripts in the library of Gonville and Caius College* (2 vols., Cambridge 1907–8), I,263–6.

44 See Beryl Smalley, *English Friars and Antiquity in the early 14th century* (Oxford 1960), p. 262; Jean Seznec, *The Survival of the Pagan Gods* (1940, trans. 1953; Harper Torchbooks, 1961), pp. 93, 174.

45 James, *On the Abbey of St. Edmund*, p. 10.

46 Their work is studied in Beryl Smalley, *English Friars and Antiquity*. See also W. A. Pantin, *The English Church in the 14th century* (Cambridge 1955), pp. 143–50.

47 Smalley, *English Friars and Antiquity*, pp. 82–3.

48 Smalley, p. 215.

49 Smalley, p. 151.

50 Germaine Dempster, 'Chaucer at work on the Complaint in the *Franklin's Tale*', *MLN*,LII(1937),16–23 (p. 20).

51 C. Muscatine, '*The Canterbury Tales*: style of the man and style of the work', in *Chaucer and Chaucerians* (ed. Brewer), pp. 88–113 (p. 95).

52 *Minor Poems*, I,71, 315.

53 From Ovid, *Amores*, II,vi.

54 See R. E. Kaske, 'The Knight's Interruption of the *Monk's Tale*', *ELH*, XXIV(1957),249–68.

55 Kingsford, *English Historical Literature in the 15th century*, p. 12.

56 Knowles, *op. cit.*, p. 267.

57 See the article with this title by E. F. Jacob in the *Bulletin of the John Rylands Library*, XVII(1933),264–90. For Elmham's chronicles, see *Memorials of Henry V*, ed. C. A. Cole (Rolls series, 1858).

58 For accounts of Whethamstede, see Knowles, pp. 193–7; Amundsham's *Annals*, ed. Riley, II, Introduction; W. F. Schirmer, *Der englische Frühhumanismus* (Tubingen 1963), pp. 73–90; R. Weiss, *Humanism in England during the 15th century* (2nd ed., Oxford 1957), pp. 30–8; C. E. Hodge, *The Abbey of St. Alban's under John of Whethamstede* (Ph.D.diss., unpub., Manchester 1933), pp. 165–223.

59 MS.Cotton Tiberius D.v., in the British Museum.

60 MS.Add.26764, in the British Museum. The catalogue calls it Part IV of the *Granarium*, but see Hodge, *op. cit.*, p. 175.

61 *Ed. cit.*, II,lvi–lviii.

62 *Ed. cit.*, I,136. 'O wretched me! Oh me! deprived, as I am, of all grace, and marked by fortune in step-dame's mood with the left hand, not her right; in that I did not recognise that star that lay hid beneath the cloud, nor had the grace to recognise it, while it was near unto me in its effulgence' (II,xxix).

CHAPTER THREE

Chaucer and the Literary Background

Lydgate's debt to Chaucer is enormous. From him he took his style, his verse-forms, his metre, and many of the genres in which he wrote; Chaucer anticipates most of the directions in which Lydgate moves, apart from the religious verse (and even here he provided at least one model for the 'literary' saint's life in the *Man of Law's Tale*) and the practical and occasional verse. Lydgate owes his very language to Chaucer, for it is unlikely that English would have been available in 1400 as a literary language of high status had it not been for Chaucer. Much has been made of the continuity of English writing in the twelfth and thirteenth centuries, and perhaps the work of R. W. Chambers and R. M. Wilson was necessary to restore a patriotic perspective to the scene,[1] but the fact remains that, when every scrap of evidence for the continuity of English as a literary language has been assembled, the literary culture of this country during those two centuries was over-whelmingly French or Anglo-Norman. Social, economic and political change help to explain the reassertion of English in the fourteenth century, but the pressure is all from below and does not necessarily affect the language of literary culture. Furthermore, there is a mass of evidence for the survival of French in all forms of written communication in the late fourteenth and early fifteenth centuries—in legal documents, public records, official and private letters as well as literature.[2] Many of the signs of change so frequently quoted for the fourteenth century—Trevisa's remark, for instance, about the growing use of English for teaching in grammar-schools, or the 1362 statute encouraging the use of English in law-courts—though they may be straws in the wind, are still in themselves very much straws. The war with France made a difference, but not a striking or immediate one, and Henry V, who spent much of his life fighting the French, still conducted his correspondence, not only with the abbey of Bury, as we have seen, but with his father, his brothers, his friends and servants, in

French.[3] Gower, who wrote major works in all three languages, French, Latin, and English, is a good example of the literary equilibrium in the late fourteenth century.

In other words, there is no reason in the nature of things for Chaucer, and whilst one would not wish to disinter old myths of Chaucer as 'the father of the English language', it is necessary to recognise that the rapid emergence of English as a status-language in the late fourteenth century is due in large part to his example. In this sense, therefore, Chaucer provided Lydgate with his language, with the example, the opportunity and the justification for writing in English, and the pressure of Chaucer's influence can be gauged from the resistance it had to overcome—not only the almost universal currency of Latin amongst Lydgate's monastic contemporaries, but also the suspicion which English had fallen under as a result of Wycliff's use of the vernacular as part of his anti-clerical propaganda campaign.[4]

The story does not end here. Lydgate's own achievement in 'fixing' English as a literary language should not be underestimated. We have seen that he enjoyed a reputation hardly less than Chaucer's in the fifteenth century, and the wide currency and popularity of his work, as well as its sheer volume, certainly helped to consolidate the process which Chaucer had begun, the assertion of the status of English and the extension of its range. It is difficult to analyse this process, except by pointing to Lydgate's influence upon subsequent writers, and this, as we have seen, extends up through the *Mirror for Magistrates* and the Elizabethan chronicle-plays to Shakespeare, but it would be well to guard against the easy assumption that it happened 'naturally'. Someone, for instance, had to introduce the large number of new words which English needed to be able to cope with its vast new range of responsibilities, and in an extraordinarily high proportion of cases it is Lydgate who does so. Reismüller[5] lists 800 words first used by Lydgate; the number is certainly exaggerated, because the *OED*, which Reismüller was using, is severely limited by the availability of texts in its day, especially in its earlier volumes, and the frequent appearance of Lydgate in first place in its entries is due to nothing more than his comparatively easy accessibility. Even Hammond's much more cautious list has to be whittled down when checked against the new *Middle English Dictionary*, though Lydgate is still left with the credit of having introduced words like *abuse, adjacent, capacity, circumspect, combine, credulity, delude, depend, disappear, equivalent,* and *excel*, some of them so much part of the English language that we can hardly imagine how it managed without them. But counting 'firsts' is a crude method of assessing Lydgate's contribution to the language. What is important is not that he used words first, but that he used new or rare words over and over again and in so doing embedded them for ever in the language. Of 25 examples of *excel*, for instance, quoted in the *MED*, 21 are from Lydgate, and so are 9 out of 10 of *adjacent*, and all 5 of *disappear*. Many words, like *confidence*, are found in isolated and obscure contexts before Lydgate, but it is Lydgate who by constant use gives them currency. Many words first used by Chaucer are not used again by others until Lydgate has worn a place for them in the language. It is this that prompts one to think of Lydgate as being partly responsible for Chaucer's impression of modernity—as compared with, say, the impression we get from *Sir Gawain and the Green Knight*. Chaucer is so accessible because the linguistic journey back to him has been worn smooth by the labours of his successor.

There is another sense in which Lydgate owes his language to Chaucer. Language is not a lexicon, and to talk about individual words in isolation is rather misleading, for language does not present itself to a writer in this way, but rather as a series of phrases, collocations, cadences, and idioms. The special quality of a traditional poetic language is that it emphasizes this aspect of language, and concentrates its resources in ways that develop a special effectiveness. Ultimately, of course, this leads to the fossilisation of poetic diction, as in the alliterative poetry of the later Old English period, or the Miltonic imitations of the eighteenth century, and there are symptoms of the same process in Chaucerian poetry of the fifteenth century, for which Lydgate is partly responsible. He certainly inherited from Chaucer a well-established and highly developed poetic language, though it would not do to think of Chaucer as having 'invented' this language, for he himself took over a whole repertoire of phrase and idiom from popular English romance[6] and other sources. Nevertheless it is he who welds these diverse materials into a distinctive style, with its wealth of traditional formula, rhetorical embellishment and conscious aureation,[7] and the fact that Coleridge could think of it as a 'neutral' style is a mark of the success of Chaucer's art not of his lack of artifice.

Lydgate took over, then, from Chaucer first of all a great stock of phrases, tags, and formulae—asseverations (*I dar wel seyn, soth to telle, I yow ensure*), intensives (*al and som, more and lasse, in every wise*), expressions of opinion (*as I wene, as I trow*), references to authority (*as olde bokes seyn, in story as I fynde*), brevity-formulae (*there is namoore to seyn, shortly for to endyte*), and others[8]—and it is these that contribute markedly to the Chaucerian texture of his verse. Needless to say, his handling of them is different, for whereas Chaucer can often turn conventional phrases to good effect by using them with a touch of irony or to convey a sense of conversational idiom, Lydgate uses them quite frankly as line-fillers. Here, for instance, is how he accommodates one of Chaucer's favourite lines—'For pitee renneth soone in gentil herte'—to the narrower limits of the octosyllabic:

> For pyte, who that kan adverte,
> Renneth sone in gentyl herte.
>> (*Reason and Sensuality*, 6915–16)

Lydgate also appropriates whole lines from Chaucer, showing by his choice a clear response to what is striking and memorable in Chaucer's idiom:

> Ther nas no good day, ne no saluyng
>> (*Knight's Tale*, CT,I,1649)
> Cf. þer was no gooday nor no saluyng   (*Troy*, II,6381)

> That Emelye, that fairer was to sene
> Than is the lylie upon his stalke grene
>> (*Kn.T.*, CT,I,1035–6)
> Cf. þat whilom was frescher for to sene
> þan þe lillye on his stalke grene   (*Troy*, II,3921–2)

> He moot go pipen in an yvy leef
>> (*Kn.T.*, CT,I,1838)
> Cf. Thou maist go pypen in an ivy leeff   (*Churl and Bird*, 276)

> Lo, here a parfit resoun of a goos!
>> (*Parlement of Foules*, 568)
> Cf. Her is a gentil reson of an hors!
>> (*Horse, Goose and Sheep*, 477)

Often it seems that a particular cadence in Chaucer's verse has stuck in Lydgate's mind, so that he keeps coming back to it, trying to catch it himself. The opening of the *Parlement*, with the memorable chiasmus of the second line—

> The lyf so short, the craft so long to lerne,

Th'assay so hard, so sharp the conquerynge—

occupies him frequently:

> The thoght oppressed with inward sighes sore,
> The peynful lyve, the body langwysshing,
> The woful ghost, the herte rent and tore,
> The pitous chere pale in compleynyng. . . .
>
> (*Complaint of the Black Knight*, 218–21)

This is probably not to much purpose, nor this—

> Our liff heer short, of wit the gret dulnesse—
>
> (*Fall*, III,22)

but the groping for Chaucer's rhythm is fascinating to watch, and on one occasion at least it sparks off two lines of great beauty:

> Fresshnesse of floures, of braunches the beute,
> Have ai on chaunge a tremblyng attendaunce.
>
> (*Fall*, III, 2201-2

Another Chaucerian cadence which hung in Lydgate's memory is the anaphora on *Lo here* in the epilogue to the *Troilus*:

> Lo here, of payens corsed olde rites,
> Lo here, what alle hir goddes may availle;
> Lo here, thise wrecched worldes appetites. . . .
>
> (V,1849ff)

Again and again, he echoes this sequence, as in the corresponding passage in the *Troy Book*—

> Lo here þe fyn of false felicite,
> Lo here þe ende of worldly brotilnesse,
> Of fleshy lust, lo here th'unstabilnesse. . . .
>
> (III,4224–6)

with its further memories of the *Swich fyn* stanza (*Troilus*, V,1828) and 'worldes brotelnesse' (1832); and again after the murder of Achilles:

> Loo here þe ende of falshed and untrouþe,
> Loo here þe fyn of swiche trecherie. . . .[9]

The striking figure which Chaucer uses in the *Knight's Tale*,

> Who looketh lightly now but Palamoun?

> Who spryngeth up for joye but Arcite?
>
> (*CT*,I,1870–1)

and repeats, with characteristic irony, in the *Miller's Tale*,

> Who rubbeth now, who froteth now his lippes
> With dust, with sond, with straw, with clooth, with
>   chippes,
> But Absolon. . . .
>
> (*CT*,I,3747–9)

is a favourite with Lydgate, echoed for instance in the lament for Troilus,

> Who wepeth now, with face ful pitous,
> Or maketh sorwe but Eccuba þe quene?
> Who wepeth now but faire Polycene?
> Who wepeth now but Paris and Eleyne!
>
> (*Troy*, IV,3056–9)

where Guido has only 'Dolet Heccuba, dolet nimium Polixena, dolet Helena'.[10]

Hints have already been given of the kind of damage Lydgate can do to Chaucer's delicate rhythms and felicities of diction when he tries to imitate them. It is proper to draw attention to this, not to stress the difference of quality, for this is obvious, but to indicate more precisely the nature of the difference. Chaucer's lines on the Friar, for instance,

> His eyen twynkled in his heed aryght,
> As doon the sterres in the frosty nyght   (*CT*, I,267–8)

are imitated thus in Lydgate's description of Fortune:

> Whos brennyng eyen sparklyng of ther liht
> As doon sterris the frosti wyntres niht.   (*Fall*, VI,27–8)

At a glance one sees the shaking loose of syntax, as a result of the characteristic substitution of participle (*sparklyng*) for finite verb; the loss of metre in the second line, resulting from the inclusion of superfluous extra detail (*wyntres*); and the attempt at a greater richness of imagery (*brennyng* as well as *sparklyng*) which involves contradiction of *brennyng* and *frosti*, and dissipates the sharp simplicity of Chaucer's image. It is not a slavish imitation by any means; in fact, it is obviously intended as an improvement, a *de luxe* version of Chaucer, but ambition painfully outruns poetic capacity.

There are many occasions when Lydgate is tempted to extended close imitation of Chaucer, because of coincidence of material. The *Thebes* draws heavily on the *Knight's Tale*, especially in the episode of Theseus's intervention at Thebes (4463–602), where the two narratives run concurrently. Several lines are copied exactly,[11] and long passages, such as the description of the funeral, are closely parallel. The freer imitations are most interesting, the way in which, for instance, the majestic repetition of:

> Thus rit this duc, thus rit this conquerour   (*CT*,I,981)

is deflated to:

> And how this Duk withoute more abood
> The same day toward Thebes rood,
> Ful lik in soth a worthy conquerour.   (*Thebes*, 4533–5)

Everything is lost, including metre, in the flood of verbiage. Again:

> He faught, and slough hym manly as a knyght
> In pleyn bataille, and putte the folk to flyght
>   (*CT*, I,987–8)

becomes, with loss of enjambement, of metre (the second line is a Lydgate trade-mark) and of idiomatic ease:

> How that he faught and slough hym like a knyght
> And all his host putte unto the flyght.[12]

Chaucer is also plundered for the *Troy Book*. Many of the amplifications of classical allusions, such as the story of Aeneas or the labours of Hercules, are drawn not from Virgil nor even from Ovid, one of the few classical authors of whom Lydgate did have direct knowledge, but from Chaucer's accounts in the *Legend of Dido* and the *Monk's Tale*.[13] In addition, Chaucer is ransacked for phrases and details, especially in the story of Criseyde's departure from Troy, where again Lydgate's narrative runs parallel to Chaucer's, in the *Troilus*. There is one occasion, the formal portrait of Criseyde, where he is rash enough to invite direct comparison with Chaucer, and an examination of the two descriptions will help to fix finally in our minds the precise differences between the great poet and the honest journeyman. Lydgate protests at length his inability to compete with Chaucer, but declares that he must, as a conscientious translator, keep to the matter of his author, Guido della Colonna, and so, stumbling along, as he tells us, like blind Bayard,

he will begin. The ingenuousness of this is undermined by the fact that
he chooses to follow Chaucer rather than Guido: he is obviously trying to show up favourably beside Chaucer. Here is Chaucer's portrait:

> Criseyde mene was of hire stature,
> Therto of shap, of face, and ek of cheere,
> Ther myghte ben no fairer creature.
> And ofte tyme this was hire manere,
> To gon ytressed with hire heres clere   810
> Doun by hire coler at hire bak byhynde,
> Which with a thred of gold she wolde bynde.
>
> And, save hire browes joyneden yfere,
> Ther nas no lak, in aught I kan espien.
> But for to speken of hire eyen cleere,   815
> Lo, trewely, they writen that hire syen,
> That Paradis stood formed in hire yen.
> And with hire riche beaute evere more
> Strof love in hire ay, which of hem was more.
>
> She sobre was, ek symple, and wys withal,   820
> The best ynorisshed ek that myghte be,
> And goodly of hire speche in general,
> Charitable, estatlich, lusty, and fre;
> Ne nevere mo ne lakked hire pite;
> Tendre-herted, slydynge of corage;   825
> But trewely, I kan nat telle hire age.
>
> (*Troilus*, V,806–26)

And here is Lydgate's imitation:

> þat was in soth of alle þo on-lyve
> On þe fayrest, þis Calchas douȝter dere,
> þer-to of schap, of face, and of chere,
> þer myȝt[e] [be] no fairer creature:
> To hiȝe nor lowe, but mene of stature—   4740
> Hir sonnysche her, liche Phebus in his spere,
> Bounde in a tresse, briȝter þanne golde were,
> Doun at hir bak, lowe doun behynde,
> Whiche with a þrede of golde sche wolde bynde
> Ful ofte syþe of acustummaunce;   4745

þer-to sche hadde so moche suffisaunce
Of kyndes wirke, withouten any were—
[And] Save hir browes joyn[e]den y-fere,
No man koude in hir a lake espien.
And, ferþermore, to speken of hir eyen,   4750
þei wer so persyng, hevenly, and so clere,
þat an herte [ne] my3t hym silf[e] stere
Ageyn hir schynyng, þat þei nolde wounde
þoru3-out a brest, God wot, and bi3onde.
Also sche was, for al hir semlynes,   4755
Ful symple and meke, and ful of sobirnes,
þe best norissched eke þat my3t[e] be,
Goodly of speche, fulfilde of pite,
Facundious, and þer-to ri3t tretable,
And, as seiþ Guydo, in love variable—   4760
Of tendre herte and unstedfastnes
He hir accuseth, and newfongilnes.

(*Troy Book*, II,4736–62)

At the beginning, Lydgate doubles the statement (and halves the effect) of Criseyde's surpassing fairness, adding a superlative (*on þe fayrest*) to the comparative (*no fairer*). He copies 807–8, destroying the metre, despite emendation, and confusing the syntax. The lively air of observation in Chaucer's description of Criseyde's hair is dispersed in a clutter of conventional detail (*sonnysche, Phebus, golde were*), worn from long use in Lydgate's descriptive armoury.[14] The syntax remains unclear. The simplicity of 809 gives way to the pretentiousness of 4745, with two lines of virtually meaningless generalisation added, 4746–7. 813 is copied, destroying the metre (unless we accept more emendation), while 814 is rearranged, perhaps to avoid the personal tone, again to the detriment of metre (a 'headless' line at best). The description of her eyes is expanded with conventional epithets (*persyng, hevenly*), and Chaucer's beautiful 817 is replaced by statutory references to wounding, 4752–4. 818–9 are ignored; perhaps Lydgate did not understand them. The stanza on her character is better handled: 821 is copied, and 4758 is probably an improvement on 822, 824, despite its shaky rhythm. There is a touch of aureation in 4759, where Lydgate recurs momentarily to the Latin (*facundia, tractabilis*). Chaucer's memorable phrase in 825 is replaced by abstractions 4760–2, where Lydgate manages to work in a reference to Guido, whilst omitting any allusion

to Chaucer's characteristic *non sequitur* about Criseyde's age. It is not
by any means a ludicrous performance on Lydgate's part (nor one of
his best), but it is an instructive one. Gone are the distinctive tone of
voice, the pure felicity of diction, the asides, the sweet smoothness of
line flowing easily into line; in their place the generalised epithet, the
conventional image, the loose syntax, the lame metre, the patches of
decoration, the pretentious abstraction.

Something needs to be said at this point about two features of
Lydgate's verse which have come in for frequent criticism in these
comparisons, his syntax and his metre. The looseness of Lydgate's syntax is notorious; his sentences often ramble on, accommodating any
stray thought or allusion that may occur to him. He is striving after
the utmost effectiveness and truth, but seems to identify this with
inclusiveness, and instead of selecting and subordinating he accumu-
lates detail laboriously in a profusion of parentheses. Sometimes syntax
breaks down altogether; it is difficult to imagine an English sentence
which contains neither subject *nor* predicate, but if there is one, it can
probably be found at the opening of *Guy of Warwick*. Starting a
poem, as I have said, is Lydgate's particular nightmare, when the in-
finity of possible things to be said presses upon him unbearably.
Technically, the explanation of this looseness of construction is to be
found in the use, or misuse, of a fairly limited number of syntactical
devices, the most noticeable of which is the use of unrelated participles
instead of finite verbs. This is almost a Lydgate 'signature', and contributes more than anything to the effect of formlessness and irresolu-
tion, especially in couplet-writing (the stanza, of its nature, is more
tightly-knit). It is to be associated with a very free use of absolute constructions, and attributed perhaps to the influence of legal and official
Latin and French, with their sonorous multiplication of qualifiers.
Other features of Lydgate's syntax which cause distress to the reader
are the loose attitude to conjunctions (especially *for*), the sudden
changes of tense, and from indirect to direct speech, the frequency of
inversion, often of the most unidiomatic kind, and the very distinctive
habit of using *as* + personal pronoun instead of the relative pronoun—

> Whan she had shewyd hir sentence,
> This lady most of excellence,
> As she that was bothe fair and good. . . .
>
> (*Reason and Sensuality*, 473–5)

Generally speaking, this looser kind of syntax is what we are used to in medieval verse, and some mention has already been made of the different context of 'publication' and delivery within which it needs to be considered.[15] A precedent for every syntactical feature mentioned above could be found in Chaucer. But the degree of looseness and confusion of syntax is not precedented, and for this two explanations may be offered. One is that Lydgate's thought-patterns are characteristically associative and encyclopaedic, and much of his poetry therefore is allusive, accumulative and descriptive, where the problems of syntax are more acute than in straightforward narrative. The other explanation must take account of the deliberate and systematic nature of his distortions of syntax, which reflect his ambition to write in an elevated style. Latinate participial and absolute constructions are part of this; Lydgate anticipates Milton's techniques, without Milton's intellectual control. But the greatest spur to ambition is the example of Chaucer, and it has been shown[16] that Lydgate's syntax is often deliberately archaic and 'poetic' in imitation of Chaucer. Lydgate seizes on a syntactical usage practised by Chaucer as an occasional licence, such as the inversion of auxiliary and verb or of verb and object-pronoun, and employs it with undiscriminating frequency, as if it were in itself a guarantee of 'poetic' utterance. He also has ambitions to emulate Chaucer's mastery of larger syntactical patterns, the famous example being the opening of the Prologue to the *Thebes*, where his model is the first sentence of the General Prologue to the *Canterbury Tales*. Chaucer's long eighteen-line sentence has a negligent ease which disguises the care taken to poise it firmly on a repeated pattern of 'Whan . . . whan . . . thanne. . . .' In itself it declares the coming-of-age of English poetry. Lydgate could hardly be expected not to respond to the challenge, but the result is disastrous. The 'whan . . . whan . . .' pattern is repeated not twice but four times, the last temporal clause slithering into a general account of the *Canterbury Tales* and eulogy of Chaucer. There is no main clause until line 66, and even that is not very distinct, and in any case by that time the reader is sunk. It is a particularly bad Lydgate sentence, but one can see that its badness is the result not of drivelling incompetence, but of lofty ambitions imperfectly fulfilled. This may not make it any easier to accept, but at least it clarifies the nature of Lydgate's relationship to Chaucer. It may be suggested that if Chaucer was the first to secure perfect control over long and complex poetic utterances, it is hardly surprising that his followers should sometimes have fallen short in their attempts to imitate him.

Lydgate's metre also presents certain problems, but the nature of the problems has not always been made clear. Older critics like Saintsbury tended to dismiss Lydgate's verse as metrically chaotic,[17] partly because the Lydgate canon was then very confused, and included spurious poems more or less innocent of metre like the *Assembly of Gods*; partly because the texts of Lydgate then available were hopelessly corrupt, being based for the most part on sixteenth century prints, not on manuscripts. The manuscripts themselves are not always reliable, since fifteenth century scribes allowed themselves unlimited freedom to add, subtract, and amend as they thought fit.[18] It is striking how many of Lydgate's lines are mended by discreet editing, according to principles which have long been considered acceptable in texts of Chaucer. There is no sense in which Lydgate is affected by the 'prosodic vertigo' which Saintsbury speaks of, quite properly, as afflicting the fifteenth century, and which we can see example of in the extraordinary *Amoryus and Cleopes* of John Metham, a follower of Lydgate. Here is total chaos, with the number of syllables to the line varying from 8 to 17, and no particular regard paid either to the number of lines in the rhyme-royal stanza. There is a spurious ending to Lydgate's *Life of St. Albon*, probably late fifteenth or early sixteenth century, in which the verse equally defies analysis:

> Yet I can not knowe what parte they shulde have
> For kynge Offa founde nothyng but the bones in his grave.
> (*St. Albon*, III,1652-3)

One is certainly disposed to look on Lydgate more favourably after reading some of the verse of his successors.

The peculiarities of Lydgate's versification are, in fact, not the result of confusion but of deliberate and systematic practice. There is an analysis of Lydgate's verse by Schick,[19] in which he divides the lines into five types, A, B, C, D, and E. A is the standard line of five stresses, with unstressed and stressed syllables alternating regularly; B and E have extra unstressed syllables at caesura and line-beginning respectively; C and D lack the unstressed syllables at caesura and line-beginning. It looks a typically Teutonic piece of analysis, an analogue for the five-type theories of Old English and Middle English alliterative verse evolved by Sievers and Luick. There is no sense, we may say, in which the infinite range of metrical variation can be classified into 'types'. The strange thing is that Schick's analysis corresponds closely to the facts of Lydgate's verse, particularly in its identification of types C (the

'Lydgate' or 'broken-backed' line) and D (the 'headless' line) as staple variants. These indeed are the peculiar mark of Lydgate's versification, and need some kind of explanation.

The standard view is that the decline of sonant final —e after 1400 played havoc with Chaucer's versification, which had made use of inflexional —e in a way that was already becoming archaic in his own day. The balance being lost, the artificial structure of the pentameter collapsed, and his successors fell back on rough four-stress native patterns,[20] Lydgate representing the transitional process of collapse. Now this is certainly true of what happened to Chaucerian verse in the sixteenth century; Spenser's idea of the Chaucerian line, in his imitations in the *Shepheards Calender*, is just such a rough four-stress line, and it is the view that persists until the eighteenth century. Furthermore, there are a good many later fifteenth-century poets—Ashby, Bokenham, Hawes, Bradshaw—in whom we do see native four-stress patterns, often with alliteration, asserting themselves against the pentameter, alongside other writers, especially of popular and dramatic verse, who use the four-stress line because it is the only one they have ever known. Loss of final —e will explain many of these phenomena, but it will not do for Lydgate, who uses final —e in much the same way and under much the same conditions as Chaucer.[21] He uses it less frequently as he grows older, it is true, but his metre does not become any worse, or better, as a result. Other poets were also using final —e with perfect ease, and writing scrupulously syllabic verse of considerable accomplishment, such as the anonymous translator of *Palladius on Husbondrie*. Hoccleve uses final —e, and writes syllabically regular verse, though it is often a forced regularity deficient in natural speech-rhythm:

> Up gooth the sail to the top of the mast
> > (*Jereslaus's Wife*, 618)

It is not possible to accept Licklider's view[22] that this accenting of unstressed syllables, or *ictus*-accent, as he calls it, is a principle of fifteenth century versification.

Nor is there much trace in Lydgate of the loose four-stress line which Lewis finds everywhere in the fifteenth century—and which, one suspects, could be plausibly squeezed out of any pentameter. A few lines drop accidentally into the pattern—

> We be so feble and þei are so strong   (*Troy*, IV,4693)

but, in so many thousands of lines, they are metrical oddities. One poem, the *Ave Maria*, seems to be written in a free four-stress eight-line stanza, quite different from the octosyllabic octave of *God is myn helpere*,[23] but the explanation here, I think, is that Lydgate is writing in imitation of the four-stress accentual lines in Latin which form the sixth and eighth lines of the stanza. It is an isolated case, and there is no doubt that for the most part Lydgate is trying to write pentameter.

The peculiarity of his metre, and in particular the hard core of broken-backed and headless lines, must therefore be attributed, again, to the elusive example of Chaucer.[24] In the first place, it should be remembered that Chaucer allowed himself a good deal more freedom than this modern editors allow him, particularly in the distribution or omission of unstressed syllables. 'Deficient' lines are frequent in all Chaucer manuscripts, and it is only the modern critical text which present him to us as syllabically regular. Amongst the licences of which Chaucer availed himself are the headless and the 'Lydgate' line, perfectly acceptable variants in themselves when supported by the rhetorical context, and it is these variants that Lydgate found, perhaps more often than we know of in carelessly written copies, and elevated into types. The consequences are not serious for the individual line, which can generally make shift for itself (few lines are totally unscannable), but they are serious for the line-flow, which is continually broken by aggressive variants which have no rhetorical point. It is an odd proceeding, but not perhaps unnatural in a man of such rigidity of mind. We might perhaps remember too the speed with which Lydgate must have written, always under pressure to fulfil some commission, with little time to polish his verses, even if he had the inclination, not enough time even to notice that he had repeated four lines wholesale (239–42 in 289–92) in his draft of the *Thebes*. The modest protestations that he makes about the roughness of his verse, his 'crokid lynys rude',[25] are to a large extent governed by convention, but it is interesting to compare a typical passage like this.

> For wel wot I moche þing is wrong,
> Falsly metrid, boþe of short and long . . .
> Late ignoraunce and rudnesse me excuse . . .
> For in metring þouȝ þer be ignoraunce,
> ȝet in þe story ȝe may fynde plesaunce . . .
> Besechyng hem, with her prudent loke,
> To race and skrape þoruȝ-oute al my boke,

> Voide and adde wher hem semeth nede
>
> (*Troy*, V,3483–92,3537–9)

with Chaucer's earnest and prophetic concern for accuracy in the transmission of his text:

> And for ther is so gret diversite
> In Englissh and in writyng of oure tonge,
> So prey I God that non myswrite the,
> Ne the mysmetre for defaute of tonge.
>
> (*Troilus*, V,1793–6)

Lydgate, perhaps, had his mind on higher things; the modesty-topos in his case is no mere convention, but conveys a genuine, and justified modesty. His frequent mention of his ignorance of 'long and short'[26] unless it refers to stress, as the *OED*, with some justification, assumes,[27] may suggest that he thought English metre might be based on quantitative analysis, like Latin. If so, one could well understand that he should be reluctant to penetrate such mysteries, and that he should fall back on a mechanical permutation of Chaucerian 'types'. This granted, one should add that only a small percentage of Lydgate's verses are seriously inadequate, that many of these can be eliminated by minor emendation, and that he can write quite smoothly for long stretches.

Lydgate's extensive knowledge of Chaucer's work has been adequately illustrated in the preceding discussion. Whether he actually knew Chaucer personally is a matter of doubt, and critics on the whole have tended to reject the possibility. His many tributes to 'my mayster Chaucer',[28] it is said, lack the personal warmth of Hoccleve, who almost certainly knew Chaucer.[29] The argument is slightly tendentious, as Lydgate is not much given to personal warmth anyway, and may conceal a somewhat less reputable feeling that if Lydgate had known Chaucer he would have learnt something at least from him, if only not to write any more poetry. The evidence is ambiguous: this passage certainly seems to indicate a personal acquaintance—

> And Chaucer now, allas, is nat alyve
> Me to reforme, or to be my rede,
> For lak of whom slou3er is my spede.
>
> (*Troy*, III,550–2)

Elsewhere he tells us that he is writing from hearsay:

For he þat was gronde of wel-seying
In al his lyf hyndred no makyng,
My maister Chaucer, þat founde ful many spot—
Hym liste nat pinche nor gruche at every blot,
Nor meve hym silf to parturbe his rest
(I have herde telle) but seide alweie þe best,
Suffring goodly of his gentilnes
Ful many þing enbracid with rudnes.

(*Troy*, V,3519–26)

The question is anyway of little importance beside our need to understand what Chaucer meant to Lydgate, for it will have become clear
that Lydgate's Chaucer was not quite our Chaucer. His closest knowledge of Chaucer's work is concentrated, as we have seen, in the *Knight's
Tale*, the *Troilus*, and the *Parlement*, whereas a modern reader would
probably pick out the tales of the Wife of Bath, the Pardoner and the
Nun's Priest, and perhaps the fabliaux, as the characteristic summit of
Chaucer's achievement. Realism, humour, irony, 'character', are what
we ask of Chaucer, and what we consequently get, or pick up in the
filter of our understanding. The rest passes us by, or seems to us of less
consequence, and it comes as something of a surprise to us, therefore,
when we find Thomas Usk talking of him as Love's servant, 'the noble
philosophical poete in Englissh'.[30] These are not words that would
occur immediately to us if we wanted to describe Chaucer, though it is
the task of criticism to understand how they should have come to be
used. The expectations of the medieval reader were different from ours,
and the ways in which Lydgate imitates Chaucer, and the terms in
which he praises him, reflect the preconditioning of these expectations.
It might even be said that his attitudes are formed, at least to some
extent, by the language of critical approbation available to him.

For Lydgate, Chaucer is above all the poet of sententious utterance
and the high rhetorical style. His admiration for Chaucer as a purveyor
of general moral truth is well illustrated in the list of Chaucer's works
that he gives in the Prologue to the *Fall of Princes*, where the tales that he
singles out as specifically worthy of mention in the *Canterbury Tales*
are those of the Clerk and the Monk, and *Melibeus* (I,346–50). His
attitude is made even clearer in this passage:

Floure of Poetes thorghout al breteyne . . .
Of wel seyinge first in oure language . . .
With many proverbe divers and unkouth,

> Be rehersaile of his sugrid mouth,
> Of eche thyng keping in substaunce
> The sentence hool withoute variance,
> Voyding the chaf, sothly for to seyn,
> Enlumynyng þe trewe piked greyn
> Be crafty writinge of his sawes swete.

(Thebes, 40–57)

But it is to Chaucer the rhetorician that Lydgate devotes his most ful-some tributes, and his praise is echoed down through the fifteenth century. Chaucer is 'þe noble Rethor þat alle did excelle' (*Troy*, III,553), who first refined and enriched the English language from its primitive rudeness:

> Noble Galfride, poete of Breteyne,
> Amonge oure englisch þat made first to reyne
> þe gold dewe-dropis of rethorik so fyne,
> Oure rude langage only t'enlwmyne.[31]

The best that his followers can hope to do is to search through his work for jewels to set among their dross. To imitate him is impossible.

> We may assaye for to countrefete
> His gaye style, but it wyl not be.

(Flower of Courtesy, 239–40)

Imagery of colour, painting and decoration recurs constantly, as well as of sugar and sweetness; style is conceived of as a glossy fixative, almost as a substance in itself, to be applied to any appropriate subject-matter. It is concept derived from the medieval rhetoricians, who de-vote most of their attention to *elocutio* or style, and specifically to the ornaments of style, the tropes, the schemes and the figures, the 'colours' of rhetoric.

We ourselves would hesitate to talk about Chaucer's style in this way, and would consider that Lydgate's attitude betrays a very naïve idea of the relationship between style and subject-matter. Rosemund Tuve spends many pages of her book on *Elizabethan and Metaphysical Imagery* trying to dissolve the image of 'style as a garment', so frequently used in classical and Renaissance writing, partly because, for her, the very naïveté of the concept stands in the way of respectable intellectual dis-cussion. Similarly, accounts of Chaucer's debt to the rhetoricians[32] have often been concerned to protect him from the consequences of

rhetorical theory, and to assert his growing emancipation from
rhetoric and his fully developed understanding of the 'organic' nature
of style. Such approaches have a modern bias, but they do not entirely
miss the point, for what they recognise, albeit in distorted form, is
Chaucer's increasing skill, subtlety and sophistication in the handling of
rhetorical style, his ability even to parody it, and his powerful sense of
decorum, or appropriateness of style. Lydgate has some sense of decorum, and a limited range of styles, but there is no doubt that he is swept
off his feet by the Chaucerian 'high style', with its 'golden' (aureate)
language and its extensive use of the devices of amplification and
figures of rhetoric. This is the style of the *Knight's Tale* and the *Troilus*,
and the one which Lydgate imitates, systematically amplifying and
exaggerating its every feature.

This is not to say that Lydgate and other fifteenth-century readers
did not know and enjoy the 'low' Canterbury tales. It is simply that
within the then prevailing canons of taste, there were no terms, no
concepts available in which they could be considered as serious literature, and therefore they go for the most part unmentioned. But they
were read, if not with such devoted attention, and one of the extraordinary sights in fifteenth-century literature is to watch Lydgate
gambolling in clumsy playfulness after his master in the Prologue to
the *Thebes*. It is a deliberate exercise in Chaucer's low style, a Canterbury link, telling how he met the pilgrims and was asked for a story—
'a mery conseyte . . . declarynge how he ajoinde the sege of Thebes to
the mery tallys of Caunterburye'.[33] Lydgate doesn't appear to know
the General Prologue very well, and he confuses the Miller, the
Pardoner, and the Summoner inextricably (32–5), but he manages
some touches of revealing description and observation, as of himself,

> Wiþ rusty bridel made nat for þe sale,
> My man toforn with a voide male. (75–6)

Similarly, in the speech of the Host, some quality of rudeness and
rough good humour comes over, though Lydgate coarsens and exag-
gerates the character and ignores a certain good sense and bourgeois
dignity in Harry Bailly. He takes care to lace his speech with Chaucerian
oaths (*by kokkis blood, a twenty develway*) and tricks of expression, but
there is little change in the loose texture of the verse, and the Host's
advice to Lydgate to belch freely (110–18), though it may have seemed
very comic in the scriptorium, is laboured. On the whole, the Prologue
is not very merry, and not very funny, but it is tolerably well done; the

surprising thing is to find it being done at all, and no stronger evidence of Chaucer's influence over Lydgate could be imagined than that he should have persuaded his disciple to such an uncharacteristic exercise.

Some evidence has been offered in this chapter of the extent and nature of Chaucer's influence on Lydgate, particularly of the way in which imitation of Chaucer, by a curious metamorphosis, produced characteristic features of Lydgate's style and technique. There is value in placing the two writers side by side, but it would not do to leave it at that, to suggest simply that Lydgate was a monk, with all that that implies, who had read Chaucer, with all that that implies. He was also part of a larger literary world, a world of patrons, publishers and readers, to whose needs and habits he adapted himself unquestioningly, and some general remarks about this milieu are necessary before we pass on to examination of individual poems.

It is a commonplace of literary history to speak of the 'decline' of English literature in the fifteenth century. Such generalisations are often meaningless, especially when they depend, as they usually do, on a stereotyped and selective reading of the literature of the period. There is anything but decline in the popular and dramatic verse of the fifteenth century, or in Arthurian romance or religious prose, and there are significant achievements even in courtly poetry (such as the *Kingis Quair*[34]) and didactic allegory (such as the *Court of Sapience*). For this reason, one is reluctant to give much weight to historical explanations of the 'barrenness' of fifteenth-century literature. The century was not wholly barren, and the explanations would explain nothing even if it were. The Wars of the Roses, for instance, are often assumed to have had a profoundly demoralising effect on society and culture, but the simplicity of such an assumption may be questioned. Literature does not respond to public events in such a direct and predictable way—on the contrary, there might even be a case for saying that it responds in just the opposite way. Civil unrest didn't stop Malory from writing; in fact it may actually have prompted his quest for a chivalric ideal in the past which he could not find in the present, as well as given him the leisure to write (in gaol). A similar scepticism might be expressed in regard to the 'disillusion' supposed to have been caused by the wars in France and their disastrous termination. Again, it is difficult to see how this could have had much effect on literature, except indirectly, through the diminishing of contacts between France and England, and any loss here was amply compensated for by closer relationships with

Burgundy. But on the whole, political and military events are not the stuff of literary history, at least in the Middle Ages; moods of national rejoicing and dismay are historians' landmarks only, and the disillusion of Arras left as fugitive a trace on literary consciousness as the illusion of Agincourt.

It is possible to suggest that the 'decline' of fifteenth-century literature is due to nothing so much as the historians' need for something of the sort between Chaucer and the Renaissance. Literary history, like the weather, must have its troughs and depressions, and this is one of them —what else could it be, with the Renaissance to come? Such uncomplicated views are pleasing, but they do scant justice to the wide range of fifteenth-century literary achievement. The grain of truth in it all, of course, is that no one after Chaucer is as good as Chaucer, not even Henryson, and that the expectations he arouses are not fulfilled. For this Chaucer himself is partly responsible, the influence of a great poet being often debilitating; but the failure of the fifteenth century to match his freedom, intelligence and sophistication, to imitate the inimitable, is hardly what one would call decline. What we witness in the fifteenth century is not a decline, but a change of temper, or, to be more precise, a reassertion of orthodoxy. Moral earnestness, love of platitude and generalisation, a sober preoccupation with practical and ethical issues (often combined with a taste for the extravagantly picturesque and decorative)—these are the characteristic marks of fifteenth-century literature, and it is in these terms that Chaucer is absorbed and redefined. Lydgate is the pattern of the new orthodoxy, though as symptom rather than cause. The high moral tone of the *Temple of Glass* is not a development of courtly tradition peculiar to Lydgate, but a typical response to the more serious temper of the age. A similar response can be discerned in the *Kingis Quair*, where the love-story is interpenetrated by a ranging Boethian discourse, and in the unsentimental eschatology of Henryson's *Testament of Cresseid*, where the moral logic of Cresseid's predicament is pursued to its conclusion with a remorselessness quite alien to Chaucer. Even a poem as comparatively light-hearted as the *Flower and the Leaf* is turned to the prevailing concern with edifying moral truth.

Lydgate's didactic and informational verse is likewise representative of a great mass of English writing in the fifteenth century.[35] It is the age of the moral compendium, of collections of pious exempla such as the *Alphabet of Tales*, and the translations of the *Gesta Romanorum* and the *Book of the Knight of La Tour Laundry*; or collections of 'sentences' such as Burgh's translation of Cato's *Distichs*. Everywhere there are books of instruction, instruction in how to live, how to die, how to bring up children, how to cook, how to carve, how to eat, how to stay healthy. It is as if for the first time a traditional body of knowledge on the conduct of life is being committed to English for the benefit of a new generation. There is also an insatiable appetite for fact and information of all kinds, much of which is satisfied in verse, such as Lydgate's *Pageant of Knowledge*. Every opportunity for purveying information is seized—a lesson in geography and a course in medicine in the *Fabula duorum mercatorum*, a popularised mythology in the *Mumming for the Mercers*—while the *Fall of Princes* has many of the characteristics of a vast dictionary of universal biography. All the evidence of marginal comment and annotation, of distribution, popularity and ownership of books, confirms that this was what the reading public wanted, and the temper of the age finds its fullest expression in Caxton, in the overwhelmingly didactic and practical nature of early printed books.[36]

It is easy to accumulate evidence for this view of the fifteenth century as dominated by moral and practical concerns, but not so easy to explain it. No doubt the Lollard purges of the early fifteenth century had some influence in reinforcing orthodoxy and putting a stop to the intellectual experimentation of the fourteenth century. As Pantin says, 'One of the most disastrous and blighting effects of Wycliffism was that, for the first time in the history of this country, it associated criticism with heterodoxy.'[37] Such a touch of frost to the intellectual life of the age must have helped to direct literature into narrower, more self-consciously moralistic channels. Some weight must be given too to the example of the court and court patronage in establishing the literary climate of the fifteenth century. Henry V, earnest, dedicated, oppressively pious, himself a great persecutor of Lollards and upholder of orthodoxy, is a striking contrast with Richard II, and an index to the change that has taken place. Like his father, his brothers, and his son, he was a man of learning—for his share of the spoils of Caen, we are told, he chose a book of histories in French[38]—but it is always learning in the service of piety, morality, or practical politics. The books that we know him to be associated with, such as Lydgate's *Life of Our Lady*, Hoccleve's *Regement of Princes*, Thomas Walsingham's *Historia Anglicana*, all illustrate these dominant concerns, and the most important of his commissions, Lydgate's *Troy Book*, is at once an instrument of national prestige and a chivalric and moral exemplar. Henry's brother, John, duke of Bedford, is not so important for English literature, since

he spent his mature years in France as Regent, but he too demonstrated
the family's interest in books; he bought up Charles VI's library of
843 volumes, and commissioned several illuminated books, including
the magnificent Bedford Book of Hours.[39] The youngest brother,
Humphrey, duke of Gloucester, is, however, the great book-lover of
the family, and it is possible that in a different climate from that of
fifteenth century England he would have been a great patron of letters.
He had close contacts with Italian humanism, and was himself a man of
taste and scholarship; yet he struck no sparks in England, and the works
for which he acted as patron—Lydgate's *Fall of Princes*, Capgrave's
Commentary on *Genesis*, the *De Studio Militari* of Nicholas Upton, the
translation of Palladius *De Re Rustica*[40]—are all solidly representative
of the practical and didactic concerns of his age. We shall see Humphrey
at work, as patron of the *Fall*, trying to stir in Lydgate a different kind
of response, but without much effect.

Lydgate is a court-poet, very definitely, but it is laughable to think
of him in the same way as Chaucer. Our picture of the Chaucerian
court audience, as it is depicted in the famous *Troilus* illustration,
elegant, witty, carelessly sophisticated, alert to every allusion and flash
of irony, may be a little exaggerated, but it is predicated in the poetry,
and none the less real even if we do allow that Chaucer must have
created the taste by which he was understood. There are traces of this
spirit in the fifteenth century, in the poems of the Duke of Suffolk,[41] in
the English translations of Charles of Orleans, in Sir Richard Roos's
translation of *La Belle Dame sans Merci*, but their elegance is lachrymose,
and their inspiration neo-French rather than Chaucerian. They are the
exceptions to the record we have; for the rest, the patronage of the
nobility reflects that of the court. It was the earl of Salisbury, for instance, who commissioned Lydgate's translation of Deguileville's
Pelerinage de la Vie Humaine, at the same time that a prose version of the
same author's *Pelerinage de l'Ame* was being written at the request of the
duke of Bedford.[42] Both are long didactic allegories, very characteristic
of the fifteenth century English writing. Henry V's interest in Hoccleve's
Regement of Princes finds a similar parallel in the prose version of the
Secreta Secretorum made by James Young for the earl of Ormonde about
1420. The *Secreta*, one of Hoccleve's sources, is a treatise of moral and
practical instruction for princes, enormously popular in the Middle
Ages and particularly in the fifteenth century. Lydgate, at the end of
his life, embarked on an ambitious verse translation which was completed by his disciple Benedict Burgh, and John Shirley did a copy of

another prose translation for Henry VI in the 1450s. Another source of
Hoccleve's *Regement* is the *De Regimine Principum* of Ægidio Colonna,
a work of similar nature to the *Secreta*; a full translation in prose was
made by John Trevisa for his patron, Lord Berkeley, along with versions of other favourite medieval encyclopaedias, Bartholomeus's *De
Proprietatibus Rerum* and Higden's *Polychronicon*. Lord Berkeley's
daughter Elizabeth was patroness of John Walton's excellent verse-
translation of Boethius (1410), and her husband, the earl of Warwick,
military administrator in France under Bedford, commissioned Lydgate's *Pedigree of Henry VI* (1427). For Warwick's third wife, Isobel,
Lady Despenser, Lydgate wrote the *Fifteen joys of our Lady*, and
Warwick's daughter Margaret, later lady Talbot and countess of
Shrewsbury, commissioned Lydgate's *Guy of Warwick* in honour of
her father's legendary ancestor. The networks of aristocratic patronage
that can be built up in this way[43] tell us something of the ubiquity of
Lydgate, and something too of the great release into English of a vast
store of encyclopaedic, didactic, and moralistic material hitherto more
at home in Latin and French. Above all, they are testimony to the
widespread and pervasive nature of the kind of tastes we have been
speaking of.

Court and aristocratic patronage, however, will not fully account for
these tastes, and may even be of only subordinate importance. The real
pressure comes from elsewhere, from the minor gentry and upper
bourgeoisie, not so much as patrons but as readers, a large and growing
audience[44] eager for information and instruction as well as entertain-
ment. It is not a new class of readers, except in the sense that the middle
class is always the new class, rising, mobile, aspirant, but it is a class
which has risen swiftly in importance, as a result of various factors.
Some are economic and general, such as the growth of trade, of towns,
of urban prosperity; others are social and particular—the rapid spread
of education in English, the decline of French, and the assertion, particularly by Chaucer, of the status of English. Nothing happened over-
night, but by the early fifteenth century the class which before Chaucer
had to be content with second-hand and second-rate versions of French
romance,[45] has the prestige and authority not only to absorb in modified form the full didactic tradition in literature, but also to annex
courtly literature to its own tastes. There is thus a broadening of the
base of literature, more sobriety, uniformity, and mediocrity, and the
effective elimination of élite culture. Developments in English painting
and manuscript illumination provide a striking parallel. Large numbers

of illuminated books are produced, but there is a levelling out of
quality as a wider audience is reached.[46] It is not a time of splendour,
and the Lancastrian kings, with their chronic shortage of money, could
do little to make it so. Agincourt was chiefly valuable to Henry, though
he may not have seen it so himself, as proof to his financial backers
that their money was well invested.

The typical member of this new literary audience is, in imagination,
the rich merchant or lawyer or country gentleman whose prosperity
has brought him confidence and prestige, a foothold in land, a knighthood, perhaps, if he couldn't afford to buy himself out of it; and with
these, cultural tastes and ambitions more earnest than sophisticated. To
buy books, to own them, perhaps even to commission one or two, will
set the seal on status. They must cover a variety of subjects, because he
cannot afford many, they must be useful and worthwhile and at the
same time have the patina of aristocratic elegance of which he is the
inheritor. Such a picture may seem to fit the facts of fifteenth century
literary production a little too closely to be true, but it is not far from
being a portrait of the Paston family, for whose literary interests and
tastes there is substantial evidence. The library of Sir John Paston,[47] for
instance, contains Chaucer's *Troilus*; a Chaucerian miscellany (the
Legend, the *Parlement*, *La Belle Dame*, Lydgate's *Temple of Glass*); another similar collection, more mixed (*La Belle Dame*, the *Parlement*,
Guy and Colbrond—probably Lydgate's *Guy of Warwick*, Lydgate's
Horse, Goose and Sheep, a didactic debate of *Hope and Dyspeyr*, the life
of St. Christopher); a miscellany of romances, predominantly historical;
a collection of didactic and religious works (an exposition of the Mass,
the *Abbeye off the Holy Goost*, a prayer for the Vernicle), with the
romance of 'Chylde Ypotis' thrown in for good measure. There is also
a religious treatise on Sapience, some Latin (Cicero and the *Somnium
Scipionis*), a copy of the *De Regimine Principum*, several books on
heraldry, and a book on the ceremony and practice of knighthood. It is
an uncommonly good library, but not an unrepresentative one. Particularly interesting is the large proportion of Chaucer (but no *Canterbury Tales*, it may be noted) and Chaucerian poetry,[48] and the emphasis
on didactic, religious, historical, and factual material. From elsewhere
we learn how Sir John commissioned books from the scrivener William
of Ebesham, including one called the 'great book' (now MS. Lansdowne
285) which includes the treatises on knighthood and war, the treatise
on Sapience, and the *De Regimine* of Hoccleve.[49] The network of
supply and demand, of author, publisher, and public, is close and is

drawn even closer if we accept MacCracken's suggestion that the *Temple of Glass* was originally commissioned for the marriage of William Paston in 1420.[50]

The Pastons are not the only East Anglian family of whose tastes in literature we have evidence. Osbern Bokenham, Austin friar of Stoke Clare, in Suffolk, who was a follower of Chaucer and Lydgate and author of voluminous verse *Legends of Holy Women*, tells us a good deal about his patrons amongst the provincial nobility and gentry. Some are members of the local aristocracy, like the countess of Oxford and lady Bourchier, others, like John and Isabel Hunt or John and Agatha Flegge, are from the class of well-to-do landed gentry, and Moore[51] has built up a convincing picture of East Anglian patronage, in which Bokenham is linked with Capgrave, Metham, and others, and portrayed as catering for a close-knit reading public of sober pious and didactic tastes. The uniformity of these tastes is remarkable. Lydgate's link with this group of patrons is to be found in two poems that he wrote for Lady Sibille Boys of Holm Hale in Norfolk, the *Epistle to Sibille*, a paraphrase of *Proverbs* 31:10–31 ('Who can find a virtuous woman?'), and the *Treatise for Laundresses*.[52] The latter illustrates, somewhat extravagantly, the use of verse for information in the fifteenth century, though no doubt it was meant to sound somewhat extravagant. In his turn, Lydgate provides the link between this kind of audience and the upper bourgeoisie. The *Mummings* that he wrote for the Mercers and the Goldsmiths of London, for performance before a civic audience, are very much like the elaborate description of the allegorical pageants at Henry VI's entry into London that he wrote for John Carpenter, town clerk of London, in their mingling of the decorative, the didactic, and the informative. One is not quite sure whether the London burgesses were getting what they wanted, or getting what they deserved, but they certainly wanted what they got. The taste was being created as well as satisfied, and continued strong into the late fifteenth century, when Roger Thorney (*c.* 1450–1515), a rich London mercer, owned several Lydgate MSS. including Trinity R.3.21 and Laud misc.557, as well as the MS., now in St. John's college, Cambridge, from which Wynkyn de Worde printed his edition of his *Thebes*.[53]

An important addition to our knowledge of the fifteenth century reading public is made by John Shirley, the ubiquitous London copyist whose life (1366–1456) spans Lydgate's.[54] Shirley held the lease on a large tenement building in London which included four shops, and from here he ran a flourishing commercial scriptorium, combining the activities of publisher, bookseller, and lending library. Like a modern publisher, he has his own 'device' incorporating his name, and also provides for the poems he copies long gossiping headings, like a publisher's blurb, in which he tells something of the provenance of the work and recommends it to the reader. He also has verse tables of contents in two of his manuscripts, in which, amongst other things, he reminds readers to return the book when they have finished with it:

> But sendeth this boke to me agayne,
> Shirley, I meane, which is right fayne
> If ye ther-of have had plesaunce.[55]

The most important of Shirley's own manuscripts are MSS. Add.16165, Trinity R.3.20 and Ashmole 59, the last written in his ninetieth year. All are in the nature of commonplace books, embracing a variety of material and appealing to the tastes we have seen to be characteristic of the fifteenth century. Add.16165, for instance, has as its principal items Chaucer's translation of Boethius and the *Boke of Huntyng* of Edward, duke of York, but it also includes Trevisa's translation of the Gospel of Nicodemus, the *Regula Sacerdotalis*, and Chaucer's *Anelida*, and is a major repository of Lydgate's courtly and sub-courtly poetry, the *Black Knight*, the *Temple of Glass*, *My lady dere*, *Doubleness*, *A Lover's New Year's Gift*, the *Servant of Cupid Forsaken*.[56] In it, very typically, we see the transmission, through translation into English, of the didactic tradition, leavened by examples and imitations of courtly idiom. The volumes that Shirley copied himself are not the only knowledge we have of his activities; there are others that bear the mark of his influence, in their maltreatment of the text, peculiarities of spelling, and informative headings, and two manuscripts in particular, Add.34360 and Harley 2251, of vital importance as sources for Lydgate's minor poetry, are derived from a lost Shirley codex.[57] John Stow, the sixteenth century antiquary, had a collection of Shirley's manuscripts and his MS. Add.29729 is a copy of Trinity R.3.20, with additions. A whole network of affiliations between these Shirley-type anthologies can be built up which show Shirley to have been at the centre of a large publishing business.

Shirley's associations with Lydgate are particularly close. He is the sole authority for some thirty of the minor poems (including all the Mummings), and the detailed knowledge he shows of provenance indicates that he was closely acquainted with the monk, at once his publisher and his literary agent. Examples have already been given of the invaluable information he provides in rubrics, of Lydgate's residences in Oxford and London, for instance, and his relationships with Henry V and Lacy. There are many other examples, scraps of information the very casualness of which is the guarantee of their authenticity, like his rubric to *That now is Hay some-tyme was Grase*:

> 'Here begyneth a balade whych John Lydgate the Monke of Bery wrott and made at þe commaundement of þe Quene Kateryn as in here sportes she wallkyd by the medowes that were late mowen in the monthe of Julii'. (MS.Add.29729)

Shirley is an indefatigable annotator; he elaborates on Lydgate's mythological references in the *Mumming for the Mercers* in a way that suggests the limitations of his audience's knowledge, as well as their eagerness to overcome them. He also provides some amusing marginal comments on Lydgate's references to women, where he seems to be playing, for the benefit of his readers, on the contrast between literary propriety and personal impropriety. When Lydgate writes of woman's 'doublenesse', Shirley adds in the margin 'Be stille daun Iohan. Suche is youre fortune', and when Lydgate follows Boccaccio in a long tirade against women in the *Fall* (extracts from which are copied in MS. Harley 2251), Shirley has a whole string of cries of mock-outrage— 'holdith your pees . . . ye have no cause to sey so . . . Ye wil be shent . . . Lat hem compleyne that neode have . . . Be pees or I wil rende this leef out of your booke'.[58] In another place, where Lydgate speaks of women's truth and fidelity, Shirley asks laconically, 'A daun Iohan, est yvray?' Shirley's enormous appetite for knowledge and for work, his lack of discrimination, his curiosity, his gossipiness, his humour, remind one vividly of Furnivall.

Shirley clearly had his eye on the reading public in producing these anthologies and miscellanies, and the taste is echoed in the commonplace books which individual owners would assemble for themselves, such as MS. Egerton 1995, which contained romance, history, Lydgate's verses on the Kings of England, his *Dietary*, treatises on etiquette and hunting, as well as miscellaneous information and gnomic verses.[59] Publishers had special techniques of mass-production to deal with the increased demand, one of which was to have poems or groups of related poems copied in loose quires which would then be held in stock and bound up to the taste of specific customers.[60] This accounts for the large number of fascicular manuscripts which have come down to us from the fifteenth century, including some, such as MSS. Trinity R.3.21, Hh.iv.12, Tanner 346, and Fairfax 16, which are of importance as sources of minor Lydgatiana. The list of Sir John Paston's books already mentioned refers to several as existing 'in quayers', which suggests that the expense of binding was often dispensed with.

There are a number of other fifteenth century anthologies in which Lydgate's minor poems figure prominently, in addition to those already mentioned. Some of them have a distinctive flavour: the Bodley group, for instance (MSS. Bodley 638, Fairfax 16, Digby 181, Tanner 346)[61] contain mostly courtly poetry of Chaucerian descent, Lydgate's and others. MSS. Lansdowne 699 and its 'partial sister', Leyden Univ. Vossianus 9, on the other hand, share the taste of Harley 2251, to which they are related, for didactic and practical verse (*Churl and Bird, Fabula duorum mercatorum, Jak Hare, Horse, Goose and Sheep, Dietary*, etc.). MSS. Jesus 56 and Laud misc.683, each with about twenty Lydgate pieces in a mass of miscellaneous verse, are lower-pitched, with some of the satirical poems (e.g. *Horns Away*) and many of the shorter and simpler religious poems without aureation. It is not possible to go into a great deal of detail, but such collections as these, fascicular or not, bear out the general truth of Brusendorff's remark, that 'Practically all late Middle English manuscripts are publishers' copies, plainly done on speculation'.[62] Many of them use famous Chaucer poems as bait, and pad out the volume with fifteenth century imitations. Others aim at a wider audience, and one of Lydgate's attractions for the fifteenth century publisher was that he could provide *everything*, so that a collection like MS. Harley 2251, which is virtually a Lydgate anthology, could cater for all tastes, didactic, religious, and practical.

However, it is well to distinguish between two kinds of publishing, for there are, roughly speaking, two kinds of commercial Lydgate manuscript: the speculative anthology, directed at the widest possible audience; and the handsome volume devoted principally to a single long poem, written to order for the better class of customer. To handle these books is to be physically aware of this difference: on the one hand, books like Shirley's MS.Add.16165, packed with all kinds of matter, well-thumbed and scribbled, manageable in size, a book intended to be read and used; on the other, MSS. of the *Fall* like MS. Royal 18.D.iv, a handsome folio volume, with large margins, beautifully regular hand-writing and floreated initials, a book which looks as though it was never opened, let alone read, but which stood, in itself, for status. The destination of some of the latter we can trace. Some were probably presentation copies, like MS. Cotton Augustus A.iv of the *Troy Book*, a very large folio volume of uninspiring magnificence. Others found homes, as we see from the insertion of coats of arms, in the libraries of the nobility and gentry, others still in monastic libraries, such as MS Sloane 4031 of the *Fall*, which was at Battle abbey, and MSS. Add. 18632 and Laud misc.416 of the *Thebes*, which were formerly at the nunneries of Amesbury and Syon respectively.[63] MS. Trinity O.5.2 of the *Troy* and *Thebes* is particularly interesting, for we can trace its passage down through the Knevet family of Norfolk and deduce something of its value to these rapidly rising members of the provincial gentry as a prestige possession.[64]

One Lydgate manuscript of great importance, MS. Harley 2255, has not been mentioned yet, partly because it seems to have no relation to the world of publishers and readers we have been speaking of, partly because it raises forcibly the question of the Lydgate canon, with a brief discussion of which this chapter must close. MS. Harley 2255 is a quarto volume, written in a spacious formal script with some quite elaborate initial decoration. It contains the arms of the abbey of St. Edmund's at Bury in the first initial, and it may be presumed that it was written at Bury for Curteys.[65] It is an old MS., a very good one, with texts of excellent authority, and it was probably prepared under Lydgate's direction as an anthology of his own religious and didactic verse, as a personal present for his abbot. The contents, even allowing for the inclusion of a satirical poem like *Horns Away*, are selected for their appropriateness to the cloister, and there can be no doubt, I think, that all the poems in it marked as Lydgate's are Lydgate's. One, however, the *Hood of Green*, has been rejected from the canon by Mac-Cracken, with the comment: 'I cannot believe that Lydgate ever sank to the abominable filth of the [Hood of Green]'.[66] The poem is undoubtedly obscene, but the evidence for Lydgate's authorship is strong. There is only one kind of testimony of authenticity which is absolutely inviolable, of course, and that is the author's own naming of himself as author. Where this fails, the establishment of the canon must depend on the testimony of contemporary scribes and other writers, and in Lydgate's case this means Shirley above all. Shirley, where he can be checked, is very accurate in his attributions, if not in his texts, and there is ample evidence for his close and detailed knowledge of Lydgate's work. MS. Harley 2255 must be given a similar if not greater authority. When these two kinds of evidence, authorial and scribal, have been exhausted, there remains internal evidence of rhyme, metre, style, and diction, which depends ultimately, for all the appearance of objectivity which can be given to it, on the editor's judgment and taste.

These are the three criteria set up by MacCracken for the establishment of the Lydgate canon,[67] and they are surely the right ones, which is why Hammond is justified in attacking him for not keeping to them, and for not distinguishing between different degrees of reliability in MS. attribution.[68] In the case of MS. Harley 2255, MacCracken has allowed personal taste to stand against a perfectly reliable MS. attribution; if external evidence is to be ignored when it does not suit us, it is difficult to know what is the point of bothering with it in the first place. All this is a lot of fuss to make about an obscene squib, but the principle is an important one, and it is also important to recognise that the kind of obscenity which is meant to provoke disgust against women is a perfectly normal and respectable part of the clerical anti-feminist tradition. Curteys, if he worried about such things, was probably a lot more worried about the courtly poems than about the *Hood of Green*. To allow modern notions of decency and respect for women to intrude is to miss the full picture.

The question of *Quia amore langueo* is more serious, for the poem is intrinsically very important, one of the most magnificent pieces of fifteenth century Marian writing. It is attributed to Lydgate by Shirley in MS. Ashmole 59, and the only grounds for rejecting it are that Shirley was too old to know what he was doing (he was over eighty when he copied this MS.). The argument is a poor one, and is not accepted for another dozen poems in the manuscript which are attributed to Lydgate on Shirley's sole authority. The real reason for rejecting *Quia amore langueo* is the conviction that it is too good for Lydgate, and that it is not in his style.[69] This argument is circular, for there is no judgment to be made of the range and quality of Lydgate's achievement except on the basis of the body of poems attributed to him by scribes, especially Shirley; but in this case a circular argument is the only possible one, for the poem, if judgment is to be at all trusted, is indubitably not Lydgate's. However, the question is worth raising, and the answer worth isolating as a purely subjective one.

In conclusion, one might recur to some of Brusendorff's doubts about the Lydgate canon, as established by MacCracken, and accepted by all subsequent scholars, including Schirmer, with very little substantive change. The poems mentioned above represent particular issues and problems, and it is not a task for this book to re-examine the whole of the Lydgate canon, which would involve a reappraisal of the whole of fifteenth century literature. But it is well to remember that the evidence on which several major poems are ascribed to Lydgate is scanty indeed, and, in particular, that the two long poems in octo-syllabic, *Reason and Sensuality* and the *Pilgrimage of the Life of Man*, have no specific attribution to Lydgate before the sixteenth and seventeenth centuries. One would not wish to put Lydgate back into the fifteenth century melting pot, but the canon is a matter on which one would like to keep an open mind.

Notes to Chapter Three

1 R. W. Chambers, *On the Continuity of English Prose*, EETS,OS 186(1932); R. M. Wilson, *Early Middle English Literature* (London 1939), pp. 3–22; *Sawles Warde*, ed. R. M. Wilson (Leeds 1938), Introduction.

2 See Helen Suggett, 'The Use of French in England in the later Middle Ages', *TRHS*, XXVIII(1946),61–83.

3 On the other hand his dispatches from France to the loyal citizens of London were deliberately written in English: see V. H. Galbraith, 'Nationality and Language in Medieval England', *TRHS*, XXIII(1941),113–28 (p. 125).

4 'The mere possession of English books, and specially of English scriptures, might make a man suspect of heresy': Margaret Deanesly, *The Lollard Bible* (Cambridge 1920, repr. 1966), p. vii. See J. A. F. Thomson, *The Later Lollards* (Oxford 1965), and, for a specific injunction against books *in vulgari idiomate*, Amundsham's *Annals (ed. cit.)*, I,224.

5 G. Reismüller, *Romanische Lehnwörter bei Lydgate* (Munich 1909). See also Hammond, *Chaucer to Surrey*, p. 87; Schirmer, *John Lydgate*, p. 74.

6 See D. S. Brewer, 'The Relationship of Chaucer to the English and European traditions' (in *Chaucer and Chaucerians*, ed. Brewer, pp. 1–38), pp. 3–15.

7 J. C. Mendenhall, for instance, in an analysis of a passage from the *Troilus*, shows how much of his vocabulary must have been rare and unusual in its day (*Aureate Terms*, Univ. of Pennsylvania, 1919, p. 39).

8 For lists, see Hammond, pp. 88–9, and the Introductions to the EETS editions of the *Temple of Glas*, *Thebes*, *Reason and Sensuality*, and the *Pilgrimage*. For some account of their general function in the economy of style, see above, p. 9.

9 *Troy*, IV,3210ff. There are further examples in the *Complaint of the Black Knight*, 400–6; *Thebes*, 4628–30; *Fall*, II,1856–9.

10 *Historia Destructionis Troiae*, ed. N. E. Griffin (Cambridge, Mass. 1936), p. 206.

11 E.g. *Thebes*, 4529–30 and *CT*, I,957–8; 4536 and 982.

12 *Thebes*, 4539–40. Compare also the vividness of *Kn.T.*, 990 with Lydgate's amplification in 4556–61.

13 See E. Bagby Atwood, 'Some Minor Sources of Lydgate's Troy Book', *Studies in Philology*, XXXV(1938),25–41 (pp. 36–9).

14 E.g. *Temple of Glas*, 271–2; *Troy*, I,1977; *Churl and Bird*, 59; and cf. *Troilus*, IV,736, 816.

15 See above, p. 9.

16 By A. Courmont, *Studies on Lydgate's Syntax in the Temple of Glass* (Paris 1912).

17 *History of English Prosody* (3 vols., 1906), I,218–34.

18 A good example of an egregiously bad copyist is the scribe of the Mostyn MS. of the *Fall* (ed. Bergen, Part IV, p. 87). Cf. Bergen's account of MS. Digby 230 of the *Troy Book* (Part IV, p. 28).

19 *Temple of Glas*, pp. liv–lxiii.

20 See C. S. Lewis, 'The 15th century Heroic Line', *Essays and Studies*, XXIV (1938), 28–41; also Fitzroy Pyle, 'The Pedigree of Lydgate's Heroic Line', *Hermathena*, XXV(1937),26–59.

21 Charlotte F. Babcock, 'Metrical use of inflexional —*e* in Middle English, with particular reference to Chaucer and Lydgate', *PMLA*, XXIX(1914), 59–92.

22 A. H. Licklider, *Chapters on the Metric of the Chaucerian Tradition* (Baltimore 1910), esp. pp. 111–61; see the account of Hoccleve's metre in J. Mitchell, *Thomas Hoccleve*, pp. 97–109.

23 *Minor Poems*, I,280,27.

24 What follows is based on Hammond, *op. cit.*, pp. 17–24, 83–6, and her article, 'The 9-syllabled Pentameter line in some post-Chaucerian manuscripts', *Modern Philology*, XXIII(1925–6),129–52. See also the Introduction to my edition of the *Floure and the Leafe* (Nelson's Medieval and Renaissance Library, 1962), pp. 59–62.

25 *Troy*, II,4705.

26 E.g. *Troy*, V,3484 (above), II,184; *St. Albon*, I,100.

27 *OED*, s.v. *long*, 13a.

28 Viz. *Flower of Courtesy*, 236–42; *Troy*, II,4677–735; III,536–64, 4077–263; V,3466–543; *Thebes*, 39–57; *Fall*, I,246–357; II,974–1001; VI,3620–33; VIII,670–9; IX,3415–21; *Pilgrimage*, 19751–84; *Life of Our Lady*, II,1628–57; *Thoroughfare of Woe*, 186–91 (*Minor Poems*, II,828). There are many other references to Chaucer, in addition to these tributes.

29 See J. Mitchell, *Thomas Hoccleve*, chap. VI.

30 *Testament of Love* (c. 1387), III.iv.249; in *Chaucerian and other Pieces*, ed. W. W. Skeat (vol. VII of the *Oxford Chaucer*, 1897), p. 123. And cf. J. A. W. Bennett, *The Parlement of Foules* (Oxford 1957), pp. 7–8.

31 *Troy*, II,4697–700. Similarly *Troy*, III,4237–43; *Fall*, I,277–8; *Pilgrimage*, 19773–6.

32 The seminal article is J. M. Manly, 'Chaucer and the Rhetoricians', *Proc. of the British Academy*, XII(1926),95–113. See also C. S. Baldwin, *Mediaeval Rhetoric and Poetic* (New York 1928); J. W. H. Atkins, *English Literary Criticism: the Mediaeval Phase* (Cambridge 1943). A recent sceptical survey of the field is J. J. Murphy, 'A New Look at Chaucer and the Rhetoricians', *RES*, XV(1964),1–20.

33 Colophon in MS.Royal 18.D.ii.

34 I take this to be a poem of southern provenance: see W. Craigie, 'The Language of the *Kingis Quair*', *Essays and Studies*, XXV(1939),22–38. The 'Scottish Chaucerians' are not brought into this argument about 'English' literature, though they could be, quite plausibly.

35 See H. S. Bennett, *Chaucer and the 15th century*, esp. pp. 104–23, 156–60; 'The Author and his Public in the 14th and 15th centuries', *Essays and Studies*, XXIII(1937),7–24; 'Science and Information in English writings of the 15th century', *MLR*, XXXIX(1944),1–8; 'The Production and Dissemination of Vernacular MSS. in the Middle Ages', *Library*, 5th series, I(1946–7),167–78.

36 See H. S. Bennett, 'Caxton and his Public', *RES*, XIX(1943),113–19; also A. B. Ferguson, *The Indian Summer of English Chivalry* (Durham, N.Ca. 1960), p. 33; C. F. Buhler, *The Fifteenth-Century Book* (Philadelphia 1960), p. 88.

37 *The English Church in the 14th century*, p. 238.

38 Kingsford, *English Historical Literature in the 15th century*, p. 4.

39 E. Carleton Williams, *My Lord of Bedford* (London 1963), pp. 249–52.

40 See K. H. Vickers, *Humphrey Duke of Gloucester* (London 1907), pp. 385–96.

41 Or, to be more exact, the poems attributed to him by H. N. MacCracken, 'An English friend of Charles d'Orléans', *PMLA*, XXVI(1911),142–80.

42 Schirmer, *John Lydgate*, pp. 121–2.

43 See further Hammond, *Chaucer to Surrey*, pp. 15–16, 39, 78; Schirmer, *passim.*; K. J. Holzknecht, *Literary Patronage in the Middle Ages* (Philadelphia 1923), esp. pp. 98–103.

44 The rapid spread of literacy in the fifteenth century is discussed by J. W. Adamson, 'The Extent of Literacy in England in the 15th and 16th centuries', *Library*, X(1929–30),163–93.

45 As in the Auchinleck MS., *c.* 1330.

46 See Margaret Rickert, *Painting in Britain: the Middle Ages*, p. 196.

47 *Paston Letters*, ed. Gairdner (1910), III,300–1.

48 Anne Paston, Sir John's sister, has also a copy of Lydgate's *Thebes* (*Paston Letters*, III,47).

49 H. S. Bennett, *The Pastons and their England* (Cambridge 1922), pp. 112–13.

50 'Additional Light on the *Temple of Glas*', *PMLA*, XXIII(1908),128–40.

51 S. Moore, 'Patrons of Letters in Norfolk and Suffolk, *c.* 1450', *PMLA*, XXVII(1912),188–207; XXVIII(1913),79–106.

52 These are MacCracken's suppositions (Canon, p. xx). The Lady Sibill, or
   Sibilla, was the widow of Sir Roger Boys, who died in 1421, and whom she
   survived by many years, dying about 1456. She administered the estate conscientiously, presented the rectors of Holm-Hale and other livings, and
   makes many appearances in the records of the time. She fits well Lydgate's
   picture of a worthy and busy matron. See Blomefield's *Norfolk* (ed. 1805–
   10), vol. VI, pp. 9, 11.

53 See Gavin Bone, 'Extant manuscripts printed from by Wynkyn de Worde,
   with Notes on the Owner, Roger Thorney', *The Library*, 4th series, XII
   (1931–2),284–306.

54 For accounts of Shirley, see Hammond, pp. 191–7; Schirmer, pp. 251–3;
   A. Brusendorff, *The Chaucer Tradition* (Copenhagen 1925), pp. 453–71; also
   A. I. Doyle, 'More light on John Shirley', *Medium Ævum*, xxx (1961), 93–101.

55 Table of Contents to MS.Add.29729, lines 81–3, in Hammond, p. 197.

56 The titles are those given by MacCracken in his account of the Lydgate
   canon (*Minor Poems*, I,xi–xxxi).

57 Eleanor P. Hammond, 'Two British Museum Manuscripts', *Anglia* XXVIII
   (1905),1–28; 'Ashmole 59 and other Shirley Manuscripts', *Anglia*, XXX
   (1907),320–48.

58 Shirley's marginalia are collected in Brusendorff, *op. cit.*, pp. 462–7.

59 Bennett, *Chaucer and the 15th century*, p. 164.

60 For the general currency of this practice, see G. S. Ivy, 'The Bibliography
   of the Manuscript-Book', in *The English Library before 1700*, ed. F. Wormald
   and C. E. Wright (London 1958), p. 32–65 (pp. 38–42).

61 For convenient accounts of these, and other 'Chaucerian' manuscripts, see E. P.
   Hammond, *Chaucer: a Bibliographical Manual* (New York 1908), pp. 326–49.

62 *Op. cit.*, p. 179. For the effect of this on the Chaucer text and canon, see
   J. S. P. Tatlock, 'The Canterbury Tales in 1400', *PMLA*, L(1935), 100–39;
   F. W. Bonner, 'The Genesis of the Chaucer Apocrypha', *Studies in Philology*,
   XLVIII(1951),461–81.

63 See N. R. Ker, *Mediaeval Libraries of Great Britain*.

64 See my 'Notes on the manuscript of *Generydes*', in *The Library*, XVI(1961),
   205–10. The Hunterian MS. of the alliterative *Destruction of Troy* was similarly passed on as 'an heyrelome': see C. A. Luttrell, 'Three North-west
   Midland Manuscripts', *Neophilologus*, XLII(1958),38–50 (p. 42).

65 See Moore, 'Patrons of Letters' (*PMLA*, XXVII), p. 207; Hammond,
   Chaucer to Surrey, p. 79.

66 Essay on the Lydgate canon (*Minor Poems*, I), p. xxxi.

67 In his essay on the Canon, *loc. cit.*, p.v. Schirmer's list of Lydgate's works is
   the same as MacCracken's, with the addition of three minor items (*op. cit.*,
   pp. 264–73).

68 See her article in *Anglia Beiblatt* XXIV(1913),140–5.

69 MacCracken, pp. xxxi–ii; Schirmer, p. 283.

CHAPTER FOUR

The Courtly Poems

Some attempt has now been made to establish a context for Lydgate's poetry, a sense of the conditions from which it sprang, the conventions according to which it operated, and the needs for which it was designed. This context is necessary if we are to read his poetry aright and use it in the way that will be most profitable to understanding. It is now time to turn to the examination and exposition of particular poems, a task of some complexity because of the vast bulk of the material and because of the problems of organisation. A literary biography would be convenient, but it would be impossible, because we lack the knowledge which would enable us to date more than a fraction of the poems with any certainty. Even if it were possible, it would involve a degree of distortion, since many of the poems owe their origin to the general influence of a traditional genre rather than to particular events of Lydgate's life. On the other hand, there are a number of poems, including most of the major ones, which can be dated fairly accurately, and it would be foolish to ignore the evidence that these can offer of the development of Lydgate's poetic career. Therefore, in the following chapters, the method adopted is a blend of literary biography and genre-study, the two major poems, the *Troy Book* (1412–20) and the *Fall of Princes* (1431–8), being used as stepping-stones, with the great mass of topical and occasional verse, which in fact does largely belong to the 1420s, the period of Lydgate's greatest fame, being dealt with in the chapter between. Other chapters are grouped around these, dealing with the courtly, moralistic, and religious verse, since it is in these areas particularly that genre is more important than occasion. Some anomalies will arise, and the genre-chapters will inevitably have a chronological 'feeling' about them which, though not always mis-leading (the courtly verse, for instance, almost certainly belongs to Lydgate's early career), will need some modifying, especially for the religious verse, which is clearly not confined to Lydgate's later years.

But it is hoped that something will be gained in terms of a sense of the shape of Lydgate's achievement; and it is, in any case, the only method of organisation which pays attention to both the extrinsic and the intrinsic reference of the poetry, and which is at once honest and manageable. It may be added that it is not the intention of this book to mention everything that Lydgate wrote.

The courtly verse, with which this chapter is concerned, includes love-complaint (the *Complaint of the Black Knight*, the *Flower of Courtesy*), and allegory (the *Temple of Glass*), as well as some minor poems, and, by an extension, *Reason and Sensuality*, with its blend of courtly and moralistic allegory. It has been suggested above that these are all poems of comparatively early date (i.e. before 1420, at the latest), though the evidence for this can only be in the closeness of their debt to Chaucer, since there is little or no external evidence. The first three poems are about love—not in any personal sense, of course—and are best regarded as exercises within the Chaucerian courtly tradition, probably occasional pieces. It is not difficult to imagine Lydgate writing such poems to order, for a lover to send to his lady; we have seen Sir John Paston using the *Temple of Glass* in a similar way, and Shirley's rubric for the same poem (in MS. Add.16165) is quite specific: 'une soynge moult plesaunt fait a la request dun amoreux par Lidegate le Moyngne de Bury'. This provides us with an external motive for the poems, and something to appease our sense of the preposterousness of a monk writing love-poems, and leaves us free to concentrate on the intrinsic nature of these three poems, which are amongst Lydgate's most significant achievement.

The *Complaint of the Black Knight*, or as its early scribes and latest editor prefer to call it, *A Complaynt of a Loveres Lyfe*,[1] is a conventional love-complaint in a conventional garden-setting. It is a mosaic of Chaucerian themes and phrases, particularly heavily indebted to the *Book of the Duchess*, for the frame-story of the poet unhappy in love and for the device of the overheard complaint, and to Chaucer's own exercises in the genre, the *Complaint of Mars*, the *Complaint unto Pity*, and the *Complaint to his Lady*. There are parallels too with the French love-vision poems of Machaut, Deschamps, and Froissart, Machaut's *Dit dou Vergier* having been singled out for particular comparison, but the parallels are general to an infinitely familiar tradition, and it is rarely necessary to go beyond Chaucer for Lydgate's specific borrowings. The poem was well-known and widely imitated in the fifteenth century, and appears in eight manuscripts, including a Shirley original

(MS. Add. 16165) and all four manuscripts of the Bodley group.[2] It was attributed to Chaucer in the sixteenth century and remained popular until its expulsion from the canon in the nineteenth, after being acclaimed as one of the best of Chaucer's shorter poems, as for instance by John Dart, co-editor of Urry's collected Chaucer of 1721.

The poem begins with the familiar spring-setting:

> In May when Flora, the fresshe lusty quene,
> The soyle hath clad in grene, rede and white,
> And Phebus gan to shede his stremes shene
> Amyd the Bole wyth al the bemes bryght,
> And Lucifer to chace awey the nyght
> Ayen the morow our orysont hath take
> To bydde lovers out of her slepe awake. . . .

It would be impossible to disentangle the 'sources' of a passage like this: the reference to Flora, to the 'clothing' of the earth, the astronomical periphrasis, with its classicising mythology of Phoebus, Taurus, and Lucifer, are all echoes of a rich and extensive tradition. But Chaucer, as always, provides the focus of the tradition for Lydgate: the 'fresshe lusty quene' is from the *Legend of Dido* (*Legend*, 1191), and the next three lines draw on the *Troilus*:

> In May, that moder is of monthes glade,
> That fresshe floures, blew and white and rede,
> Ben quike agayn, that wynter dede made,
> And ful of bawme is fletyng every mede;
> Whan Phebus doth his bryghte bemes sprede,
> Right in the white Bole. . . . (II,50–55)

There is a memory too of the *Merchant's Tale*,

> Phebus hath of gold his stremes doun ysent (*CT*,IV,2220)

and, in the next line, of the English translation of the *Romaunt of the Rose*:

> Sped thee to sprede thy beemys bright,
> And chace the derknesse of the nyght. (2637–8)

It is a tissue of borrowings, and it is through the borrowings that the passage achieves its coherence, which is internal and literary, not external and naturalistic. Lydgate is not describing spring-time, but working variations on a series of literary motifs in the description of spring, the reference of which is aesthetic, humane, and philosophical. Nature is not being imitated, but re-created, in the context of a formal tradition which lays stress not only on the beauty (decorum) of Nature but also on the ordered inevitability of its processes and on its usefulness. The development of this tradition is summarised by Rosemond Tuve in an article rebuking over-simplified interpretation of the opening of the General Prologue to the *Canterbury Tales*:

> This tradition may be traced from Lucretius and Virgil through later poems (such as the *Pervigilium Veneris*), through Carolingian poetry, Goliardic poets, encyclopaedists and comput-writers, through Old French lyric and romance, was given new emphasis and relationships because of the importance of the seasons in astrological and other 'scientific' treatises, and in art, and appears in Middle English (particularly in Chaucer and Lydgate) with the varied and rich characteristics which so long a history and process of accretion would inevitably give it.[3]

Often, as Miss Tuve suggests, literary seasons-description takes over the pictorial conventions of art. When Lydgate later in the poem speaks of the 'chare of gold' and 'rowes rede' of Phebus (595–6), he is drawing, not on observation, but on the pictures in calendar-books which showed the sun as a chariot of gold passing across a sky of unnaturally vivid and unvaried hue, with red or golden rays descending from it in a formal design. Again, Lydgate is not describing Nature, but describing pictures of Nature's work which in their turn are mythological and philosophical in function.

The tradition, however, both in literature and art, was wearing thin in the fifteenth century. Skies were beginning to look like real skies, with shades of blue and other colours, and poets were beginning to introduce realistic detail of a non-traditional nature. Lydgate's response to the formal tradition is extraordinarily full and rich. The spring-description in the *Black Knight* is only one, and that by no means the longest, of a continuing series of such descriptions which he goes on elaborating all through his life, in all kinds of poems. But some sense of loss is apparent, by comparison with Chaucer, not so much in the intrusion of realism, which is quite foreign to Lydgate's nature, but in the profusion of surface ornament at the expense of inner significance. Imitation often betrays him, as in this passage, a few stanzas on from the opening of the *Black Knight*:

The dewe also lyk sylver in shynyng
Upon the leves as eny baume suete

Til firy Tytan with hys persaunt hete
Had dried up the lusty lycour nyw
Upon the herbes in the grene mede   (26–30)

which is clearly an attempt to improve on Chaucer:

And firy Phebus riseth up so bright
That al the orient laugheth of the light,
And with his stremes dryeth in the greves
The silver dropes hangynge on the leves.

                            (*Kn*, *T.*, *C.T*,I,1493–6)

Nothing need be said of the loss of vigour and delight; what is significant is the use of *lycour* to mean 'dew' instead of 'sap', as in the opening
of the General Prologue. A word of strong scientific and philosophical
connotation in Chaucer thus loses its fullness of sense and becomes
another element in surface decoration.

    The poet goes on to tell how he went out on a spring morning to
hear the birds sing, and to solace the pains of love. He follows a river
till he enters a park through a small gate in the wall.

And by a ryver forth I gan costey
Of water clere as berel or cristal
Til at the last I founde a lytil wey
Towarde a parke enclosed with a wal
In compas round; and by a gate smal
Whoso that wolde frely myghte goon
Into this parke walled with grene stoon.

And in I went to her the briddes songe
Which on the braunches bothe in pleyn and vale
So loude song that al the wode ronge
Lyke as hyt shold shever in pesis smale.
And, as me thoghte, that the nyghtyngale
With so grete myght her voys gan out wrest
Ryght as her hert for love wolde brest.

The soyle was pleyn, smothe and wonder softe,
Al oversprad wyth tapites that Nature

7

> Had made herselfe, celured eke alofte
> With bowys grene the floures for to cure
> That in her beaute they may long endure
> Fro al assaute of Phebus fervent fere
> Which in his spere so hote shone and clere.
>
> The eyre atempre and the smothe wynde
> Of Zepherus among the blosmes whyte
> So holsom was and norysshing be kynde
> That smale buddes and round blomes lyte
> In maner gan for her brethe delyte
> To yif us hope that their frute shal take
> Ayens autumpne redy for to shake.
>
> I saw ther Daphene closed under rynde,
> Grene laurer and the holsom pyne,
> The myrre also that wepeth ever of kynde,
> The cedre high, upryght as a lyne,
> The philbert eke that lowe doth enclyne
> Her bowes grene to the erthe doune
> Unto her knyght icalled Demophoune.
>
> Ther saw I eke the fresshe hawethorne
> In white motele that so soote doth smelle,
> Asshe, firre and oke with mony a yonge acorne,
> And mony a tre mo than I can telle.
> And me beforne I saw a litel welle
> That had his course (as I gan beholde)
> Under an hille with quyke stremes colde.
>
> The gravel gold, the water pure as glas,
> The bankys round, the welle environyng,
> And softe as veluet the yonge gras
> That therupon lustely cam spryngyng.
> The sute of trees aboute compassyng
> Her shadow cast, closyng the welle rounde
> And al the erbes growyng on the grounde.   (36–84)

The landscape is so familiar that any medieval poet could find his way about it blindfold. The tradition is that of the *locus amoenus* which, as

Curtius says, 'from the Empire to the sixteenth century, forms the principal motif of all nature description',[4] with its six 'charms of landscape'—shaded site, grove of trees, smooth greensward, flower-carpet, birdsong, and soft breezes. For later medieval poets, the focus of the tradition was the *Roman de la Rose*,[5] and Lydgate draws heavily on the English translation. Specific borrowings include the river by which he walks ('costeiyng', *RR*,134), the walled park, the small gate, the list of trees, the well-spring and the grass as soft as velvet (*RR*,1420). From the *Parlement of Foules* he takes the 'park walled with grene ston' (*PF*,122), and also the idea of amplifying the tree-catalogue with characteristic attributes (*PF*,176–82), Such description, it will readily be seen, has little to do with realistic observation of nature. Laurels, pines, myrrh-trees, and cedars do not occur together in English gardens, any more than lions appear in the forest of Arden. The ideal here is, as Curtius puts it, 'richness of décor and an elaborate vocabulary' (*loc. cit.*). Elsewhere, the classical origin of such descriptions is obvious in the emphasis on shade and running water, for instance. Flowers in England hardly need protection from the burning heat of the sun in early May (cf. *RR*,1395), and springs and conduits are not necessary to make the grass grow soft and green, as they are in a Mediterranean garden (*RR*,1417–26).

The function of such description is not to imitate but to idealise. The forms of nature are systematically distorted in the interests of 'love of order, light, intelligibility, and symmetry'.[6] The delight in nature is certainly there, but it is a nature which has been subdued to human concepts of beauty and usefulness. Wild landscape had little appeal for the Middle Ages and only appears in literature as the setting for martyrdoms and temptations, or for *rites de passage* in romance, as in *Sir Gawain and the Green Knight*. Gawain has to pass through a Wordsworthian landscape of rocks, mountains, and waterfalls, but he is not there to admire the scenery, and neither is the poet. Nature, to be appreciated, has to be made courteous, it has to be enclosed within a wall, emblematic of civilisation itself. 'The walled garden became the centre of all that was fair and peaceful in love, in life, and in religion'.[7] Within the wall, all is pattern, harmony, symmetry, brilliance of colour and definition of outline. Nature is systematically interpreted and re-ordered in images of human sway and human beauty. Water is clear and pure like beryl or crystal or glass; grass has the texture of velvet; the flowers are a tapestry spread by Nature on the ground; the boughs form a canopy or roof, so that the ideal garden seems to be the one that best repeats outside, the trappings of civilised existence inside. The most extravagant example of such artifice is the effect of the birds' song:

> So loude song that al the wode ronge
> Lyke as hyt shold shever in pesis smale.   (45–6)

Here Lydgate is copying Chaucer again:

> The noyse of foules for to ben delyvered
> So loude rong, 'Have don, and lat us wende!'
> That wel wende I the wode hadde al to-shyvered
> (*Parlement*, 491–3)

but whereas in Chaucer the image is left unresolved as a playful hyperbole, Lydgate enforces a literal reading by his 'pesis smale', in which the wood takes on the character of fine porcelain, ready to crack when the birds' song reaches a certain intensity. It is an extraordinary image, and it anticipates Dunbar in its neglect of actual textures and concentration on an artificial surface:

> The cristall air, the sapher firmament,
> The ruby skyes of the orient,
> Kest beriall bemes on emerant bewis grene;
> The rosy garth depaynt and redolent,
> With purpur, azur, gold, and goulis gent,
> Arayed was. . . .   (*Golden Targe*, 37–42)

Lydgate is still writing in a recognisably metaphorical way, but the significance of his metaphors is inward, not outward. They are not there to provide vivid sensuous analogues, but to offer images of control and explicability, and the idea of Nature imitating an elegant and well-ordered civilisation is brought out even more strongly in the systematically 'human' interpretation of her activities. Sun and flowers operate together in mutual trust, with branches intervening to care for the flowers when the sun grows too strong; the nightingale sings her heart out for love, and the buds and blooms 'delyte' in the soft breezes, giving hope of fruit in the autumn. The poetic eye which views these landscapes is one which has been trained to interpret more than to see.

A passage like this demonstrates what I have called Lydgate's 'usefulness', because in it he captures the essence of a general tradition, anthologising and indexing its major functions, which are not merely formal and lietrary, as Curtius suggests, but conceptual also. But the very clarity with which we can see the general tradition laid open suggests

Lydgate's limitations, for the landscape here described is not complicated by a particular function in the poem. There is a sense of beauty
and harmony and fecundity, but it is unrelated to the complaint that
follows, and remains no more than a setting, a backcloth. One is forced
to make the contrast with Chaucer, and the way he uses similar description in the *Parlement* as an integral part of the allegorical structure of the
poem. Above all, Lydgate's constant echoes of the *Romance of the Rose*
remind us that what we are witnessing is the 'defusing' of allegory. The
Romance had a walled park, but the specific allegorical significance of
the wall was clear not only from what was outside and inside but also
from the 'wiket small' which was its only entrance, guarded by
Ydelnesse. Lydgate keeps the park and keeps the 'gate smal', but
explicitly denies the allegorical sense of privilege by his next two lines:

> Whoso that wolde frely myghte goon
> Into this parke walled with grene stoon. (41–2)

Lydgate, like the *Romance*, also has a well-spring, but deprives it of all
its potent allegorical significance as the source and fountainhead of love
(the eyes of the beloved) by declaring it to be 'nat lyche' the well of
Narcissus, whereas the fact that it *is* the well of Narcissus is the whole
point of its presence in the *Romance*. The poet in Lydgate drinks from
it, is much refreshed, and goes on his way. It might just as well be a
real garden, with a real wall, and a real well. One sees how easily
Lydgate is led along by his own fluency in imitation, until he realises
that the vein is exhausted, that the well has nothing to do with the case,
and promptly drops it. The whole seasons and landscape description at
the beginning of the *Black Knight* is beautifully organised and polished,
and demonstrates fully the formal and conceptual nature of such
description in medieval poetry, but it lacks coherence with the poem
of which it forms part, chiefly because Lydgate is not interested in
larger allegorical structures. Paradoxically, his garden, though less
realistic, is more real than those of his predecessors.

After describing the garden the poet comes upon an 'erber grene', in
which there is a man clad 'in blake and white', lamenting his pitiful
state. The poet prepares to record his complaint, first calling for help
from Niobe and Myrrha to produce in him the right mood of anguish,

> For unto wo accordeth compleynyng (183)

and declaring his own inadequacy to the task, since he is a mere

'skryvener'. There is a good deal of imitation here of the opening of
the *Troilus*, but it is typical of Lydgate to begin by laying down this
sort of preliminary barrage, softening up the audience with salvoes of
invocatio, *dubitatio*, rhetorical precedents and modesty-topics, before
actually moving forward. The Complaint itself (218–574) is the centre-
piece of the poem, describing the lover's hopeless state and the allegorical forces ranged against him (Daunger, Malebouche, etc.). The god of
Love always seems to be cruellest to those who are most faithful to him,
as is shown in a long series of examples (323–406), e.g.

> What shal I say of yonge Piramus?
> Of trwe Tristram for al his high renoune?
> Or Achilles or of Antonyus?
> Of Arcite, or of him, Palamoune?
> What was the ende of her passion
> But after sorow, deth and then her grave.
> Lo, her the guerdon that thes lovers have.   (365–71)

Truth and virtue go unheeded by Love, while Falsehood is rewarded,
and the lover laments Love's blindness, and the bitterness of having to
seek pity from the one who wounded him. He describes how Nature
endowed her with every beauty and virtue,

> And altherlast Dysdeyne
> To hinder Trouth she made her chambreleyne.   (503–4)

He ends with repeated avowals of his intention to die in her service so
that she may know his truth.

This Complaint is entirely conventional, in a mode which had long
been the staple of medieval love-lyric. It is *de rigueur* for the lover in the
Romaunt of the Rose:

> Among eke, for thy lady sake,
> Songes and complayntes that thou make;
> For that wole meven in hir herte,
> Whanne they reden of thy smerte.   (2325–8)

The attraction of the form is that it substitutes for the flux of experience
of unrequited love a pattern of desire and rejection which is in complete equilibrium—'For ever must thou love and she be fair'. The
Complaint takes the notion of 'service', isolates it as a mode of behaviour self-sufficient in itself, deprives it of any motive, origin, or issue
into action, and presents it in this eternal moment of stasis. There is no
movement, no action, only the lover and his mistress for ever frozen

into ritual gestures of beseeching and disdain. The only 'action' is in the inset allegorical narratives, where abstract personifications engage in precise and formalised manoeuvres, within a framework of military (250–6) or legalistic (257–87) allegory:

> And Male-bouche gan first the tale telle
> To sclaundre Trouthe of Indignacion,
> And Fals-Report so loude rong the belle
> That Mysbeleve and Fals-Suspecion
> Have Trouthe brought to hys damnacion. . . (260–4)

Relieved thus from the disturbing pressures of reality, the love-complaint is open to the poet as a 'theme' for amplification and decoration. It is ideally suited to the display of rhetorical skills, since it is in itself a form of persuasion and has the formal identity of a plea or complaint in law. This, no doubt, is why the form was so popular in other fields, Alain de Lille's *Complaint of Nature*, for instance, or the genre of political complaint-poems, or, to go back to the progenitor of the form, Ovid's *Heroides*.

Chaucer showed early dissatisfaction with the formal love-complaint. After some experiments with the genre in its purer form, in poems like the *Complaint of Venus*, the *Complaint to Pity*, and the *Complaint to his Lady*, he tends in his maturer work to establish it within a narrative framework, as in the *Book of the Duchess*, the *Complaint of Mars*, and *Anelida and Arcite*, thus returning it to the context of human motive and situation, and ultimately to reintegrate it completely in narrative so that it almost loses its formal identity, as in the *Knight's Tale* and the *Troilus*. The final metamorphosis is near-parody, in the Franklin's jaunty dismissal of Aurelius's furious languishing:

> He seyde he lovede, and was biloved no thyng. (*CT*,V,946)

Lydgate, however, betrays no such desire to complicate matters. The formal love-complaint, with its high rhetorical tone, strong formal definition, its opportunity for amplification by examples, and continual deflection into abstraction, is the perfect vehicle for the display of the skills of which he is master. He copies Chaucer in providing a narrative frame for the Complaint, but it is a frame in the most literal sense, for it acts only to surround and define the Complaint, not to influence or penetrate it. The poet overhears the lover, as in the *Book of the Duchess*, but he engages in no dialogue with him. The Complaint exists in a void, as far as real life is concerned. It represents the final purification of *fine amour*, a crystalline vision purged of the taint of earth and reality, a hypostatisation of the life-processes, like a game of chess left on the board for centuries, its significance not in its relation to real life but in the harmony of its parts. One can see how well-suited this insulation of love-poetry was to Lydgate himself as a monk, but it would be a mistake to attribute it to his 'monkishness', since it is a characteristic late medieval phenomenon. Alain Chartier's *La Belle Dame sans Merci* is typical of the tendency towards formal abstraction, and Sir Richard Roos's English translation preserves the tone of the original with some success. The same tendency is shown in the series of debate-poems by Baudet Herenc, Achille Caulier, and others, prompted by the *Belle Dame*, where the legalistic framework of the complaint is further extended, and merciless beauty is brought to the bar for trial and judgment.[8]

The love-complaint in the *Black Knight*, demanding of Lydgate what he is uniquely well qualified to give, draws from him one of his most splendid sustained pieces of high rhetorical writing. Leaning heavily on Chaucer, especially the *Troilus* and the *Knight's Tale*, he adds to the ingenious allegories and antitheses of the conventional form a rich apparatus of classical and philosophical allusion. The style is highly wrought, with elaborate but unostentatious figuring and a sure control of conventional metaphor and diction. The exuberant flow of examples and parallels is for once restrained within a dominant pattern, as in the catalogue of lovers betrayed, or the fine stanzas (400–34) where the complainant piles up the case against Love of virtues scorned and vices rewarded. The passage begins with an imitation of the 'Lo her' stanza of the *Troilus*, as if Lydgate's imagination was first stirred by the form, the figure, rather than by the literal reality. It is the same with the opening stanzas of the Complaint (218–45), which begin with the imitation already quoted of the first lines of the *Parlement of Foules*:

> The thoght oppressed with inward sighes sore,
> The peynful lyve, the body langwysshing. . . .

Lydgate seems to use the literary reminiscence as a spur, and the stanzas that follow, with their elaborate patterns of repetition, parallelism, antithesis, chiasmus, echoing, alliteration, exclamation, and oxymoron, are good examples of the rhetorician's art at its purest:

> This ys the colde of ynward high dysdeyn,
> Colde of dyspite and colde of cruel hate.

This is the cold that ever doth besy peyn
Ayenes trouth to fighten and debate.
This ys the cold that wolde the fire abate
Of trwe menyng (alas the harde while):
This ys the colde that will me begile.   (239–45)

It is important to recognise how the formula, in this case the rhetorical figure, releases, not inhibits, what is best in Lydgate. 'The finest fruit ripens on espaliers'.

Nor is this true only of style: it is the very essence of a rhetorical poetic. It would be possible to talk about the Complaint as 'frigid', and many of the images I have used in the attempt to identify its special nature have been of this kind. But we must be clear about what we can usefully expect. To use 'frigid' as a term of disapprobation makes about as much sense as to talk of Lydgate's landscape-description as 'artificial', with the censure that that word usually carries in criticism. It should be clear by now that real life, experience, 'the sensuous apprehension of reality', whatever one calls it, play only a minimal part in Lydgate's poetry, except of course in low-style writing, where a different set of conventions operate. Experience, to be poetically assimilable, must come to him strained through the medium of literary convention and literary formula. The Complaint does not exist to imitate the reality of passion and carry it alive into the heart, any more than any other medieval love-poetry does; the fact that it would have been improper for Lydgate to attempt anything of the sort is a side-issue. What counts is not recognition of the accuracy of the emotions displayed, but delight in the ordering of those emotions into a formal pattern which is internally coherent and harmonious and basically conceptual. Anyone can fall in love, just as anyone can take pleasure in spring-time, but only the poet can make sense of them. No doubt this is true of all literature, even the most overtly naturalistic; again, the usefulness of Lydgate is that he demonstrates the operation of the truth in its purest form, for there is no chance for us to be distracted by anything else.

This claim, of course, is double-edged. In recognising the purity of the poetic experience, it recognises also its thinness. The *Black Knight* is alien to our ways of thinking about what poetry should be, but fundamentally it is a very easy poem, almost a template of a poem. There is nothing in the body of it to match the rich elaboration of the style, as we see in the passage where Lydgate amplifies the familiar oxymoron of the lover's fever:

With hote and cold myn acces ys so meynt
That now I shyver for defaute of hete
And hote as glede now sodenly I suete.

Now hote as fire, now colde as asshes dede,
Now hote for cold, now cold for hete ageyn,
Now colde as ise, now as coles rede
For hete I bren; and thus betwexe tweyn
I possed am and al forcast in peyn;
So that myn hete, pleynly as I fele,
Of grevous colde ys cause everydele.   (229–38)

A similar delight in paradox, in contrarieties, can be found in the
Romaunt of the Rose and in the *Troilus*,[9] Lydgate's direct sources, but
whereas in those two poems the metaphors of paradox correspond to a
wealth of knowledge, or perception, of sheer 'matter', the metaphors in
Lydgate correspond to nothing. The impression of copiousness is misleading, and the pattern created, though pleasing and by no means
meaningless, lacks depth. The passage in fact is very characteristic of
Lydgate in the way it elevates a formal structure (oxymoron) into a
structure of thought. It is a habit of mind to which we shall have to
recur on other, more significant occasions.

There is not much more to the poem. The Knight retires to his wood-
land 'logge', where he is wont to spend May in complaint. Night draws
on, in a beautiful descriptive set-piece (589–97), and the poet prays to
the evening-star, Venus, that the knight may be better rewarded for his
loyal service. He goes home, and commends his poem to all true lovers,
hoping that they too may meet with better success before the night is out:

That eche of yow may have such a grace
His oun lady in armes to embrace.
I mene thus, that in al honeste,
Withoute more, ye may togedre speke
Whatso ye liste at good liberte. . . .   (657–61)

The retreat into abstraction, from the hint of action back to the eternal
dialogue, is amusing, and is meant to be so, suggesting a shared awareness on the part of Lydgate and his audience of the strict decorum
beyond which he must not trespass. The poem ends, characteristically,
with two envoys; Lydgate always begins with a flourish, and he never
retires from our presence without a good deal of bowing and scraping.

But there is no lapse of consistency, and the construction of the frame, when complete, is as perfect as that of the Complaint.

I have dealt with this poem at length, partly because it is one of Lydgate's best, but more because it is so characteristic of his work. In comparatively brief compass, it provides an introduction to some of his major techniques and habits of mind, and therefore, if what I have said of Lydgate's role as a representative of his age is true, to those of the general medieval tradition of formal love-poetry.

The *Flower of Courtesy*, another love-complaint, is Lydgate's by supposition only. There is no manuscript extant, and the poem first appeared in Thynne's collected Chaucer of 1532. It was subsequently attributed to Lydgate by John Stow the antiquary. Stow, like Thynne, had access to a good deal of manuscript material now lost, but his ascriptions are not always reliable, and the poem must depend for its place in the canon on internal rather than external evidence. Fortunately, unless there was an anonymous poet who could write more like Lydgate than Lydgate could himself, this internal evidence—of style, diction, descriptive technique, characteristic allusion, use of and reference to Chaucer—is overwhelming: fortunately, for the poem is a near-flawless piece of craftsmanship.

On St. Valentine's eve the poet hears the lark calling to lovers to renew their allegiance to love's service, and he goes out after rising to a grove to see the birds choosing their mates, as in the *Parlement of Foules*. But he is love-sick, and sits down beneath a 'laurer grene' to make complaint, and to protest, in two very effective stanzas (53–70), against the 'purveyaunce' that allows to birds 'free election', while man 'Constrayned is, and by statute bounde'.

> For I my herte have set in suche a place
> Wher I am never lykely for to spede.   (78–9)

Nevertheless, he vows that he will serve her till he dies, and proposes to write for her sake something in honour of the day. Thus formally introduced begins the description of his lady (113–224), 'the floure of curtesye', which is the central set-piece of the poem and virtually its whole substance. The description is worth attending to as a *tour de force* of non-visual abstraction. Like similar descriptions elsewhere in Lydgate, particularly that in the *Temple of Glass*, which is very close, it consists entirely of eulogistic topics of surpassing and inexpressible excellence, lists of abstract virtues, praise of Nature's feat of creation,

In her is naught that Nature can amende   (189)

and comparisons with other famous ladies. There is, in the hundred
lines and more, not a single detail of descriptive visualisation, almost as
if Lydgate were responding to a sense of challenge. This type of description (or non-description) seems to have been, at least at such length and
so systematically constructed, Lydgate's own development, and he
developed it probably because the more familiar type of female description was now outworn. This older technique of description was in the
form of an inventory or catalogue of physical excellences.[10] The poet
would begin at the top, with the lady's hair, and then work his way
steadily downward, through eyes, nose, mouth, teeth, and so on, with
a wealth of predictable detail and conventional imagery. There was, it
may seem, an element of suspense in such description (usually frustrated
—'taceo de partibus infra'), which may account for its long popularity,
but by Lydgate's time the inventory of female charms must have been
vieux jeu, for in translating the *Troy Book* he rejects a long description of
Helen on these lines,[11] and we can be sure that the change of taste was
decisive indeed if it persuaded the monk of Bury to leave anything
out.[12]

Possibly, though, he thought such descriptions improper—in which
case he has certainly established new standards of propriety—and saw
the appropriateness to himself and the usefulness to the 'amoureux' of
this kind of universalising abstraction (no lady could fail to recognise
herself in this kind of portrait, any more than on the blank page in
Tristram Shandy). To be truthful, he has invented nothing. What he
has done is to take particular traits of descriptive technique and, as
usual, to amplify them and elevate them into systematic principles.
Again, he lays open a whole medieval convention by allowing us to
see it operate in a vacuum. For instance, medieval description, especially
personal description, is traditionally idealising, whether *ad praeconium* or
ad vituperium,[13] 'good' or 'bad'. So the *descriptio feminae pulchritudinis* is
always more a celebration of womanhood than a description of a
particular woman:

> And there to speke of femynyte,
> The leste mannysshe in comparyson.   (148–9)

To describe a woman by saying that she is very womanly, and not at
all mannish, may seem to us tautologous at the least, but it is an idea
rather than a picture that the medieval poet is trying to get over, and

Chaucer too, at the significant moment of Criseyde's introduction into the *Troilus*, where a novelist might provide a 'thumbnail sketch', concentrates on the *idea* of her womanliness:

> She nas nat with the leste of hir stature,
> But alle hire lymes so wel answerynge
> Weren to wommanhod, that creature
> Was nevere lasse mannyssh in semynge.   (I,281–4)

It is worth noticing how little we know of Criseyde's actual appearance. The low-style description of Alysoun in the *Millers' Tale*, with its spicy physical detail and toothsome imagery, provides a striking contrast, and a useful reminder that abstraction is employed by medieval writers because it is decorous to the high style, not because they couldn't think of anything else.

The list of virtues also contributes to the idealisation of woman, in the moral sphere. Lydgate, comprehensive as always, attributes to the lady every virtue, regards her indeed as the very exemplar of virtue:

> For every vertue is in her at reste,
> And furthermore, to speke of stedfastnesse,
> She is the rote, and of semelynesse
> The very myrrour, and of governaunce
> To al example, withouten varyaunce. . . .
> She is the welle, aye devoyde of pride,
> That unto vertue her-selven is the gyde.
>
> (129–33, 139–40)

Such terms as 'rote', 'myrrour', 'welle', idealising in their very essence, are the characteristic marks of personal description in Lydgate. Hector, for instance, in the *Troy Book*, is described thus:

> He was þe rote and stok of chevalrie,
> And of knyȝthod verray sovereyn flour,
> þe sowrs and welle of worschip and honour;
> And of manhod, I dar it wel expresse,
> Example and merour; and of hiȝe prowesse
> Gynyng and grounde.   (*Troy*, II,244–9)

Phrases like 'crop and rote', 'sours and welle', are systematically used to express this perfection of quality, whether admirable, as with Hector or, later, Polyxena,[14] or vile, as with Aeneas,

> Crop and rote, fynder of falsnesse,
> Sours and welle of unkyndenesse.
>
> (*Troy*, IV,6443-4)

Sometimes the whole description consists in the systematic variation of such terms, as in the description of Leonidas in the *Fall of Princes*—

> Of chevalrie callid the lode-sterre,
> The sunne of knyhthod, that shon so briht and sheene. . . .
> Charboncle of armys, merour of policie
>
> (*Fall*, III,2304-9)

or that of Arthur and his court:

> Welle of worshep, conduit of al noblesse,
> Imperial court al wrongis to redresse,
> Hedspryng of honour, of largesse cheef cisterne,
> Merour of manhod, of noblesse the lanterne.
>
> (*Fall*, VIII,2853-6),

Amplification by systematic variation is characteristic of Lydgate's description, in fact of all his writing. His method is always to obtain copiousness by accumulation, as in the opening of the description of the 'floure of curtesye':

> Ryght by example as the somer sonne
> Passeth the sterre with his beames shene,
> And Lucyfer amonge the skyes donne
> A-morowe sheweth, to voyde nyghtes tene,
> So, verily, withouten any wene,
> My lady passeth, who-so taketh hede,
> Al tho alyve to speke of womanhede.
>
> And as the ruby hath the soveraynte
> Of ryche stones and the regalye,
> And the rose of swetenesse and beaute,
> Of fresshe floures, withouten any lye,
> Ryght so. . . . She passeth al. . . . (113-25)

This imagery of surpassing excellence is highly conventional. The comparison of sun and star, for instance, is taken in the first place from the description of Nature in the *Parlement of Foules* (299), but beyond that it goes back through Machaut and Petrarch to Chretien and the

Carmina Burana and ultimately to Seneca and Ovid.[15] Lydgate himself uses it frequently, in describing Hector, for example, in the *Troy Book* (II,8471), or Chaucer in relation to himself in the *Fall* (II,995). At the end of his life, in the *Secrees of Philisoffres*, he is still pressing the same image into service (344–8). The other images are also very common in Lydgate, and the whole sequence is repeated item by item, almost word by word, in the *Temple of Glass* (251–64). It is the contrastive form of the image that attracts him, not its content, and above all the repetition of the form in a systematic pattern. It is as if Lydgate felt a compulsive need to go through his limited list of categories of excellence, ticking them off one by one, before he could feel satisfied.

One senses similar pressures at work in the later part of the description, where the method of amplification is by comparison with famous ladies of history and fiction: his lady is as good as Polyxena, as fair as Helen, as steadfast as Dorigen, as constant as Cleopatra, as 'secree' as Antigone of Troy, and so on. The direct ancestor of this passage (190–217) is the *balade* in praise of Alceste in the Prologue to the *Legend of Good Women*, where many of the same names occur, and where the function of the comparisons is similarly eulogistic. But the topos is a familiar one, particularly in the praise of women, and much favoured by Lydgate. It is the very structural principle of his *Ballade of her that hath all the virtues*, and is important too in *A Lover's New Year's Gift* and the *Epithalamion for Gloucester*. The same women appear in the *Life of Our Lady*:

> Late be, thow Grece, and speke not of Eleyn,
> Ne thow, Troy, of Yong Polexene,
> Ne Rome of Lucresse, with hir eyn tweyne,
> Ne thow, Cartage, of thy fresshe quene,
> Dido, that was so fayre some tyme to seen;
> Late be your boste, and take of hem noon hede
> Whose beaute fayleth as floure in frosty mede.   (I,302–8)

Panegyric of men is amplified on the same principle. Gloucester in the *Epithalamion* has the virtues of Solomon, Julius Caesar, Tullius, Hannibal, Pompey, and Scipio (148–54). The systematic elaboration of such topics had been made easier by the establishment of the Nine Worthy as standard ideals of comparison, as in the *Ballade of King Henry VI's Coronation*, though the origin of the Nine is not in panegyric but in moralistic amplifications of the transience of worldly glory (the *Ubi sunt* formula): their significance is that they are all dead.

It is easy to see the eulogistic function of comparison-topics in description, but Lydgate's use of the technique is so systematic and extensive that one looks for some further explanation. Partly it is that he tends to systematise everything, using mechanical principles of accumulation as his mode of organisation. Partly it is that the opportunity to use classical and Biblical names stimulates his passion for encyclopaedism. Collecting allusions becomes almost an end in itself, as it did for the English friars of the early fourteenth century, Robert Holcot, for instance, assembling detail for a praise of good women.[16] Lydgate's range is much smaller, but his ambitions are the same. Psychologically, the mania for lists recalls, as Hammond points out, the phenomenon of total recall. A particular stimulus, usually a point of literary technique, triggers off a torrent of examples, parallels, analogues, and images, and the poet cannot move forward until the whole contents of his memory have been regurgitated.

However, as I have said, Lydgate only demonstrates in extreme form, and at extreme length, characteristic medieval preoccupations. The three types of descriptive idealisation and amplification mentioned above are all typical of Chaucer as well as Lydgate, and to them one should add a fourth, exemplified in the two stanzas of the *Flower of Courtesy* which begin thus:

> I am to rude her vertues everychone
> Cunnyngly to discryve and write. . . .   (176–7)

This technique of description through assertion of inability to describe is an example of what Curtius, or his translator rather, calls the 'inexpressibility topos',[17] and it is very common in Lydgate. The term topos, or topic, which has been used with some frequency in the last few pages, is a useful one to denote the sources or 'common places' of material for amplification. Fuller discussion of the 'topics', and their importance to an understanding of Lydgate and medieval verse, will be reserved for the chapter on the *Troy Book*, where Lydgate's techniques of amplification are more extensively developed.

I have called the *Flower of Courtesy* a near-flawless piece of craftsmanship, and so it is, but it is worth remembering the limitations of craftsmanship. Chaucer's examples of conventional *descriptio feminae* are usually brief, as in the *Complaint of Mars* (173–81) and *Anelida* (71–84), but the *Book of the Duchess* offers more extended comparison. Here we find Chaucer using many of the same techniques: the image of sun surpassing stars (821), the list of abstract virtues (826–9, etc.), brief hints of Biblical (987), and classical (1081) comparison, suggestions of indescribability,

> Allas! myn herte ys wonder woo
> That I ne kan discryven hyt! (896–7)

But all of this is broken up and embedded in a context of varied and personalised detail and vivid physical concretion; and this in its turn is constantly brought alive and given an extra dimension by being part of the lover's process of reminiscence and growing realisation of what he has lost. If Chaucer was dissatisfied with the old-fashioned kind of descriptive catalogue, he showed it by moving outwards towards the immediate and the individual, where Lydgate circles inward towards the abstract and universal. What Chaucer does, even in this early poem, he does better than Lydgate at the height of his powers, but it would be wise to be aware of the difference between what they are trying to do, and singularly pointless to criticise Lydgate for lacking precisely what he has spent the resources of a very considerable art in trying to avoid.

A word may be said here of the half-dozen shorter love-poems. Most of them are complaints, though two are avowals of requited love: *My lady dere*, traditionally associated with the *Balade at the Departyng of Thomas Chaucer*,[18] and *A Lover's New Year's Gift*. They were all probably written to order, like the *Ballade of her that hath all the Virtues*, 'whiche þat Lydgate wrote at þe request of a squyer þat served in loves court',[19] though *A Gentlewoman's Lament* looks like an exercise in prosopopeia, and the *Servant of Cupid Forsaken* has a bitter twist in the envoy which links it with the satirical anti-feminist poems. All are graceful exercises in a conventional idiom, dependent for their very existence on their form, and often constructed on strict formal principles, like the *Ballade*, with its topics of comparison, and *My lady dere*, with its accumulated illustrations from nature of the lover's mood. The diction is highly stylised, and so is the imagery, as in the *Complaint for lack of mercy*, which rings the changes on sickness, tears, and the sword of Achilles; but Lydgate makes the most of it, and the image in *A Gentlewoman's Lament*,

> And Love þoo gaf me for my meede
> A knotte in hert of remembraunce (23–4)

is susceptible of quite complex analysis on a particular level: it is a knot between her heart and her love, a knot tied for memory, and a 'knotting'

8

of the heart in grief, but pathetically falls short of what she really
wants, a knot between her and her love.[20] Such images reward attention, and the poems themselves, though their surface is too smooth to
give the illusion of passion, have the muted charm of faded tapestry
designs.

The *Temple of Glass* is an altogether more ambitious poem, the longest
sustained composition in which Lydgate does not work from a direct
source. It appears in eight manuscripts, including Shirley's MS. Add.
16165 and the Bodley group, and was extremely popular in the fifteenth
century, particularly as a quarry for other poets, both practising and
aspiring, to draw from. For this it was well suited by its sprawling and
eclectic construction. The poem is cast as a dream and set, like the
House of Fame, in December. The poet,

> Al desolate for constreint of my wo,
> The longe nyȝt waloing to and fro,   (11–12)

dreams of a 'temple of glas'

> That foundid was, as bi liklynesse,
> Not opon stele, but on a craggy roche,
> Like ise ifrore.   (18–20)

This, too, is taken from the *House of Fame*, which Lydgate is using as
a springboard, just as he used the *Book of the Duchess* in the *Black Knight*.
The poet enters the temple, which turns out to be the temple of Venus,
and finds the walls painted with famous lovers[21] and the temple full of
lovers making their complaint to Venus. They complain of absence,
disdain, poverty, falsehood, and every other possible frustration to
which the lover is subject; groups of ladies complain, with a specific
bitterness which is rare in the genre, of having been forced into marriages for wealth, or as children, and of having been dedicated to the
cloister when too young to know love. It is rather difficult to see what
the last group are doing in the temple of Venus in the first place, and
the lines have often been taken to be personal on Lydgate's part, a
belated *cri de coeur* for what he has missed. But the lines refer specifically
to women (207–8), and are chiefly an example of how the urge to be
comprehensive leads Lydgate into slightly indecorous irrelevance.

Amongst the complainants the poet sees a lady, whose surpassing
beauty is described (251–97) in the systematically abstract and idealising
terms of the *Flower of Courtesy*. Her complaint to Venus is of constreint

in love, of being bound to one she does not love, so that her true love
cannot be fulfilled. She is presumably referring to marriage:

> For I am bounde to þing þat I nold:
> Freli to chese þere lak I liberte,
> And so I want of þat myn herte would,
> The bodi knyt, alþouȝe my þouȝt be fre;
> So þat I most, of necessite,
> Myn hertis lust outward contrarie—
> Thogh we be on, þe dede most varie. (335–41)

The particular nature of the complaint thus follows on from the general
problem raised earlier, of loveless marriages. Venus replies in vaguely
hopeful terms (419–22) and the Lady thanks her. These three set speeches
are in rhyme-royal, and thus formally distinguished from the narrative
frame, which is in couplet. Lydgate returns to couplet for the narrative
link which introduces the Knight, and for the Knight's own complaint,
which is in the form of a soliloquy and plays neat variations on the
familiar imagery of eyes, wounds, battles, traps, and, in particular, the
'sterelees boot' of *Troilus* (I,416):

> Alas, when shal þis tempest overdrawe
> To clere þe skies of myn adversite. (610–11)

The poem again uses rhyme-royal for the Knight's Complaint to Venus,
and for Venus's reply, in which she promises him help, providing that
his love is pure:

> She shal not have, ne take of þe non hede
> Ferþer þen longiþ unto hir womanhede. (874–5)

She advises him to approach the Lady with his complaint, and another
brief narrative link in couplet, chiefly devoted to the poet's invocation
of Thesiphone and her sisters to help him write,

> Nou lete ȝoureteris into myn inke reyne,
> With woful woordis my pauper forto blot,
> This woful mater to peinte not but spotte (961–3)

introduces the final sequence, in which the Knight's complaint to his
Lady is followed by her reply,

> For unto þe time þat Venus list provyde
> To shape a wai for oure hertis ease,
> Boþe ȝe and I mekeli most abide (1082–4)

and Venus's admonitions to the lovers. Venus unites the lovers in what appears to be a quasi-marital bond:

> Eternalli, be bonde of assuraunce,
> The cnott is knytt which mai not ben unbound.
>
> (1229-30)

The poem ends with a beautiful ballade in honour of Venus the day-star, sung by the lovers in the temple; the singing wakes the dreamer, who promises to make a 'litil tretise' for the Lady of the dream,

> In prais of women, oonli for her sake.   (1381)

The dreamer seems to have fallen in love with the Lady himself, or else the Knight was his own dream-surrogate, it is not clear which. The whole of the narrative epilogue is extremely ambiguous, probably because Lydgate has not fully worked out his relationship to the *persona* of the poem.

The *Temple of Glass*, it will be seen, is ambitious in design. Lydgate has devised for it, working from hints in *Anelida*, *Mars*, and the Prologue to the *Legend of Good Women*, a formal metrical design in which blocks of stanzas, used for lyrical and rhetorical set-pieces, stand in relief against narrative introduction and links in couplet. The opening of the poem shows the same deliberate attention in its unusual winter-setting and weirdly effective description of the temple of glass. The significance of this temple is not so much that it is made of glass and founded on ice. These are simply details that Lydgate has picked up from Chaucer's description of the House of Fame for their decorative effect; as symbols of instability they are irrelevant to this poem, which deals with constancy in love. The significant passage comes a little later, where the dreamer describes how he is blinded by the light reflected from the glass, and cannot see his way to enter until the sun is obscured by clouds. This passage, if it means anything, and it is precise enough to suggest that it does, anticipates the argument of the poem that love (=the sun) can only be truly known by the experience of its loss or frustration.[22] But this is all. After these opening lines, we hear only of the paintings on the walls of the temple and the lovers' complaints, and these are evidence only of Lydgate's encyclopaedic tendencies, not of any allegorical intention. There is nothing of the luminous allegorical description of the temples of Venus in the *Parlement of Foules* and the *Knight's Tale*, at once pictorially decorative and meaningful. **The** presence of Venus is didactic: she represents no particular facet or synthesis of love or lovers' behaviour, but is simply a mouthpiece for advice and instruction. The whole frame of the poem, in fact, shows what a feeble hold allegory had on Lydgate's imagination. Even when he copies some traditional allegorical image, he more or less empties it of content.

The real originality of the *Temple of Glass* is not in its superficial imitation of allegory, but in the way it takes as its 'story' a literal human situation, in which the true love of the Knight and his Lady is temporarily frustrated by the fact that she is married. This at any rate is the purport of the lines quoted above, and of many other dark hints in the course of the poem, though Lydgate does not make the situation very explicit.[23] The reason for this is obvious: he was reluctant to be seen to be celebrating an extra-marital union, however pure and however distant the prospect of its consummation. At the same time, the insistence on the priority of the earthly contract, its inviolability until Venus decides otherwise (presumably by removing the husband), gives Lydgate the opportunity to sing the praises of loyal, hopeful, bodiless love in a manner which suits him perfectly, for it relieves the emotion of all the pressure of sexual reality.

Lydgate did not arrive at this compromise without a struggle, for the manuscripts show that the poem was extensively revised. Two MSS. of good authority (MS. Gg.iv.27 and Shirley's MS. Add.16165) contain an earlier version; two (Fairfax 16 and Bodley 638) are intermediate, perhaps as a result of scribal mixture; while the final version is best represented in MS. Tanner 346, the basis of the edited texts of the poem. The early version[24] varies in several details, and especially in the portrayal of the Lady. She is represented as complaining, not of the frustration of her true love by a rather vaguely identified and unmalicious husband, but violently and bitterly against 'Jelusye':

> The vile serpent, the snake tortyuous,
> That is so crabbit and frounynge of his ye,
> And evere grochynge and suspecyous,
> Ifret with eysel that makyth hym dispytous
> Of every thing the werste for to deme,
> That ther is no thyng that may his herte queme.[25]

Jealousy is not meant altogether as an abstraction, however, as the following lines suggest:

This is the maner of krokede fer in age
Whan they ben couplyd with ȝouthe: þey can no more
But hem werreyen, which wemen beyeth ful sore.
Thus evere in tourment and yre furyous
We ben oppressed (allas the harde stounde!)
Ryght as ȝoure selve were with Vulcanus
Ageyn ȝoure wil and ȝoure herte bounde.   (353–9)

The analogy of Vulcan, Venus, and Mars, particularly, suggests that this is a complaint against an old, crabbed, and jealous husband, which Lydgate later rejected, like the Lady's call to Venus to punish Jealousy,[26] because he saw how inappropriate in its violent tone and language it was to the Lady. Suppressing it involved some loss of connection with the early general complaints about forced marriages, while the revision, which supplies the Lady with a true love (that is, makes out that she already knows about it), makes the Knight's complaint of unrequited love and lack of pity rather ungrateful, and Venus's promise of help unnecessary. Lydgate makes some other changes too: the Lady is clad in green and white (299), instead of black and red, as in the earlier version, in order to match the hawthorn leaves which Venus bestows on her in token of constancy (503); these in their turn replaced the red and white roses of the original, because Lydgate remembered that the roses in Venus's traditional chaplet signified the fading transience of human love. He also changed the Lady's motto from *Humblement magre* to *De mieulx en mieulx* (310). This motto was used in England in the fifteenth century by the Pastons, and the change is the basis of Mac-Cracken's argument that the poem was written for the Pastons, specifically for the marriage of William Paston and Agnes Berry in 1420.[27] There is no reason to reject a general association with the Pastons, but the idea that it was specially commissioned for a marriage is wholly untenable and most improper, as will be seen from the story outlined above.

One other change needs mentioning. The two early manuscripts (G and S) have a truncated form of the epilogue which introduces a long 628-line *Compleynt*, written by a lover on leaving his mistress Margaret (the name given to the Lady in the GS version of the *Temple of Glass*) the last day of March. He begs for her favour, deplores her cruelty, describes his anguish, and her beauty, praises the daisy and complains upon Fortune. It is a slack, ill-disciplined, sprawling inventory of commonplaces, the sort of thing that Lydgate might have written in his sleep, though it is universally rejected from the canon. It looks to have been added by a literal-minded scribe to fulfil the promise of a 'litel tretise in prais of women', though it doesn't correspond at all closely with what we might have expected.

The revisions of the *Temple of Glass* are interesting, and valuable in the record they give that Lydgate could take an interest in the particular structural coherence of a work, but it would be a mistake to regard them as very significant. Any number of such changes could be introduced, in fact the whole frame-story could be dropped altogether, despite its ambition and originality, for all the difference it would make to the fundamental nature of the poem. 900 of the 1,400 lines are devoted to complaints and other set-speeches, and it is as an anthology of set-pieces that we should surely regard the poem, not as an allegorical narrative. If we look for a story, we are bound to come to a conclusion like Schick's—'The action is poor, and overweighted by long, tiresome speeches'.[28] There is no action, in fact no movement at all; nothing happens except that Venus gives the stamp of approval to what has already happened. It is like a tableau, the dummies disposed in an attractive composition around the central figure of Venus. There is only the faintest attempt to sketch in the human realities of the situation; the characters have no past, and they certainly have no future, the very reason for the choice of subject being that there is absolutely nothing to be done.

Within this frame, however, Lydgate develops the set-speeches with skill and energy. He is always at his best thus, writing within a strong convention, where the material is already to some extent selected for him. Our delight in well-ordered patterns, and rhetorical skills properly applied, is not marred by the excesses to which Lydgate is prone. Furthermore, the patterns have a depth, for they are rooted in a moralistic view of life which is Lydgate's most extraordinary achievement in this poem. It is not a poem about love; Lydgate's psychology of love is of the simplest, and he is quite content to reach for the familiar apparatus of arrows and wounds. It is really a poem about suffering. The temple of Venus is a vale of suffering, like life, and the Knight's complaints to himself, to Venus and to his Lady give expression to an ideal of 'service' so highly attenuated that it comes close to being a didactic code of behaviour in itself. The doctrines are made explicit in Venus's replies and advice to the lovers. Love is an opportunity for suffering, and for learning the virtues that come from patient endurance. The lovers will be purified by pain, as gold is refined by fire (1191); love will be the more, being bought with woe (1256), as heaven was granted to the martyrs:

For holi saintis þuruȝ her passioun
Have heven iwonne for her soverain mede.   (414–5)

It is quite easy to forget that one is reading a 'love'-poem, the content
of Venus's exhortions being not at all different from the instructions in
the search for Do-wel. It is only a shift of emphasis, of course, for
Venus's admonitions could all be paralleled in true courtly poems like
the *Romance of the Rose* and the *Court of Love*, a late pastiche for the
form, which draws specifically on the *Temple of Glass*; but it is clear
that what moves Lydgate to eloquence is not love but 'service', not the
prospect of reward but the satisfaction of duty well performed.

Instead, therefore, of an allegorical situation decked out in realistic
detail, which is the characteristic medieval mode, what we have is a real
situation treated abstractly. In other words, Lydgate rejects the realism
which allegory in its decline was beginning to promote, and returns to
the conceptualisation of experience from which allegory originally
sprang. These concepts, moreover, are organised in so systematic a way
as to expose for us a very anatomy of medieval thought. The basis of
the pattern is that a thing can only be defined, experience can only be
analysed, in terms of its opposite.[29] Perception of colour, sensation of
pain or pleasure, knowledge of truth or falsehood, all depend on contrastive structures in which the flux of experience is polarised. It is this
that provides the 'philosophy' of the poem, that love's joy can only be
defined through its contrary:

> For white is whitter if it be set bi blak,
> And swete is swettir eftir bitternes,
> And falshode ever is drive and put abak
> Where trouþe is rotid withoute doubilnes.
> Wiþoute prefe may be no sikirnes
> Of love or hate; and þerfor, of ȝow too
> Shal love be more, þat it was bouȝt with wo.
>
> (1250–6)

To call it a 'philosophy' is perhaps to misrepresent it; it is really a kind
of proverbial folk-wisdom, a wisdom of the status quo, from which
spring most platitudes about the nature of experience. The fundamental
nature of this system of contraries in its reference to the mental processes
is borne out by the way the language of evaluation is structured in pairs
of opposites—good and evil, truth and falsehood, pain and pleasure.
The nature of language enshrines and perpetuates the system of thought,

and as a system Lydgate found it completely satisfactory. For the literary
expression he draws first on Chaucer:

> By his contrarie is every thyng declared.
> For how myghte evere swetnesse han ben knowe
> To him that nevere tasted bitternesse?
> Ne no man may ben inly glad, I trowe,
> That nevere was in sorwe or som destresse.
> Eke whit by blak, by shame ek worthinesse,
> Ech set by other, more for other semeth,
> As men may se, and so the wyse it demeth.
>
> (*Troilus*, I,637–44)

but beyond that on the *Roman de la Rose*:

> Ainsinc va des contraires choses:
> Les unes sont des autres gloses;
> Et qui l'une en veaut defenir,
> De l'autre li deit souvenir,
> Ou ja, par nule entencion,
> N'i metra diffinicion;
> Car qui des deus n'a quenoissance
> Ja n'i quenoistra diference,
> Senz quei ne peut venir en place
> Diffinicion que l'en face   (21573–82)

and ultimately on Boethius:

> And of thise thinges, certes, everich of hem is declared and schewed
> by othere. For so as good and yvel ben two contraries, yif so be
> that good be stedfast, thanne scheweth the feblesse of yvel al
> opynly; and if thow knowe clerly the freelnesse of yvel, the
> stedfastnesse of good is knowen.[30]

For all medieval poets, the system of contraries was available as a category of thought, a way of explaining the apparent arbitrariness of life,
and nowhere is it more strikingly used than in the speech of Peace to
the daughters of God in *Piers Plowman*,[31] where it provides an analogous
construct for the Fall, the Incarnation, and the Atonement.

Lydgate, in his usual way, raises a category to a system, viewing the
universe as a well-regulated clock. The vagaries of Fortune are resolved
by Venus, in her reply to the Lady, into a simple alternation of tick and
tock:

> And þinkiþ þis: within a litel while
> It shal asswage and overpassen sone.
> For men bi laiser passen meny a myle,
> And oft also, aftir a dropping mone,
> The weddir clereþ, and whan þe storme is done
> The sonne shineþ in his spere briȝt,
> And joy awakiþ whan wo is put to fliȝt.
>
> Remembreþ eke, hou never ȝit no wiȝt
> Ne came to wirship withoute some debate,
> And folk also rejosshe more of liȝt
> That þei wiþ derknes were waped and amate.
> Non manis chaunce is alwai fortunate,
> Ne no wiȝt preiseþ of sugre þe swetnes
> But þei afore have tasted bitternes.   (391–404)

And since the mode of the poem is generally optimistic, the sequence ends

> Thus ever joy is ende and fine of paine.   (411)

Pandarus agrees,

> And also joie is next the fyn of sorwe,
> > (*Troilus*, I,952)

but at other times, the reverse can be equally true:

> The ende of blisse ay sorwe it occupieth
> > (*Troilus*, IV,836)
> Cf. For evere the latter ende of joye is wo.
> > (*NPT, CT*, VII,3205)

For other poets, the system of opposites is a mode of thought, a way of organising their thinking; for Lydgate it is a substitute for thought. The images of sun and storm, dark and light, sugar and gall, used in the passage above, are repeated in endless patterns of variation by Lydgate to describe the mutability of human fortune, the alternation of joy and sorrow, briefly, as in *Guy of Warwick*,

> The sonne is hatter after sharpe schours,
> The glade morwe folweth the dirke nyght,
> After wynter cometh May with fresshe flours,

And after mystys Phebus schyneth bright,
After trouble hertys be maad lyght. . . . (81–5)

or at length in the *Troy Book* and the *Fall of Princes*.[32] Sometimes he
amplifies the pattern by extending the literal or surface range of the
metaphor, as we saw him doing with the 'root-source-well' group:

To somme sugre and hony sche distilleth;
And of somme sche þe botel filleth
With bitter galle, myrre, and aloes. . . .
For sche to somme, of fraude and of fallas,
Mynystreth pyment, bawme, and ypocras:
And sodeynly, whan þe sote is past,
Sche of custom can ȝeven hem a tast,
For to conclude falsely in þe fyn,
Of bitter eysel and of egre wyn,
And corosyves þat fret and perce depe,
And narkotykes þat cause men to slepe.

(*Troy*, II,51–64)

There is not much enrichment of reference in such amplification: it is
mostly a matter of surface decoration.

Lydgate's mind, like a computer, operates thus on a binary system,
which provides not only his philosophy but also his psychology. The
contrastive patterns of imagery developed above to describe mutability
are further pressed into service for human duplicity and hypocrisy,
especially in the *Troy Book*, as we shall see later. The psychology of the
lover is represented by extended formal play with the oxymoron of
'hot' and 'cold', as in the *Black Knight*, or by a pseudo-allegorical
dialogue between Hope and Drede in the Knight's soliloquy in the
Temple of Glass:

For Hope biddiþ pursue and assay,
And Drede againward answeriþ and saiþ nai.
And now wiþ Hope I am iset on loft,
But Drede and Daunger, hard and noþing softe,
Have overþrowe my trust and put adoune.
Nou at my laarge, nou feterid in prisone,
Nou in turment, nou in soverein glorie,
Nou in paradise and nou in purgatorie. . . . (643–50)

And so for another thirty or more lines, all amplified from a line in the
Troilus:

Bitwixen hope and drede his herte lay.   (V,1207)

All passion is synchronised to this mechanism of contrast, so that every human situation becomes a dilemma, and every shade of feeling is resolved into a straight antithesis. The Lady's complaint, where Lydgate is writing out of a comparatively unconventional human situation, falls immediately into this sort of pattern:

> Devoide of joie, of wo I have plente:
> What I desire, þat mai I not possede:
> For þat I nolde is redi aye to me,
> And þat I love, forto sue I drede:
> To my desire contrarie is my mede.
> And þus I stond, departid even on tweyn,
> Of wille and dede ilaced in a chaine.   (349–55)

Again Chaucer prompts the form of expression,

> For bothe I hadde thyng which that I nolde,
> And ek I nadde that thyng that I wolde,[33]

and again Boethius supplies the original suggestion:

> 'Certes', quod I, 'it ne remembreth me nat that evere I was so fre of my thought that I ne was alwey in angwyse of somwhat.'
> 'And was nat that', quod sche, 'for that the lakkide somwhat that thow woldest nat han lakkid, or elles thou haddest that thow noldest nat han had?'
> 'Ryght so is it', quod I.   (III,pr.3, 34–42)

At every possible point, Lydgate reaches out towards an antithetic structure of thought and expression, imposing the stereotype even on a straightforward statement like 'I can say no more', in the Knight's complaint to Venus:

> A mouth I have, and ȝit for al my peyne,
> For want of woordis I may not nou atteyne
> To tellen half þat doþ myn herte greve.   (823–5)

Here the formal antithesis remains unrealised, but Lydgate was to return to it with more success in the *Troy Book*,

> He had a mouþe, but wordis had he non,   (III,4178)

and again in the *Fall*, in a highly affective context:

A mouth he hath, but woordis hath he noone.   (I,6931)

This brings us back to the influence of figures of expression on Lydgate's imagination, but the question is not a separate one, for a mode of thought which works in contraries is not really different from a mode of expression which depends on parallelism and antithesis, nor can one say which comes first. Clearly, the systematisation of both is basic to Lydgate's method, and basic too, at least as one method of operation, to all medieval writing, indeed to language itself. Chaucer alone has provided sufficient illustration of this. Any method is better than none, and there is no doubt that the sense of unity, order, pattern, and control that one gets from the set-speeches in the *Temple of Glass*, the sense of a well-made *artefact*, is due in large part to elaborately developed contrastive patterns. But not much is being controlled, and the experience is thin. Chaucer uses the same techniques to suggest the immense variety and richness of life, and above all to identify the special nature, the uniqueness, of what he writes about. Lydgate manages, with considerable simplification and enormous amplification, to suggest the sameness of everything.

Despite all this, the *Temple of Glass* is an important poem, for itself and for its influence, because it reveals what dominated Lydgate's mind when he was working on his own. *Reason and Sensuality* is not so important, being a translation, or partial translation, of a French poem, *Les Echecs Amoureux* ('Love's Game of Chess'), but it is one of the easiest and pleasantest to read of Lydgate's poems, a leisurely progress through the familiar landscape of the *Romance of the Rose*. At the beginning, after the statutory spring-description, Nature appears to the poet and declares the potentialities of the microcosm, Man, provided that the Sensitive Virtue, out of which springs Sensuality, is under the control of Understanding or Reason (896). She departs, and the poet, out walking, sees four deities, who are elaborately described, Minerva, goddess of wisdom and battles, Juno, of riches, and Venus, of love, all led by Mercury, god of eloquence and science (1846). Mercury appeals to him for a review of the judgment of Paris, and when the poet, after a perusal of the contestants, agrees with Paris, Venus promises him a fairer prize than Helen, and allays his fears about Nature's advice by assuring him she is Nature's chief officer. She tells him of her two sons, Deduyt (Delight) and Cupid, and advises him to seek the Garden of Deduyt (2700). On his way there he enters a forest of unfading green and meets Diana, who reproaches him and laments that Venus is now so popular. She warns him against the treacherous delights of the Garden, gives examples of unfortunates betrayed by love, and compares her own forest of Chastity (4778). The poet, unimpressed, pursues his way to the Garden, which is described explicitly as the Garden of the Rose (4818), with wall, springs, birds, Cupid's bow and arrows, music, and the well of Narcissus (5798). He finds Deduyt playing chess with a lady, and Cupid insists that the poet should play the next game. The chessboard is elaborately described, as are the lady's pieces, each piece representing some desirable quality in love (there is much ironical anti-feminist comment in this passage). He then describes his own pieces, and has just got to the fourth pawn when the translation breaks off (7042).

The French original continues, at some length. The game of chess is played, and the poet loses. Love takes him as one of his retinue and teaches him how to serve; greatly heartened, he challenges the lady to another game, but Pallas (Minerva) intervenes, accusing him of surrendering to Sensuality. She offers remedies of love, and recommends the contemplative life (as at the university of Paris) or the active practical life. This leads on to a consideration of human society, its ranks and their duties, the institution of marriage, the upbringing and education of children, the siting and design of the house, and much other useful information. The poem ends with advice on investment and making money. This latter part of *Les Echecs* is a prize example of the medieval love of information and instruction; the material is derived from widely known encyclopaedic compilations like the *Speculum doctrinale* and *Speculum naturale* of Vincent of Beauvais, Brunetto Latini's *Tresor*, and the *De Regimine Principum* of Aegidio Colonna. The encyclopaedia, in fact, has taken over completely, and this is why the comparison with the *Romance of the Rose*, which is clearly the inspiration of this kind of poem, should not be pressed too far. Both Guillaume de Lorris and Jean de Meun organise their material in accordance with dominant allegorical patterns, and Jean de Meun particularly, for all the weight of knowledge that his part of the poem carries, is basically a philosophical poet. The function of allegory in *Les Eechecs*, however, is merely schematic, and the material might just as well be organised alphabetically. Later, it was.

The French poem runs to about 30,000 lines. The English translation tackles only the first 4873 lines, expanding these to just over 7000 lines in short couplet. There are two MSS., Fairfax 16 and Add.29729. The first is a familiar 'Chaucerian' miscellany, and contains, in addition to the

text, some quite elaborate marginal annotation in Latin, chiefly designed
to elucidate the allegory. There is a suggestion that this MS. was revised
by Shirley.[34] The poem is headed 'Reson and sensuallyte compylid by
John Lydgat', but this is in a later hand, the hand in fact of John Stow,
who is also responsible for the second copy of the poem in MS. Add.
29729, which is his own anthology of Lydgate's works. This is the only
external evidence of authorship that there is,[35] and it is interesting that
this poem and the *Pilgrimage*, the other major poem ascribed to Lydgate
without contemporary evidence, are the only poems in the canon which
are in octosyllabic couplet. But the coincidence may simply be that this
is the form of the French original in both cases, and on other grounds
there are strong reasons for accepting Stow's word. The style is
Lydgate's, especially the methodical padding-out of the original in this
sort of way[36]:

> Ceste dame ot nature nom   (*Les Echecs*, 231)
> Cf. This emperesse, I you ensure,
> I-called was Dame Nature   (247–8)

> Par envie ou par negligence   (*Les Echecs*, 31)
> Cf. Oonly of malyce and envye
> Or collateral necligence   (30–1)

The habits of mind are also Lydgate's, in so far as they are revealed by
his amplifications of the original, for what clearly attracted him in the
poem was the opportunity it gave to display his knowledge of classical
mythology and fable, within a moralistic framework. In this respect,
the poem is like a thesaurus, or, to use Whethamstede's terms, a
'granary' or 'storehouse' of good things. He elaborates the portraits of
the classical deities, giving a specifically Christian allegorical significance, for instance, to the armour of Pallas (1188), and turns to his purpose every scrap of classical lore that he possesses, like the fable of the
swan's dying song, in the same description (1247). Diana's conversation
with the poet is full of exemplary stories and allusions,

> Ful many story newe and olde
> To my purpose I shal applye,   (4234–5)

and Lydgate cannot resist the open invitation to expand the stories of
Venus and Adonis (3685), Venus and Mars (3760), Pyramus and Thisbe
(3954, nine lines expanded to forty-eight), Icarus and Phaeton (4162,
twenty lines expanded to sixty-six), and others. The story of Jason and

the Golden Fleece (3524), introduced as pure digression (the poet's perils if he enters the garden will be worse than Jason's), is given the same treatment. Lydgate also systematically unfolds the significance of the allegory, like the Fairfax annotator, though not to the same degree. This presumably is a sign of allegory's waning hold on the medieval imagination. The fact that Lydgate finds it necessary to *explain* why the pictures of Age, Poverty, Envy, and the others are on the outside of the wall of the Garden (4960) suggests that allegory was not now being read in the same way as in the days of Guillaume de Lorris.

The lady's chess-pieces in *Les Echecs* are given an allegorical significance, carefully contrived from bestiary and lapidary symbolism. Here, too, Lydgate introduces a mass of original material, expanding ninety-two lines of the original to 776 of his own. Each piece signifies a quality in women, and Lydgate embarks on ironically extravagant praise of women for possessing these qualities. The first pawn bears a moon, symbolic of change—but this is no property of women,

> They be so stable and so sure
> In ther trouthe to persever,
> For ther hertys chaunge never.   (6172–4)

and so on for thirty-four lines, all original. The Fairfax annotator comments, for safety's sake, 'per Antifrasim', and later, 'per contrarium', reminding us, as if it were necessary, that we are witnessing a conventional exercise.[37] Women, Lydgate goes on, are also very humble and quiet, and never argue:

> Ther ys no man that wyl sey nay
> That hath hem preved at assay.   (6271–2)

They are governed by 'mesure', and are good at keeping secrets ('Cuius contrarium est verum'). They are generous—though some say they are greedy (this view is expounded at length) and deserve to have their tongues clipped. They never bear malice, and there is none

> But she ys goode or ellys wolde
> At the leste so be holde.   (6509–10)

They never dress showily, and they hate high horned head-dresses.[38] They never vary, and are always meek, true, and obedient:

> Recorde I take of her husbondys
> That knowe best experience
> Of her mekenesse and pacience.   (6584–6)

And so on. Lydgate clearly finds the subject congenial, but his view of it, and his technique of irony, is limited by the same mechanical systematisation that we have seen in his attitude to all human experience. He simply says the opposite of what he means, without inflexion. But it makes a change from Lydgate's usual deathly seriousness, and it is a mood we shall see him indulging in riper vein later.

Lydgate's additions to *Les Echecs* show him very much at home and at his ease. It is one of only two major works that he undertook without a commission, and the only one that he left unfinished—an encouraging sign, if it suggests that he felt free to do what he wanted, though it may be due to nothing more than that he came to the end of what he had of the French. The modest success of the poem is that it gives Lydgate a rare opportunity to be himself in a Chaucerian 'landscape'. The machinery is all traditional to the love-vision poem, decorative, digressive, allusive, in a manner that he had at his fingertips from Chaucer, and which he manages here with relaxed ease. He catches, too, better than anywhere else, Chaucer's conversational tone of voice, especially in the narrator's dialogue with Venus (e.g. 6603, 4733). Even the use of tags and padding formulae seems part of this tone of voice (e.g. 1340–52, 1433–43). Much of this success may be attributed to the metrical form, the short couplet, which discourages the kind of heavy rhetorical figuring to which Lydgate is given, and where the characteristic sentence-patterns are inevitably simpler. The verse is light and easy—often, of course, too easy, for it would not do to linger over these lines.

Something of the geniality of Chaucer seems to have touched him too. The moralist is always there, as well as the anthologist, but the moralising is polite, and does not grind out momentous platitudes in quite the usual way, even manages to suggest some of the potential wealth and range of human experience along the wrong road:

> But I desire the knowleching
> Of the hevene and his mevying,
> And also of the salte see . . .   (4611–13)

It is not much, and it could hardly be said that Lydgate conveys the imaginative power of the medieval view of Nature, for instance,[39] but there is some richness of substance, in allusion as well as theme, and the best of it is bright, clear, and colourful in the manner of good medieval painting.

The date of *Reason and Sensuality* is not known, but it has a relaxed

9

and carefree assurance which is incompatible with the heavy weight of responsibility Lydgate was about to take up, as 'official' poet. One would think of it as a last excursion into the world of polite love-allegory before the *Troy Book*.

Notes to Chapter Four

1 The latest editor is J. Norton-Smith, in his selection of Lydgate's poems for the Clarendon *Medieval and Tudor Series*. Quotation of the *Black Knight* and of the *Temple of Glass*, and of other poems which Norton-Smith prints complete, is from his edition. The usual title is kept, however, since there must be a rooted objection to changes in familiar titles, except where they are positively misleading.

2 See above, p. 76.

3 'Spring in Chaucer and before him', *MLN*, LII(1937),9–16 (p. 9).

4 E. R. Curtius, *European Literature and the Latin Middle Ages* (1948; English trans. by W. R. Trask, 1953), p. 195.

5 See Rosemond Tuve, *Seasons and Months* (Paris 1933).

6 Ruskin, 'Mediaeval Landscape', in *Modern Painters*, vol. III (*Works*, ed. Cook and Wedderburn, V,248–316), p. 257.

7 Joan Evans, *Pattern: a Study in Ornament in W. Europe* (2 vols., 1931), I,58.

8 See the articles by A. Piaget in *Romania*, XXX–XXXI, XXXIII–IV; also Italo Siciliano, *François Villon et les Thèmes Poétiques du Moyen Age* (Paris 1934), chap. IV: 'L'Amant martyr et la Dame sans Merci'.

9 *Romaunt*, 4703; *Troilus*, I,420.

10 E.g. Matthew of Vendome's description of Helen in the *Ars Versificatoria*, or Geoffrey of Vinsauf's similar description in the *Poetria Nova*, 563–621 (both in Faral, *op. cit.*); see also E. de Bruyne, *Etudes d'esthétique médiévale* (3 vols., Bruges 1946), II,173–202; D. S. Brewer, 'The Ideal of Feminine Beauty in Medieval Literature', *MLR*, LX(1955),257–69.

11 *Troy Book*, II,3674–9.

12 It is interesting that the alliterative *Destruction of Troy*, only a few years earlier than Lydgate, translates Guido's description in full (3019–84), while the alliterative *Alexander A* fragment actually introduces a catalogue-description of Olympias (178–99) which is not in the Latin source at all. There is some evidence here that alliterative poets, though not unsophisticated, were somewhat out of date.

13 Matthew of Vendome, in Faral, p. 132.

14 *Troy*, II,4801–8, 5016–34. See Sieper's note to *Reason and Sensuality*, 282.

15 Hammond, *Chaucer to Surrey*, pp. 452, 457.

16 See above, p. 39.

17 *Op. cit.*, p. 159.

18 See below, p. 162.

19 Shirley's heading in MS.Trinity R.3.20.

20 See J. Norton-Smith, 'Lydgate's Metaphors', *English Studies*, XLII(1961), 90–3; also A. Renoir, 'The Binding Knot: three uses of one image in Lydgate's poetry', *Neophilologus*, XLI(1957),202–4.

21 See above, p. 39.

22 See J. Norton-Smith, in his selected edition of Lydgate, p. 177. His account of the poem is extremely valuable.

23 Renoir takes it that the Lady's complaint is against the conventions of courtly love, which force her to conceal her real affection under a guise of coldness: 'Attitudes towards Women in Lydgate's *Siege of Thebes*', *English Studies*, XLII(1961),1–14, and *The Poetry of John Lydgate*, p. 93. The literal reading is Lewis's (*Allegory of Love*, p. 241).

24 Schick considered it to be the later (ed. *Temple of Glas*, p. xlix), but Norton-Smith's account is definitive: 'Lydgate's Changes in the *Temple of Glas*', *Medium Aevum*, XXVII(1958),166–72.

25 343–8, in the notes to Norton-Smith's edition, p. 184.

26 497–517, in Norton-Smith, p. 186.

27 *PMLA*, XXIII(1908),128–40. See above, p. 73.

28 Schick, *op. cit.*, p. l; or to share the exasperation of a fifteenth-century reader of MS.Bodley 638, who got lost in the tangle of complaints and replies and wrote at the end of one speech (847) 'Hoc usque nescio quis' and at the beginning of another (970) 'Who in all godly pity maye be' (Schick, p. xx).

29 Norton-Smith, *Lydgate: Poems*, p. 177.

30 Book IV, prose 2, lines 10–17 (in Chaucer's translation).

31 C-text, XXI,209–39.

32 E.g. *Troy*, II,451,2005,3311,4089; V,30; *Fall*, I,3109,4536,6079; III,355; V,57,1818; VI,20. And see Sieper's note to *Reason and Sensuality*, 3363.

33 *Parlement of Foules*, 90–91; and cf. *Pity*, 99–104.

34 *Reson and Sensuallyte*, ed. E. Sieper (EETS,ES, 84,1901), p. xii.

35 As with the *Flower of Courtesy*: see above, p. 97.

36 For extended illustration, see 613–30, 683–96, 1735–54, etc.

37 Cf. Lydgate's own *Ballade per Antiphrasim* (*Minor Poems*, II,432), and see below, p. 216.

38 Lydgate elsewhere devotes a poem, *Horns Away*, to satirising this extravagance of dress.

39 In Alain de Lille's *De Planctu Naturae* or in the *Roman de la Rose*.

CHAPTER FIVE

Troy and Thebes

The story of Troy was, in medieval eyes, the great story of classical antiquity. Thebes was insignificant by comparison, the adventures of the Argonauts and Ulysses mere appendages, and though Alexander himself was a more dominating figure than any single personage of the Troy-story, his life, with its crude monotony of conquest and heaping-up of sensation and fantasy, lacked the interwoven drama and tragic conflict of the siege and fall of Troy. In one instance, indeed, the story of Troy is assigned a historical dignity and authority commensurate with that of the Bible: Sir Thomas Gray, at the beginning of his Anglo-Norman prose chronicle called the *Scalacronica*, has an image of the ladder of history, reaching up from the past to the present, beneath which lie, as the foundations of history, the Bible and the story of Troy.[1]

Western Europe had a special reason for reverencing Troy, for most of its nations traced their ancestry to Trojans scattered after the fall of their city:

> Ticius to Tuskan and teldes bigynnes,
> Langaberde in Lumbardie lyftes up homes,
> And fer over þe French flod Felix Brutus
> On mony bonkkes ful brode Bretayn he settes
> With wynne.
>
> *(Gawain and the Green Knight, 11–15)*

Virgil had initiated this cult, bringing Aeneas from Troy to found Rome, his intention being to give authority to the imperial dynasty by establishing for it a lineage of antiquity at least equal with that of the Greeks. What Virgil claimed for Rome, his admirers claimed for Rome's descendants, and it was a mark of Theodoric's emancipation from the barbaric genealogies of heathen deities that Cassiodorus should provide him with a Trojan family-tree.[2] The cult persisted, along with the pro-Trojan sympathies which it naturally entailed, and which are a characteristic feature of all medieval treatments of the Troy-story—and which survive in our language in expressions like 'to fight (or work) like a Trojan'. The most famous and most influential presentation of the myth of Trojan descent was Geoffrey of Monmouth's description, in his *Historia Regum Britanniae* (1135), of how Brutus came from Troy to Britain and founded Troynovant, or New Troy, better known in later years as London, and established the dynasty of British kings.[3] This story was accepted as history throughout the Middle Ages, and provided the basis for the passage in *Gawain* quoted earlier. Much later, Ronsard based his epic of the *Franciade* on the legendary exploits of Francus, who left Troy to found France,[4] while Jean le Maire des Belges, in his *Illustrations de Gaule et singularités de Troie*, 'distributed the names of the various Trojan heroes, like spoils of war', among the nations of Western Europe.[5]

With all this fervour of national and dynastic interest, it must be admitted that the Troy-story found its way down to the Middle Ages by a peculiar route. Homer himself was little known, and what little of him was known was not much liked: for one thing, he was a Greek, and therefore prejudiced against the Trojans; for another, he was unreliable, as witness his habit of mixing gods and goddesses with the affairs of men. It is rich that the medieval mind should have found anything far-fetched, but the genre was history, not romance. In any case, Greek being a rare accomplishment in the Middle Ages, Homer was available only in the crude Latin epitome of Silius Italicus, the *Ilias latina* of the first century A.D.

The real 'authorities' for the story of Troy were Dictys Cretensis and Dares Phrygius, who had the advantage over Homer of being eye-witnesses. Dictys was a Cretan who bore arms at the siege of Troy and, like a good soldier, kept a journal in Phoenician characters. The journal was buried with him in a tin trunk and lay there until exposed by an earthquake in the thirteenth year of the Emperor Nero. The manuscript was carried to Rome and translated on the orders of Nero as the *Ephemeris Belli Troiani*. Actually written in Latin in the fourth century A.D. (though based on a slightly earlier Greek original, fragments of which have been recovered), this forgery is fluently written, coherent and matter-of-fact, but still labours under the disadvantage of being by a Greek. Fortunately, inside the walls of the beleaguered city was another eye-witness, Dares the Phrygian. Homer does in fact mention a Trojan priest called Dares, and to him antiquity ascribed a lost earlier

Iliad. The *De Excidio Troiae Historia* purports to be a Latin translation of this by Cornelius Nepos. It is in fact a crude summary of the Troy-story—typical of the way in which many of the great stories of classical antiquity came down to the Middle Ages—written in the sixth century in wretched Latin prose, but mercifully brief. Its influence was enormous.

These two works extended the range of the story—Dictys by retailing the adventures of the Greek heroes on their return home, right up to the death of Odysseus, and Dares by going back to the Argonauts. They both pack out the narrative with a mass of factual detail, especially Dares, whose story reads at times like a casualty report. For those who wanted history, this was clearly superior to Homer, who dealt with only a few weeks of the war. Furthermore, they are both scrupulously matter-of-fact, and both systematically demythologise and humanise the story. For instance, the first destruction of Lamedon's Troy (which preceded Priam's) was due in classical myth to his failure to pay Poseidon (the earth-shaker) his wages for building it—and excavation suggests the basis of this myth in that this layer of Troy was in fact destroyed by an earthquake.[6] Dares, however, has Lamedon's Troy destroyed by Jason's followers as an act of deliberate revenge for his rudeness in not allowing the Argonauts to provision on his territory on their way to Colchos. This in turn prompts the abduction of Helen, and so the circle of rational 'explanation' is complete. Dares and Dictys also insist on the humanity of their characters, placing Hector's parting with Andromache, for instance, so that it precedes, not the battle with Ajax, but his death, where it is much more humanly touching.

Dares and Dictys were the authorities, but the real source of the medieval Troy-story was the work of a talented and imaginative French poet, Benoit de Ste. Maure, who produced in 1165 a vast conflation in over 30,000 lines of the Latin prose annals of Dictys and Dares, the *Roman de Troie*. Into the bare summaries of his originals, Benoit intercalated much new material of his own invention, including the story of the ill-fated love of Troilus and Briseyde (it was Boccaccio who changed the name to Criseida), and threw over the whole the trappings of medieval romance, thus setting a fashion in the treatment of classical legend in general which was to influence the whole Middle Ages. A close translation of Benoit into Latin prose was made by the Italian Guido della Colonna in 1287, the *Historia Destructionis Troiae*. Guido, in what looks to us like a startling piece of literary robbery, acknowledges no source, and was widely credited with the inventivenes and originality which properly belong to Benoit. Guido shows some added interest in science and pagan worship, but little more. However, his translation served its purpose, for it brought the medieval version of the Troy-story to a much wider audience. There was a copy of Guido in the Bury library, and Guido was Lydgate's main source for the *Troy Book*.

Lydgate began the *Troy Book* in 1412 at the command of Henry, prince of Wales, who was to succeed to the throne in the following year, and he finished it in 1420.[7] The commission was the fruit of an association which may, as we have seen,[8] have dated back several years. For Henry, the Troy-story was an obvious choice, as an authentic historical narrative and as an exemplar of ancient chivalry: Lydgate says that he writes at the bidding of his lord,

> Whiche hath desire, sothly for to seyn,
> Of verray kny3thod to remembre ageyn
> The worthynes, 3if I schal nat lye,
> And the prowesse of olde chivalrie. (Prologue, 75–8)

Lydgate, for his part, welcomed the opportunity to apply to a larger theme the elaborate amplificatory style that he had developed in his Chaucerian imitations. But there was something more. Henry was concerned about the reputation of English, and authorised the translation

> By-cause he wolde that to hy3e and lowe
> The noble story openly wer knowe
> In oure tonge, aboute in every age,
> And y-writen as wel in oure langage
> As in latyn and frensche it is. (Prologue, 111–15)

The work is thus a status-symbol, an attempt to define and consolidate the new status of English by tackling the greatest epic story of antiquity. It reflects a concern for English similar to that of the Elizabethans in their translations of the classics.[9] It builds on Chaucer, but also presses consciously beyond Chaucer, annexing larger territories to literary English. Chaucer uses a vernacular source for his *Troilus* (though he claims a Latin one) and tells only an episode from the Troy-story; Lydgate takes a Latin source, a true 'auctoritee', and tells the whole story, expanding enormously on everything—the moralising, the invocations and apostrophes, the learned digressions—that contributes to the story's *sentence*. Looking back, one can even see a kind of pattern in the way Lydgate uses academic rhetoric to fortify (in Dryden's term) and improve upon successive Chaucerian models: the *Black Knight* upon the *Book of the Duchess*, the *Temple of Glass* upon the *House of Fame*, *Reason and Sensuality*, with its pictorial allegory, garden, and analysis of different kinds of love, upon the *Parlement of Foules*, and now the *Troy Book* upon the *Troilus*. The 'improvement' is generally of the kind that assumes that two lines are an improvement on one, and three lines better still, but the pattern is interesting, especially in view of Lydgate's frequent and fulsome tributes to Chaucer.

The serious and self-conscious nature of Lydgate's attention to his task is reflected in the elaborate 384-line Prologue (and in an equally elaborate Epilogue), where he not only translates Guido's Prologue but adds as much again of his own, including an apostrophe to Mars and also, most interesting, a precise astronomical dating for his beginning the poem (125–46). The motions of sun, moon, morning and evening star are fixed in their relative positions to signal the momentousness of the occasion, 4 p.m. on Monday, October 31st, 1412, just as in a later poem, *The Title and Pedigree of Henry VI*, Lydgate gives the exact position of the sun and *all* the planets (287–323) to mark the date when the earl of Warwick commissioned the work. The sense of occasion is precisely that which prompted the designers of some Italian churches and palaces to incorporate in their vaults and ceilings complete sky-maps, in which the aspect of the sky for a particular date— the date of the consecration, or of a patron's birth—was completely reconstructed.[10]

In addition to this reverent self-consequence, there is the prestige of a Latin source, to which Chaucer's invention of Lollius is apt testimony. English poets of the time approached Guido with something of the awe that later ages reserved for Homer, and it is interesting that at the time when Lydgate began his *Troy Book*, two other English translations of Guido had just been completed—the alliterative *Destruction of Troy* (14,044 lines) and the Laud *Troy Book* (18,664 lines). The former is skilful and fluent, but tame, and the poet is so overawed by the *matiere* that he attempts little in the way of innovation—the few additions are mostly short seasons-descriptions or storms at sea.[11] The Laud *Troy Book* has connections with popular romance but it is a good deal nearer to Lydgate than to romance, being fairly elaborate in its treatment, with apostrophes, *sententiae*, moral comment, *exempla*, and extended descriptive topics.[12] The language is colourless, but is goaded into

vigour occasionally when the author applies the stimulus of the alliterative style. Both these poems are unremarkable in themselves, and their
dissemination cannot have been very wide, since they both exist in
unique manuscripts, but they are evidence, with Lydgate, of some sort
of cult of the Troy-story in the early fifteenth century, for which the
growing number of Troy tapestries is added corroboration.[13] Perhaps
the original stimulus was the popularity of the Brutus story of Trojan
descent in alliterative tradition,[14] as a by-product of interest in the
Arthurian legend.

Lydgate shares the humility of these two unknown poets before his
Latin exemplar,

> Whom I schal folwe as nyȝe as ever I may, (Prologue, 375)

but his whole treatment is loftier and more grandiose, and the final
product has a massiveness (30,117 lines) which makes even their bulk
look insignificant. He reiterates frequently his scrupulous fidelity to
Guido, his reluctance to omit or alter anything, even when Chaucer
has shown the way to a new interpretation:

> And but I write, I mote þe trouþe leve
> Of Troye boke, and my mater breve
> And over-passe and nat go by and by
> As Guydo doþ in ordre ceryously.   (II,4687-90)

Even when he cannot understand the relevance of an incident, such as
that of king Menon, he sets it down faithfully (V,2871), and at the end
of the poem he stops simply because there is no more,

> I have no more of latyn to translate,   (V,3360)

and to add anything would be mere vain presumption. His idea of
translation is that which is accepted as standard in the Middle Ages, and
which is concisely expressed for us in the *Danse Macabre*:

> Out of þe frensshe I drewe it of entente
> Not worde by worde but folwynge þe substaunce.
> (665-6)

Chaucer makes the same sort of comment, and avows the same fidelity
to his 'auctour'; such statements are habitual in medieval poetry. The
difference with Lydgate is that in his case the statements are true, for he
makes no attempt to re-order or re-interpret the narrative, no new
'sens' of the old 'matiere', nothing remotely approaching Chaucer's

reappraisal of the Troilus story. He moralises constantly, but even his moralising is external and factitious, rather than interpretative, so that, when the material is not immediately susceptible of a Christian moral, the result is self-contradiction. The falseness of men to women, and of Jason to Medea in particular, is roundly condemned (I,2868), but this sorts oddly with earlier attacks on Medea and the falseness of women (I,1845, 2072). Lydgate, when it fits the 'matiere', vigorously upbraids the common people for their fickleness and mutability,

> Þe trust of peple is feint and untrewe,
> Ay undiscrete and ful of doubilnes,   (IV,302–3)

but at another point he clearly stands behind Priam when he says

> For whan a þing toucheþ a communte. . . .
> Of alle þe comoun it ouȝte be confermed.   (II,3142–4)

Chaucer treats the *Troilus* seriously as a story, in which the imitation of life is itself substantive, in which the fiction *is* the meaning. In so doing, he contradicted, though implicitly and incompletely, the traditional medieval assumption that fictions are exemplary, and exist to demonstrate truths outside themselves. Christian doctrine provided a complete and coherent scheme of truth, and there was no story which could not be adapted so as to illustrate some part of this scheme. The *Gesta Romanorum* are almost an object-lesson in the impossibility of any alien scheme of values. On a higher level, *Piers Plowman* demonstrates systematically the subordination of story to truth. It is full of narratives, but they are always contained within a larger frame, so that they are never self-sufficient or explicable in terms of human values but only in terms of a spiritual diagram which Langland is plotting. Its interest is not in human behaviour as such, but in aspects of human experience and behaviour as exempla of a system of moral and spiritual truth. Other medieval writers, however, explore what Silverstein calls 'the border where the exemplary and the imitative meet'.[15] Gower casts his *Confessio Amantis* in the form of love-stories illustrative of different aspects of the seven deadly sins, but as he writes he is continually drawn to interpret the stories in terms of their human significance.[16] Malory too moves, tentatively at first, but with growing confidence, towards a version of the Arthurian story which is internally consistent. But it is Chaucer above all who haunts this border-ground, sometimes making elaborate jest of the whole idea of externally imposed 'moralitee', as in the *Nun's Priest's Tale*, sometimes missing his footing and achieving neither allegorical nor mimetic consistency, as in the *Clerk's Tale*. In the *Troilus*, though, Chaucer releases character into dramatic action with such confidence that he can even shift perspective at the end to the Christian world-view without destroying the poem's own powerful integrity.

Chaucer is interested in Boccaccio as a story, but Lydgate is interested in Guido as a text. It is immovable, it has quasi-Biblical authority, but it exists not for its own sake, but for the truth that can be drawn from it. It may be history, but it has no historical reality, for the ultimate purpose is to destroy history in the interests of truth, so that Hector, Achilles, and the rest may take their place in the universal diagram. Truth may be of two kinds, moral and factual, and Lydgate systematically exploits the narrative for both. The *Troy Book* is a homily first, an encyclopaedia second, and an epic nowhere. In it, Lydgate draws upon every resource of medieval rhetoric to amplify his treatment of the story, to broaden its scope and to drive home its moral lessons. Amplification, the elaboration of any given subject-matter through conventional techniques of expression, which we have seen to be Lydgate's characteristic mode of thought and style, is here applied on a colossal scale. Endless digression, description, astronomical periphrasis, apostrophe, exclamation, prophesy, lament, philosophical reflection, moral exhortation—these are what Lydgate adds to the translation, but they are in a sense the body of the work, for it is through them that Lydgate makes sense in his own terms of a historical narrative which for the Middle Ages could make sense in no others. The *Troy Book* cannot be recommended for readers who wish to make an acquaintance with the story of Troy, but it is of endless interest for those who wish to understand the medieval mind and its characteristic operations.

Lydgate's amplifications could be studied in themselves and analysed. They do, on analysis, as in the list above, bear a strikingly close relation to the eight devices of amplification recommended by Geoffrey of Vinsauf, in his *Poetria Nova*,[17] or for that matter to those of a more recent writer, Brunetto Latini, Dante's teacher, who lists in his encyclopaedic *Livres dou Tresor*[18] eight ornaments of discourse or *colores rhetorici—interpretatio*, periphrasis, comparison, exclamation, fable (exemplum), transition, description, and repetition. But such analysis would tell us only what we know already—that Lydgate was a skilful and practised rhetorician. In a work so vast one must examine the particular, the actual sequence of events, in order to illustrate the processes by which Lydgate systematically subdues the narrative to non-narrative purposes.

Guido does much of his work for him. Book I begins with the
account of how Peleus, king of Thessaly, plans to get his nephew Jason
killed by sending him to Colchos to win the Golden Fleece. No more
than eight lines have passed before Lydgate is following Guido into a
long digression from Ovid on the origins of the Myrmidons, Thessaly's
inhabitants (9–86). The motive of this is purely encyclopaedic: it is like
a commentary or a footnote to a text, which immediately swamps the
text, and its relationship to the text is merely formal, as Lydgate indicates by his self-conscious *transitio* back to his matter (87–91). The
introduction of Aeson, Jason's father, prompts a discussion of Ovid's
story that he was later cured of his madness by Medea, but no attempt
is made, now or later, to relate the discussion to the story—to suggest
that Jason ought to have been grateful to Medea, for instance, as Gower
does.[19] The dislocation of human and historical reality is complete, and
the attitude to the story rather like that of Biblical glossators to variant
readings—it was difficult to choose the right one, but it didn't matter,
because all had the same relation to universal truth. All this is in Guido,
but the next episode, the account of Peleus's plot, is much expanded by
Lydgate from the merest hint in Guido:

> Quare disquisiuit in corde suo uiarum ymaginata proposita
> quibus posset Iasonem perdere absque sui sugillatione pudoris.[20]

Lydgate first locks Peleus's behaviour into his code of contrastive
formulae for 'duplicity',

> His felle malys he gan to close and hide,
> Lyche a snake that is wont to glyde
> With his venym under fresche floures. . . .
> In porte a lambe, in herte a lyoun fel,
> Dowble as a tygre sli3ly to compasse,
> Galle in his breste and sugre in his face,   (I,209–18)

and then traces it to its universal ground in *cupiditas*:

> And grownde of al, so as I can divise,
> Was the Ethik of false covetise,
> Whiche fret so sore, falsly for to wynne,
> As crop and rote of every sorowe and synne,
> And cause hath ben, sythen goo ful 3ore,
> That many a rewme hath a-bou3t ful sore
> The dredful venym of covetyse, allas!   (I,237–43)

Lydgate's method of moralising all character and action back to fundamental abstractions is analogous to sermon-technique in reverse, for
where sermons move from abstract truth (the text) to concrete illustration (exemplum), Lydgate moves from narrative concretion to
abstract truth.

Such moralising is often highly inappropriate, indeed, as I have said,
totally destructive of any values for which the story itself might stand.
Lydgate follows Guido, for instance, in condemning the pursuit of the
Golden Fleece,

> Whos pursute roos oute of covetise,
> Grounde and rote of wo and al meschaunce,
> By veyn reporte hem silfe to avaunce,   (I,356–8)

which seems to place all the participants in the action, not merely the
traitor Peleus, beyond the pale of moral relevance. This impression is
strengthened by frequent incursions into the story to throw scorn on its
superstitious ignorance, as when Lydgate (not Guido) speaks thus of the
metamorphosis of Diomedes' followers into birds:

> But of our feithe we ouȝte to defy
> Swiche apparencis schewed to þe eye,
> Whiche of þe fende is but illusioun.   (I,909–11)

Later, both Guido and Lydgate belabour Ovid for saying that Medea,
or anyone but God, could produce eclipses (1711). It is as if Chaucer
had put his

> Lo here, of payens corsed olde rites

at the beginning of the *Troilus* instead of the end, and reminded us of it
continually. Exposed to such contempt, the narrative in Guido and
Lydgate withers in significance.

Guido goes on with the account of the fitting out of the Argon, and
of those who join Jason on the expedition, including Hercules. Here he
inserts an account of the pillars at Gades, which Lydgate expands with
reference to all twelve labours of Hercules (568), derived ostensibly
from Ovid but more directly from Chaucer. At such points the poem
is close to being a dictionary of mythology, though there is nothing
here to compare with the enormous digression on idolatry in book II,
which Lydgate expands with a mass of detail (II,5480–940), blandly
admitting that it is there simply for information:

> And, as I trowe, þe verray cause why,
> Þat myn auctor rehersith by and by
> Grounde and gynnynge of ydolatrie—
> Þis þe cause, for ouȝt I can espie,
> For þat he sawe þe mater was nat knowe. . . .
>
>   (II,5925–9)

The account of Hercules is followed by the journey to Colchos, and a discourse on navigation and the stars, which Lydgate retails at length, reserving his full powers of amplification, though, for Guido's prophetic digression on Lamedon's inhospitality to the Greeks and its far-reaching consequences for Troy and, through the Trojan diaspora, for the whole Western world. Lydgate seizes, as usual, on the central abstract antithesis of the issue—that slight quarrels lead to great wars, or simpler still, that little things lead to big things—and grinds away at it vigorously:

> For of griffyng of a lytel braunche
> Ful sturdy trees growen up ful ofte;
> Who clymbeth hyȝe may not falle softe;
> And of sparkys þat ben of syȝte smale
> Is fire engendered þat devoureth al. . . .   (I,782–6)

This building-up through accumulated metaphorical analogy is characteristic of Lydgate, as we have seen.[21]

It would be impossible to go through the whole poem in this sort of detail, but perhaps enough has been said to give some idea of the general texture of the narrative. Book I continues with the landing of the Argonauts near Troy, and their expulsion by Lamedon. They arrive at Colchos and Jason wins the Fleece with Medea's help. On their return to Thessaly, they equip a punitive expedition and the book ends with the siege and first destruction of Troy. Lydgate keeps fairly close to Guido, rarely adding, but always expanding, like a candy-floss machine. Set speeches are an obvious target for amplification, and characters, once they have started to speak—and this is no easy matter[22]—often spend some ten or twenty lines saying how briefly they will say what they have to say. Medea's first speech to Jason is a good example (I,2297). This is all quite basic to Lydgate's amplificatory style: he would have been hardly conscious of it. Guido's moralising, too, he expands more or less by automatic reflex—on Fortune, on men's falsehood, on Oetes' duplicity, on the mutability of the common people,

on the punishment of Medea.[23] But with all this, there is no deeper
penetration to the human reality and drama of the story than the
platitudes Guido has provided him with. The trouble with Lydgate is
his incredible facility: he never struggles. The stimulus is suggested—
'duplicity' or 'covetousness'—and the machine slides easily into gear,
churning out the stock responses. This is the treatment given, too, to the
love of Jason and Medea, which is the central human drama of book I.
The coming of love to Medea is plotted as an access of alternating lily
and rose colouring, of hot and cold (1949), and the inner conflict which
she undergoes is mechanised in the familiar contrastive formulae of
desire and shame (2160), hope and fear (2744). It is the same when he
comes to deal, later, with the love of Achilles and Polyxena (IV,597–
625), or even of Troilus and Criseyde, where the parting of the lovers is
described in a formal antiphon:

> For she of cher pale was and grene
> And he of colour liche to ashes dede;
> And fro hir face was goon al þe rede,
> And in his chekis devoided was þe blod,
> So wofully atwene hem two it stood.
> For she ne myȝt nat a worde speke
> And he was redy with deth to be wreke
> Upon hym silfe, his nakid swerd beside;
> And she ful ofte gan to grounde glide
> Out of his armys, as she fel a-swowne,
> And he hym silf gan in teris drowne;
> She was as stille and dowmb as any ston,
> He had a mouþe, but wordis had he non.
> Þe weri spirit flikered in hir breste,
> And of deth stood under arreste.   (III,4166–80)

Lydgate pays elaborate tribute to Chaucer's version of the story, and
uses it skilfully in the passage above, but he is totally incapable of being
touched by its view of the complexity and ambiguity of human experience, and immediately after his eulogy (III,4264) he slips back into
Guido's comfortable abstractions, reproaching Criseyde for her fickleness and Troilus for believing in it. The mechanical nature of Lydgate's
responses is nowhere better illustrated than in book V, where Ulysses
addresses his dream-maiden in fifteen lines of the most conventional
and ludicrously inappropriate courtly complaint:

> Now have I al, a-twexe hope and drede,
> My silf declared to ȝoure wommanhede.   (V,2999–3000)

Guido has 'Volo ut insimul conjungamur ut te forte cognoscam', which is very proper in the context, but Lydgate, needing to amplify, can amplify only in the one way he knows. A switch is pulled, in this case labelled 'love', and the process of response follows automatically.

However, it is in this realm, in the treatment of narrative as a series of 'themes' for amplification, that the *Troy Book* achieves whatever significance it can be said to possess. It is when the narrative allows him to write more or less separate poems in conventional rhetorical moulds that Lydgate is at his best. The passages on women are a case in point. Guido's attacks on women, for which the story of Troy, in Medea, Helen and Criseyde, provided him plenty of opportunity, are retailed with relish and at length, as in book I, 1845–1904 and 2072–2137. In the latter Lydgate has twenty-four lines of invective against women's deceitfulness from one not over-long sentence in Guido, and then forty lines of ingenious apology, highly spiced with irony:

> For þouȝ amonge þei chese hem lovis newe,
> Who considreth, þei be no þing to blame,
> For ofte tyme þei se men do þe same.
> Aei most hem purveie whan men hem refuse,
> Itnd ȝif I koude I wolde hem excuse.
> It sitteth nat a womman lyve alone;
> Þ is no stor but þei have more than oon.[24]

He commends himself to all women, committing Guido to his fate,

> For ȝif he died withoute repentaunce,
> I am dispeired of his savacioun.   (I,2124–5)

Guido's attacks on Helen and Criseyde are fallen upon with similar delight, expanded with much new material (II,3531–631, III,4264–417), and then repudiated with mock-outrage. The disclaimers are commendably straight-faced, letting slip the irony in an innocent-sounding remark:

> For ȝif wommen be double naturelly,
> Why shulde men leyn on hem þe blame?   (III,4408–9)

The attack on Criseyde's final treachery (IV,2148) is based on a casual aside in Guido ('tamquam varia et mutabilis, sicut est proprium mulierum', p. 198), and is much more bitterly ironic:

Loo! what pite is in wommanhede,
What mercy eke and benygne routhe,
Þat newly can al her olde trouthe
Of nature late slyppe asyde
Raþer þanne þei shulde se abide
Any man in meschef for hir sake!
Þe change is nat so redy for to make
In Lombard Strete of crowne nor doket—
Al paie is good, be so þe prente be set;
Her lettre of change doth no man abide!
So þat þe wynde be redy and þe tyde,
Passage is ay, who-so list to passe.   (IV,2148–59)

By contrast, the story of Penelope prompts a straightforward defence
of good wives (V,2192–2219) and reproof of Guido:

And, o Guydo, þou shuldest ben ashamed
To seyn of wyves any þing but wele.   (V,2198–9)

Here and in the attack on Criseyde the elements previously held in
suspension through irony are resolved into a simpler pattern of praise or
blame, but in the rest of the poem it is possible to see how an extra
richness of interest attaches to Lydgate's work in the conventional
genre of anti-feminist satire *per antiphrasim*,[25] partly because of the very
fact that it is conventional. Convention allows a controlled and limited
sort of ambiguity and humour which Lydgate could rarely allow himself and which he can exploit successfully in closed contexts. It can
even, in this one matter, touch tentatively his interpretation of the
narrative. Of Helen's recovery from her grief for Paris, for instance,
he says,

And ȝit she roos ageyn fro deth to lyve.   (IV,3700)

This is neat, and it is brief, as is his comment on Clytemnestra's taking
of Aegisthus as her lover,

Suche drede hadde she for to lyn allone.   (V,1109)

Beside it, drawing on the same vein of humour, we may put the extraordinary heavy archness of his account of the lovemaking of Jason and
Medea[26]:

And sche abood sleples for his sake,
Wonder devoutly desyryng, as I gesse,

With hym to trete of som holynes,
Touching maters of contemplacioun;
For sche was smete with a devocioun
Of fresche Venus to holden a memorie
With hym allone in hir oratorie. . . .   (I,3546–52)

It is a trick he has caught from Chaucer, but the heavy playfulness is all
his own, and not unwelcome. It is certainly to the taste of fifteenth
century readers, for there is more marginal annotation in MS. of these
passages about women than of any others.

   The other feature that I want to mention here, as an example of the
way the narrative draws its richest material from non-narrative sources,
is Lydgate's use of descriptions of times and seasons, as of dawn and
dusk, spring and autumn. As a form of narrative punctuation, this was
of ancient lineage, especially when combined with astronomical-
mythological periphrasis, and it is current convention in medieval
romance (e.g. *Kyng Alisaunder*) as well as classical epic.[27] Guido often,
but not always, provides the hint, but Lydgate draws on a far richer
tradition, and provides in the *Troy Book* some of the great *loci classici* of
medieval seasons-description.[28] Here, for instance, is how he expands
'Insurgente igitur roseis aurora splendoribus et sole aureo luce modica
cacumina montium illustrante, Iason . . ' (Guido, p. 27):

Whan þat þe rowes and þe raies rede
Estward to us ful erly gonne sprede,
Evene at þe tweyliȝt in þe dawenyng,
Whan þe larke of custom gynneth syng
For to salue in hir hevenly lay
Þe lusty goddesse of þe morwe gray—
I mene Aurora, þe whiche afor þe sonne
Is wont t'enchase þe blake skies donne
And þe dirknes of þe dymme nyȝt;
And fresche Phebus, with comfort of his liȝt
And þe briȝtnes of his bemys schene,
Hadde over-gilt þe hiȝe hilles grene;
And floures eke ageyn þe morwe-tyde
Upon her stalke gan splaie her levis wyde,
Whan þat Iason. . . .   (I,3093–107)

The literary provenance of such description has already been discussed
(the use of 'I mene' or, elsewhere, 'This is to seyne', is a direct echo of

the expository *dico* of the rhetoricians),[29] and there is no need to join
Professor Schirmer in his speculative walks with Lydgate along the
banks of the river Linnet.[30] The descriptions are often highly technical,
both in their astrology and their natural science (e.g. IV,3363), and
handle mythology with a freedom and tenderness Lydgate could never
show elsewhere:

> Whan Aurora, with silver dropes schene,
> Hir teris shadde upon þe freshe grene,
> Compleynynge ay in wepinge and in sorwe
> Hir childis deth, every somer morwe—
> Þis to seyne, whan þe dew so sote
> Enbawmed hath þe flour and eke þe rote
> With lusty lycour, in April and in May;
> Whan þe larke, messanger of day,
> Of custom ay Aurora doth salue
> With sondry notis, hir sorwe to transmue
> Or Phebus ryse to joye and gladnes,
> Þoruȝ armonye to leve hir hevynes,
> Takyng hir leve, with seinte John to borwe—
> Þe same tyme, Grekis. . . .   (III,2745–58)

It is difficult not to go on quoting these passages, for they have an
accumulated richness of reference which in itself is a reward.[31] Paradoxically, too, they are a source of real originality in Lydgate, for, safe
within the convention, he is prepared to experiment with descriptions
of February (II,5067) and autumn (V,585) which have little debt to the
tradition. But this is not the chief significance of these passages, for
what happens is that they come not only to serve their immediate
function as decorative narrative transition, but to suggest also, in their
science and philosophy, their sense of order and the due establishment
of things, a kind of counterpoint to the swift and arbitrary fluctuation
of human fortune. They may do more, in their context, than Lydgate
was aware of, and it is interesting again that at the very point where he
appears to retreat from the narrative Lydgate should come closest to
grounding it in his own proper concerns.[32]

These concerns, however, are not yet clear for Lydgate, and are not
to be for some time. Book II deals with events from the rebuilding of
New Troy to the first fight of Greeks and Trojans, and is enormously
swollen with extraneous matter such as the digression on Idolatry, the

elaborate portraits of Greeks and Trojans, and the dispositions of the
Greek navy. The mania for fact finds here its full expression, and Lydgate is not slow to add to Guido from the riches of his encyclopaedic
learning. The building of the New Troy and of the palace of Ilion
(479–1066) is packed with new and enlivening detail, as on the origins
of chess (816), the performance of plays (860), or the value of *pi* (946).
Lydgate revels in the allegorical exposition of Mercury and the three
goddesses on mount Ida (2488), with some side-glances at the frauds of
cosmetics (2672)—all this, with characteristic neglect of dramatic propriety, contained *within* Paris's narrative. He preserves and expands
Guido's digressions on Aeneas (7122) and the pillars of Hercules (7436)
while adding similar material of his own, on Aeneas (327) and Iphigenia
(6215).

Above all, and endlessly, he expands and adds passages of moralisa-
tions—complaints against Fortune,[33] apostrophes and exclamations
against the evil effects of rancour (1067) and upon Priam for his repeated
folly (1797, 2812) warning against women's evil influence (7849),
against gambling (827, prompted merely by the mention of dice-
games), against drink (5746). These, many of them, are set-pieces, the
sort of thing Lydgate does well, where the material falls into pre-set
rhetorical moulds, but they bear little upon the narrative, which is
dramatic only where Lydgate, with a limited sense of the style appropriate to character in set speeches, distinguishes between the blunt,
brusque earthiness of Ajax (1479), for example, and the confident
power and nobility of Agamemnon (4337). For the rest, the narrative
is washed out in floods of moralising. Some of it is political, as if
Lydgate were thinking of his patron's inclinations (though most of it is
adumbrated in Guido). Henry V was not at all averse to listening to
political advice, providing it was comfortably general, *vide* Hoccleve's
Regement of Princes, and he could hardly have taken offence at Lydgate's
admonitions to be kind to strangers, unlike Lamedon,

> Þerfor, ȝe kynges and lordis everychon,
> Make ȝow a merour of þis Lamedoun,   (II,83–4)

or to seek peace before war,

> And it is bet by pes to han redresse,
> Þan gynne a werre without avisenesse,   (II,1265–6)

or not to act hastily,

And late Priam alwey ʒour merour ben,
Hasty errour be tymes to correcte.   (II,1898–9)

The narrative also gives plenty of opportunity, here and in later books, to preach the disastrous consequences of discord among rulers[34]:

For whan discord and false discencioun
Allied ben in hertis for to strive
Among lordis, þat kyngdam may nat þryve.
                                            (III,2350–2)

This is good advice, but it hardly entitles Lydgate to be treated as a serious political commentator, grey eminence to the Lancastrian kings, as some recent writing on Lydgate comes near to suggesting. Some of it may have had, or come to have had relevance as years went by, such as the frequent expression of preference of peace to war, but it is all too general to be any more than a public expression of private morality—which is what the medieval 'Mirror of Princes' always is—and far too commonplace to have any particular topical import. There is sufficient evidence against such interpretation within the poem, in such passages as Lydgate's outburst on the murder of Agamemnon:

O myʒti God, þat with þin inward loke
Sest every þing þoruʒ þin eternal myʒt,
Whi wiltow nat of equite and riʒt
Punishe and chastise so horrible a þing,
And specialy þe mordre of a kyng?   (V,1046–50)

Only a poem totally innocent of contemporary reference could permit such an outburst so soon after the death of Richard II, and the same may be said of Lydgate's reflections, in the same story, on murder and adultery,

Whiche bringeth in alyenacioun,
By extort title fals successioun,   (V,1139–40)

which could have been tactless, to say the least, at a time when the Beauforts, legitimised descent of John of Gaunt's adultery with Katharine Swynford, were beginning to be powers in the land. It may be that in other works Lydgate is more specific, but in the *Troy Book* the 'political' advice and reflection are really the traditional wisdom of the *Secreta Secretorum*, or of contemporary works like the *De Officio Militari* of Richard Ullerston addressed to Henry of Monmouth, or the *Sophilo-gium* of Jacobus Magnus.[35] For real political comment, we have to go outside the work of the monastic professionals, to George Ashby or the *Libel of English Policy*.

After the diversity of book II, book III is something of a disaster, for it is totally preoccupied with the interminable battles of Greeks and Trojans, ending with the death of Hector. Even the indefatigable Furnivall, whose head-lines and side-notes provide *divertissement* in many a weary early English text, is finally reduced to 'Various Kings and Dukes are unhorst by their Foes' (p. 479). Guido is chiefly to blame: he has a maniac appetite for recitals of battalions, wards, and encounters, and this is the sort of thing Lydgate's eye would fall upon as he ploughed ahead with his translation:

> Ayax et Hector in bello conueniunt, ambo deiciunt se ab equis. Menelaus interfecit quendam amiratum Troyanorum. Celidonas autem interfecit Moles de Orep, nepotem regis Thoas. Madon uero de Clara irruit in regem Cedium, quem tam dire percussit in facie quod oculum eius euulsit. Sardellus autem quendam alium Grecorum amiratum interfecit. Margariton uero in Thelamonem irruit sed Thelamon ipsum grauiter uulnerauit. Fanuel autem regem Prothenorem deiecit ab equo. Sic et ceteri fratres naturales filii regis Priami contra Grecos letaliter offendendo uiriliter se gesserunt.[36]

It is against Lydgate's nature to omit anything, but he does everything he can to enliven and heighten the colour of the battle-descriptions, for instance by adding a long, detailed, and scrupulously accurate con-temporary description of arms and armour (44–108)—this, like the account of the siege of Tenedos in book II (6416), would no doubt have pleased his patron—and by frequent detail of banners, devices, love-tokens, the bray of trumpets, and the neighing of horses. In this way, by implicit contemporising, and explicitly, by drawing out the chivalric behaviour worthy of imitation (1298, 1450, 2075) as well as criticising Hector when he falls short of these ideals (5354), Lydgate keeps his promise of making the work an exemplar of ancient chivalry. But it is hard work, and the episode of the parting of Troilus and Criseyde, however inadequate by Chaucerian standards, makes a welcome interlude.

It may have done more for Lydgate. The lament of Troilus and

Criseyde at their parting (4077) is one of the first truly affective passages in the *Troy Book*,[37] and it initiates a movement in the poem in which the imaginative response is enormously heightened and intensified. Partly it may be the memory and example of the fifth book of the *Troilus* that provoke this heightened response, but above all it is Lydgate's sense of the inevitable ruin that Time and Fortune make in human grandeur. Here at last, as Troy's heroes decline and the city falls into the shadows, the rich and intractable diversities of the story resolve into a tragic pattern in which the Christian can take a passionate concern. Lydgate may have begun the poem to please Henry and to keep alive the memory of ancient days, but Troy has little meaning for him until he is drawn to contemplate its fall, the great tragedy of pagan times. It is in this that the moral commentary, up till now factitious and indiscriminate, finds at last its centre, in the contemplation of the inexorability of Fate, the mutability of Fortune, the transitoriness of worldly bliss and the inevitability of retribution, to the memorial of which book IV is chiefly dedicated.

The close of book III prepares the ground, in the lament for Hector and solemn apostrophe to Troy:

> A Troye, allas! wel maist þou wepe and crie
> And make a woful lamentacioun,
> Whiche hast of newe, to þi confusioun,
> Loste þi diffence and þi stronge wal,
> Þi berer up, þi surete royal,
> Be whom þin honour chefly was begonne.
> Allas, allas! for now þi briȝte sonne
> Eclipsed is, and þou stanst desolat
> Of al comfort, and discounsolat.   (III,5480–8)

Book IV takes up the burden of sorrow, outrage, and pity, and a series of richly expanded laments—for Troilus (3004), for Achilles (3237), for Paris (3654)—lead up to the final great lament for Troy:

> Now fare wel Troye, farwel for everemore!
> Farwel, allas! to cruel was þi fal!
> Of þe no more now I write shal.
> For þi sake, in soþe, whan I take hede,
> Of inward wo myn herte I fele blede;
> And whan þat I remembre in my þouȝt
> By ruyne how þou art brouȝt to nouȝt,

Þat whilom were so noble and so riche,
Þat in þis world I trowe noon was liche,
Nor perigal, to speken of fairnesse,
To speke of knyȝthod and of worþinesse,
As clerkes seien þat þi bildyng knewe;
Þat al þe world ouȝte for to rewe
On þi pitous waste walles wylde,
Whilom so rial whan men gan to bilde
Þin touris hiȝe, and kyng Priamus
Þe first began, moste riche and glorious,
And sette his se in noble Ylyoun.
O, who can write a lamentacioun
Convenient, o Troye, for þi sake?
Or who can now wepe or sorwe make,
Þi grete meschef to compleyne and crie?
Certis, I trowe nat olde Jeremye. . . .
. . . nor þou Ezechiel. . . .
Nor Danyel. . . .
Alle ȝoure teris myȝte nat suffise
To have bewepte her sorwes everychon,
Be tresoun wrouȝt, as wel as be her foon.
Here-of no more, for it may nat availle.   (IV,7036–85)

Combined with these goes a systematic repudiation of the humane values
for which the classical story stands (not difficult, for the tale here is of
unrelieved treachery and intrigue): attacks on the treachery of Achilles
(2668, 2768), and on the inhuman cruelty of Pyrrhus (6866), where he
ignores Guido's careful religious explanation of Pyrrhus' motive in
sacrificing Polyxena; constant reflection on the instability of the common people (300, 4987, 5411), on the mutability of worldly joy (6222),
on Fortune (2401, 3499, 4270); all culminating in the reproach to Mars
(4440–4537), which we may set beside the opening invocation in the
Prologue, and a final prolonged, fierce and comprehensive attack on
the pagan gods of antiquity (6930–7035), which immediately precedes
the lament for Troy. These last two passages are completely original,
and most of the others virtually so.

Lydgate's expansive method can be intolerably tedious in exposition,
narrative, or the development of ideas, but for anything of a set
rhetorical nature—complaint, lament, apostrophe, invocation, description, formal oratory—it is well suited. The success of book IV is that it

offers a multitude of such themes for amplification, and offers them within a narrative context of ruin, destruction, and loss which enables Lydgate to come to grips finally with a significance in the story which is profoundly meaningful to him, namely, its profound meaningless-ness. The style has a solemn and moving and ruined grandeur to match its theme, for here at last Lydgate can destroy the story along with Troy.

Book V has a faintly posthumous air. It deals, in the comprehensive medieval way, with the subsequent adventures of Agamemnon, Menelaus, Diomedes, Orestes, and Ulysses, and is totally lacking in form. Lydgate takes little interest in it, and seems in haste to finish. He rarely amplifies, even refuses the bait of a seasons-description at one point (1557), and the narrative transitions are more than usually slack and nerveless (1180, 2866). It justifies all the worst that can be said of Lydgate's incompetence in narrative. But out of this miscellany of murder, treason, adultery, and vengeance grows an Epilogue, modelled on that of the *Troilus*, where he recaptures the high style of book IV, and, meditating on the story of Troy, concludes that there is no trust in the world, our lives here being but a pilgrimage, so that we must put our faith in Christ, in whom alone is surety (3544–92). It is a fine passage, and demonstrates that if Lydgate had no skill in beginning, where there is everything to be said, he had at least a gift for ending, where there is nothing more to be said. The poem actually ends with two envoys, one to Henry V, the other to his 'litel bok'.

The *Troy Book* requires patience, but it yields its riches, mostly in an unprecedented extension of techniques of amplification. These tech-niques have been identified and discussed, but not analysed, and it is here, I think, that we may introduce a consideration of the 'topics' and their importance in Lydgate and in medieval poetry. The currency of the term 'topic' (or, less ambiguously, topos, *pl.* topoi) in stylistic theory is largely due to Curtius, but his discussion of the feature,[38] though charac-teristically rich, allusive, and suggestive, is not entirely systematic. In classical rhetoric, pre-eminently in Cicero, the topics are the *argu-mentorum sedes*, the 'storehouses of trains of thought'. They are the places, the *loci communes* ('common places'), where material can be found for argument, and they provided not merely mnemonics but a series of categories of thought, whereby the orator, assembling his arguments, could consider the case in the light of cause, effect, simi-larity, difference, the whole, the parts, time, place, and so on. A systematic attempt was made by Matthew of Vendome to apply Cicero's theory of topics to his own theory of poetic description.[39] Given the circumstances of the general transfer of rhetorical teaching to the *artes poeticae*, such an attempt was almost inevitable, and since it is a peculiarity of Matthew's to regard description as more or less synonymous with poetry, he was bound to make it in this way. There is a spurious justification for him in the way he provides, for instance, a 'systematic' basis for *descriptio temporis* and *descriptio loci*, but the whole exercise is faintly unreal, and persuades one to the belief that the proper home of the topics in the Middle Ages was in dialectic not in rhetoric, and that from there its influence on poetry would be difficult indeed to ascertain. As a recent writer on the subject says, 'One cannot fail to find examples of the dialectical topoi in any poetry of statement, whether the author is aware of them or not.'[40] The subject is a complex one, and cannot be treated here, but it may be observed that the system of contraries which forms such an important category of Lydgate's thought is an example of the application in poetry of just such a dialectical topos. One wonders whether the elucidation of this feature, offered above,[41] might not profitably be extended to other and better poets and to other topoi, so that we might find what happened to *inventio* in medieval poetry.

However, the point at the moment is to distinguish between the dialectical topics of thought, which originated in forensic and deliberative oratory, and the rhetorical topics of expression, which were developed particularly in epideictic oratory (panegyric). The latter were less systematised in formal teaching, but they are a consistent feature in medieval poetic style, which shares with classical panegyric the desire to amplify, to heighten and to idealise, and in Lydgate these topics are raised almost to the level of new modes of invention. Various kinds of topic blend one into another, but for the purpose of discussion they may be identified thus (in an imaginary eulogy of a hero):

1. I have not the skill to tell of him (modesty-topic)
2. I have not the time to tell of him (brevity-topic)
3. He has the virtues of all others (topics of comparison)
4. His excellence is inexpressible (inexpressibility-topic)
5. He surpasses all others (outdoing-topic)

Of these, the third has already been sufficiently dealt with in speaking of courtly poetry.[42]

The topics of modesty are first of all a means of ingratiation, and thus have a clearly defined function in both rhetoric and poetry. They are widely employed in classical poetry, but the *locus classicus* for Lydgate is the Prologue to the *Franklin's Tale*. The poet laments his 'rude' and 'boistous' style, declares that everything is said 'under correccioun', and that he would never have dared write but for the insistence of his patron. His pen quakes at his temerity:

> And here an ende of þe firste book
> I make now, with quakyng hond for drede,
> Only for fer of ȝow þat schal it rede.
>
> (*Troy*, I,4426–8)

Sometimes it quakes too at the prospect of a particularly harrowing passage,[43] with the literal extension of the metaphor that is typical of Lydgate:

> For whiche, allas, my penne I fele quake,
> Þat doth myn ynke blotten on my boke
>
> (*Troy*, V,1044–5)

> O Hercules, my penne I feele quake,
> Myn ynke fulfillid of bittir teris salte
>
> (*Fall*, I,5517–18)

> And shede of grace the aureat lycoure
> Into my penne, quakyng of verray drede.
>
> (*Legend of St. Margaret*, 56–7)

The references to his rude and barren style are similarly extended,

> And þouȝ my stile, blottid with rudenes,
> As of metre, be rusty and unfiled
>
> (*Troy*, IV,7096–7)

> For I shal now, lyk as I am wont,
> Sharpen my penne, boþe rude and blont
>
> (*Troy*, V,2923–4)

particularly in allusion to the image of 'coloures' or 'floures' of rhetoric:

> And for þou art enlumined with no floures
> Of rethorik, but with white and blak
>
> (*Troy*, Envoy, 100–1)

> Al-be þat I ne can þe weye goon
> To sue þe floures of his eloquence;
> Nor of peyntyng I have noon excellence

> With sondry hewes noble, fresche and gay;
> So riche colours biggen I ne may;
> I mote procede with sable and with blake.
>
> (Troy, II,192–7)

The 'variation' of this metaphor is completed in the *Secrees*:

> I have no colour, but only chalk and sable.   (337)

It is not difficult to see in the literal application of this metaphor an origin for the concept of 'aureate' style, a sense of the surface textures of words expressed in imagery of painting and jewels.

Ingratiation, however, is only one function of the modesty-topos. It can also heighten and idealise in a simple way:

> I wante connynge by ordre to discrive
> Of every cours þe diversytes . . .
> Myn englische is to rude and eke to pleyn
> For to enditen of so hiȝe a þing.[44]

It can also serve, by disclaiming knowledge of artifice, to assert the writer's concern for plain truth:

> I toke non hede nouþer of schort nor long,
> But to þe trouþe, and lefte coryouste
> Boþe of makyng and of metre be.
>
> (Troy, II,184–6)

Traditionally, such disclaimers were associated, as in the Franklin's Prologue, with a display of rhetorical fireworks, and Lydgate's confessions of inadequacy are rich in allusions to the mount of Parnassus he has never slept on, or the well of Helicon he has never drunk from, or the garden of Tullius where he has never gathered flowers. These allusions, like the use of modesty-topics in general, are particularly common in prologues and epilogues, which are always very extensive in Lydgate, and the Envoy to *St.Edmund* is an anthology of such allusion:

> Save blak and whyt thow hast noon othir wede,
> Of Tullius motles a dyrk apparence;
> The hevenly botler, callyd Ganymede,
> The to refresshe lyst do no dilligence;
> Of Mercurye the aureat influence
> The t'enlumyne dystylled skarsly doun. . . .
> At Elycon welle thow drowh but smal foysoun. . . .

The sugre of Omer was fer off be absence. . . .
Callyope lyst nat hyr bawme shede
The t'enbelysshe with colours of cadence;
Thy auctour gadred no flours in the mede
Under Pernaso, to have ther assistence;
Daunger of Muses gaf hym no licence
For t'approche the hyl of Cytheroun:
For which be soget to al correccioun.

Lydgate is assuring us of his stylistic sophistication, but the real function of such passages—as also of the elaborate allusions to Chaucer, which are almost invariably introduced through modesty-topics—is to broaden the reference of the poem. Coghill speaks of the way Chaucer draws the substance of his narratives from the world he knows—'do that it be lik'⁴⁵—but medieval poets do not usually do this. They prefer to draw substance from books, from literary tradition, to create an impression of accumulated richness by reference to material outside the narrative. This is the basic function of much of the description of wall-paintings and tapestries in medieval poetry, as it has been argued to be of the similes in *Paradise Lost*. The modesty-topos is thus analogous to what we have seen of seasons-description in Lydgate, that is, it provides the opportunity for a strictly conventional kind of bravura writing in which his imagination can operate with a freedom (as in his handling of the 'colours') denied to it in the interpretation of straight narrative.

Brevity-topics are common in Chaucer's longer narratives, particularly the *Knight's Tale*, and are also prominent in the *Squire's Tale*.⁴⁶ They draw attention to the swift prosecution of the narrative, and the poet's praiseworthy refusal to linger over details, and usually indicate the opposite. At the beginning of his *Legend of St. Giles*, for instance, Lydgate spends thirty-four lines saying how briefly he is going to tell the story, thus emphasising his own skill in amplification. Often brevity-topics function as superlatives, like the topics of excellence. Lydgate cannot describe the sorrows of the Trojan women for

A large boke it wolde occupie.

(*Troy*, III, 5562)

If he were to describe the armour of the combatants in the *Thebes*,

It wer in soth almost a dayes werk. (2667)

There are at least two occasions in the *Troy*, however, where such

topics are genuinely abbreviatory (IV,3251, 3728): both concern pagan
burial rites, in which Lydgate takes a good deal less interest than Guido.

The most popular form of the brevity-topos is the *occupatio*, the
refusal to describe which accompanies the description. A classic
example is in the building of the New Troy:

> And if I schulde rehersen by and by
> Þe korve knottes by crafte of masounry,
> Þe fresche enbowyng, with vergis riȝt as linys,
> And þe vowsyng ful of babewynes,
> Þe riche koynyng, þe lusty tablementis,
> Vynnettis rennynge in þe casementis—
> Þouȝ þe termys in englisch wolde ryme,
> To rekne hem alle I have as now no tyme.
>
> (*Troy*, II,651–8)

After an exhaustive account of the Trojan arms and armour in book III,
Lydgate adds:

> I have no konnyng every þyng to telle,
> And unto ȝow it were to long to dwelle.
>
> (*Troy*, III,109–10)

Elsewhere he spends thirty lines describing Ulysses' reunion with
Penelope, declaring meanwhile that if he did so,

> It were to long tariyng for my boke   (V,2287)

though beside this we may set the disarming honesty of

> It were but veyn to make mencioun
> Of her revel ne her gret array,
> Nor of þe fest made þe same day,
> Eke in þe story I fynde it nat, in soth.   (V,2698–701)

Occupatio gives the illusion of getting on with the story, but its main
function is to signal passages of bravura description, as with Arcite's
funeral in the *Knight's Tale*.

The last two topoi offer rhetorical substitutes for description, and are
superlative in function. The inexpressibility-topos in its simpler form is
represented in the *Testament*:[47]

> Ther is no speche nor language can remembre,
> Lettre, sillable, nor word that may expresse,

> Though into tunges were turned every membre
> Of man, to telle the excellent noblesse
> Of blessed Jesu.... (57–61)

Sometimes, characteristically, Lydgate refers literally to his pen:

> For alle her sorwes ʒif I shulde telle....
> Mi penne shuld of verray routhe rive
>
> > *(Troy*, IV,6374–6)
>
> Yif I sholde writen in sentence
> Lik his demerites hooli the maneer,
> It wolde thoruh perse and blotte my paper.
>
> > *(Fall*, IV, 2728–30)

But the most notable extended use of the topic is in the laments for Troilus and Troy in book IV of the *Troy Book*, which have already been quoted.[48] Here again Lydgate uses the topic as a source of enrichment as well as heightening, the reference to the Prophets in the latter giving a biblical portentousness in which narrative 'sens' and rhetorical amplification are conjoined.

Finally, of all topics the commonest, the assertion of surpassing excellence. This can take many forms, some of them very simple:

> Þat it alone was incomperable
> Of alle cites þat any mortal man
> Sawe ever ʒit, sithe þe world began.
>
> > *(Troy*, II,586–8)
>
> Þat in þis world was never wiʒt so wo (II,416)
> Þat in þis world was to it noon lyche (II,549)

The extent of the 'world' is often specified—as far as India:

> That from Cartage into Inde
> Men myghte nat a bettre fynde,
>
> > *(Pilgrimage*, 7305–6)

and the 'India topos' is only the epitome of many such in medieval poetry in which rhyme supplies the geography:

> Si n'i ot bube ne malan:
> N'avoit jusqu'en Jerusalen
> Fame qui plus bel col portast.
>
> > *(Roman de la Rose*, 541–3)

Another group of topics develop the idea of 'never' (in all my life, etc.)
rather than 'nowhere'; others resort to hyperbole:

> Hir cruel wo and lamentacioun,
> Whiche wolde meve to compassioun . . .
> Any herte þouȝ it were made of stel.
>
> (*Troy*, IV,3713–16)

Sometimes the topic is desperately assertive:

> Ther may no whitenesse be compared
> To that whittenesse, I dar telle,
> For al whitenesse yt dyd excelle.
>
> (*Reason and Sensuality*, 2822–6)

A whole series of topics are evolved from the image-patterns that we
saw operating in the *Flower of Courtesy*: as the sun among stars, the
ruby among gems, the rose among flowers, so she, etc. But the richest
development of the outdoing-topos again involves allusion, and as such
merges with the topics of comparison. The classic form is 'Some talk of
Alexander', as in a *Valentine to her that excelleth all*:

> Men speke of Lucresse. . . . [and twenty others]
> But I love oone, þat excelleþe alle.   (22–70)

In book IV of the *Troy*, the topic again provides a basic technique of
amplification, particularly in Helen's lament over Paris:

> I trowe þat never man before
> No woman sawe falle in swiche distresse. . . .
> Nat Cleopatre goynge to hir grave,
> Nor woful Tesbe, þat fro þe kave sterte,
> Whan she hir silfe smote unto þe herte,
> Nor þe feithful trewe Orestille. . . .
> Nor þe sorwe of trewe Julya,
> Nor þe fervence of feithful Porcia. . . .
> But al þe wo and þe furious sorwe
> Of þese echon ȝet may nat atteyne
> Unto þe sorwe of þe quene Eleyne.
>
> (IV,3654–82)

What one has to say about the rhetorical topics in the *Troy Book* is a
reflection on a small scale of what has been said about its methods of
amplification: that most of the riches of the poem are drawn from

outside the narrative. Lydgate is not, for the most part, interested in the story, but he is interested in writing, and the remarkable achievement of the *Troy Book* is that at the climax of the narrative, in book IV, the rhetorical skills are employed on 'themes' which display perfectly the inner significance of the narrative to the Christian moralist. Lydgate comes into his own amidst the ruins of Troy, and, with his mind on the eternal platitudes of existence, the facility of his style curbed and fortified through conventional patterns of expression, he can rise to a solemn and powerful eloquence.

The *Troy Book* is extant in twenty-three MSS., the *Siege of Thebes*, Lydgate's next major work, exists in twenty-nine, most of them of the same type, that is, 'quality' texts prepared for aristocratic or upper-class patrons. In three of these manuscripts,[49] it occurs together with the *Troy Book*, and the two works are clearly associated in many ways. Lydgate began the *Thebes* at the end of 1420, after delivery of the *Troy Book* to Henry V, and completed it by 1422, certainly before the death of Henry V in August, which made the prophecies of peace at the end of the *Thebes* into pipe-dreams. He had no patron for this work, which gives it an added importance since it encourages us to assume that he wrote it because he chose to. The immediate reasons for this choice are not very inspiring: the story of Thebes existed in the medieval mind as a pendant to Troy, and had done ever since the composition of the *Roman de Thebes* in the late twelfth century as a pot-boiler to Benoit's *Roman de Troie*. Versions of the two regularly occur together in French MSS.,[50] and a writer as systematic and inert as Lydgate would have drifted naturally from the one to the other. However, it is possible to suggest that, having embarked on the story, he saw ways in which he could deal with it significantly.

The story may be briefly told. It begins, in the medieval way, at the beginning, with the building of Thebes by Amphion, and then passes on to tell of king Layus and his queen, Jocasta, and their son, Edippus, who, it is predicted, will kill his father. He is cast out to die, but is found and brought up by king Polibon. He grows up, kills Layus at a tourney, meets and slays the Sphinx and, on arrival at Thebes, marries his mother. The first part ends with the discovery, and Edippus' death. The whole episode demonstrates the gratuitously accumulative nature of medieval narrative, and the disintegration of classical myth. In this myth, the destruction of Thebes was the dreadful consequence of Oedipus' curse upon his unnatural offspring, but Lydgate makes little or nothing of this, and contents himself with warnings against marrying one's mother (787) and adjurations to honour one's parents (1019) which, in the circumstances of Oedipus' error, are ludicrous.

In Part 2, Edippus' sons, Eteocles and Polynices, quarrel over the succession and eventually agree to rule in alternate years, Eteocles first, as the elder. Polynices goes to Argos where he clashes with the noble knight-adventurer Tydeus, but the two are reconciled by king Adrastus and marry his daughters. At the end of the first year of Eteocles' rule, Tydeus goes to Thebes to make Polynices' claim, but is unsuccessful and, after a narrow escape from an ambushing party, finds himself in the garden of king Lycurgus where, in a pastoral interlude, the king's daughter cares for him. He returns to Argos.

In Part 3, Adrastus resolves to help Polynices and gathers a great army to attack Thebes, despite the warnings of 'bishop' Amphiorax. On the way to Thebes they run short of water, and, in another odd interlude, are helped to find a water supply by Ipsiphyle, the nurse of Lycurgus' baby son. While she is away, the child is stung by a serpent and killed, but Adrastus intervenes with Lycurgus for Ipsiphyle's life. At last the siege of Thebes begins (3556). Jocasta tries to make peace, but hostilities erupt when the Greeks kill the Thebans' tame tiger (a silly episode). Tydeus, the two brothers and all except Adrastus are slain. Creon becomes king and refuses burial to the Greek dead, whereupon Theseus is called in:

> ʒif ʒe remembre, ʒe han herde it to-forn
> Wel rehersyd at Depforth in the vale,
> In the bygynnyng of the knyghtys tale.   (4522–4)

Lydgate repeats here the events of the opening of the *Knight's Tale*, with a good deal of close imitation of Chaucer.[51] Thebes is destroyed, and the poem ends with condemnation of war and praise and prayers for peace.

The whole poem is framed as a Canterbury tale, with a prologue in which Lydgate the monk meets the pilgrims as they leave Canterbury and is cajoled by the Host into telling this tale. The fiction is kept up through the tale, with more realism than Chaucer ever admitted, with references to the progress of the journey as he tells the tale (324, 1044–60) and the allusion already quoted, but the ending does not refer to the frame. The Prologue is not badly done, except in so far as it challenges comparison with Chaucer. Lydgate's presentation of himself is quite amusing, and the Host's language has a certain liveliness, but it is all rather mechnical: there is no illusion of drama, no interplay, no real dialogue, only a self-consciously 'low' speech by the Host in which character simplifies into caricature. The other pilgrims are blurred, out of focus, and Lydgate is not at all clear which is which.[52] The point of interest, though, as I have said before, is not how well it is done, but that it should have been done at all. Such a close imitation of Chaucer, on his own ground, argues an extraordinary confidence on Lydgate's part. The opening of the Prologue, with its elaborate astronomical periphrasis, is clearly an attempt to improve on Chaucer, and the tribute to Chaucer (39–57) contains none of the usual protestations of modesty. In fact, the modesty-topics are conspicuously absent from the whole poem. We may assume that the access of confidence is due to the completion of the *Troy Book*, which thus takes a place in Lydgate's poetic career similar to that of the Homeric translations in Pope's. The *Thebes* is then the final stage in Lydgate's re-creation of Chaucer's poetic development, a new and improved version of the Canterbury tale, specifically the *Knight's Tale*, tackling the whole Theban epic where Chaucer merely worked a romantic episode from its sequel. Such may have been Lydgate's ambitions. The association with Chaucer was also convenient in that it provided a literary 'occasion' for the poem. All Lydgate's poems, as I have said, are in a sense occasional poems, for he was not the kind of poet who writes from the pressures of his own creative imagination.

His source for the *Thebes* is some late French prose redaction of the *Roman de Thebes* similar to the *Roman de Edipus*. Lydgate was well aware of the inferior 'authority' of such vernacular romances: he makes no specific mention of his source, but laces the narrative with more or less relevant passages from the encyclopaedic works of Boccaccio,[53] to whom he alludes frequently, so that the uninitiated reader might assume that his source was Boccaccio throughout. In the absence of a known source, it is difficult to say much about Lydgate's handling of the details of the story. Renoir assumes that Lydgate actually worked from the *Roman de Edipus*,[54] and is able therefore to give him the credit for some minor improvements in the logic of the narrative of Oedipus. One would like to follow him in this, but such changes are quite alien to Lydgate's method of working from sources, which is always to add, never to alter. In any case, the 'improvements' are insignificant in relation to the colossal irrelevance of the Oedipus-story as Lydgate tells it, or, later, to the irrelevance of the two Lycurgus episodes. Far from 'rectifying the logic' of the narrative, Lydgate makes no pretence of relating these episodes to the general narrative, even seems unaware that they are mutually contradictory. His modest image of himself as 'blind Bayard', stumbling purposelessly but patiently along, never seemed truer. Renoir also places stress on Lydgate's growing 'humanism' in this poem, represented in his comparatively mild treatment of the pagan deities. It is true that Lydgate omits some attacks on pagan superstition which are made in the *Edipus*, but it is hard to make much of a case out of this when the *Edipus* is only a source by hypothesis. Lydgate also treats Amphiorax fairly leniently, but this presumably is because he happens to be right about the outcome of the war, and when Amphiorax is swallowed up into hell, Lydgate weighs in, just as he did in the earlier account of Apollo (539–44), with a diatribe against pagan belief,

> Lo here the mede of ydolatrie,
> Of rytys old and of fals mawmetrye (4047–8)

which has all the fierce conclusiveness of the *Troy Book*.

However, the *Thebes* is very different from the *Troy Book*. For one thing, it is much shorter (4716 lines). Though there are one or two passages of encyclopaedic expansion, like the account of who was (Cerberus, Erebus, Megaera, Thesiphone, etc.) and who was not (Hymen, Clio, Calliope) at the wedding of Oedipus and Jocasta (823), they are few and brief. Some of the pressure to be elevated is relaxed, as a result of the different status of the story, and the fact that Lydgate has no patron to impress. The whole handling of the story is more subdued, less highly coloured and rhetorical. There are no elaborate protestations of modesty, no fulsome tributes to Chaucer, no seasons-description, except for the briefest phrases in transition.[55] Favourite topics of complaint and lament are introduced and dismissed almost casually (1866, 3401), and invitations to expand on 'love' (1487, 3954) or even on the steadfastness of women (2841, 2869, 4449) are barely acknowledged. References to Fortune (887, 4250) and Fate (1233) are like shorthand compared with the *Troy Book*, and brevity-topics are genuinely abbreviatory in function (1209, 1562, 2661), though Lydgate cannot resist an extended imitation of the funeral *occupatio* of the *Knight's Tale* (4565–602). It would not be right to give the impression that the narrative is brisk and economical: certain habits are too deeply ingrained for this to be possible, and the twelve lines in which Tydeus proclaims his intention of being brief (1901) are in a familiar vein. But amplification is not a systematic and deliberate policy, and it is possible to read the story as a story, which is what one is never tempted to say of the *Troy Book*. There are even moments, such as Tydeus' embassy to Thebes, when the narrative has a sweep and authenticity quite compelling in its own right. Lydgate catches the sarcasm of Eteocles (1974) very effectively, and the grand disdain of Tydeus' exit, and the whole episode of the ambush (2111–235).

It is, indeed, through the portrayal of Tydeus and, to a lesser extent, of Adrastus that Lydgate establishes for himself a moral significance in the narrative. There is a most striking contrast between the factitious handling of the Oedipus story, with its ludicrously inapposite moralising, and the deep moral integrity of the rest of the poem, demonstrating as it does the virtues of wise, just rule, the consequences of unwise governance, and the horror and futility of war.[56] It is here that the narrative is subdued to the proper concerns of the moralist, and that the political interests of the *Troy Book* are given a systematic and convincing expression. History is of use in providing examples of moral and political action, and Lydgate here pays enough respect to the narrative to make it a true 'Mirror for Princes'. He begins early, using the story of Amphion to emphasise the virtues of benignity in a ruler (244–85):

> Her may ȝe see how myche may avaylle
> The goodlihed and lownesse of a kyng.   (244–5)

Eteocles' failure to keep his promise prompts an excursus on truth (1721–84):

> For which ȝe kyngges and lordes beth wel war
> ȝour bihestes justly for to holde!   (1774–5)

Adrastus' generous treatment of his army is also followed by the moral elucidation—the need of a king to be liberal, and especially not to live sumptuously while his people suffer (2688–2722):

> For which eche prince, lord, and governour,
> And specialy every conquerour,
> Lat hym be war, for al his hegh noblesse,
> That bounte, fredom, plente and largesse
> Be on accord that they his brydel lede,
> Lest of his puple whan he hath most nede
> He be defrauded: whan he is but allone,
> Than is to late for to make his mone.   (2701–8)

Above all, the poem debates the question of peace and war. Jocasta

advises solving problems by negotiation (3655), while Adrastus' council
give expression to the other view (4134), that we cannot betray our
brave progenitors (i.e. Edward III and the Black Prince, as Henry V
might have said). The poem ends with a vigorous condemnation of
war, backed by readings from Old and New Testaments and from
common sense, which asserts that war proceeds always from covetousness and ambition, and brings desolation to all. Witness the waste walls
of Thebes. The Epilogue closes on a note of hope, prophesying peace
and concord between realms,

> Pees and quyet, concord and unyte,   (4703)

in words strongly reminiscent of the terms of the treaty of Troyes
(1420):

> Item, ut Concordia, Pax, et Tranquillitas inter praedicta Franciae
> et Angliae Regna perpetuo futuris temporibus observentur. . . .[57]

Troyes was Henry V's supreme achievement: peace, the union of
England and France through his marriage with Katherine, and the
designation of their issue as king of both countries. It was a hollow
achievement, largely because of Henry's death. But to Lydgate, writing
in 1421, it was the fulfilment of the whole historical teaching of the
Thebes-story, to which he may have turned in the first place partly
because of its close relevance to the theme of peace that he began to
develop in the *Troy*-epilogue (V,3399–458). No doubt he would have
been less emphatic for peace had it seemed less certain that the debate
was now concluded in the treaty—but his immediate remarks are not
less convincing for that. The consistency with which these politico-
moral themes are worked out, and the skilful handling of the narrative
to give them their greatest effectiveness, are the real achievements of
the *Thebes*. In little, it represents much of what is best in Lydgate—deep
moral concern, good sense, a sober solemnity of style—indeed, something of what is best in English. It is a far cry to Shakespeare, but the
history-plays, with their sober and practical reflections on government,
are the true inheritors of Lydgate's concerns. There is even the possibility that Shakespeare may have known the *Thebes*, for it appeared
as a Canterbury tale in Stow's 1561 Chaucer, and in successive collected
editions of Chaucer.

Notes to Chapter Five

1 Beryl Smalley, *English Friars and Antiquity*, p. 14.
2 Gilbert Highet, *The Classical Tradition* (Oxford 1949), p. 54.
3 See T. D. Kendrick, *British Antiquity* (London 1950).
4 This tradition goes back to the Burgundian Fredegarius of the seventh century: see A. M. Young, *Troy and her Legend* (Pittsburgh 1948), p. 57.
5 J. Seznec, *The Survival of the Pagan Gods* (Harper Torchbooks, 1961), p. 24.
6 Margaret R. Scherer, *The Legends of Troy in Art and Literature* (New York 1963), p. 24.
7 Prologue, 124; V,3368.
8 See above, p. 30.
9 See R. F. Jones, *The Triumph of the English Language* (Stanford 1953).
10 Seznec, *op. cit.*, pp. 77–9. William Worcester wrote for Fastolf a *Versificatio omnium Stellarum fixatum pro anno 1440* (Holzknecht, *Literary Patronage* p. 94).
11 This is a marked characteristic: see 1983, 3686, 4625, 12487, and also 1055, 7618, 9636 (ed. D. Donaldson and G. A. Panton, EETS,OS 39, 56, 1869–74).
12 For examples of these features, see 3303, 3352, 5393, 5909, 9878, 10999, 13687, etc. (ed. J. E. Wulfing, EETS,OS 121–2, 1902–3).
13 See Young, *Troy and her Legend*, p. 120.
14 It appears in *Winner and Waster* as well as *Gawain* (and most extensively, of course, in Laȝamon) and is referred to familiarly in both.
15 Theodore Silverstein, 'Allegory and Literary Form', *PMLA*, LXXXII (1967),28–32 (p. 30).
16 This is the theme of my article, 'Gower's Narrative Art', in *PMLA*, LXXXI (1966),475–84.
17 Viz. *interpretatio* (tautology), periphrasis, comparison, apostrophe, prosopopeia, description and *oppositum* (antithesis): see *Poetria Nova*, 220–686, in Faral, *ed. cit.*
18 Ed. F. J. Carmody (Berkeley and L.A., 1948), III,13. See Hammond, *Chaucer to Surrey*, pp. 452–3.
19 *Confessio Amantis*, V,4175.
20 *Historia Destructionis Troiae*, ed. N. E. Griffin (Cambridge, Mass. 1936), p. 6.
21 Above, p. 100. It is characteristic of medieval poetry, in fact, though Chaucer recognises its comic potential by making it characteristic of Pandarus (e.g. *Troilus*, I,946).
22 See, for instance, how Lydgate expands Guido's 'Castor irato sermone respondit' (Griffin, p. 54) in II,1592–6.
23 I,2251, 2868, 3470, 3506, 3599.
24 I,2108–14. Nothing could be more irrelevant to these literary exercises than Renoir's view that they express a 'Renaissance' attitude to women, in which 'women are human beings, and each human being must be judged according to his own merits' (*Poetry of John Lydgate*, p. 86).

25 See above, p. 118.

26 It replaces some salacious pseudo-technical jargon in Guido (p. 25).

27 Gervaise of Melkley, the twelfth-century rhetorician, says: 'Perfecto versi-ficatori non hyemet, non estuet, non noctescat, non diescat sine astronomia.' See Curtius, *European Literature and the Latin Middle Ages*, pp. 275–6, and above, p. 86.

28 Viz. I,623, 1196, 1284, 2723, 3093, 3431, 3906; II,2378,3319,5067; III,1, 2667, 2745, 3564, 4449; IV, 629, 3363, 3579; V,1, 585.

29 E.g. III,15, 2749; IV,629, 3583. And it does not, of course, carry the faintly satirical flavour of the Franklin's 'This is as muche to seye' (*CT*, V,1018).

30 *John Lydgate*, p. 47, cf. p. 251. 'Lydgate must often have . . .' is a major technique of amplification in Schirmer's book.

31 The echoes of Chaucer, for instance, in I,3907–36.

32 Neither the alliterative *Destruction of Troy* nor the Laud *Troy Book* do any-thing of this sort, but both have to do a version of Guido's *locus amoenus* at Colchos (Griffin, p. 14), and provide an epitome of their styles in so doing, the former dense, vivid, substantive (326–48), the latter fluent, thin, and diffuse (539–52), against the richly derivative orotundity of Lydgate (I,1265–309).

33 E.g. 1–72, 1857, 2005, 3240, 3280, 3307, 4255.

34 Lydgate wrote a prose treatise on the theme, the *Serpent of Division* (ed. H. N. MacCracken, 1911), using the civil war of Caesar and Pompey as the classical model.

35 E. F. Jacob, *The Fifteenth Century* (Oxford 1961), pp. 305–7.

36 Griffin, p. 144; cf. *Troy Book*, III,1786–821.

37 The illustrator of MS.Royal 18.D.ii echoes the text in his highly expressive portrait of Criseyde on f. 88a.

38 *Op. cit.*, pp. 79ff, 154–65, 411–13, 487ff.

39 *Ars Versificatoria*, in Faral, *ed. cit.*, pp. 136–50.

40 M. J. Woods, 'Sixteenth-Century Topical Theory', *MLR*, LXIII(1968), 66–73 (p. 71).

41 See p. 110.

42 See above, p. 101.

43 There is a definitive note on quaking pens in Hammond, p. 448.

44 I,1556–7, 1562–3. See also I,160–1, II,552–60.

45 'Chaucer's Narrative Art', in *Chaucer and Chaucerians*, ed. Brewer, pp. 114–139 (p. 120).

46 A 'dramatic' reason for this is suggested in my article, 'The Squire as Story-teller', *Univ. of Toronto Quarterly*, XXXIV(1964),82–92.

47 It is parodied, like most rhetorical topics, in Shakespeare (*Midsummer Night's Dream*, IV.i).

48 IV,3004–53, 7054–95. See above, pp. 41 and 141.

49 Viz. Trinity O.5.2, Royal 18.D.ii and Digby 230. In MS.Add.18632 it

appears alongside Hoccleve's *De Regimine Principum*; in MS.Laud misc. 416 with the English translation of Vegetius *De Re Militari*. Both MSS. found their way into monastic libraries.

50 See A. Renoir, *The Poetry of John Lydgate*, p. 112. Note also the English MSS. mentioned above. Chaucer has an elaborate allusion to the story of Thebes in *Troilus* (V,1485–512), Diomede being Tydeus' son; and Criseyde was listening to it in her 'paved parlour' (II,84).

51 See above, p. 55.

52 See above, p. 66.

53 Especially the *De genealogia deorum* and *De claris mulieribus*. See the accounts of Amphion (186), Cadmus (293), the early life of Tydeus (1272), and Ipsiphyle (3171), and Lycurgus (3510).

54 See *The Poetry of John Lydgate*, pp. 117ff, and the articles by Renoir referred to there.

55 1051, 2298, 3992, 4014, 4256.

56 See the excellent article by R. W. Ayers, 'Medieval History, Moral Purpose, and the Structure of Lydgate's *Siege of Thebes*', *PMLA*,LXXII(1958),463-74.

57 Quoted in the EETS edition of *Thebes*, Part I, p. vii.

CHAPTER SIX

Laureate Lydgate

After the completion of the *Troy Book* and the *Thebes*, Lydgate moved into a larger world, and his poetic production during the next ten years reflects his contact with the many public concerns of this world. His pen was in demand for all kinds of occasions—a coronation, an entry, a piece of propaganda, a feast or celebration—and Lydgate was always willing. This was the period when Lydgate had the *de facto* status of an 'official' poet—not a court-poet, in the Chaucerian sense, but more of a public orator, who could be relied upon to produce something appropriately dignified for any occasion—and this status brought him commissions from ruling and middle classes alike. It is probable that he spent a good deal of time away from Bury during these years, and a lease of land in February 1423,[1] may be as much a recognition of his need of an independent income as a belated reward for the *Troy Book*. Further preferment was to follow in June of the same year when he was made prior of Hatfield Broadoak in Essex, near Bishop's Stortford. This was a small alien priory which had recently been appropriated to Bury: many of these small houses, often no more than cells, which owed their only allegiance to the founding-houses in France, had felt the cold wind of the Hundred Years' War, and expropriation, which Henry V carried on vigorously, was politically inevitable and often beneficial, for they were difficult to administer under the old system. Lydgate may have spent some time at Hatfield, but we may regard the post as essentially a sinecure. Between about 1426 and 1429 Lydgate was for a time in Paris, in the train of the duke of Bedford, and particularly closely associated with the earl of Warwick. In the years following he was back in England, dividing his time between the capital, the royal residence at Windsor, and Bury, but by 1432 he had relinquished the priorate of Hatfield, and on 8th April, 1434, he received official permission to return permanently to Bury, in a document which sanctioned a move he had probably already made.[2] By now, Lydgate was deeply committed to another colossal task, the translation of the *Fall of Princes* for the duke of Gloucester; he was chronically short of money; the flirtation with the world was over, and, as an old man, Lydgate returned to spend his last fifteen years in the monastery.

To trace Lydgate's poetic progress through the 1420s is not a difficult task, though it involves a degree of speculation. We can start from Ewelme, the home of Thomas Chaucer, and the poem that Lydgate wrote, as Shirley tells us (MS.Add.16165), 'at the Departyng of Thomas Chaucyer on Ambassade into France'. That Thomas Chaucer was the son of the poet we can now take, after a good deal of debate, as more or less certain.[3] He was a man of some eminence in the service of the state in the early fifteenth century, sheriff at various times, chief butler of the royal household, M.P. for Oxfordshire on many occasions between 1400 and 1430, Speaker of the House of Commons five times, and—the summit of any commoner's ambition—member of the Council, 1424–5. He was frequently on royal commissions, especially for raising money, but he was not an ambitious man, and much of his public career was as an instrument of Henry Beaufort, bishop of Winchester (later Cardinal), to whom, of course, he was related through his mother Philippa, sister of Katharine Swynford. Thomas Chaucer married Maude Burghersh, a rich Oxfordshire heiress, in 1393, and settled at the Burghersh manor of Ewelme, just south-east of Oxford. It is wholly probable that Lydgate made the acquaintance of the Chaucer family during his years at Oxford, and he kept up a close connection afterwards. The frequent and glowing references to Chaucer the poet in the *Troy Book* may be one result of this association; another may be the incorporation into Shirley's MSS. of a good deal of traditional information about the poet Chaucer, derived perhaps from the Chaucer family via Lydgate.

Thomas Chaucer, like his father, went on several diplomatic missions to the continent, and it was for his departure on one of these, whether in 1414, 1417, or 1420 it is hard to say, that Lydgate wrote his *propemticon*. Though the occasion is a classical one, the derivation of the poem is Chaucerian. The opening invocation of Lucyna and Neptune, to provide a calm sea and prosperous voyage, alludes to Aurelius' prayer in the *Franklin's Tale*, and Lydgate's praise of Thomas Chaucer's hospitality, of his civilised and bounteous household, reminds one of the Franklin:

'Saint Julyan, oure joye and al our glorye,

Come hoom ageyne, lyche as we desyre,
To suppowaylen al þe hole shyre.'[4]

Lydgate presumably knew this hospitality himself, and he refers also,
very politely, to Thomas's wife,

Lat be your weping, tendre creature,   (50)

and to 'gentyl Molyns', Sir William Moleyns, Chaucer's closest friend
among the local gentry, whose daughter Eleanor later became his
ward. The poem is altogether pleasing, and gives a picture of a gentle,
leisured and ordered life. It has no independent literary significance, but
any man going on a tedious and dangerous journey would have been
pleased to receive it, and to understand this is enough.

The love-poem called *My lady dere* is attached to the *Balade at the
Departing* by Shirley, as if it were offered by Lydgate as Thomas's
parting gift to his wife. The poem is so conventional and so innocent
of real allusion that this cannot be proved, but Lydgate probably had a
little stock of such poems that he kept for appropriate occasions, and
this was one of them. One MS adds a stanza, a 'Devynayle par Pycard',
with an anagrammatic explanation of the lady's name, but it has not
yet been deciphered.[5] It probably has nothing to do with Lydgate's
poem as originally written.

The Chaucer household provided Lydgate with a number of important contacts, probably, for instance, with Gloucester, of whom we shall
hear much, and certainly with the earls of Warwick and Salisbury, who
both commissioned works from Lydgate when he was in France.
Thomas Montacute, earl of Salisbury, was the second husband of
Alice, Thomas Chaucer's only child, and it was presumably at Alice's
instigation that Salisbury commissioned the *Pilgrimage* in 1426. She
continued her good offices on Lydgate's behalf after the death of
Salisbury and her marriage to William de la Pole, earl of Suffolk, who
was later to become the most powerful man in the country and the
engineer of Henry VI's marriage with Margaret of Anjou (1445).
Alice herself, as countess of Suffolk, was patroness of Lydgate's instructional poem on the *Virtues of the Mass*, and Suffolk too had an interest
in Lydgate. He owned the best MS. (Arundel 119) of the *Thebes*, and
supported Lydgate's application, in 1441, for the renewal of his grant
from the crown.[6] As a great East Anglian landowner, Suffolk was constantly associated with Bury, and sat on commission several times with
William Curteys, Lydgate's abbot. Here too he would have met Sir

Miles Stapleton, who, as sheriff of Norfolk, paid part of Lydgate's annuity in 1439,[7] and who was also the patron of the East Anglian poet John Metham, a great admirer of Lydgate.[8] Suffolk was himself a poet: Shirley ascribes a number of poems to him in MS.Trinity R.3.20, and there are more in MS.Fairfax 16 which are attributed to Suffolk by MacCracken.[9] Amongst these is the poem which Hammond prints and calls 'A Reproof to Lydgate'.[10] It begins as a praise of the daisy, to which, as he says, only Chaucer could do justice: but Chaucer is dead,

> And to the monke of Bury now speke I,
> For thy connyng ys syche and eke thy grace
> After Chaucer to occupye his place;
> Besechyng the my penne enlumyne
> This flour to prayse as I before have ment,
> And of these lettyrs let thy colours shyne
> This byll to forthir after myn entent.   (26–32)

There is a suggestion of parody, in the participle, of Lydgate's invocatory style, and Suffolk goes on to take Lydgate to task for being so rude about women:

> A fye! for schame, O thou envyous man!
> Thynk whens thou came and whider to repayr. . . .
> Knoke on thy brest, repent now and ever
> Ayen therwyth, and say thou saydyst yt never.   (64–70)

He advises him to get an attorney for when he is brought to court, and to be ready to pay compensation. The poem is a neat literary spoof, and the tone of playful condescension is what we might expect of an aristocratic poet who was also a friend (and gaoler) of that most aristocratic and sophisticated of poet-exiles, Charles d'Orléans.[11]

The *Balade at the Departing*, to return for a moment to Lydgate's poem, is eminently 'practical'; it depends upon its occasion, but within this context it has a civilised quality, an urbanity, which reminds one of Chaucer's minor poems. Most of Lydgate's poems during this period, however, were written for much more elevated occasions and patrons, and their style is appropriately inflated. The poem called *A Praise of Peace* takes up the theme of the *Troy*-epilogue and the *Thebes*, and develops it, with hypnotic ceremonial repetition of the word *pees*, through an elaborate series of Biblical and classical 'finding-places', down to the late wars of England and France and the present peace. It must have been written soon after the death of Henry V (see 182), and bears witness to Lydgate's continuing preoccupation with the theme of war and peace, as well as to his consistently accumulative techniques. To the same period belongs the poem that he addressed to the queen-mother Katherine, Henry's widow, and the pathetic survivor of the dream of Troyes. The *Valentine to her that Excelleth all* is a praise of the Virgin, with an envoy to the Queen which must precede her association with Owen Tudor in 1425. It is pure amplification, consisting almost wholly of topics of comparison drawn from classical sources ('Men speke of Lucresse . . .', 22–70) and of biblical allusions (71–105), but the familiar catalogues are framed in an invocation of secular love-poetry and the custom of choosing a lover on St. Valentine's day, which give the refrain

> But I love oone whiche excelleþe alle

a happy twist. Lydgate also refers to flower-poetry, like Chaucer's *Legend*-Prologue and the poem of Suffolk's just mentioned:

> I chase þat floure siþen goon ful yoore,
> And every yeere my choyse I shal renuwe.   (15–16)

At the end, in a surprising little cascade of Chaucerian allusion, he returns to the Valentine frame:

> Frome yeere to yeer for necglygence or rape,
> Voyde of al chaunge and of nufanglenesse,
> Saint Valentyne hit shal me not escape
> Upon þy day, in token of stedfastnesse,
> But þat I shal conferme in sikurnesse
> My choys of nuwe, so as it is befalle,
> To love hir best, whiche þat excelleþe alle.   (120–6)

The technique of offering an amorous 'bait' in a religious poem is familiar in the Middle Ages, as in the *Luve-Run* of Thomas of Hales or in a number of the Harley lyrics, but it is interesting to see how Chaucerian imitation acts as a spur to the often mechanical processes of Lydgate's mind.

   Lydgate wrote another poem for queen Katherine, according to Shirley's rubric (in MS.Add.29729) for *That now is Hay some-tyme was grase*, 'made at þe commaundement of þe Quene Kateryn as in here sportes she wallkyd by the medowes that were late mowen in the monthe of Julii'. The poem is one of the group of gnomic pieces with

refrain, to be dealt with in the next chapter, and it falls immediately
into systematic patterns of amplification: the multiplying of instances
of the world's transience, with particular reference to the *Ubi sunt* topos
of the Nine Worthy (65–88), followed by four whole stanzas of
miscellaneous antithesis,

> Nowe it is day, nowe it is nyght;
> Nowe it is fowlle, nowe it is feyre;
> Nowe it is derke, nowe it is lyght;
> Nowe clowdye mystes, nowe bryght ayre. . . .   (89–92)

The theme is universal in didactic poetry, and has always a potential
grandeur, but in this particular poem of Lydgate's it is made to sound
like the scratching of an old gramophone record—and it is difficult even
to tell when the needle has stuck.

Katherine was of the past, but Lydgate was already in contact with
Gloucester, the man of the future. Before the death of Henry V, he
wrote his laudatory piece *On Gloucester's Approaching Marriage* to
Jacqueline of Hainault (1422). Nothing could better illustrate Lydgate's
lack of contact with political realities, for Gloucester's marriage was by
any accounts a political disaster, alienating as it did the duke of Burgundy, the ally upon whom England's presence in France depended. But
even if he had understood this, it would have been hard to refuse such
a commission, and he solves any problems by retreating into abstract
generalities. Marriage, he says, is divinely established, and can bring
peace between realms, and he passes from this to eulogise Jacqueline,

> Truwe ensaumple and welle of al goodenesse,
> Benyngne of poorte, roote of goodelyheed,
> Sooþefast myrrour of beaute and fayrnesse   (65–7)

with extended use of the topics of comparison:

> Feyre was Heleyne, liche as bookes telleþe . . . .
> But sheo in goodnesse fer above excelleþe.   (78–80)

He does the same for Humphrey, culling his first examples, with frank
economy, from the recently completed *Troy* and *Thebes*—Paris,
Troilus, Hector, Tydeus—and ends with an invocation of the gods to
favour the marriage. It is not an Epithalamion in the usual sense of the
word; the celebration is of marriage purely as a dynastic arrangement,
and the rest is panegyric, but if it had to be done it is hard to know how

it could have been done better—flattering without being fulsome, dignified without being too ponderous.

Gloucester soon lost interest in Jacqueline and her territories, and if Lydgate wrote the *Complaint for my Lady of Gloucester* (1428) he could at least be said to be more consistent than his master. Gloucester's disloyalty provoked some outcry from Londoners, amongst whom he was generally very popular, and the *Complaint* expresses sympathy for Jacqueline and hope that the duke may break free of the sorceries which have made him neglect her. The ascription to Lydgate is a casual one in the late Shirley MS. Ashmole 59, and is contradicted by Shirley's own rubric, that it was written by 'a Chapellayne of my lordes of Gloucestre'. It is wholly unlikely that Lydgate would write a poem critical of his patron's personal conduct, and there is nothing in the style to argue for his authorship. The basing of the rhyme-royal stanza on a four-stress line is unusual for Lydgate, and the whole setting and narrative technique is foreign to his manner, as is the directness of the opening:

> A Solytarye, soore compleynyng,
> Sat weping by a water syde . . .

The *Complaint* should surely be rejected from the canon.

Lydgate's association with Gloucester was to bear fruit later in the *Fall of Princes*, but meanwhile Lydgate was in France. It was presumably at Warwick's instigation that he went, and the contact with Warwick may again have been Thomas Chaucer, who went with Warwick to France on the armistice negotiations of 1417. A number of poems are connected with Lydgate's stay in France, including major works like the *Pilgrimage* and the *Danse Macabre*, which we shall deal with later, as well as minor pieces like the *Devowte Invocacioun to Sainte Denys*, written at the request of Charles VI. The most immediate public consequence of his presence in France was the poem on the *Title and Pedigree of Henry VI*. Lydgate tells us that he began this on 28th July, 1427, giving a comprehensive 'sky-picture' for the day and hour,[12] and that it is a translation, made at Warwick's request, of the pedigree of Henry VI that Laurence Calot, king's secretary in France, did for the duke of Bedford. With what degree of satisfaction Warwick, himself an accomplished poet,[13] could have contemplated the final product it is difficult to say, for it is loosely constructed, repetitive, and sometimes difficult to follow (couplets tend to bring out the worst in Lydgate), but presumably its very size (329 lines), and the fact that it accompanied

Lydgate with a palmer presenting the book of *The Pilgrimage of the Life of Man* to Thomas Montacute, earl of Salisbury (see p. 173).

Lydgate praying for inspiration at the shrine of St. Edmund: *Life of St. Edmund.*

British Museum MS. Harley 2278, f.9a.

an impressive-looking genealogical tree, were sufficient to further the cause of English propaganda.[14] It is not well done, and Lydgate seems to miss the control of systematic 'topics', but that is his fault. It is not because the subject is fundamentally 'unpoetic': Shakespeare handled much the same sort of material in the Archbishop of Canterbury's speech in *Henry V*. Shakespeare gains in dramatic indirection what Lydgate loses in practical commitment to the world of action, but clearly both have the same notion of what can be done in poetry.

The mention of the earl of Warwick as a poet prompts a brief digression on another network of patrons with which Lydgate was connected. Warwick married, as his first wife, Elizabeth, daughter of Thomas, lord Berkeley: she herself, as we have seen,[15] inherited her father's literary interests (he was Trevisa's patron) and commissioned John Walton's verse translation of Boethius, and her daughter Margaret, who later married John Talbot, earl of Shrewsbury, continued the tradition of patronage by asking Lydgate to write the history of *Guy of Warwick* in honour of her father's family, probably about 1425. The story of Guy originated as an ancestral romance in the thirteenth century, one of many which celebrated the heroic exploits of the spurious founder of a noble family. So effective was the historical colouring in this case that the story was subsequently incorporated into English history, and was so regarded until the sixteenth century, and it is the Latin history of Gerardus Cornubiensis that Lydgate uses as his source. This version deals only with the 'historical' part of the original romance, that is, Guy's return to England as an unknown pilgrim to take up the single combat with the Danish champion Colbrand and so save Athelston's England from the Danes. The poem ends with Guy's return to Warwick, still in disguise, and his pious death in the arms of his wife, Felice.

There is a tradition that regards *Guy of Warwick* as Lydgate's worst poem, but the choice seems rather arbitrary. The only part of the poem that shows any power is the indignation at the beginning at the cruel ravages of the Danes, where Lydgate is probably drawing on the emotional associations of the St. Edmund story, but the rest is consistently serious and elevated in language, and must have served its purpose well. Lydgate uses the modified techniques of amplification of the *Thebes*, elaborating for instance on the Danish invasion as God's punishment for sin, with parallels from Biblical and classical story (33–72), and alluding briefly to the change of fortune in the sorrow-joy nexus of images:

12

The sonne is hatter after sharpe schours,
The glade morwe folweth the dirke nyght,
After wynter cometh May with fresshe flours,
And after mystys Phebus schyneth bright,
After trouble hertys be maad lyght. . . .   (81–5)

The narrative is comparatively economical, and the complex eight-line
stanza is managed without egregious padding. The effect of the whole,
however, is dull and ponderous, chiefly because Lydgate lacks any
power of highlighting the narrative so as to draw out its significance.
All he can do is relate it to moral commonplaces and these in themselves
are insufficiently developed to give it the weight of the *Troy* or the
Thebes. Selection and emphasis are alike lacking, and the narrative
slithers forward without perceptible motion, so that one is not even
aware, for instance, that the battle of Guy and Colbrand, the central
event of the story, has begun (381). It is not a failure in the portrayal of
character, such as Hammond speaks of,[16] but a failure in administration,
a 'contempt of interval' which is not counterbalanced by any effective
drawing-out of larger non-narrative significances.

Lydgate has a further association with Warwick through Warwick's
third wife, Isabella, daughter of Lord Despenser, for whom he wrote
the *Fifteen Joys of Our Lady*. This in its turn was one of several commissions for religious and devotional poems that Lydgate executed for
noble patronesses. For Anne, countess of Stafford, widow of the Stafford
killed at Shrewsbury, he wrote his *Invocation to St. Anne* (the practice
of commissioning works on a sainted namesake was common), and
for her daughter Ann, whose first husband was Edmund Mortimer,
5th earl of March, he wrote his *Legend of St. Margaret*. The further
ramifications of this family are interesting: the countess of Stafford
married as her second husband William Bourchier, head of the prominent East Anglian family, and their son Henry married Isabella, sister
of Richard, duke of York. Isabella was patroness of the *Life of St. Mary
Magdalen* by Osbern Bokenham, and important follower and admirer
of Lydgate,[17] and it was for her son William that Benedict Burgh,
Lydgate's closest disciple and the continuator of the *Secrees*, wrote his
version of the *Disticha Catonis*.

The cross-connections between these aristocratic families are endless,
and the multiplication of literary contacts and commissions would be
easy. There is one more lady-patron of Lydgate's whom we might
mention, however, who seems to belong to a slightly different class.

This is Lady Sibille Boys of Holm Hale in Norfolk, for whom it is suggested he wrote the *Epistle to Sibille* and probably the *Treatise for Lavenders*. The former is a skilful amplification of *Proverbs* 31:10–31 ('Who can find a virtuous woman? for her price is far above rubies'), its main theme being

> Þat moder of vyces is wilful ydelnesse,
> And grounde of grace is vertuous besynesse.   (132–3)

The mode of address and subject-matter of both poems suggest that they were written for a lady who had a good many day-to-day domestic concerns, and belonged therefore to the class of non-aristocratic gentry, like Agnes Paston. Lady Sibille perhaps stands as representative of a group of readers and patrons who played a larger part in Lydgate's literary production than we now know. The poems to her, like those to the other ladies, were probably written in this period of 1422–33, when Lydgate was in more general circulation.

Lydgate returned from France in time for the coronation of Henry VI, now nearly eight years old, at Westminster in November, 1429. In his capacity as poet-propagandist to the Lancastrian dynasty, he was asked to provide a number of poems for the occasion, and above all to celebrate the union of the two crowns of England and France in Henry VI. This he does in the *Roundell* to be sung 'ayens his coronacioun', and in the verses he composed to accompany the 'soteltes' at the coronation banquet. 'Soteltes' were a form of table-decoration, the ancestors of representational cake-icing, and were brought in, to the accompaniment of great ceremony, with each course. At this banquet they were ingeniously designed to emphasise the theme of union, one showing, for instance, the young king kneeling before St. Edward and St. Louis, another before St. George, St. Denys, and the Virgin, and Lydgate composed verses to be written on scrolls or tablets beside them, and read out, presumably, as the course was eaten. The food itself was not without significance, if we are to judge by 'Custade Rooial with a leparde of golde sittyng theryn' or 'Flampayne poudred with lepardis and floure de lices of golde', and the whole banquet is interesting as an example of fifteenth century 'applied art', though it lacks the extravagance of the Burgundian fête at Lille in 1454, where the table-decorations included

> 'a rigged and ornamented carack, a meadow surrounded by trees
> with a fountain, rocks and a statue of Saint Andrew, the castle

of Lusignan with the fairy Melusine, a bird-shooting scene near a
windmill, a wood in which wild beasts walked about, and lastly,
a church with an organ and singers, whose songs alternated with
the music of an orchestra of twenty-eight persons, which was
placed in a pie.[18]

Lydgate is more at home in the *Ballade to Henry VI on his Coronation*,
where he proclaims his descent from Edward and Louis, Arthur and
Charles, and urges him to unite the qualities of all of them, and of a
whole sonorous roll-call of kings and emperors (the Nine Worthy
topos expanded), ending with praise of his father and mother and a
compact orison-like envoy which recalls Polonius and the rich tradition
of classico-Christian gnomic platitude:

> Prynce excellent, be feythful, truwe and stable;
> Dreed God, do lawe, chastyce extorcyoun,
> Be liberal, of courage unmutable,
> Cherisshe þe Chirche with hoole affeccyoun,
> Love þy lyeges of eyþer regyoun,
> Preferre þe pees, eschuwe werre and debate,
> And God shal sende frome þe heven adoune
> Grace and goode hure to þy royal estate.   (121–8)

A king can rarely have been better served by his laureate: within its
unenviable limits, the *Ballade* is about as good as it could be.

The same may be said of the *Prayer for King, Queen and People*,
written not long before the Coronation (see lines 78–81). This solemn
invocation is based, stanza by stanza, on the sentences of the Latin
prayer 'Ab inimicis nostris defende nos, Christe', and it offers a further
demonstration of Lydgate's ability to handle any kind of material
competently. Like a good public speaker, he can always say something
appropriate to the occasion, which will sound impressive, never offend,
and at worst only send the audience to sleep. For, like the public
speaker, his role prevents him from ever saying anything striking or
unexpected, and he can never draw our attention to the language he is
using as anything but serious, consistent, and decorous.

After his coronation at Westminster, Henry VI was taken to France,
where he was crowned in Paris amidst scenes of great apathy. Determined to erase the memory of this fiasco, the authorities arranged a
great triumphal entry for the young king on his return to London.
Lydgate has left us a long verse-account of this occasion, describing

how the king was met at Blackheath by the Mayor, aldermen, and citizens and then led in procession through the streets of London in which, at seven fixed stations, a series of elaborate allegorical tableaux enacted the hopes, joys, and exhortations of the king's loyal subjects. First, at the entrance to London Bridge, was a giant champion, with an inscription declaring that he would put down all the king's enemies; he was supported by two antelopes bearing the arms of England and France. In the middle of the bridge a tower bore three empresses, Nature, Grace, and Fortune, who offer their gifts of wisdom, strength, and prosperity, and seven virgins clad in white, who offer the seven gifts of the Holy Ghost. At Cornhill was the tabernacle of Dame Sapience, with the Seven Liberal Arts and their representatives (Logic with Aristotle, Rhetoric with Cicero, &c.), and so on through Cheapside and past St. Paul's to Westminster, where the great sceptre of St. Edward was delivered to the king:

> Thouh it were longe, large, and of grete weyht,
> Yitt on his shuldres the Kyng bare it on heyht. (480–1)

This pageant, with its mixture of Biblical and classical learning and its strongly moral and hortatory purpose, is clearly the work of Lydgate, who is thus in the position of an artistic director, or 'devisor',[19] who writes his own souvenir programme. He was given the commission partly because of the loyal work that he had already done for the crown, partly because of the evidence he had provided of his skill in devising 'mummings' for the London guilds at various festivals. And if Lydgate was the director, the producer was John Carpenter, town clerk of London, a man of some learning, and similar tastes to Lydgate. His library was large, mostly in Latin, and included many of Lydgate's favourite moral-encyclopaedic works, such as the *Secreta Secretorum* and Vincent of Beauvais' *Speculum morale*, as well as the works of Alanus and more recent books such as Richard of Bury's *Philobiblon* and Petrarch's *De remediis utriusque Fortunae*.[20] Carpenter probably provided the Latin inscriptions actually incorporated in the tableaux (which Lydgate expands in English in his account) and co-operated with Lydgate in the devising of the pageant.

The flexibility of our concept of poetry is given a sharp test by Lydgate's verses for the *Triumphal Entry*. Ultimately, of course, it cannot stand as a 'poem' and can relate only to the event; a souvenir programme may mean a lot to the person who was there, at the performance, but precious little to anyone who was not. But the performance itself, in this case, is of great interest, for, as Wickham points out,[21] these 'pageant theatres of the streets' were extremely influential in the development of drama and stagecraft, probably more so than the miracle plays themselves. They were genuinely national, communal, and popular experiences and included in their *dramatis personae* both 'real' and allegorical characters. They lead, claims Wickham,

> 'in a patently direct line through Tudor chronicles to plays like *Gorboduc*, *The Misfortunes of Arthur* or *Endymion* with their exposi-tional dumbshows and acutely personal allegory and thus to Shakespeare's History Plays with their thinly veiled sermons on government' (*op. cit.*, p. 63)

Here is another link between Lydgate and Shakespeare, and another mark of how Lydgate could combine a total lack of originality with an extraordinary readiness to experiment. Lydgate's desire to verbalise the whole experience is also interesting: he will not allow the tableaux to speak for themselves, for fear of misunderstanding, and he elaborates the point of each with great care; and finally he embodies the whole performance in literary form. Providing words for pictures (the oppo-site of *ut pictura poesis*) is a characteristic occupation of Lydgate's, as we shall see later in this chapter, and perhaps it is another indication of the completely non-visual nature of his imagination.

It is time now to turn from these genuinely occasional works to the two poems, written or commissioned during the years in France, which have, or should have, a claim as literature. The first is the long *Pilgrimage of the Life of Man*, a translation of the *Pèlerinage de la Vie Humaine* of Guillaume de Deguileville. Deguileville was a Cistercian monk of the early fourteenth century, and, just as his fellow-Cistercians took over the Arthurian legend, particularly the Grail, for spiritual-didactic pur-poses, so he took over the techniques of the *Roman de la Rose* to offer an allegorical account of man's life on earth, from cradle to grave. He followed this up with the *Pèlerinage de l'Ame*, describing the progress of the soul after death, and completed a neat trilogy with the *Pèlerinage de Jésus-Christ*, in which the life of Christ, as in *Piers Plowman*, is nar-rated as model and exemplar, with much attention, again as in Lang-land, to the debate of the Four Daughters of God on the doctrine of the Atonement. Langland does not appear to have known Deguileville (nor does Bunyan), but in the fifteenth century he had something of a vogue and several translations and versions of the first two *Pèlerinages* appeared, in addition to Lydgate's.[22] The duke of Bedford was particularly active in promoting his work. Lydgate's own translation was begun in France in 1426, as he tells us, at the request of Thomas Montacute, earl of Salisbury, second husband of Alice Chaucer, who was presumably instrumental in bringing patron and poet together. It was finished by 1428, when Salisbury died, unless we assume that the abruptness of the end, and the lack of the usual dedicatory epilogue, indicate that the patron was already dead. It should be made clear that Lydgate's authorship of the *Pilgrimage* is only presumptive, since he does not name himself in the poem, which is perhaps somewhat unexpected in such a long work. Ascriptions in the three manuscripts (one is a mere fragment, and one is a Stow MS.) are of the sixteenth century or later, and the famous drawing of 'Lidgat presenting his Booke, called the Pilgrime, unto the Earle of Salisbury' is not a frontispiece to a 'luxurious dedication copy' of the *Pilgrimage*, as Schirmer calls it,[23] but a paste-in on the title-page of MS. Harley 4826, which is a manuscript of *St. Edmund*, the *Secrees* and Hoccleve.[24] The drawing itself is fifteenth century, but the inscription quoted above is of the late sixteenth century. None of this would deny Lydgate's authorship: sixteenth century traditions usually have some basis in fact, and Stow is not always unreliable. The Prologue is certainly authentic, with its elaboration of man's life under Fortune as a series of antitheses,

> Wo after joye, and after song wepyng   (31)

its development of the idea of life as a pilgrimage, as in the *Troy*-epilogue,

> Trusteth ther-for, ye folk of every age,
> That yowre lyff her ys but a pylgrymage   (45-6)

and the string of modesty-topics with which it ends:

> Nor I drank no-wer of the sugryd tonne
> Of Jubiter, couchyd in hys celer,
> So strange I fonde to me hys boteler,
> Of poetys i-callyd Ganymede.   (176-9)

The Prologue is in pentameter-couplet, and in one of Lydgate's richer veins. The rest of the poem is in short couplet, and the lack of amplification and the poverty of style prompt one to a tentative suggestion that it may have been sub-contracted out by Lydgate, who must have been under heavy pressures during these years. It would thus be like a good deal of contemporary painting, the work of a 'school' rather than a master. Lydgate would still bear the responsibility for it, however, and I shall write of it as his.

After his own Prologue, Lydgate goes on, as in the *Troy Book*, to translate his author's, where Deguileville tells how this was the second version of a dream he had in 1330, the first having been pirated (308). The dream follows. After seeing a vision of the Holy City and deciding to be a Pilgrim, the dreamer is taken, after a delay of nine months, into the house of Grace-Dieu, 1330 years old (860), and there initiated into the mysteries of baptism and confirmation, with much advice from Reason on his conduct in the pilgrimage (3230). The eucharist is defended against the objections of Aristotle and Nature, and Penance and Charity explain their offices (6197). Grace-Dieu advises him on the custody of the senses, on keeping his eyes in his ears, and gives him lengthily allegorised scrip and staff, Latin poems on the Creed, etc., and various pieces of allegorical armour which his fleshly weakness makes it hard for him to bear (10304). He now meets, as he at last sets out on the pilgrimage, Rude Entendement (i.e. Ignorance), who is put down by Reason, and then Youth, who leads him off on the wrong route at the fateful fork in the way where sit Labour and Idleness (12749). He meets various sins, who explain themselves politely and then attack him, usually being thwarted by the intervention of Grace-Dieu in the form of a white dove—Gluttony, Venus, Sloth, Pride, Envy, Wrath, Tribulation (whose commission is ambiguous), and Avarice (18470). He now starts meeting more intellectual obstacles, Necromancy, Heresy, and the like, and has a difficult time in the sea of Satan and on Fortune's wheel (19974). He has arguments about astrology, meets Idolatry, Sorcery, and Conspiracy, and a Siren explains the whirling Tower of worldly Gladness and throws him in the sea (21716). Grace-Dieu arrives with the Ship of Religion, upon which he chooses the Cistercian castle; here he is introduced to people like Hagiography, Poverty, and Prayer, seeing something too of abuses within the church, and of Apostasy (24130). Old Age and Sickness now come to warn of Death's approach, and his prayers to God precede his awakening.

Lydgate expands 18123 lines to 24832 but adds very little of his own —some etymologising on *glaive* (2449), explanations of hard words like *elenchus* (1671) and *synderesis* (4963), and one brief excursion into the old world of spring-description (3451-92) in Nature's account of her work. Mostly he relies on familiar techniques of padding—tags, reduplication, and tautology—techniques too basic to be called amplification. Here for instance is how he tackles God's promise of eternal life to Adam and Eve:

> Il leur fist si grant courtoisie,
> Et leur donna tele franchise,
> Qu'ilz povoient vivre sans languir,
> Sans necessite de mourir.[25]

> Cf. God, of hys gret curteysye,
> To hem dyde suyche gentrye
> As to the I shal devyse.
> He gaff to hem so gret fraunchyse
> T'a'lyved evere, thys no lesyng,
> In elthe withoute languysshyng,
> Lusty and fressh in o degre,
> Never t'ave had necessyte
> Of deyyng. . . .   (1015–23)

There is some ludicrous use of the litotes-formula, e.g.

> And hyr ovene was of old
> Verray hote and nothyng cold.   (5445–6)

The technique of reduplication is well illustrated in this passage:

> Or est le point, comme tay dit,
> Que te tiengne mon conuenant.

> Cf. The tyme ys good and covenable,
> As I ha sayd, and acceptable
> That I my promys and my graunt
> Holde unto the, and my covenaunt.   (7199–202)

When all else fails, the French can be put in as well:

> I love no thyng, thys the cas,
> Hih nor lowe, hault nor baas.   (14897–8)

The tags are more obvious, more gross, raw and undigested than any-where else in Lydgate, though it must be admitted that the editors' habit of bracketing them makes them stand out even more glaringly.[26] One would have thought that the couplets where *both* rhymes are provided by tags might have been avoided.

Lydgate seems to have been dead to Chaucer here. A passage comparing bad priests to negligent shepherds (17981–99) evokes no reminiscence of lines in Chaucer that seem imperishable by contrast. He does, however, dutifully quote Chaucer's translation of Deguileville's ABC poem to the Virgin at the appropriate point in the narrative (19791), with a tribute to Chaucer which echoes the *Troy Book*, and there is another prayer to Mary, four ballade stanzas (16947), in a totally distinct style, very similar to Lydgate's other poems to the Virgin, which is like an oasis in a desert, or, as Furnivall puts it, a nugget of ore in his acres of clay.

The allegory is strangely literal, the correspondences intellectual rather than imaginative, involving a degradation and diminishing of the concept rather than a heightening of awareness: Penance appears with a hammer (to break the resistance of the Flesh) and a besom in her mouth (to cleanse); Memory has eyes in the back of her head; Detraction is Envy's cook and makes her a broth of the good names she has stolen from men; Tribulation is heaven's goldsmith, with a hammer of persecution and tongs of distress; Astronomy is half-hidden, the lower half being astrology. It is curiously Bosch-like at times, as in the sea of Satan the Hunter, where pilgrims swim, some feet uppermost, some flying, some with their feet clogged in weeds (19069). There is very little action to sustain the allegory, and little attempt to actualise it, to make it mean more, not less, than what it represents: thus Venus, for instance, is portrayed as foul and ugly from the start (13097). The problem that Langland solved so superbly, that is, of giving a transcendental meaning to life without denying the nature of life or destroying its reality, the problem that Chaucer faced briefly at the end of the *Troilus*, is here hardly recognised as a problem. The literal level is treated with contempt, and it is this contempt which pervades the poem, giving the impression that its attitudes are harsh, narrow, and doctrinaire, whereas in fact they are no different from those of Langland or any other orthodox medieval writer. The failure of the poem, it must be stressed, is a failure of literary, dramatic, and imaginative technique, specifically a failure to embody spiritual concepts in meaningful literary form.

All this, of course, is Deguileville's responsibility,[27] but the prospects for a Lydgate-translation are bleak indeed. With no stimulus from Chaucer, with his general imperviousness to allegory as a form, and with the task of handling an allegory so mechanically conceived, Lydgate had really no chance of success. From him we get no comment, no heightening, no rhetoric, no attempt at communication—in a word, no style—but only a raw, barren, arid waste of words. Verse never seemed cheaper. One would gladly salvage the prologue and the poems to the Virgin and consign the rest to the outer darkness.

Writing of the *Danse Macabre*, the other poem of the French years, is a more congenial task. This work is a close translation of the French text originally inscribed on the cloister walls of the Church of the Holy Innocents in Paris in 1424. There it accompanied a fresco showing death, in the form of a decomposing corpse, leading figures representative of the various grades of society, from the Pope down to the labourer, in a grim dance. This theme of the 'dance of death',[28] best known to us from Holbein's engravings, became widespread in the fifteenth century, in murals, painting, and literature, drawing with increasingly morbid elaboration on a medieval preoccupation with death which was at once imaginatively rich and morally salutary. The origins of the dance of death are associated with the motif of the Three Living and the Three Dead, which appears frequently in wall-painting, as at Longthorpe tower, near Peterborough;[29] but a more specific original for the dance may be in dramatised sermons, in which figures of death and his victims passed before the pulpit as the preacher thundered his warnings—and no doubt he would have made his own connections between this 'dance' and the dancing in the churchyard which so horrified the clergy and the wave of compulsive dancing that seems to have swept Europe after the Black Death. The name *Danse macabre* has been the subject of some speculation: the likeliest explanation is that *macabre* is the name of a French writer who wrote an early *danse*. Lydgate's reference to 'the daunce of Machabre' (46) supports this interpretation.

Lydgate tells us that he made his translation at the request of 'frensshe clerkis' (22). He received a further request from John Carpenter in 1430 to have the verses inscribed on the cloister walls of Pardon churchyard, near St. Paul's, where the dance of death, 'commonly called the dance of Pauls', was 'artificially and richly painted'. Stow's account, from which these quotations come,[30] makes it sound that Carpenter's was the original commission, but this cannot be, in view of what Lydgate says. However, there do seem to be two distinct groups among the twelve manuscripts of the *Danse Macabre*, which indicate an unusually extensive revision on Lydgate's part, and it may have been Carpenter's request that prompted him to take up the work again. The cloister was pulled down in 1549 for the building of Somerset house.

In the *Danse Macabre*, what Lydgate had to do for once happily coincided with what he could best do. There is no need for any development of ideas, no narrative, no exposition, only variation, reiteration, insistence on the call of death and man's reply, a prolonged and varied antiphon—'You must die': 'I must die'. Moreover, the French octo-syllabic eight-line stanzas are compact and forceful, and Lydgate clearly relishes the gnomic last lines of each stanza:

> Alle be not mery wich þat men se daunce   (392)
> Some have faire eyȝen þat see nevere a dele   (408)

With such a good source and such clear direction, Lydgate's translation is extremely skilful. He catches well the grim satire of Death's words to the fat Abbot,

> Who þat is fattest, I have hym behiȝt,
> In his grave shalsonnest putrefie   (239–40)

and the way Death adapts his language to the office of the victim, to the Bailiff, for instance,

> ȝe must come to a newe assise,
> Extorciouns and wronges to redres   (267–8)

or to the Empress:

> Lat se your hand, my lady, dame Empresse,
> Have no disdeyn with me for to daunce.
>   (65–6, Lansdowne MS. only)

The replies too have a sharp dramatic propriety, like the wry self-awareness of the King,

> I have not lernyd here aforn to daunce,
> No daunce in sooth of footyng so savage   (113–14)

or the bluster of the Sergeant-at-Law:

> Howe dare þis deþe sette on me areste,
> Þat am þe kinges chosen officere!   (369–70)

Even to the child is given a strange pathetic reality:

> A, A, A, o worde I can not speke;
> I am so ȝonge, I was bore ȝisterday. . . .
> I cam but nowe and nowe I goo my way.   (585–9)

Lydgate's own additions to the French, particularly the women (the Princess, the Abbess—with hints from Chaucer—and the 'Gentil-womman amerous'), concede nothing to the original. He is the most perfect of imitators.

The prevailing tone is not one of morbid excess. There is little prolonged contemplation of the physical fact of death, but rather a grim
satisfaction in the levelling of rank: death is inevitable, but it is some
compensation to know that it is inevitable for everyone. Nor is the
gloom unrelieved: the note of affirmation is sharp by contrast, first in
the words of the Carthusian,

> Unto þe worlde I was dede longe agone   (353)

and finally in the measured calm of the Hermit,

> Life in desert, callid solitarie,
> May aȝein deþe have no respite ne space.
> At unset our his comyng doth not tarie,
> And for my part, welcome be goddes grace   (617-20)

to which Death, stripped of the splendid necrophily of art, can only
reply 'That is wel seide'.

The intrinsic interest of the *Danse Macabre* is not limited by its
practical function, as the occasional poems are by their occasion, and it
may be worth making this distinction. The occasions and roles of
poetry, however, are in continuous, unbroken relation with life, inter-
lock at every level, and the flexibility and comprehensiveness of this
concept of poetry are well illustrated in a particular way in the *Danse
Macabre*, in the free exchange between text and mural illustration. The
word is not sealed off from the picture, as it is after the invention of
printing, and it is interesting to recall in this connection the subtle
associations between text and illustration in medieval manuscripts,[31]
and also the habit of incorporating scrolls and writing in pictures,[32] a
technique which is now confined in degraded form to cartoons. Lydgate was particularly active in exploring this borderland of word and
picture, though he did so quite unconsciously and would not have been
aware of a borderland. We have seen examples of this already in the
Title and Pedigree, in the *Soteltes* and in the *Triumphal Entry*, as well as
the *Danse*, and there are others, even more striking.

The poem *Bycorne and Chychevache*, for instance, deals with two
legendary monsters, the former fat, since he feeds on patient husbands,
the latter lean (*chiche*, as in *Havelok*, 1763), since she feeds on patient
wives. It was an old fantasy of anti-feminist literature, and Chaucer
makes reference to Chichevache in the Envoy to the *Clerk's Tale*. It
became popular in murals and tapestries in the fifteenth century, the

most famous example being the mural paintings in the castle of
Villeneuve-Lembron in France.[33] Shirley's rubric tells us that Lydgate's
verses were written to accompany a painted cloth:

> Loo sirs þe devise of a peynted or desteyned clothe for an halle a
> parlour or a chaumbre devysed by Johan Lidegate at þe request of
> a werþy citeseyn of London.

Lydgate develops the theme, with a good deal of allusion to the *Clerk's
Tale* and its Envoy, in a series of 'scenes', in which the beasts speak, and
their victims, and finally 'an olde man with a baston on his bakke
manassing þe beest for þe rescowing of his wyff'. Schirmer assumes that
this indicates a pantomimic mumming (and one of Shirley's running
titles calls it 'þe fourome of desguysinges'), with the poet speaking the
verses, but the use throughout of the expression 'And þane shalle þeer
be purtrayed'[34] suggests that the verses were actually meant to accompany the painted cloths, perhaps a sequence of them, like a strip cartoon,
with the words written on scrolls between, as in the Villeneuve paintings. It should be made clear that the pictures referred to in Lydgate's
poem are painted or stained cloths, as the rubric says, not tapestries, as
Hammond and Schirmer assume. Citizens of London, however 'werþy',
were not likely to be able to afford tapestries as elaborate as this.[35]

The poem *Of the Sodein Fal of Princes in oure dayes* has usually been
referred to as another 'tapestry' poem.[36] It is a tiny offshoot of the *De
Casibus* tradition, dealing with more recent princes (perhaps in imitation of Chaucer's 'modern instances' in the *Monk's Tale*) such as
Richard II, Thomas of Gloucester and John of Burgundy. Its seven
stanzas clearly refer to some form of pictorial representation—
'Beholde.... Se howe.... Se nowe.... Lo here'—though there is no
rubric. Robbins believes it to be a mumming, like the Christmas
Mumming of the Seven Philosophers in MS. Trinity R.3.19,[37] but its closest
associations are with the processional, in which a series of figures pass
before the reader or in the movement of the spectator's eyes. The
medieval technique of isolating significant figures in a series of 'stills',
related by concept rather than by organic composition,[38] to which the
very nature of glass-painting and panel-painting lent itself so readily, is
here translated directly into a technique of verbal composition. Saints
in their niches or vertical lights, the Nine Worthy in a tapestry sequence
such as that in the Cloisters, New York (where they are portrayed in
architectural niches), are evidence of the same principle of conceptual
organisation as the processional sequences of the *Fall* literature or, for

that matter, of the *Danse Macabre*. For a writer so close to basic medieval habits of thought as Lydgate, one would extend the principle even further, for it enters into his handling of material which naturally resists such organisation, namely narrative: the *Troy Book* achieves its greatest effectiveness when Lydgate turns it into a series of formal laments on the falls of princes.

The religious poetry will be dealt with later, but some of it is interesting for this discussion of word and picture. Shirley's rubric to the *Legend of St. George* tells us that it is 'þe devyse of a steyned halle of þe lyf of Saint George . . . made with þe balades at þe request of þ'armorieres of London for þ'onour of þeyre broþerhoode and þeyre feest of Saint George', and the poem begins:

> O yee folk þat heer present be,
> Wheeche of þis story shal have inspeccion,
> Of Saint George yee may beholde and see
> His martirdome, and his passyon.

The poem was presumably read out when the series of mural paintings were first presented to the guild. As befits the occasion and the audience, it is remarkably straightforward and free of the amplification that Lydgate generally introduced in purely literary treatment of saints' lives. The poem *Mesure is Tresour* was written for a similar occasion: it goes through the estates of society, showing the importance of moderation in all human affairs, and referring to the 'portrature' (108) which it accompanies. In the last two stanzas a shepherd, symbolic of the church, speaks in his own person, and these verses were probably inscribed beside a portrait of such an allegorical shepherd, placed at the entrance of the house as if to protect it (149).

More obvious, and more practical, are the poems which 'explain' pictures, like the poem on *The Image of Our Lady*,

> Beholde and se this glorious fygure,

which Lydgate wrote to accompany a copy, made for Ralph Gelebronde at the request of Archdeacon John Thornton, of the painting of Our Lady by St. Luke in the church of St. Maria del Populo in Rome. The purpose of these verses was to explain the precise indulgence (i.e. remission of penance in purgatory) granted to those who came to pray before this image at particular feasts. *The Dolerous Pyte of Crystes Passioun* is similar:

> Erly on morwe, and toward nyght also,
> First and last, looke on this fygure. . . .
> My bloody woundis, set here in picture,
> Hath hem in mynde knelyng on your kne.   (1–2, 5–6)

For those who pray before this *imago pietatis*, the last stanza specifies an indulgence of 26,000 years and thirty days. This type of picture is associated with an iconographic theme which is characteristic of the fifteenth century, and which provided one of the most familiar motifs of mural decoration, 'Christ covered with wounds, and surrounded by the implements of the Passion'. Caiger-Smith draws attention to a German MS. in which such a picture is linked with a written exposition,[39] while Rosemary Woolf says of Lydgate's *Dolerous Pyte*, 'Like many of Lydgate's poems it would seem to demand an illustrated, devotional manuscript. . . . Possibly, however, the poem is primarily intended to supply the kind of devotional thoughts which should precede the liturgical exercise, which itself will be performed in church.'[40] Lydgate's poem on *Cristes Passioun*, an address by Christ from the cross, was intended, judging from the Envoy, to be hung on a scroll beside the crucifix:

> Go, lytel bylle, with al humylyte
> Hang affore Jesu, that list for man to bleede,
> To-fore his cros pray folk that shal the see,
> Onys a day this compleynt for to reede.   (113–16)[41]

The poem *On the Image of Pity* accompanied a *Pieta*,

> Turne hidder in hast, knelle doun, behold and se
> The moder of Cryst, whose hert was woo begon   (3–4)

explaining its purpose as a memorial and a call to penance:

> To suche entent was ordeynt purtreture
> And ymages of dyverse resemblaunce,
> That holsom storyes thus shewyd in fygur
> May rest with us with dewe remembraunce.   (37–40)

Lydgate's poems may look to us rather lengthy to be inscribed on a wall or scroll, but there is near-contemporary evidence of the practice in the Clopton chapel of Holy Trinity at Long Melford. This Suffolk church, which belonged to Bury, was rebuilt by the monks in the late fifteenth century, and they incorporated into the wall-decoration six stanzas from Lydgate's *Lamentation of Mary Magdalen* and twenty-six from his *Testament*, the former on a ceiling-beam at the west-end, the latter on a series of plaques running round the chapel at the top of the wall.[42] At one time the whole wall-space seems to have been covered with inscriptions, mottoes, and pictures. Such extensive use of 'textual decoration' is not usual, but it provides striking testimony to the free interplay of word and picture, book and wall.

The last of this group of poems is rather different, for its relation to its pictorial occasion is itself a literary device. In the *Fifteen Joys and Sorrows of Mary*, Lydgate tells how he opened a book of meditations in the small hours and came upon a picture of Mary:

> Lyke a pyte depeynt was the figure
> With weepyng eyen, and cheer most lamentable.
>
> (10–11)

Before her knelt one in devout prayer, intermingling the prayers with ballades in reverence of her fifteen joys and sorrows. Lydgate's poem purports to be 'the said balladys'. The imitation of the real in the imaginary occasion[43] is an interesting extension of the interchange between word and picture I have been discussing, and the device is repeated in *Horse, Goose and Sheep* (line 18), but the fictional use of a picture to prompt a poem is of course not really separate from the fictional use of a book, as in Chaucer or Henryson, and that is a much larger issue.

Many of the poems that have been mentioned in the preceding pages, such as the *Triumphal Entry* and the *Life of St. George*, relate to occasions which verge on the dramatic. The *Mummings* carry this idea of dramatic performance a stage further, in some cases as far as the distribution of speech, though various forms blend one into another. The simplest form is represented in a poem which is not called a Mumming at all, but a *Pageant of Knowledge*. The textual history of this piece is complex, since parts of it could be detached at will, but the first part of the complete text (in MS. Trinity R.3.21) is clearly a tableau-presentation of the seven estates, the seven virtues of Sapience, the founders and exemplars of the seven liberal arts, the seven planets and the twelve signs of the zodiac. Some passages are more obviously pantomimic than others, and there is one stanza where the tableau-group, the seven estates, each speak a line individually, the scribe having inserted speech-prefixes as in a play. The second part of the text in MS. Trinity R.3.21 is really a separate piece, and corresponds, with some variation, to what is copied as a separate poem in MS. Harley 2255. It is a systematic exposition of the four elements, the four complexions and the four seasons, designed to demonstrate the mutable disposition of the world:

> Tytan somwhyle fresshly doþe appere,
> Then commeþ a storme and doþ hys lyght deface;
> The soile of somer with floures glad of chere
> Wynters rasure doþe all awey rase;
> All erþely þynges sodenly do passe
> Whyche may have here no seker abydyng,
> Eke all astates false fortune doth manase;
> How shuld a man þan be stedfast of lyvyng! (264–71)

It is a didactic poem with no reference to performance at all.

The Mummings themselves are seven in number, all preserved in Shirley MSS. alone. They are semi-dramatic in form, consisting of verses designed to accompany dumb-shows or 'mummings' presented before court and civic audiences on festival occasions. They are of great importance in the history of drama,[44] and one of them is a considerable achievement in its own right. Five of them are short, about a hundred lines each, and represent the basic form: all five are in rhyme-royal, whereas the two longer and more significant ones are in couplet.

The *Mumming at Eltham* was the first to be composed, 'made at Eltham in Cristmasse, for a momyng tofore þe kyng and þe Qwene', probably in 1424. The king is the three-year-old Henry VI, the queen his mother. The verses for the mumming are spoken by one speaker, maybe Lydgate himself,[45] who presents Bacchus, Juno, and Ceres sending gifts,

> Wyne, whete, and oyle by marchandes þat here be, (5)

betokening peace, gladness, and plenty. There is the suggestion of two groups of actors, one group of three deities in a tableau, another group of 'marchandes' who present the actual gifts. The whole piece is extremely formal, and adheres closely to literary convention, even to the ballade-like repetition of the last line of each stanza.

The *Mumming for the Mercers* was written for a performance put on by the silk-merchants before Mayor Eastfield on the feast of the eve of Epiphany (January 6th), 1429. The presentation this time is by Jupiter's herald, who describes how he has come to visit the Mayor,

Doune coosteying, as bookys maken mynde,
By Lubyes landes, thorughe Ethyope and Ynde;
Conveyed doune, where Mars in Cyrrea
Haþe bylt his paleys upon þe sondes rede,
And she, Venus, called Cytherrea,
On Parnaso, with Pallas ful of drede.   (6–11)

The mention of the well of the Muses, by which he has passed, introduces a catalogue of poets, and the whole passage is an excursus into
classical geography which would have delighted an audience of aspiring
civic dignitaries: it appealed very much to Shirley, who adds much
marginal comment ('Ovyde and Virgilius weren olde poetes'). But
the climax of the evening was to come, for, as he approached England,
Jupiter's herald saw a series of allegorical ships—and presumably so did
the audience in the mercers' hall[46]—from which 'certein estates'
descended to greet the Mayor. The mummers were probably dressed as
oriental merchants[47] bringing rich gifts of silk to Eastfield.

    The *Mumming for the Goldsmiths* followed less than a month later, on
February 2nd, 1429, 'upon Candelmasse day at nyght, after souper',
again before Mayor Eastfield. The presenter is Fortune, who introduces
David and the twelve tribes of Israel, bringing the Ark of the Covenant,
'bright as the sonne beeme', with its gifts of wisdom, peace, and justice.
The Ark would be of gold, befitting the occasion, and contained a
scroll, inscribed with advice,

        Where yee shal punysshe and where as yee shal spare,
        And howe þat Mercy shal Rygour modefye.   (87–8)

A feature of this performance was the song of the Levites who bore the
Ark:

        Syngeþe for joye, þatþe earke is sent
        Nowe to þe Mayre with hoole and truwe entent.
                                                        (34–5)

This would come in the middle of the Mumming.

    Later in the same year, Lydgate did another Christmas mumming for
Henry VI, the *Mumming at Windsor*, showing 'howe þ'ampull and þe
floure de lys came first to þe kynges of Fraunce by myrakle at Reynes'.
Since the king was about to leave for France to be crowned, and
anointed from this very ampulla, the subject was highly appropriate.
The presentation is again extremely formal: the verses are spoken by

an unnamed speaker, almost certainly Lydgate himself, and precede, not accompany, the dumb-show of the events they describe. There is one moment of levity, when Lydgate speaks of the faith and truth of St. Clotilda, and adds, blandly,

> It is no wonder, for wymmen soo beon echoon.   (49)

Shirley comments, 'A daun Johan, est y vray?'

One of the most interesting of the Mummings, though it does not seem to vary much the simple method of performance, is the *Mumming at Bishopswood*, 'sente by a poursyvant to þe Shirreves of London, accompanyed with þeire breþerne upon Mayes daye at Busshopes wod, at an honurable dyner, eche of hem bringginge his dysshe'. Schirmer thinks of this as a picnic, but the idea is ludicrous. The 'poursyvant', or herald, introduces Flora, Veer (*ver*, spring) and May, and celebrates the happiness that they bring, with elaborate allegorical interpretation:

> Wynter shal passe of hevynesse and trouble,
> Flowres shal springe of perfite charite,
> In hertes þere shal be no meninge double,
> Buddes shal blosme of trouþe and unytee. . . .   (43–6)

Norton-Smith, who edits the poem in his selections, suggests that the mummers brought branches and flowers as 'soteltes' to grace the table (p. 123). Despite the pretty occasion, there is not much reason to congratulate Lydgate on the execution of his task, for the verse, though it refers to some of his most cherished notions of the scientific and philosophical basis of spring-description, is cumbersome and awkward.

The *Mumming at London*, presented 'to-fore þe gret estates of þis lande, þane being at London', in 1427, is more elaborate and more precise. It portrays in turn Fortune, and the four ladies whose power can overcome Fortune—Prudence, Righteousness, Fortitude, and Temperance (the four cardinal virtues). The tone is lofty and serious, drawing on familiar material to preach a clear and effective lesson on the mutability of fortune and the way to govern it. The performance ended with a song:

> And yee all foure shal nowe sing
> With al youre hoole hert entiere
> Some nuwe songe aboute þe fuyre,
> Suche oon as you lykeþe best;
> Lat Fortune go pley hir wher hir list.   (338–42)

This may serve to remind us that the Mummings were very much *part* of a celebration, an interlude in festivities, more like a cabaret at a night-club than an evening at the theatre. It was typical of Lydgate to turn such an occasion to moralistic purposes.

The last of these pieces, the *Mumming at Hertford*, is one of Lydgate's unexpected triumphs. It was written by Lydgate at the request of John Brys, Controller of the Royal Household, and presented before the king at Hertford castle in 1430. It presents 'þe rude upplandisshe people compleynyng on hir wyves, with þe boystous aunswere of hir wyves', with a final superbly evasive reply from the king, in which Lydgate seems to parody his own style, postponing for a year a decision on women's right to rule their husbands. The presentation of the rustics, however, is the real delight of the piece, and it shows us Lydgate working far more successfully in the 'low' style than in the *Thebes*-prologue. There is a heavy debt to Chaucer, especially the Wife of Bath (who is referred to, 168), throughout, but Lydgate repays the debt with couplets of rare crispness:

> For þey afferme þer is noon eorþely stryff
> May beo compared to wedding of a wyff,
> And who þat ever stondeþe in þe cas,
> He with his rebecke may sing ful offt ellas! (21–4)

The presenter introduces first Robin the Reeve, who returns home after a hard day's work to his wife, Beatrice Bittersweet, hoping to find his dinner ready:

> Þanne sitteþe Beautryce bolling at þe nale,
> As she þat gyveþe of him no maner tale;
> For she al day, with hir jowsy nolle,
> Hathe for þe collyk pouped in þe bolle,
> And for heed aache with pepir and gynger
> Dronk dolled ale to make hir throte cleer. (37–42)

If he speaks a word, she hits him with her distaff. The scene, and the language, are reminiscent of the world of popular lyric,[48] or of the Noah-plays. Colin Cobbler has the same trouble with his wife Cicely Sour-cheer:

> Sheo qwytt him ever, þer was no thing to seeche,
> Six for oon of worde and strookes eeche.
> Þer was no meen bytweene hem for to goone;

What ever he wan, clowting olde shoone
Þe wykday, pleynly þis is no tale,
Sheo wolde on Sondayes drynk it at þe nale.   (65–70)

And so with Bartholomew the butcher, Tom Tinker, and the rest. This is all well done, but from the dramatic historian's point of view the striking innovation is the wives' reply, which is spoken in their own person (163–214). The language is here a cento of reminiscences from Chaucer, especially the Clerk's Envoy (e.g. 172–8). Maybe one can exaggerate, because it is so unexpected, the effectiveness of Lydgate's excursion into the low style here, but there is no denying that he had stumbled, with Chaucer's encouragement, into something new.

One last poem remains, the *Procession of Corpus Christi*, 'an ordenaunce of a processyoun of þe feste of corpus cristi made in london'. The verses are designed to explain the significance of the various pageants in the procession, which was organised annually by the furriers:

For now þis day al derkenesse t'enlumyne,
In youre presence fette out of fygure,
Schal beo declared by many unkouþe signe
Gracyous misteryes grounded in scripture.   (5–8)

Each stanza expounds a 'figure' of the sacrament of the eucharist—Adam, Melchisedech, Abraham, Isaac, down to the evangelists and the Church fathers. The familiarity of figural techniques of interpretation to Lydgate is useful confirmation of Kolve's view that they played an important part in the structure of the mystery-cycles,[49] but it would be interesting to know why Lydgate makes not the slightest allusion in the poem to the Corpus Christi plays.

Notes to Chapter Six

1 Steele, ed. *Secrees*, Appendix, p. xxiii.
2 See Schirmer, *John Lydgate*, pp. 90–2.
3 See A. Brusendorff, *The Chaucer Tradition*, pp. 31–42; M. B. Ruud, *Thomas Chaucer* (Research Publications of the Univ. of Minnesota, Studies in Lang. and Lit., no. 9, Minneapolis 1926), esp. pp. 68–86.
4 68–70: text from the edition of J. Norton-Smith, p. 6.
5 MacCracken makes it RER; Ethel Seaton, of course, produces ROZ (*Sir Richard Roos*, p. 222). 'Pycard' is also a puzzle. It could be the name of a code or cipher-system; or it could be a person. A 'maister Picard' is

mentioned as Prince Edward's tutor (and an expert on poetry) in the *Balade to my gracious Lord of York* (*c.* 1448), formerly attributed to Hoccleve (and printed by Furnivall among his *Minor Poems*, EETS,ES 61,1892), but now known to have been written long after his death in 1426.

6 Steele, *op. cit.*, p. xxvii.

7 Steele, *op. cit.*, p. xxvi.

8 See S. Moore, 'Patrons of Letters' (*loc. cit.*), p. 200; also Metham's *Works*, ed. Hardin Craig (EETS,OS 132,1916), pp. x–xii.

9 'An English Friend of Charles d'Orléans', *PMLA*, XXVI(1911),142–80.

10 *Chaucer to Surrey*, pp. 198–201. In quoting from her text, I have added punctuation.

11 Charles' acrostic poem to *Anne Molins* may provide a link, through Suffolk, with the Chaucer household and the Moleyns whom Lydgate knew: see E. P. Hammond, in *MP*, XXII(1924),215–16.

12 Not a horoscope for Henry VI, as Schirmer says (p. 119). See p. 126, above.

13 There is an elegant *virelai* in Shirley's MS.Add.16165.

14 A pictorial manuscript genealogy was posted, with Calot's poem, on the walls of major churches in N. France; Lydgate's version was designed to lull more the English anxieties about the dual monarchy. Copies of the genealogy can be seen in MS.Royal 15.E.vi and in C.U.L. MS. LI.v.20: both are reproduced in the article by J. W. McKenna, 'Henry VI of England and the Dual Monarchy: Aspects of Royal Political Propaganda', *Journal of the Warburg and Courtauld Institutes*, XXVIII(1965),145–62. McKenna shows how coins, novelties and tableaux, as well as poems and posters, were all used as instruments of propaganda. See also B. J. H. Rowe, 'King Henry VI's claim to France: in Picture and Poem', *The Library*, 4th series, XIII (1933),77–88.

15 See above, p. 71.

16 *Chaucer to Surrey*, p. 33.

17 See S. Moore, 'Patrons of Letters' (*loc. cit.*), pp. 87–90; Schirmer, *John Lydgate*, p. 155.

18 J. Huizinga, *The Waning of the Middle Ages* (London 1948), pp. 231–2. See also G. Wickham, *Early English Stages 1300–1660*, vol. I, 1300–1576 (London 1959), pp. 211–15.

19 Instructions for the design of medieval buildings were given in the form of a *devise*, or written specification, not in plans or drawings, and the same is true of paintings, decorations, pageants, and masques. See G. Webb, 'The Office of Devisor', in *Fritz Saxl: Memorial Essays*, ed. D. J. Gordon (London 1957), pp. 297–308. Lydgate's poem is presumably a 'literary' reworking of the original *devise* for the *Entry*. Webb's article does not mention Lydgate, but gives some attention to similar work done by Alexander Barclay, Lydgate's follower, at Guisnes in 1520.

20 See T. Brewer, *Memoir of the Life and Times of John Carpenter* (London 1856), p. 130.

21 *Early English Stages*, pp. 51–111.

22 See Schirmer, *John Lydgate*, pp. 120–3; *Pilgrimage*, ed. Furnivall and Locock, Part III (EETS,ES 92,1904), pp. xiii, lxiii–v; Rosemond Tuve, *Allegorical Imagery: Some Mediaeval Books and their Posterity* (Princeton 1966), pp. 146–50. There is a possibility, Dr. Peter Newton tells me, that a window of the second quarter of the fifteenth century in Allexton church, Leics., may incorporate a motif from the *Pilgrimage*.

23 *Op. cit.*, p. 121.

24 *Catalogue of the Harleian MSS.* (1808), III,208–9. See J. Norton-Smith's Preface to his edition of Lydgate's poems.

25 The French passages are quoted from Furnivall's notes. The standard edition of *Le Pélerinage de Vie Humaine*, by J. J. Stürzinger (Roxburghe Club 1893), is of no use for comparison, since it is based on the first, unexpanded version. The editor apparently thought that the revised version would be included in the EETS edition of Lydgate (Preface, p. vi).

26 For some particularly thickly-strewn passages, see 6769–78, 11881–92.

27 Lydgate gives a poor view of Deguileville, it must be admitted, especially since he chose to use Deguileville's own more verbose second version. Deguileville's importance as a writer is undeniable, and one can understand Rosemond Tuve's professional enthusiasm for his work as the total allegorical fiction (*Allegorical Imagery*, chap. III). At the same time one would recognise her own misgivings about the way he 'consistently re-literalises metaphors' (p. 198).

28 See Hammond, *Chaucer to Surrey*, pp. 124–42 (text of the poem—from which I quote here—with introduction); *The Dance of Death*, ed. Florence Warren and Beatrice White (EETS,OS 181,1931); Schirmer, *op. cit.*, pp. 126–9; and, for the theme of death, Siciliano, *Francois Villon et les Thèmes poétiques du Moyen Age*; Huizinga, *op. cit.*, chap. XI; Rosemary Woolf, *The English Religious Lyric in the Middle Ages* (Oxford 1968), chap. IX, esp. pp. 347–51.

29 See A. Caiger-Smith, *English Medieval Mural Paintings* (Oxford 1963), pp. 45–9.

30 Quoted in Warren and White, *ed. cit.*, p. xxiii.

31 Perhaps the best parallel is to be found not in the more sumptuous illuminated MSS., with their conscious artistry, but in collections of didactic treatises such as MS.Add.37049, designed for the use of lower clergy and laity, where text and illustration blend and overlap in the manner of a modern scientific text-book. See *Piers Plowman*, ed. Elizabeth Salter and Derek Pearsall (York Medieval Texts, 1967), pp. 15, 35; Rosemary Woolf, *The English Religious Lyric, passim*.

32 And, even closer to the *Danse Macabre*, in funerary monuments, such as that of the Black Prince, with its long French inscription mourning the passing of life and its pleasures: see Joan Evans, *English Art 1307–1461* (Oxford 1949), p. 156.

33 Reproduced in R. S. Loomis, *A Mirror of Chaucer's World* (Princeton 1965), plates 161–2.

34 As opposed to 'showeth', 'kometh', and 'demonstrando' in Shirley's rubrics to the mummings. But the question can hardly be called decided: see Wickham, *op. cit.*, p. 195. The confusion and misreadings in MacCracken's footnotes (p. 433) do not make things easier: see Hammond, p. 115, and Schirmer, p. 100.

35 For the distinction of class, see Joan Evans, *English Art 1307–1461*, p. 138. On this same page, incidentally, we are told of some painted cloths in the possession of John Baret of Bury, who was regularly associated with Lydgate in the grants of his annuity (Steele, *op. cit.*, pp. xxvi–xxx).

36 Following Hammond, in *Englische Studien* XLIII(1910–11),10–26.

37 *Secular Lyrics of the XIVth and XVth centuries* (Oxford 1952), p. 110; and see *Historical Poems of the XIVth and XVth centuries* (New York 1959), p. 342.

38 See D. W. Robertson, *A Preface to Chaucer*, pp. 187, 258, and chap. III *passim*.

39 *Op. cit.*, p. 56.

40 *Op. cit.*, p. 199.

41 The crucifix which he describes himself seeing, as a boy, in part IV of the *Testament*, is similarly accompanied by exhortations, 'wrete there, besyde': 'Vide . . . Behold my mekenesse, O child, and leve thy pryde'.

42 See J. B. Trapp, 'Verses by Lydgate at Long Melford', *RES*, VI(1955),1–11.

43 Which in turn becomes 'real' in MS.Trinity R.3.21, where the text of the poem is accompanied by a Pieta.

44 See Wickham, *op. cit.*, pp. 191–207.

45 This is how Lydgate understood classical plays to be presented, according to his account in the *Troy Book*, II,896.

46 Chaucer alludes in the *Franklin's Tale* to feasts where 'tregetours' brought on barges rowing up and down (*CT*, V,1144).

47 Wickham, *op. cit.*, p. 202.

48 Especially nos. 43 and 44 in Robbins' *Secular lyrics of the XIVth and XVth centuries*.

49 V. A. Kolve, *The Play called Corpus Christi* (London 1966), chap IV.

CHAPTER SEVEN

Fables and Didactic Poems

Most of the poems dealt with in the last chapter were related to a specific period in Lydgate's life, 1422–33, when he was at the height of his fame, and many of them to specific occasions within that period. In this chapter, by contrast, the arrangement of the material is chronologically quite arbitrary. One good reason for this is that no other arrangement is possible, since, though one or two of the fables can be plausibly assigned to different phases of Lydgate's poetic career, the vast majority of the poems are unrelated by allusion or occasion. Furthermore, these poems being essentially exercises in a variety of traditional genres, a chronological arrangement, even if it were possible, would probably distort their relationships and inter-relationships. There is no need, either, to concern ourselves with Lydgate's 'development': the moralistic and didactic preoccupations of these poems are the permanent preoccupations of Lydgate and, indeed, of the Middle Ages, and the manner in which he wrote changed little through the years. The same words, figures, topics, and strings of allusions appear in the latest works as in the earliest, and the only development discernible is a slight and sporadic enfeeblement, which may be associated with the declining power of Chaucer to stimulate Lydgate's imagination.

Of the fables, the *Isopes Fabules*, seven in number, are generally regarded as the earliest. The evidence is in Shirley's rubric in the very late MS.Ashmole 59 (which contains only one, the last, of the *Fabules*), where he states that it was 'made in Oxforde'. Stow copies this in MS.Trinity R.3.19, but there is no mention of it in the other complete text, MS.Harley 2251, a codex derived from Shirley. There is no reason to doubt Shirley's information: we know for certain that Lydgate studied at Oxford around 1405–10, and a translation of Aesop would be a natural outgrowth of such studies. 'There is ample evidence that fables did serve as paraphrase vehicles for teaching composition',[1] and they were included as the first of a series of paraphrase exercises in

Priscian's *Praeexercitamina*, the standard advanced Latin grammar in the Middle Ages. Beast-fables were also widely current in sermons and sermon-teaching as exemplum-material, and this would have been another avenue of approach for Lydgate. The reservation one would make about Shirley's rubric is that it refers specifically only to the one fable, and that one by far the shortest. One might conclude that the *Fabules* were a task that Lydgate returned to at odd times, and that their unity in the two complete MSS. is scribal. In particular, the first four, which, with the Prologue, follow the traditional opening order of the Aesop-collections, and are quite lengthy and elaborate in their treatment (749 lines out of a total of 959), may be distinguished from the last three, which are much slighter, and disturb somewhat the usual sequence. In MS.Trinity R.3.19 these two groups appear in widely separated parts of the manuscript.

Aesop's Fables, or the Aesopic fables, as they perhaps ought to be called, were very popular in the Middle Ages, and particularly familiar as school-texts. The version in which they had come down was, as usual, late Roman, the prose translation made by Romulus in the sixth century of the verse fables of Phaedrus (first century), unknown in the Middle Ages, which in their turn claimed to be directly from Aesop's Greek. Romulus was the source of all medieval knowledge of the Aesopic fables; he was turned back into verse by an unknown 'Walter' in the twelfth century, and Walter's version was the basis for the *Esopus Moralisatus* of the thirteenth century, which added much extra moralisation, and proved the most popular of all the collections. It is difficult, and not important, to know what was Lydgate's precise source, but it was probably some French or Latin version of this last descendant of Romulus. The Aesopic collections attracted large numbers of similar fables called *fabulae extravagantes*, and an extensive compilation, with variants and German translation, was made by Steinhöwel in 1476. Caxton's *Aesop* (1483) is drawn from a French translation of Steinhöwel.

The Fables had another claim on the Middle Ages, for they provided a basic and obvious embodiment of the medieval theory of the function of poetry, which was an essentially allegorical one:

> The reality of poetry is dependent on its allegorical foundations;
> its moral teachings are to be sought in the hidden meanings
> discoverable beneath the literal expression.[2]

Boccaccio provides the fullest discussion of this theory in books XIV and XV of the *De genealogia deorum*, and elsewhere. The image that he uses is a favourite one: 'Poetry is essentially a veil of fiction which clothes the naked truth'.[3] Fifteenth-century poets, especially Hawes,[4] recur again and again to these theories, and Lydgate provides a clear formulation in the *Churl and the Bird*:

> Poetes write wondirful liknessis,
> And undir covert kepte hem silf ful cloos:
> Bestis thei take, and fowlis, to witnessis,
> Of whoos feynyng fables first arroos.   (29–32)

The Prologue to the *Fabules* pays particular attention to the 'lowness' of the form:

> Where sylver fayleþ, in a pewter dyssh
> Ryall dentees byn oft tymes seyne,
> And semblably poetes, in certeyne,
> In fables rude includyd gret prudence
> And moralytees full notable of sentence.   (17–21)

Further analogies are made to the finding of precious stones in the 'blak erþe' and of pearls in oysters. Henryson, whose version of the *Moral Fabillis* (c. 1485) is at points quite closely related to Lydgate's, embodies the idea in what is perhaps the most notable image of all:

> The nuttis schell, thocht it be hard and teuch,
> Haldis the kirnill and is delectabill;
> Sa lyis thair ane doctrine wyse aneuch
> And full of fruit under ane fenyeit fabill.   (15–18)[5]

This image goes back to St. Augustine[6] and, with the related image of grain and husk, nucleus and cortex, is a metaphorical cornerstone of medieval aesthetic.

With such a strong traditional backing in theory for his own pre-occupation with moral generalisation, and with his contempt for narrative as such, it is not surprising that Lydgate's *Fabules* should be heavily didactic. It is interesting to compare Chaucer, whose handling of fable, in the *Nun's Priest's Tale* and the *Manciple's Tale*, reflects in miniature his exploratory progress through various 'exemplary' forms of narrative, and his gradual sloughing-off of the externally imposed moralisation. The *Nun's Priest's Tale* explodes the fable in a cascade of literary fireworks, so that the mock-serious injunction at the end,

> Taketh the moralite, goode men,

> (*CT*, VII,3440)

can evoke only the bewildered response, 'Which one?' The moral is
mortified into absurdity and irrelevance, and our attention directed
back to the body of the tale, which contains its own 'moralite'. In the
Manciple's Tale Chaucer provides as the moral a string of unctuous
platitudes which reflect back not upon the tale but upon the narrator,
and upon the whole concept of the fable as a vehicle of moral wisdom.
These very platitudes, parodied by Chaucer, are presented by Lydgate
with a perfectly straight face.

The first fable is of the Cock and the Jewel. It is of twenty-four
stanzas and Lydgate takes eight to get to the jewel, giving us a long
description of the Cock, with some echoing of Chaucer,

> Of custom namyd comon astrologere
> In throwpes smale to make þeyr hertis lyght   (66–7)

as the type of the wakeful Christian, who keeps 'þe tydes of the nyght'
and praises the Trinity in his crowing 'with treble laudes'. Having got
to the jacinth, Lydgate then goes off for another four stanzas in praise
of the Cock's industry in scraping for his food:

> Vertu gynneþ at occupacion,
> Vyces all procede of idelnesse.   (134–5)

In Henryson, by contrast, the Cock finds the jasp in the sixth line, and
the poet explains how it got there, swept out carelessly by the maids,
whose only interest is to get their work done as quickly as possible,

> Thay cair nathing swa that the flure be clene   (74)

and go out to flaunt themselves on the streets. This is the realising
imagination at work, giving the narrative a substance and density such
as we are used to in Chaucer, 'making it like'. To Lydgate the jewel is
simply something there, something given; his mind never probes or
questions, but slithers instantly into the apt generalisation. So in the
Cock's speech rejecting the jewel: Henryson is brisk, business-like,
seems to have entered into the Cock's nature himself, while Lydgate's
Cock, after referring to the lapidary of Evax, gravitates inevitably to
the commonplace of 'Everything according to its nature' and amplifications thereof. In style there is a world of difference: it is not that
Lydgate is elaborate and Henryson simple, for Henryson does not disdain long words; but Henryson is forceful, compact and varied, where
Lydgate is loose, heavy-handed and monotonous. Here are their styles
in epitome, in the Cock's address to the jewel:

Twene þe and me ys no convenience.   (161)

Thow ganis not for me, nor I for the.   (112)

The envoys are different. Henryson sees the moral in the rejection of
the precious stone of wisdom and learning by the ignorant, while
Lydgate labours the points already made—the need for diligence and
acceptance of one's station in life. Henryson is not so 'advanced' as
Chaucer: he has a lot of respect for the attached moral, but he has too
the late-medieval belief in realism which allows the narrative to make
its own way independently. Lydgate, however, pushes the moral back
into the narrative so that the narrative is engulfed: like the nutshell, it is
disposable.

In the Fable of the Wolf and the Lamb, Lydgate prefixes the narrative with three stanzas on a favourite commonplace, the contraries that
exist in nature, between vice and virtue, proud and humble, great and
small, wolf and lamb. Even the actual detail of the narrative, the wolf's
angry approach to the lamb, for instance, is made to seem like an
illustration of a previously stated general truth:

Who þat is froward of condicion
And disposyd to malyce and outrage,
Can sone seke and fynde occasion
Pyke a quarell for to do damage;
And unto purpose malycious of corage
The furyos wolfe out with hys venym brake. . . .

(253–8)

Henryson, however, pays attention to the detail, to the actual:

The wolff him saw and rampand come him till.
With girnand teith and awfull angrie luke. . . .

(2629–30)

In Lydgate, the wolf kills the lamb halfway through, leaving the poet
to a series of commonplaces (the usefulness of the lamb, the neglect of
allegorical shepherds), whereas Henryson keeps up the cruel legalistic
debate almost to the end, and then embarks on a *moralitas* full of fierce
indignation against tyranny and compassion for the poor. Lydgate's
moral, that, as lamb is served at the king's table, so the poor go to
heaven, is more typically medieval, but its quietism is made to sound
feeble beside Henryson.

In the Frog and the Mouse, Lydgate prefixes the story of the frog helping the mouse over the river with the frog's visit to the mouse's humble home (a variant of Town and Country Rat). He moralises from the start about fraud being quit with fraud, about deceivers being deceivers ever, since it is their nature, and only just holds himself back from another excursus on the theme of 'Everything according to its nature' (372). The mouse praises 'glad povert with small possession' in eight stanzas of commonplaces and familiar allusion (Croesus, Midas, Diogenes), and the conclusion returns to the satisfactory equilibrium of

> Who useþ fraude, with fraude shal be quyt.   (525)

Henryson takes the two fables separately, handles each brilliantly, with wit, irony, acute observation, a pure effortless narrative technique, and exquisite play on the human-animal situation:

> Ane lytill mous come till ane rever-syde;
> Scho micht not waid—hir schankis were sa schort;
> Scho culd not swym; scho had na hors to ryde:
> Of verray force behovit hir to byde.   (2778–81)

Lydgate's mouse, by contrast, sounds like Lydgate, neither mouse-like nor human:

> The mowse answeryd quakyng in hys drede:
> 'I have of swymmyng noon experience'.   (484–5)

In the Fable of the Hound and the Sheep, which is directed against false witnesses and legal corruption, Henryson shows again his readiness to take the narrative seriously. He accepts that law relates to human reality, and works his poem out as if it were a real law-suit, with wit, cruelty and passion. Lydgate, knowing nothing of the law nor of reality, retires into commonplaces and moral generalisations, drawing on the book of Proverbs and Holcot on *Sapience* for his information.

The other three fables, of the Wolf and the Crane, the Sun's Marriage, and the Hound and the Cheese, are slight, and have no parallel in Henryson, which takes away a good deal of their interest. Comparison with Henryson is deadly for Lydgate, one must admit—it is sometimes not even very favourable for Chaucer—but it is useful in demonstrating to us the difference between the bookish, moralistic, typically medieval tradition and the realism, the sense of a significance attaching to life in its literary imitation, which always threatens to erupt into that tradition and which, when it does, provides some of its most memorable writing. Style and narrative technique reflect these differences, and so do the systems of thought which underlie them. Henryson is disturbed and disturbing: his poetry can contain, but only just, his indignation and compassion. Lydgate encases life in a shell, blurs all its dangers and sharp edges; he has no sense of outrage or pity, only sets of consoling platitudes and balanced contraries to which all experience may be referred and which cannot be disturbed. It is an equilibrium which could be majestic, and is, in some medieval poetry, and can make post-medieval poetry look fretful and sentimental, but in this case it is too easily won, too cheap, to be effective. There is nothing wrong with the medieval tradition, but Lydgate represents it here in his most undistinguished manner.

The *Churl and the Bird* is much better. Quite short (386 lines), it was very popular in its day, was included in a number of the sub-Chaucerian anthologies, and appears in six early printed editions, a record for Lydgate. It is a little moral fable on the lines of the *Manciple's Tale*, but simpler and more straightforward, without the ironic undertones. Lydgate tells us he drew it from a French 'paunflet', which must be some version of the story as told in the *Disciplina Clericalis* of Petrus Alfonsus, a work of instruction and advice which uses brief *exempla* to enforce its points (the *Knight of La Tour Laundry* is a more familiar example of the genre). It was a work very familiar to Lydgate, and he must have had it by him for several poems we shall mention in this chapter: there was a copy in the Bury library.[7]

The story is quite ingenious. A churl traps a bird, but the bird says she will never sing if she is not free, and she is not much to eat, but promises three great wisdoms if freed. Once freed, she moralises on hidden perils and gives the wisdoms—do not be credulous, do not desire the impossible, and do not regret the past. She adds that he was a fool to let her go because she has a jacinth in her body of magical properties, though he wouldn't have appreciated it anyway. The churl complains at his loss, whereupon the bird reproves him for forgetting so quickly all three pieces of advice. How could she, so tiny, carry about a great stone inside her? But then, you can't expect to teach a churl any sense.

Lydgate is not markedly different from his usual self in this poem. He extracts every ounce of morality, for there are not only the three wise sayings proved true, but also the bird's discourse on freedom, with its typically antithetic amplification of hidden perils (sugar/poison, *triacle/venym*, quail/net, 176–89), and some elaboration (253–66, 337–57) of the theme of the churlishness of churls, everything to its nature:

> Ech þing drawith unto his semblable:
> Fissh in the see, bestis on the stronde,
> The eyr for fowlis of natur is covenable,
> To a plowman for to tyle his londe,
> And to a cherl, a mookfork in his honde;
> I lese my tyme any moor to tarye,
> To telle a bouir of the lapidarye. (260–6)

We have seen this in the *Fabules*; another poem uses the first line of the above stanza as its refrain. Elaborate prefatory and concluding material ensure that we shall not miss the point of the poem: a long Prologue discourses on the value of allegorical fables and the conclusion has, in turn, a *Verba auctoris*, an Envoy and a *Go litel quaier*. There is also a garden-description at the beginning, in Lydgate's best vein:

> Al th'aleys were made pleyn with sond,
> The benchis turved with newe turvis grene,
> Sote herbis with condittes at the hond,
> That wellid up ageyn the sonne shene,
> Lich silver stremys, as any cristal cleene,
> The burbly wawis in ther up-boylyng
> Round as berel, ther bemys out shewyng. (50–6)

All the accustomed Lydgatian paraphernalia, in fact, is here, which makes it all the more interesting to decide why the poem is such a delight. Some things are obvious—it is short, and the story is neat—but there are two other reasons. One is Chaucer, who has laid his hand lightly on Lydgate's handling of narrative and language; the other is the French source. Having admitted to a vernacular source for his fable, and to one, furthermore, which has no Aesopic 'authority', Lydgate is under less pressure to put on a performance. Once the Prologue, the language of which is very turgid, is out of the way, he relaxes into a dry, colloquial, almost terse idiom, especially in the exchanges of speech, and especially in the language of the bird when she is being patronisingly superior to the churl:

> To heeryn a wisdam thyn eris ben half-deeff,
> Lik an asse that listeth on a harpe,
> Thou maist go pypen in a ivy leeff;
> Bett is to me to syngyn on thornes sharpe
> Than in a cage with a cherl to karpe,
> For it was seyd of folkis yoore agoon
> A cherlis cherl ful oft is woo-bigoon! (274–80)

14

There is more than one echo of Chaucer here,[8] but Lydgate can take the credit for the crispness of delivery. It is almost impossible to believe that the poet of this stanza wrote the opening lines, quoted on p. 11 above. The doctrine of the decorum of styles has a lot to answer for.

It is not possible to date the *Churl and the Bird*, but it is usually regarded as early. The *Debate of the Horse, Goose and Sheep*, which is not radically dissimilar, was written soon after 1436, since it contains an allusion (413) to the Duke of Burgundy's attack on Calais in that year, an event which marked the final breakdown of the long-fostered Anglo-Burgundian alliance. The *Debate* had the same sort of popular currency in manuscript and print as the *Churl and the Bird*, and exploits some of that poem's success in the low style, but it is longer (659 lines) and carries a correspondingly heavier load of miscellaneous erudition. It is couched in the traditional form of the medieval debate, in which various animate or inanimate objects argue their usefulness to man:

> Which of them to man was most profitable.   (28)

Such debates were common as school-exercises (they still are), and made their entry into literature as displays of skill in assembling and styling arguments. Some debates are coloured by beast-fable, and raise the level of their reference by varied play upon the human-animal ironies. The *Owl and the Nightingale* is the best example in Middle English. Lydgate has no such pretensions; his animals present their case with a wealth of curious detail, but have no ambition to be anything but animals, even though Lydgate does at one point, rashly, evoke the *Parlement of Foules* (477).

The structure of the poem is simple: each animal presents its case, and then there is a brief exchange between them before the Lion and the Eagle give judgment. The Horse quotes famous horses of antiquity, Chaucer's steed of brass in the *Squire's Tale* and Zachariah's vision of four horses, refers to his usefulness in war and peace, and makes interesting use of etymology as a category of argument (57). The Goose, though it does not neglect to mention the usefulness of its turds in curing burns, concentrates on the arrows flighted with its feathers, and the pens made from its quills, echoing the Prologue to the *Legend of Good Women* (36):

> For, yiff pennys and writyng were away,
> Of remembraunce we had lost the kay.   (188-9)

The Sheep, who is so shy that the Ram speaks for her, mentions the trade in wool, England's major export, but reserves her strongest argument, and loftiest terms, for another, somewhat incongruous role:

> Lat be thi bost, thou Hors, and thi jangelyng!
> Ley doun thi trapurs forgid of plate and maile!
> Cast of thy brydyl of gold so fressh shynyng!
> What may thi sadil or bos the availe?
> This gostly Lamb hath doon a gret bataile;
> Bi his meknesse he offred up for man,
> Clad in pur purpil venquysshid hath Satan.
> The Goos may gagle, the Hors may prike and praunce;
> Neithir of hem in prowes may atteyne
> For to be set or put in remembraunce
> Ageyn the Lamb, thouh their ther-at disdeyn:
> For comon profite he passith bothe tweyne. (337-48)

The horse takes up the sheep's claim to be the exemplar of peace, pointing out that Burgundy's attack on Calais was motivated by the desire to close it to English wool-exports, and furthermore that peace always produces wealth (as through the wool-trade), wealth causes pride, and pride causes wars, concluding,

> Werr is brought in al only bi the Sheep, (476)

which successfully disposes of the sheep's argument that she is for Peace, but in doing so gives her the credit for War, which both Horse and Goose support. The argument is really rather tangled here, which suggests that Lydgate is responsible for it. Argument is not his *forte*, and he is much happier with the verdict, which declares that each animal has its place, and he elaborates on it in a very long Envoy. All is for the best, and nature's plan accommodates all kinds of variety and contradiction:

> Thynges contrarie be founde in every kynde. (597)

Lydgate's mind is by this date so ready with examples to amplify these generalisations that they flood in upon him in wild and curious disorder. It is characteristic of him when he is working on his own, as here, and in some of the moralistic poems, to offer such a wealth of illustration in support of a comparatively simple point that in the end he begins not to make sense at all. Associated with this tendency is a peculiar kind of gnomic syntax, which adds to the obscurity. I suspect that this is not all unintentional, and that Lydgate believed that his recondite and allusive method was a mark of the high style. To us, though, the Envoy looks like a loose rag-bag of platitudes.

The debate itself is more interesting, chiefly as a lively and varied exercise in a familiar form, and the plain idiom is often admirable:

> Hors in the feeld may mustre in gret pride,
> Whan thei of trumpetis her the blody soun;
> But whan an arwe hath perced thoruh his side
> To ground he goth and cast his maistir doun;
> Entryng the feeld he pleyeth the leoun;
> What folwith aftir? his careyn stynkith sore;
> Sauf skyn and shoon men leve of hym no more.   (218–24)

Some interest adheres to Lydgate's discussion of the wool-trade, though it is ridiculous to think of it in the same terms as the economic *real-politik* of the *Libel of English Policy*.[9] However, there are verbal corre-spondences between the two poems[10] which suggest that one writer knew the other—surely that the author of the *Libel* had read Lydgate. The only point that one could make concerning Lydgate's political awareness is that he thinks of England as a country—

> Bi bowe and arwis sith the werr began
> Have Ynglysshmen, as it is red in story,
> On her enmyes had many gret victory—   (215–17)

in a way that Chaucer never did, but Renoir's argument that this is a sign of the new nationalism[11] will not hold. Such references go back a very long way, especially in monastic tradition, and Ralph Higden, Robert of Gloucester, even the anonymous monks of the Anglo-Saxon Chronicle, are no less 'nationalistic' than Lydgate. It is Chaucer, with his Europeanness, who is the exception.

The *Debate of the Horse, Goose and Sheep* is mixed in style and varied in interest. The *Fabula duorum mercatorum*, the last of this group of fables, is by contrast a systematic application of high-style rhetoric to a simple exemplum taken from the *Disciplina Clericalis*.[12] It is a fable of friendship, like *Amis and Amiloun*, telling of how one merchant sacrifices his bride-to-be and the other confesses to a murder he did not commit, both to save their friend. To this simple tale, which might take up half a page of the *Gesta Romanorum*, Lydgate, at the height of his powers, brings the full resources of his style and techniques of amplification, working from the model of Chaucer in the *Man of Law's Tale*. There is extensive moralising, often in the form of *exclamatio* or apostrophe, on favourite themes, such as

Unto his semblable thus every thyng can drawe   (83)

or on the virtue of patience (589) or the variability of Fortune (666); there is an *exclamatio* on the bitterness of absence (120), a long, elaborate and highly rhetorical complaint by the unlucky merchant (549), and a lofty and powerful prayer of remorse by the murderer in the crowd, beginning thus:

> O rihtwys God, to whom ech pryvyte
> Is pleyn and open to thy magnyficence,
> O Lord, that knowyst myn hyd iniquite:
> Beholdyng al, O Sonne of Sapience,
> Ne take no vengaunce of myn hih offence,
> That I so longe concelyd have the trouthe;
> But of thy mercy, Lord, have on me routhe.   (792–8)

There is elaborate Chaucerian invocation of the Furies when the story veers toward tragedy (498), a formal love-complaint by the love-sick merchant (221) and a typically abstract *descriptio feminae* (379)—as well as a passing dig at the patience of wives (484). The love of fact is satisfied by a carefully signalled digression on the geography of Egypt (8–35) and an even longer one, full of medical detail (like the *Knight's Tale*), on the disease of *malencolye* (274–343). The topics of excellence are exploited as nowhere else outside the *Troy Book*, and the figuring is heavily rhetoricated, even to rarer figures like *dubitatio*:

> This straunge marchaunt thankyth hym with herte:
> Nay, 'straunge' nat; allas, why seid I soo?   (183–4)

It is an extraordinary performance, and we have to add to this familiar apparatus an exceptional care and precision in vocabulary (many words occur here and nowhere else in Lydgate), a smooth and uncluttered syntax and metre, an unusual felicity in the individual line, e.g.

> My liff, my deeth is portrayed in hir face   (413)

and an unprecedented fondness for alliteration:

> Al merthe of makyng my mateer mot refuse.   (501)

The following stanza demonstrates some of these qualities:

> Revolvyth ech by contemplacioun
> Al of his freend the lyknesse and ymage:
> Thynkyng hath grave with deep impressioun

> Ech othris fourme, stature and visage;
> Her hertys eye did alwey her message,
> And mynde medleth in the memorial
> And fet his foode in the fantastical.   (50–6)

One must confess to a certain bafflement before this poem. The story, of course, sinks beneath such a weight and is lost from sight, but as an exercise of style it is superb. One is inclined even to think of it as an imitation of Lydgate's manner by a far superior poet, and the acuteness of Dr. Ethel Seaton's literary perceptions is well demonstrated by her ascription of the poem to Roos on precisely these terms.[13] The attribution cannot be accepted, any more than the nonsense about anagrams, and Lydgate's authorship is clearly authenticated in the very reliable MS.Harley 2255, which I have described as being written at Bury under Lydgate's supervision. The poem must stand, and stand as a warning against any underestimation of the range of Lydgate's skills. The story, with its neat balances and reversals, and pat moral, like the *Man of Law's Tale*, can have little presence for us, but for the techniques displayed in the telling one must have ungrudging admiration.

It is a far cry from the grandiloquence of the *Fabula* to the group of moralistic poems that MacCracken calls 'little homilies with proverbial refrains'. These poems aim low, and are in a different style altogether from his epic or high style, free from rhetorical elaboration and ornament, free too from the grosser forms of amplification, solider, more weighty and serious, duller, more in tune with the mind of Lydgate himself. The lines are self-contained, end-stopped, aphoristic, heavily weighted lexically and metrically, as in this stanza from *A Song of Just Mesure*:

> Where mesure reygnith, subgettis lyve in peas;
> Roote of discorde is froward tyrannye:
> Favour in mesure causith grete incres,
> And out of mesure it causith grete envye.
> Men must by mesour rigour modifye;
> Atwixt love and hate mesure doth equyte;
> Wherfor late soverayns use this policye,
> Whatever they do late it in mesure be.   (65–72)

Their most characteristic identity as a group is in the refrain, and they are represented in their simplest form where Lydgate takes some proverbial saying, e.g.

Ful weele is him þat fyndeþe a freonde at neede;

He hastuth weele þat wysely can abyde,

and proceeds to demonstrate its truth with series of allusions and examples culled from classical, Biblical, bestiary, and other sources, even life.
As might be expected, many of these illustrations have seen the light
of day before in Lydgate, and there is a good deal of cross-pollination
within the poems as a group. Whole sequences of illustrations are often
reproduced, with permutation, and one is reminded again of the
phenomenon of 'total recall' in Lydgate's mental processes. For all this,
the impression is often one of wealth rather than poverty.

The form of such poems, most of which are in eight-line stanzas, is
derived partly from the *ballade*, partly from the religious lyrics, especially those which use as refrain a familiar liturgical text and relate each
verse, often in shifting and sophisticated ways, to the sense of the text.
One of Lydgate's poems, *Timor mortis conturbat me*, is specifically of
this type. Lydgate seems to have developed the form more systematically than anyone else, but there is no lack of precedent and parallel, as a
glance through the lyric-collections of Brown and Robbins will readily
confirm. Particular collections of poems, like that in MS.Digby 102,[14]
written by a monk, possibly prior of his house, between 1400 and 1420,
are very close to Lydgate, with verses based on refrains like

Man, knowe thy self, love god, and drede   (I)

Man, knowe thy self, and lerne to dye   (VII)

Eche man be war, er hym be wo   (XIV)

Sometimes the refrain is not a complete line, but based on the repeti-
tion, in varied contexts, of a key-word like *mede* (II), as in Lydgate's
Amor vincit omnia. Even closer to Lydgate is the group of poems in the
Vernon MS.,[15] with moralistic and proverbial refrains like

Uche mon ouȝte himself to knowe   (6)

Hos seiþ þe soþe, he schal be schent   (9)

Þis world fareþ as a fantasye   (12)

Selden i-seiȝe is sone forȝete   (19)

Fond evermore to sey þe beste   (22)

But he sey soth, he schal be schente   (29)

The soil from which such poems sprang was again, as with the Fables, the school-text. Every schoolboy would be familiar with the *Disticha Catonis*, a collection of proverbial maxims running to just over 300 lines. They have no connection with Cato, any more than the *Proverbs of Alfred* have with Alfred—the name simply provided 'auctoritee'—but represent the residual wisdom of the age, or any age, sifted clean of complexity. They provided a neat solution to the school-master's two problems—how to teach Latin, and how to instil basic morality into the pupils—and there is no doubt that they exerted a profound influence in the formation of young minds, Shakespeare's as well as Lydgate's. They are Christian by implication, but chiefly practical, worldly, and strictly limited in their view of human behaviour:

Quod potes, id tempta   (III,14)

Res age, quae prosunt   (IV,7)[16]

There are at least five Middle English verse translations, including one in the Vernon MS., standing next to a collection of 'Proverbes of diverse profetes and of poetes', principally Seneca. Lydgate's disciple, Benedict Burgh, did a version in rhyme-royal of the *Distichs*, a remarkably successful piece of low-style 'practical' writing to set beside his ridiculous attempts to ape his master's aureate style.

The taste for proverbs, however, was not confined to schoolmasters and schoolboys. At a higher level it produced the collections of *sententiae* culled from classical writers, which were circulated in *florilegia*, and soon acquired proverbial status, quite detached from their authors. Most of Lydgate's knowledge of the classics, apart from Ovid, was derived from such collections. Often the attribution was quite spurious, as with Cato, or Seneca, the other major 'source' of medieval aphorisms. Systematic collections were made, in which biblical quotation, especially from the book of *Proverbs*, rubbed shoulders with quotations ascribed, with more or less accuracy, to Plato, Aristotle, Socrates, and Cicero. The *Dicta Philosophorum* is one of the most comprehensive of these: various versions in English exist, including one in verse by George Ashby, clerk to the Signet in the mid-fifteenth century, and of course the prose translation by Anthony Woodville, earl Rivers, the *Dicts and Sayings of the Philosophers*, which was the first book printed in England (1477). The popularity of such moralistic literature needs no attestation: Chaucer's own *Tale of Melibeus* is little more than a collection of proverbs strung out on a narrative line, and, a century later, one of Wynkyn de Worde's most profitable publishing ventures was his *Proverbs of Lydgate*, garnered from this group of poems and from the envoys to the *Fall of Princes*.

The Lydgate refrain-poems are not quite as widespread in MS. as one might expect. For the twenty poems there are only just over sixty MS. occurrences, and, of those, twenty are of the three most popular, *A Song of Vertu*, *As a Mydsomer Rose*, and *Look in thy Merour*. They nearly all appear in Shirley MSS. and MSS. derived from Shirley (Harley 2251, Add. 29729, Ashmole 59) or else in Harley 2255. The poems are remarkably homogeneous, but some internal groupings can be made.

The basic form offers a piece of proverbial advice in the refrain and weaves a discourse around it to prove it true. The first, *Amor vincit omnia: mentiris, quod Pecunia*, takes a Latin proverb as its theme and title, and develops the refrain

Love is sette bakke, gold goth byfore, and mede.[17]

It is a catalogue of instances, with considerable classical reference, not all of it very apt—Lydgate's range of knowledge is limited and he is quite accustomed to press the same allusion into service for different purposes at different times—but the real structure of the poem is in the variation of the refrain, particularly the twist in stanza 14, where, 'mede' becomes 'eternal mede', the reward of God's love. The language is plain, unvarnished, clipped and compressed: the ideal of style is brevity, and the characteristic syntactical figure is *articulus*, the deliberate omission of conjunctions, a feature of gnomic verse in Latin, in Old English, or in any language:

> Take it for a custome, it wil be non other,
> In worldly quarels lucre goth toforn.
> A man for wynnyng wil forsake his brothir;
> Some tyme for lucre weede above the corn;
> For lucre alday men wil be forsworn;
> Chaunge hath be founde som tyme in wommanhede;
> In al suche case love blowith the bukkis horn,
> Where olde acqueyntaunce is sette abak for meede.
>
> (49–56)

The theme is an obvious one, and there are many popular songs about the power of money and 'Sir Peny', but the sophistication of Lydgate's allusions, ordering and variation can be measured by comparing nos.

57–60 in Robbins' *Secular Lyrics of the XIVth and XVth centuries*: the second misses, in line 122, precisely the twist that makes Lydgate interesting.

Amor vincit omnia is one of the Shirley texts of MS.Ashmole 59, and Shirley performs a characteristic and valuable office by offering in the margin the Latin proverbs from which Lydgate is drawing his material. Thus, for

> Al nys nat golde that shyneth bright, parde!   (77)

he suggests 'Non teneas aurum totum quod splendet ut aurum'; and for

> The faire behestis maken foolis gladde   (97)

'Pulchrum promissum facit stultum esse gavisum'.[18] No clearer evidence of the community of this proverbial wisdom could be afforded than Shirley's instant recognition of its source.

A Freond at Neode has a courtly opening,

> Late whane Aurora of Tytane toke leve. . . .

with the pretty device of a bird singing the refrain,

> Ful weele is him þat fyndeþe a freonde at neede,

but it soon devolves into a systematic cataloguing of examples—Orestes and Pylades, Achilles and Patroclus, David and Jonathan, Amis and Amiloun—and authorities: Cicero *De Amicitia*, the book of *Proverbs*, the book of *Wisdom*, and something that Lydgate calls the 'doctrinal' (57), for which Shirley again provides the Latin original—'Sepe viatorem nova non vetus orbita fallit'.[19] In the last stanza Lydgate repeats the shift to a spiritual context,

> O Cryste Jhesu, whos frenship may not fayle. . . .   (129)

a *Troilus*-epilogue in miniature.

The *Ditty upon Haste* is altogether similar. Azael and Phillis apart, all the examples of

> He hastuth weele þat wysely can abyde

are from the Troy-story, evidence of Lydgate's economy of method, and also of the ease with which any human misfortune can be accommodated to a set moral scheme. The 'twist' in the last three stanzas reverses the sense of the refrain completely:

That hast is good wheche hastuth to vertue,
And slouthe is good þat vengaunce doth differre.
Best of all hastus is haste towarde Jhesu,
Haste hym to serve, for suche haste may not erre. . . .
Lette parfyt cherite be þy loode sterre,
Suche haste is beste who can þer-on abyde. . . .
Haste in all perylys to Cristus Passion,
Embrace þat baner, and do þer-by abyde.   (137–60)

One can see Lydgate practising an 'effect', one which he will put to excellent use in a later poem.

Consulo quisquis eris, the last of this group, is a peculiar piece of work. Lydgate takes as his text a proverbial maxim equivalent to 'When in Rome, do as the Romans do', using as refrain

Lyke the audience so uttir thy language,

but the multiplication of instances leads him into such pointless absurdity,

With wachmen wake; with sloggy folkes sleepe;
With wood men wood; with frentyk folk savage;
Renne with beestys; with wilde wormys creepe;
And like the audience uttir thy language.   (53–6)

that he is compelled to add another eight stanzas of *Verba translatoris* in which he makes his usual 'turn' on the refrain,

Wher vertu regnyth, ther uttir thy language,   (64)

and then develops the theme,

Be paied with litel, content with suffisaunce.   (65)

Cato is quoted, and the story of Diogenes plays a large part; the last stanza suggests that we 'uttren our language' to please Christ. The whole poem is awkward and fumbling: the limited applicability of the original proverb leaves Lydgate with no clear directive, and he gropes forward as if every breath will be his last.

The next group of poems develops a very popular medieval theme, the wisdom of silence. If there is one major recurrent idea in the Cato, it is that keeping quiet is on the whole better than speaking, and a number of the best-known distichs, as well as the very nature of gnomic verse, reaffirm the truth of this:

Virtutem primam esse puta conpescere linguam;
proximus ille deo est, qui scit ratione tacere.   (I,3)

Rumores fuge, ne incipias novus auctor haberi,
nam nulli tacuisse nocet, nocet esse locutum.   (I,12)

It is this theme, of course, and this last distich in particular, that Chaucer
exposes so comically at the end of the *Manciple's Tale*, but Cato's influence was more pervasive than Chaucer's, and there was a great vogue
for poems with titles or refrains like 'Whate ever thow sey, Avyse the
welle', 'Lerne say wele, say litel, or say noȝt', and 'Hyre and see and
say not all'.[20] Lydgate's *Say the best and never repent* is an example,
though it is really two poems: one is in a lively four-stress ballade
stanza, and begins with a spring-scene and a variant of the bird-song
motif:

> When the silver dewes sote
> From the hevyn down gan still
> To bryng the bawme oute of the rote,
> Aftyr kalendes of Aprill,
> Within a park I found a bill
> Undir a bank beside a bent,
> Directid to folk þat lyst speke yll,
> 'Who seith the best shall never repent'.   (36–43)

The other precedes it, and is a meditation, in Lydgate's more opaque
manner, on the refrain which it quotes as its first line. There is only one
MS.,[21] and no Lydgate ascription: the first part is certainly Lydgate's,
the second probably not. Lydgate often wrote poems as commentaries
on other poems, or embedded their fragments in his own new fabrics,
as if the materials of poetry were like old bricks (as in some sense they
are), that could be used over and over again. Another poem, *See myche,
say lytell, and lerne to soffar in tyme*, should certainly be rejected from the
canon. It is not a refrain-poem at all, but simply repeats the first line
as the last. Stow is the only one to attribute it to Lydgate, whereas a
contemporary ascription in another of the manuscripts (Corpus Christi
Oxford 203) calls it 'Proverbium R. Stokys', which surely qualifies as
a *durior lectio*.[22]

The two other poems in this group are more interesting. *A Wicked
Tunge wille sey amys* is an epitome of Lydgate's techniques: it develops
the theme of slander first in a series of contrastive statements (whether
you are married or single, fat or thin, sober or merry, etc., people will

say ill of you), and secondly by accumulating topics of comparison (though you had the virtues of David, Solomon, Joshua . . .). It has life, and a clear direction. *The Cok hath lowe shoone*, however, is more complicated. The general basis of the poem is the contrariousness of life, which suggests that keeping quiet is best:

A good 'be stille' is well wourth a groote.   (153)

The form is a cryptic catalogue of allusions, with extensive use of animal-analogies (as in the refrain), and reference to the familiar topos of 'the world upside-down'.[23] In this sense it is a 'contraries' poem, like some others that we shall meet, but not a very clearly designed one. There is about it a deliberately hermetic quality, like true gnomic poetry: each line or stanza has a kernel of truth, but the articulation of these truths is left to the reader, with the help provided by the refrain. Or perhaps it is that the systems of contraries were by now so mechanical to Lydgate that he could short-circuit normal mental and syntactical processes. Whatever the reason, *The Cok hath lowe shoone* is an extraordinary production. It would repay study and annotation, though not as a poem.

There are two poems in praise of 'measure', one of which, *Mesure is Tresour*, has already been mentioned as a picture-poem. The other, *A Song of Just Mesure*, relates the theme of moderation to a variety of human affairs, including poetry:

If mesure lak, what vailith eloquence?   (45)

The method is straightforward, and the treatment of little interest except for its connection with the great medieval tradition of *ne quod nimis*, which finds expression in Chaucer, Langland ('mesure is mede-cyne'), Hoccleve, and, at vast length, in Hawes' seven-stanza anaphora on *Mesure* in the *Pastime of Pleasure*.[24]

The next group, which we may call, following Carleton Brown, 'Songs of Mortality', is of greater significance. Mortality, death, the transitoriness of the world, are the major single theme of medieval moralistic poetry, and it was a theme to which Lydgate responded with some of his richest writing. His technique, in *That now is hay some-tyme was Grase* (written for queen Katherine), in *Timor mortis conturbat me*, and in *A Thoroughfare of Woe*, is unfailing—the accumulation of great names, particularly those of the Nine Worthy, as exemplars of the power of death. The last named is particularly elaborate: the refrain is taken from Chaucer, as Lydgate explains at the end:

> Remembre sothly that I the refreyd tooke,
> Of hym that was in makyng soverayne,
> My mayster Chaucier, chief poete of Bretayne,
> Whiche in his tragedyes made ful yore agoo,
> Declared triewly and list nat for to feyne,
> How this world is a thurghfare ful of woo.   (186–91)

In fact, of course, the line is not from Chaucer's 'tragedyes', by which is meant the *Monk's Tale*, but from Aegeus's speech in the *Knight's Tale*, where it represents, in its narrative context, something of the premature resignation of senility. Theseus' speech offers a truer, more truly philosophical resignation. Again Lydgate accepts quite straightforwardly a commonplace that Chaucer undermines by embedding it in a rich dramatic context. The genres are different, admittedly. *A Thoroughfare of Woe*, which is a solid and sober piece of work, has further interest in that it carries its examples of the proud fallen down to recent times, and speaks of Henry V, Clarence, Exeter and Salisbury, Lydgate's own patron for the *Pilgrimage*. *They that no while endure* is a good deal less interesting, being simply a list of those who will not endure (knights, squires, gluttons, thieves, etc.), without even the sonorous roll-call of names; but it exists in two versions, one in rhyme-royal, the other in ballade-stanza, of which the second must be Lydgate's, so that we do get the chance to see Lydgate at his joinery-work —and a sadly obvious sight it is. In other poets one searches long for some clue to the mystery, some objective criteria of style by which the uniqueness of the poet's way with language can be explained. In Lydgate there is no mystery and no search: all his techniques are laid out before us like a tidy craftsman's tools.

But whenever one tires of Lydgate's solid and workmanlike virtues, and thinks of him, like Colonel Brandon in *Sense and Sensibility*, as a man of nothing but sterling qualities, he does something which restores one's faith in the power of poetry to raise a man above his common level. *As a Mydsomer Rose*, the last of these songs of mortality, is such a poem. The opening line,

> Lat no man booste of konnyng nor vertu,

with its echoes of the great laments of the *Troy Book*, leads into a quiet meditation on the mutability of things,

Al stant on chaung like a mydsomyr roose.

There are some fine stanzas of natural description, drawing analogies for the theme of change from the seasons, and from the golden dawn:

> The nyht doth folwe, appallith al his cheere
> When western wawes his streemys over-close.
> Rekne al bewte, al fresshness that is heere:
> Al stant on chaung lyke a mydsomyr roose. (53–6)

The *Ubi sunt* follows, but the climax of the poem is the variation of the refrain in the last two stanzas, where the martyrs of Christ are introduced, and the rose takes on a new significance:

> Ther bloody suffraunce was no somyr roose.
> It was the Roose of the bloody feeld,
> Roose of Jericho that greuh in Beedlem:
> The five Roosys portrayed in the sheeld,
> Splayed in the baneer at Jerusalem.
> The sonne was clips and dirk in every rem
> Whan Christ Jhesu five wellys lyst uncloose
> Toward Paradys, callyd the rede strem,
> Of whos five woundys prent in your hert a roos.
>
> (112–20)

The first line here has an extraordinary power, and Norton-Smith has written well of the whole passage:

> The poetic activity which translates the natural rose, symbol of organic decay, into the highest expression of martyrdom through the traditional symbolism of Christ, the rose of Jericho, and, further, translates the image into a meditational emblem, is original and unparalleled elsewhere in medieval poetry.[25]

For a final point, the version here quoted is a revision, and we can in this instance trace the process by which Lydgate moved from the ordinary to the unique.

The last group of moralistic poems are almost archetypal Lydgate. Working on the basis solely of contrastive and parallel statements, with no internal logic or development at all, they circle endlessly, with infinite convolutions of allusion, around a theme of bewildering simplicity: 'life is as it is, everything according to its nature'. Words cannot describe the breathless vacuity of their utterance, like that of a man compelled to stammer but with nothing to say. *Look in thy Merour and deeme noon othir wight* has the courtly opening, with a 'feldefare' singing the refrain, but soon settles to a pattern of disjunctive one-line statements which add-up, roughly, to 'Some are one thing, some another'. Much use is made of bestiary-material. It is really very much like what Beryl Smalley calls Lathbury's 'mincing-machine' at work,[26] except that it not only comes out the same, but goes in the same too—as in the sequence of images for hypocrisy in 109-15. *Look in thy Merour* is the longest of all the refrain-poems (216 lines), and *Everything to his Semblable* is only slightly shorter. The refrain was announced in the *Fabules* and in the *Churl and the Bird*, and the catalogue here is exhaustive, working its way systematically through all the estates of society:

> Þe pyebaker leteþe heos pyes blode,
> With stobul-geesse selleþe garlec dere,
> Þe vynter, gladde of vendages goode,
> Of beestis fatte rejoyeþe þe bochier. . . .   (105–8)

There is a touch of satire on clergy and the law (121, 129), and a 'turn' on the refrain at the end, where man is urged to draw toward God, 'to whome he was semblable'. *A Song of Vertu* is a string of associations amplifying the idea that virtue follows virtue as things follow their nature; characteristically, the system of correspondences on which the poem is constructed is left to speak for itself:

> The fissh for beit goth to the angil-hook,
> The larke with song is Phebus massageer,
> A thryvyng scoler riht eerly to his book—
> Who sewith vertu, vertu he shal leere.   (37–40)

The World is Variable seems to be related to this group, but it is difficult to tell, for the poem is virtually unintelligible, so complete is the collapse of its syntax (e.g. 49–56).

The last two poems are simple expressions of the contrastive habit of thought which we have seen to be basic in Lydgate. *Ryme without Accord* is an expanded oxymoron, a catalogue of antinomies, but the catalogue is so miscellaneous that one cannot be entirely sure that Lydgate is aware of the play of irony within the paradoxes:

> A leche to thryve where none is sore ne sike,
> An instrument of musyk withouten a sown,

A scorpion to be both mylde and meke,
A cloyster man ever rennyng in the towne,
First to kille and sith to graunt pardoun,
To yeve a stone to hem that of brede the besought,
To make a shippard of a wielde lyoun—
It may wele ryme, but it accordith nought.   (49–56)

Some of these, it will be seen, are straightforward contradictions, like 'Merlin's prophecy' allusions[27]; others are traditional sources of satirical comment; but Lydgate presents them all in the same tone of voice, like a man making an inventory of books without any awareness of what is in them. *Tyed with a Lyne* is easier, and better. It lists the contraries to which man is subjected by Fortune, concluding that there is no surety in this life,

The gretter lord, the lasse his assurance;
The sikerest lyffe is in glad poverte;
Both high and lough shal go on dethis daunce,
Renne unto Powlis, beholde the Machabe. . . .   (64–7)

and that man should turn to the stability of God. The first stanza is copied from the poem attributed to Halsham in MS. Fairfax 16,[28] and with it the two-line refrain which runs through the poem (it is varied in the last four stanzas):

Is this fortune, or is it infortune?
Though I go loose, I tyed am with a lyne,

There is no need to assume that Lydgate misunderstood Halsham's *lune* 'leash for a hawk', as 'line': the spellings *lyne* and *luyne* both appear in the Lydgate text, and the scribe must be responsible for the former. It is interesting to see Lydgate working again quite obviously from a literary stimulus—a phrase, a proverb, here a stanza from another man's poem. Nothing could be further from his habit than to respond to the stimulus of experience or life.

However, life does creep in, and it is one of the qualities of these last two poems, and to some extent of the other moralistic poems too, that the very fixedness of the moral schemes permits a degree of illustrative realism which Lydgate finds impossible in narrative, where the pressure to moralise is self-imposed and therefore more imperative. It is the same sort of creeping, non-academic (i.e. not specifically associated with low-style narrative) realism as one finds in the *Knight's Tale*, where

15

everyday life is introduced by allusion, in the accounts of planetary
infortune, and above all in sermons, which are a major source of
naturalistic observation of common life in medieval literature.[29]

These tendencies towards realism are carried further in what are
usually called the 'satirical' poems of Lydgate, though the category is a
loose one. Some of them are distinguished from the moralistic poems
only by a lighter tone of voice, like *So as the Crabbe goth forward* and
Ryght as a Rammes Horne, which are refrain-poems *per antiphrasim*.
Both present pictures of an ideal world,

> Marchauntes of lucre take noon hede,
> And Usure lith fetred yn distresse;
> And for to speke or write of womanhede,
> Thei banished han from hem Newfangelnesse;
>
> (*Rammes Horne*, 17–20)

which are turned upside-down in the refrain. These poems, with their
simple verbal trickery, are like some children's game, or like the
punctuation-poems in Robbins' *Secular Lyrics of the XIVth and XVth
centuries* (nos. 110–12). In the first, which is a loose paraphrase of a
French poem (which MacCracken prints), Lydgate not only points
up the contradiction by translating

> Aynsi come le cravisse va

as

> So as þe crabbe goþe forward

but even finds it necessary to explain the joke in the last stanza:

> Howe þat þe crabbe gooþe bakward!

(And even this he gets wrong, though the weight of medieval authority
would have supported him.)

The favourite target of these satirical poems, as might be expected,
is women.[30] The *Ballade per Antiphrasim* demonstrates both the kinship
of form with the moralistic poems—it uses again the refrain 'As I goo
loos, and teied am with a lyne'—and also the mechanical nature of these
antifeminist ironies. Like the more popular rendering in Robbins (no.
38), and like the chess-passages in *Reason and Sensuality*, it is a matter
simply of 'Cuius contrarium verum est'. *Beware of Doublenesse*, in
which we move away from refrain-poem to true ballade, is subtler.

The scribes, Shirley in particular, label it *per antiphrasim*, but the poem itself keeps the ironies nicely suspended. What enables Lydgate to preserve his poetic balance, and to resist the usual strident anti-feminism, is the example of Chaucer's Envoy to the *Clerk's Tale*, to which he alludes in the last stanzas. *Beware of Doublenesse* was, in fact, long attributed to Chaucer: the four-stress ballade-stanza is not characteristic of Lydgate, but one would like to accept Shirley's ascription.

More conventionally medieval are the straightforward attacks on women and marriage in *The Pain and Sorrow of Evil Marriage* and the *Examples against Women*. There is no irony here, and a rather listless air:

> Thise olde ensamples ought inowgh suffice. . . .
>
> (*Examples*, 99)

Most medieval poets would have an allusion somewhere to such 'examples': they are always available as raw material, and the readiness with which they come to mind is illustrated in Gawain's complaint against the fickleness of women in his confrontation with the Green Knight, and his reference, like Lydgate, to Adam, Solomon, and Samson. But the best poets make some use of the material, transmute it to some larger poetic purpose, dramatic, as in *Sir Gawain and the Green Knight*, or quasi-dramatic, as with Chaucer's references to 'the sorwe and wo that is in mariage' in the *Envoy to Bukton*. The Wife of Bath, of course, carries the whole anti-feminist tradition off into a different sphere altogether, first standing it on its head by herself acting as its representative, and then subtly undermining all its assumptions. Lydgate, as so often, seems to be working in the cellars and storehouses of literature, shifting about its bales and barrels with barely a glimpse of light coming through.

The subject of *Horns Away*—the extravagant horned headdresses worn by women in the early fifteenth century[31]—is an obvious one for satire, but Lydgate's poem, which was, to judge from the number of MSS., the most popular of all these moralistic and satirical pieces in the fifteenth century, turns out to be quite different. Anyone else would have produced a lively squib—Hoccleve, for instance, who writes brilliantly of a similarly ridiculous fashion, for long sleeves, in the *Regement of Princes* (470, 533)—but Lydgate, beginning

> Of God and Kynde procedith al bewte,

offers a serious and considered explanation, with analogies from nature and history, of how horns are philosophically unacceptable within the doctrine of natural beauty. The clinching argument, in an Envoy nearly as long as the poem, is the Virgin:

> She wered a kovercheef, hornes wer cast away.   (56)

The only perceptible lightening of tone throughout is in another allusion to the *Clerk's Tale* Envoy (37). Lydgate's seriousness is often deadly: here it is endearing and not ineffective, though the reason may be simply in the lift that his poetry always takes when he speaks of Mary:

> This rose of Jericho, ther greuh non suych in May.   (62)

The whole poem, of nine ballade-stanzas, is on three rhymes.

There remain, apart from the *Order of Fools*, a dull catalogue, two satirical exercises in low-style realism which confirm what I have said of Lydgate's versatility: *Against Millers and Bakers*, which suggests, amongst other things, a chapel for false millers and bakers under the stocks, since they spend, or ought to spend, most of their time there; and the *Ballade of Jak Hare*, or 'Tale of Froward Maymond'.[32] This poem, an offshoot of Lydgate's reading in the *Disciplina Clericalis*,[33] is a portrait of a slovenly, idle, drunken cook's boy.

> His mouth wel wet, his slevis riht thredbare,
> A turnebroche, a boy for Hogge of Ware.   (4–5)

The model, as may be gathered from the allusion, is Chaucer's *Cook's Tale*, and, though there are no comparisons to be made, the sharpness of the language and the observation,

> As barkyd leder his face ys schynyng,   (30)

and the vigour of expression,

> Wassail to Maymond and to his jousy pate,
> Unthryft and he be togedre met   (49–50)

are enough to persuade one that Lydgate could have written that masterpiece of fifteenth century low satire, *London Lickpenny* (though we must accept that he did not).

There is a residue of 'didactic' verse which resists classification by any of the methods that have been employed in this chapter, since it is avowedly informational or practical. I am thinking of the *Verses on*

Cambridge, the *Kings of England*, and some pieces already mentioned, in one capacity or another, such as the *Pageant of Knowledge*, the *Cartae Versificatae* and the *Treatise for Lavenders*. Such pieces reflect the sober and business-like tastes of the age, just as they reflect a comprehensive concept of poetry which thinks nothing alien to itself. More to the point, though, they appear now, in the fifteenth century, because this is the age in which a large body of knowledge is being made available, for the first time, to an English-speaking audience which has no Latin or French. The clearest example of this movement is *Stans puer ad mensam*, a poem instructing young boys how to behave at table, which takes its place among the many 'Books of Courtesy' which were being produced in the fifteenth century. The literature of social etiquette in English has moved up a degree: whereas parental instruction in English in the fourteenth century, such as *The Good Wife taught her Daughter*, is addressed to middle-class readers,[34] here in the fifteenth century it concerns the upper classes as well. The fifteenth century was a particularly pragmatic age, fond of information and fact, but many of its literary phenomena are the product of the change of language, not the change of taste. These instructional and informational pieces appear in English because that is now the language of the audience which needs them, not because the audience is new.

Stans puer ad mensam, which originates again from the *Disciplina Clericalis*,[35] was very popular in its day, and something like twenty-three manuscripts survive. It is written in sharp, clear, disjunctive statements:

> Be symple of cheer, cast not thy look asyde,
> Gase nat aboute, turnyng over all;
> Ageyn the post lat nat thy bak abyde;
> Make nat the merour also of the wall;
> Pike nat thy nase, and in especyall
> Be riht weell war, and set hit in thy thouht,
> To-fore thy sovereyn cracche ne rubbe nought.   (8–14)

It manages to combine mnemonic advice about basic habits with an air of literary polish, and the literature of etiquette could hardly ask for more. The popularity of this piece, however, is eclipsed by that of the *Dietary*, which, with over fifty manuscripts, is by far the most widely disseminated of all Lydgate's poems. As Robbins points out,[36] this number is exceeded only by the *Prick of Conscience*, the *Canterbury Tales*, *Piers Plowman*, and the *Confessio Amantis*. No more, surely, need be said. The poem exists in many different versions and permutations, longer and shorter, and some MSS. include a *Doctrine for Pestilence* ('eschewe mystis blake') which is really a separate poem, of ballade-construction. The title, too, is a little misleading, since advice on diet and health inevitably, at least in Lydgate's hands, evolves into general moral advice, of the usual gnomic kind:

> Suffir in tyme, in thi riht be bold,
> Swer non othis, no man to begyle,
> In youthe be lusti, sad whan thou art old:
> No worldly joie lastith her but a while.   (149–52)

The work is usually thought of as educational, and is often found, as Robbins says, in collections of instructional poems used by children. Presumably they made what they could of advice like this:

> With women aged flesshly have na a do.   (29)

Literary criticism has no part here, except to say that what had to be done is well done, and with assurance, and that the manner is well suited to the matter.

The few other pieces reflect the enduring medieval concern to classify information and moral instruction by enumeration. *The Nine Properties of Wine* is of the same type as the *Four things that make a man a fool*, a translation of a Latin proverb ('Quatuor infatuant, honor, etas, femina, vinum') of which Lydgate did no fewer than three versions: both employ a technique of numerical organisation which is at bottom mnemonic and practical, 'a means of intellectual orientation', as Curtius puts it,[37] and which finds its fundamental expression in number maxims like

> Kepe well x   And flee fro vii;
> Rule well v   And come to hevyn.[38]

Lydgate's poem on the *Twelve Abuses* is again based on a Latin original ('Rex sine sapiencia . . .') which was of very wide currency: there are fifty distinct versions of it in English alone[39] and we may be sure that this is only the tip of the iceberg. It must have been part of the very structure of medieval thought. Furthermore, like most medieval habits of mind, 'numerical composition' is the visible remnant of an elaborate philosophical system, in this case based on the concept of number as divine. We should do well to have in mind the larger reference of even such commonplaces as Lydgate provides us with.

Notes to Chapter Seven

1 *Caxton's Aesop*, ed. R. T. Lenaghan (Harvard U.P. 1967), p. 12.

2 J. E. Spingarn, *A History of Literary Criticism in the Renaissance* (New York 1899), p. 9.

3 C. G. Osgood, *Boccaccio on Poetry* (Princeton 1930), p. xxxviii.

4 See *Pastime of Pleasures*, 36–42, 50–6, 715–21; Hammond, *Chaucer to Surrey*, pp. 409, 488, 492.

5 Quotation from *Robert Henryson: Poems*, ed. C. Elliott (Clarendon Medieval and Tudor Series, Oxford 1963).

6 D. W. Robertson, *A Preface to Chaucer*, p. 54.

7 The *Disciplina Clericalis* is edited by A. Hilka and W. Söderhjelm in *Acta Societatis Scientiarum Fennicae*, XXXVIII (Helsinki 1911–12), nos. 4 (Latin text) and 5 (French text). The 'Exemplum de rustico et avicula' is on p. 30 (French text, p. 26).

8 Compare *Troilus* I,731; *CT*, I,1838, IX,163–74, IV,1637.

9 As Schirmer does, p. 232.

10 Especially 536 and *Libel*, 1100: see Lydgate's *Horse, Goose and Sheep*, ed. M. Degenhart (*Münchener Beiträge zur Romanischen und englischen Philologie*, XIX,1900), p. 23.

11 Renoir, *The Poetry of John Lydgate*, p. 101.

12 'Exemplum de integro amico', *ed. cit.*, p. 4 (French text, p. 3).

13 *Sir Richard Roos*, p. 275.

14 In *Twenty-Six Political and other Poems*, ed. J. Kail (EETS,OS 124,1904).

15 Ed. Furnivall, in *Minor Poems of the Vernon MS.* (EETS,OS 117,1901), pp. 658–746.

16 There are four books of maxims, mostly in couplets, preceded by the 'little Cato', a collection of two or three-word gnomes. The modern edition is by M. Boas (Amsterdam 1952).

17 Also used in *Fall*, III,3088–115, the envoy on unjust judges.

18 The Latin proverbs are nos. 18575 and 22868 in *Lateinische Sprichwörter und Sentenzen des Mittelalters*, ed. H. Walther (5 vols., Göttingen, 1963–7). For others quoted for lines 22, 90, and 106, see nos. 23941, 31228, 20088.

19 Not *nona* as in MacCracken: no. 27350 in Walther.

20 Carleton Brown prints the first of these (*Religious Lyrics of the XVth Century*, p. 280) and refers to the others (p. 349),

21 Laud 598, which has a few other Lydgate pieces in it.

22 For the pleasant suggestion that 'R. Stokys' is the Richard Stokes 'who moved in the outer fringes, at least, of the Chaucerian circle', see Carleton Brown, in *MLN*, LIV(1939),131–3.

23 See no. 63 in *Historical Poems of the XIVth and XVth Centuries*, ed. Robbins; also, for the topic in general, Curtius, *European Literature and the Latin Middle Ages*, pp. 94–8.

24 2591–639. See Hammond, *Chaucer to Surrey*, pp. 445, 451; Sieper's note to *Reason and Sensuality*, 4194; Owst, *Literature and Pulpit in Medieval England*, p. 185.

25 *Op. cit.*, p. 138. Quotation is from Norton-Smith's text.

26 *English Friars and Antiquity*, p. 226.

27 As in 'When to Trust Women', no. 114 in *Secular Lyrics*, ed. Robbins.

28 Printed in *Religious Lyrics of the XVth Century*, ed. Brown, p. 262. For Halsham, see Helen P. South's article in *PMLA*, L(1935),362–71. Lydgate, with customary economy, uses the first stanza of Halsham's poem in the *Pageant of Knowledge*, 160–6.

29 See G. R. Owst, *Literature and Pulpit in Medieval England*, p. 22 and *passim*; also Margaret Schlauch, *Antecedents of the English Novel 1400–1600* (Warsaw and London 1963), pp. 40, 83.

30 See above, pp. 118 and 135.

31 See Hammond's introduction to her text of the poem, *Chaucer to Surrey*, p.110; Owst, *Literature and Pulpit*, pp. 399–403.

32 So entitled in the best MS. and by Norton-Smith in his edition.

33 'Exemplum de Maimundo servo', *ed. cit.*, p. 38 (French text, p. 32).

34 See the edition by T. F. Mustanoja (Helsinki 1948), which has an excellent introduction ranging widely over instructional literature as diverse as Cato and the *Disciplina Clericalis*.

35 'De modo comedendi', *ed. cit.*, p. 37 (French text, p. 31).

36 *Secular Lyrics*, p. 251.

37 *Op. cit.*, p. 510 (in the excursus on 'Numerical Apothegms').

38 *Secular Lyrics*, ed. Robbins, no. 83.

39 *Historical Poems*, ed. Robbins, p. 327.

CHAPTER EIGHT

The Fall of Princes

It is time now to return to the chronology of Lydgate's life and to the *Fall of Princes*, which, with its 36,365 lines, is his longest single work. By about 1433 or 1434, Lydgate had returned to live permanently at Bury, and his decision to do so may have been prompted by the vast commission of translating the *Fall*. He needed the leisure, and he also needed the security which monastic life afforded, since the financial support he received from his patron was at best erratic. Lydgate's acquaintance with Humphrey, duke of Gloucester, younger brother of Henry V, and Protector of England during the minority of Henry VI, goes back at least to 1422, when he wrote the poem on Gloucester's approaching marriage to Jacqueline of Hainault, and may go back further. There were plenty of opportunities for earlier contact, through Henry V, or through Thomas Chaucer, or through the abbey of Bury itself, and for the continuation of the association in Lydgate's laureate work in the later 1420s. The Prologue to the *Fall* tells us that Humphrey, having a high opinion of Boccaccio's *De Casibus Illustrium Virorum* as a 'Mirror for Princes', asked Lydgate to translate it,

> To shewe the chaung of worldli variaunce.   (Prol., 434)

The date of this commission must be 1431, since Lydgate makes reference elsewhere in the Prologue (403) to Humphrey's stern suppression of Lollard heretics in that year. The translation occupied the next eight years of Lydgate's life, with some intervals to fulfil commissions like the writing of the *Life of St. Edmund*, and it was not completed until 1438 or 1439.

In his Prologue, Lydgate speaks in very complimentary terms of Humphrey's love of learning and scholarship:

> Of hih lettrure, I dar eek of hym telle,
> And treuli deeme that he doth excelle

> In undirstondyng alle othir of his age,
> And hath gret joie with clerkis to comune:
> And no man is mor expert of language. . . .
> His corage never doth appalle
> To studie in bookis of antiquite,
> Therin he hath so gret felicite
> Vertuously hymsilff to ocupie,
> Of vicious slouthe to have the maistrie.　　(I,384–99)

This last statement should prepare us for a paradox in the relationship of patron and poet. Lydgate justifies Humphrey's interest in classical antiquity, an interest which entitles him to some claim as the first humanist patron of letters in England, in terms of the specifically medieval—and specifically Benedictine—injunction to 'eschew idleness'. Humphrey was touched, however superficially, by the spirit of the Italian Renaissance and the reawakening of interest in classical literature, and his commissioning of a translation of the *De Casibus* is part of his admiration for anything that came out of Italy, but Lydgate responds only fitfully to the stimulus, and at almost every point reasserts, if that is the right word for so inert a habit of thought, the medieval commonplaces upon which Boccaccio's work is so largely based.

Perhaps the difference between Humphrey and Lydgate should not be emphasised too much. So much has been written of Humphrey as a patron of letters[1] that one is in danger of rating him too highly, as a dedicated lover of classical learning, instead of what he was, an erratic, unprincipled and attractively unsuccessful politician who dabbled in letters partly because he saw in them a way to prestige and profit. His claim as a humanist patron only looks strong for lack of contenders. Beaufort's encouragement of Poggio Bracciolini, for instance, was disastrously premature. Poggio, whom Beaufort had met at the council of Constance, came to England (1418–22) with a great reputation as a classical scholar and as a professional 'discoverer' of lost classical texts such as Lucretius *De Natura Rerum* and Statius' *Silvae*. Beaufort offered him employment, not because of a love of scholarship, but because he understood the simple fact that epistolography was a form of power and that it would assist his political ambitions and add to his prestige if the letters from his chancery were in the polished curial style. Poggio's visit, however, was a disappointment. He found nothing to interest him in the libraries and catalogues that he examined (in this he was unfortunate, considering what there was at Christ Church and Bury), and had to fall back for his reading on the Church fathers and on medieval translations of Aristotle and Chrysostom. Beaufort, busy with politics, lost interest in him, and he returned to Italy with sad tales of the ignorance—and gross eating-habits—of the English.

Gloucester was certainly more successful than this. His first contacts with Italian humanism would have been through Papal officials in this country, such as Giulano Cesarini in 1426, and especially Piero del Monte, who was Papal collector in England from 1435 to 1440 and who dedicated a moral treatise to Gloucester. He seems to have acted as some sort of adviser on taste to Gloucester, and he was in close touch too with Gloucester's own chancery officials, such as Thomas Beckington, his chancellor (1420–38), who was well aware of the need for an effective Latin epistolary style and severely critical of Whethamstede. Piero del Monte, however, like a true opportunist, cultivated Whethamstede, not because he admired his extraordinary Latin style, but because he coveted the rich library of St. Albans.

Gloucester's most important contact was Zano Castiglione, bishop of Bayeux. He went to the council of Basle in 1434 with Humphrey's commission to buy books, and when the council adjourned to Florence, met Leonardo Bruni, one of the foremost Italian humanists of the time. Gloucester commissioned a translation of Aristotle's *Politics* from Bruni, but it came to nothing. Pier Candido Decembrio also heard of Gloucester from Zano, now acting as Gloucester's literary agent, and wrote to ask him to act as patron of a translation of Plato's *Republic*. Gloucester was enthusiastic, though he seems more interested in the dedication than in the work itself. He also asked Candido to obtain for him certain books for his library, which was now growing to considerable proportions. The translation of the *Republic* was eventually completed, but the association of the two men ended soon afterwards in some acrimony, and there is more than a suspicion that it was due to Humphrey's reluctance to pay what he was thought to have promised.

Gloucester also brought over Italian scholars to work as his secretaries. One was Tito Livio Frulovisi, who came over about 1436, and from whom Gloucester commissioned a life of his brother, the *Vita Henrici Quinti*, which has some importance in English historiography. His motives, as usual, were not entirely disinterested: he wanted Livio to glorify Henry as a war-leader, since he himself was of the war-faction in England at the time. Another work of Livio's, the *Humfroidos*, written in praise of Humphrey's martial exploits 1435–7 (the relief of Calais, and the pointless raid on Flanders), casts some doubt on the quality of his humanism, since it is written in a mannered and florid style similar to that of Whethamstede.[2] Livio was succeeded as Gloucester's secretary about 1438 by Antonio Beccaria, who did some translations for him and also conducted his correspondence with Decembrio. Gloucester's own scholarship is dubious: he seems to have preferred French translations and himself invariably wrote in French. His encouragement of English writers does not give much ground, either, for thinking of him as a humanist, though he probably did the best he could with the talent available. There was Lydgate, and Hoccleve, who airily discusses Gloucester as a possible patron in the *Dialogue* (534). There was John Capgrave, monk of Lynn, who dedicated a commentary on *Genesis* to him in 1438, and is said to have written a *Vita Humfridi Ducis*; and Nicholas Upton, who did a translation of the *De Studio Militari* for him. John Russell, author of the *Boke of Nurture*, George Ashby, and Thomas Norton, who wrote a poem about alchemy, had all been in his service or in his household. Most detailed is our knowledge of the translation of Palladius *On Husbondrie* (1440), the prologue to which speaks at length of Humphrey and of his gifts of books to Oxford. The author seems to be a member of the Duke's household and shows a far closer acquaintance with him than Lydgate, as well as a more extravagant turn of praise:

> Serenous prince! or thus: O princis flour!
> Or thus: O prince in pees and duc in werre!
> Or nay: O Goddis knyght and Cristis tour!
> Or ellis thus: O londis lif and sterre
> Of light! Or ellis: Thynge of thyngis derre!—
> Or y noot what, excedyng so nature,
> That who thow art to sayn my wittis erre,
> Not oonly god ner oonly creature.
> But God, me semeth, best thou mayst resemble
> For verite, justice, and mansuetude. . . .[3]

Perhaps the sharpest comment on Gloucester's taste is the fact that he was closely associated with Whethamstede, abbot of St. Albans, who acted as literary adviser to him. Whethamstede is in the medieval encyclopaedic tradition,[4] and his attitude to the classics is as of a repository of information, fable, curious lore, and anecdotal wisdom. His favourite modern author was Boccaccio (the Latin Boccaccio, of course, not the Italian one), and it may well have been he who suggested a translation of the *De Casibus* to Gloucester.

To be fair to Gloucester, it should be said that, though he himself was no scholar and no humanist, he had the energy and variety of interests which would have made him an excellent patron in a more favourable climate. England was not ready for him, and his real achievement was posthumous. His generous gifts of books to Oxford—129 in 1438, 134 in 1444, and others—formed the nucleus of the university library, indeed forced the university, by their numbers, to establish an organised library. The books themselves reflect the utilitarian nature of Glouces-ter's approach to learning—there are large numbers of books on medicine, agriculture, and astronomy—but there were enough classical and neo-classical writers to make Oxford the springboard for English humanism in the later fifteenth century. A man like William Grey, for instance, later bishop of Ely, certainly took his first inspiration from Gloucester's books. Gloucester also helped, through his Italian secre-taries, to raise the standard of epistolary Latin style in England, and opened channels of communication with Italy from which later scholars profited. It was the Englishmen who went to Italy for their post-graduate education who made the classical revival in England possible, men like Robert Flemmyng, the first Greek scholar that England pro-duced, and John Free, the first to approach the professional standards of the Italian humanists.

There will be more to say later about Gloucester's actual influence on Lydgate's translation of the *Fall*. Meanwhile, we can trace the course of their association, during the eight long years of the work, through Lydgate's own comments. The opening Prologue is full of vigour, and contains, as an outgrowth of the modesty-topos—

> Bu O allas! who shal be my muse,
> Or onto whom shal I for helpe calle? . . .
> My maistir Chaucer, with his fresh comedies,
> Is ded, allas, cheeff poete of Breteyne—   (I,239–47)

Lydgate's longest allusion to Chaucer, with an invaluable, though occasionally obscure, list of his works. Scholars have assumed that this allusion was put in at Gloucester's suggestion, but this seems unneces-sary: no catalogue of Gloucester's books ever so much as mentions Chaucer, and it is on the contrary characteristic of Lydgate to invoke Chaucer at moments of high poetic activity or ambition.

The Prologue also contains a eulogy of Gloucester, for which Lydgate must have thought he had good occasion. But by the end of book II,

Gloucester's promises were wearing thin, and Lydgate penned to him a *Letter* (not part of the *Fall*) in which he complains of the poor state of his purse[5]:

> Tokne of mornyng, I weryd clothys blake
> Cause my purs was fal in gret rerage,
> Lynyng outward, his guttys wer out-shake:
> Oonly for lak of plate and of coignage.   (5–8)

The next stanza develops with some wit the metaphor of the sick purse:

> I souhte leechys for a restoratiff,
> In whom I fond no consolacioun,
> Appotecaryes for a confortatiff:
> Drag nor dia was noon in Bury toun.
> Botme of his stomak tournyd up-so-doun
> A laxatif did hym so gret outrage,
> Made hym slendre by a consumpcioun:
> Oonly for lak of plate and of coignage.   (9–16)

Succeeding stanzas play off nautical, monetary, medical, and alchemical images in a skilful and complexly precise manner. The whole poem is a minor masterpiece of the occasional epistolary art. What is more, if we accept Hammond's interpretation of events, it produced immediate results. In the Prologue to book III Lydgate takes up Boccaccio's image of the pilgrim, weary from his journey, and develops it with wry feeling:

> Support was non my dulnesse for to guie;
> Povert approchid; in stal crokid age:
> Mercurie absent and Philologie;
> Mi purs ay liht and void of al coignage.
> Bachus ferr off to glade my corage;
> An ebbe of plente; scarsete atte fulle,
> Which of an old man makth the sperit dulle.
>
> (III,64–70)

But hope is renewed, and the outlook brightens, through his lord's 'bounteuous largesse':

> A, how it is an hertli rejoishyng
> To serve a prynce that list to advertise

> Of ther servauntis the feithful just menyng,
> And list considre to guerdone ther servise.
>
> (III, 78–81)

The mists of despair clear, and he presses forward with his task. 'There are many begging-letters', as Hammond says, 'and many adulatory poems; but it would be hard to match this case of plea and thanks both remaining to us'.[6]

But by the end of book III, Lydgate was in trouble again, and he inserts a 'Chapitle on the governance of Poetis', in which he complains that poets have no land or wealth to support themselves and need the munificence of patrons to give them security from worldly cares:

> Thei shold be quieet fro worldli mocioun,
> And it sequestre out of their remembraunce.
>
> (III,3839–40)

Other men have their resources,

> Men of the cherche of gold have habundaunce,
>
> (III,3852)

but poets nowadays have to beg for their livelihood. He concludes with a request for money to his patron, the 'welle of fredam'. The request seems to have gone unanswered, and it was probably at this point that Lydgate, tired of 'worldli mocioun', decided to find his own security by returning permanently to Bury. He seems, in fact, despite his many commissions, always to have been chronically and famously poor. His friend Shirley refers to his poverty in his verse table of contents to MS. Add.16165,

> God wolde of nobles he hade ful his hoode,   (86)

and again, more pointedly, in MS. Add. 29729:

> His nobles bene spent, I leve, ychon,
> And eke his shylinges nyghe by:
> His thred-bare coule woll not ly.
> Ellas, ye lordis, why nill ye se
> And reward his poverte?   (40–4)[7]

He even adds a marginal allusion to Lydgate in transcribing Chaucer's line about the Clerk,

> And yet had he but litill gold in cofre.[8]

Lydgate received no more money from Gloucester, it appears. Translating the Prologue to book VIII, with its conversation between Boccaccio and Petrarch, he applies Petrarch's words of encouragement to himself:

> Haste on thi way, lat Grace crosse þi saille,
> Fall on no sond of wilful necligence,
> Lat goode will be cheef of thi counsaille,
> To guye thi rother set enteer dilligence;
> Yif vitaille faille and wyn to thi dispense,
> Yit at the laste, thynk, for this socour
> Sum roial prince shal quyte thi labour.　　　(VIII,141–7)

Nothing came of it, and in the Envoy to the whole work Lydgate, after describing the difficulties of the task he had completed—the scarcity of rhyme in English, his age, lack of skill, 'the Frenssh unkouth compendyously compyled'—returns patiently to the theme of reward:

> Trustyng ageynward your liberal largesse,
> Of this cotidien shal relevyn me,
> Hope hath brought tydyng to recure myn accesse;
> Aftir this ebbe of froward skarsete
> Shal folwe a spryng flood of gracious plente,
> To wasshe away be plenteuous influence
> Al ground ebbys of constreyned indigence.
>
> 　　　　　　　　　　　　　　　　(IX,3345–51)

The imagery, so playfully exercised in the *Letter*, now has a tired and worn air, like much in the later books of the *Fall*.

Lydgate's source for the *Fall of Princes* was a French translation of Boccaccio's *De casibus illustrium virorum*. Boccaccio is best known today for his *Decameron*, and to Chaucer for his Italian poems, such as *Il Filostrato* and *Il Filocolo*, but his great reputation before the Renaissance was based on the Latin encyclopaedic works written in the latter part of his life, the *De Casibus*, the *De Claris Mulieribus* and, above all, the *De Genealogia Deorum*. The last-named work, a comprehensive account of classical mythology, is often regarded as 'humanist' in its affiliations, and certainly the range of its classical knowledge is wide; but its spirit is essentially medieval. Boccaccio is undiscriminating in his use of sources, encyclopaedic in ambition, and systematically allegorical in his interpretation of the material. He claims to have gone back to the classics, but his chief debt is to medieval compilers like Albericus of London, and Albericus' own sources—the *Mythologiae* of Fulgentius, the *Fulgentius metaforalis*, Servius' commentary on the *Aeneid*, Martianus Capella, and Isidore's *Etymologiae*.[9] The real precursor of the Renaissance in fourteenth-century Italy is Petrarch, who distinguished the Biblical from the classical, and had a sense of historical perspective in which classical writers and writings could be seen to have their own separate and independent existence, quite apart from their usefulness as repositories of fact and fable. He carried the medieval admiration of Rome to its extreme by coming to regard all the period between then and now as a long interval, so laying the foundation for the concept of the 'Dark Ages', which is the main and often the only distinguishing characteristic of what we call the Renaissance. The Renaissance, in other words, is a 'fact' because it so often proclaimed itself to be one.

The *De Casibus*, completed about 1358, is a history of Fortune, of the crushing blows dealt to the most illustrious characters in history and mythology, based mostly on Biblical and classical sources, with the object of teaching princes wisdom and virtue by showing them the misfortunes brought on by pride, ambition, and sin, or simply the salutary lesson of misfortune. As Boccaccio sits in his study, a long procession of unfortunates, from Adam and Eve to King John of France, captured at Poitiers in 1356, pass before him in a vision, and he tells their stories. Sometimes they address him and begin their own stories, like Adam and Hercules[10]; or else they appear to him dolefully complaining and he then proceeds with their stories (this is usual); or they interrupt him, as Thyestes does (p. 34) as he was about to tell of Theseus, saying that his story was far more woeful. There are occasional disputes, as between Atreus and Thyestes (p. 35), or Fortune and Poverty (p. 70), or conversations between Boccaccio and his characters, such as Petrarch (p. 185) or Brunnhilde (p. 209). The material is further varied by digressions in which he enlarges on the vices that have brought men into adversity, and offers warnings, as against disobedience in reference to the fall of Adam (p. 27), against the pride of princes, with reference to Nimrod (p. 29), against hasty credence and rashness in princes (p. 38), against trust in worldly riches and praise of poverty (p. 43), and against the falsehood and malice of women (p. 46). Boccaccio also varies the procession by changing the perspective, so that longer accounts alternate with group-chapters, in which numbers of the unfortunate ('Conventus Infoelicium' or 'Pauci Flentes') pass by with a mere mention.

16

The *De Casibus* does, systematically and comprehensively, what the Middle Ages did as a matter of habit, that is, teaches virtue by multiplying examples of the mutability of Fortune to those who put their trust in the world. Both concept and form were ingrained in medieval consciousness, and every reflection on death, mortality or fortune that catalogued the illustrious dead as a *memento mori*, or elaborated the *Ubi sunt* formula, was contributing to the *Fall* tradition. The long passage in the *Roman de la Rose*, where Reason speaks to the Lover of the instability of Fortune and quotes as examples Seneca, Nero, Croesus, and Manfred (5921–6900), is particularly important in providing the widest possible currency for the tradition, and in establishing precedent for more elaborate exempla and for 'modern' instances (Manfred). Chaucer was probably more influenced in the *Monk's Tale* by the *Roman* than by Boccaccio. What Boccaccio added to the tradition was an enormously expanded range of exempla, a greater vigour and skill in individual narratives, and a rhythmic structure for the whole, in the form of the processional, which is never completely obscured, and to which the alternation of close-up and receding perspective (in the group-chapters) contributes considerably.

There are eighty-three MSS. of the *De Casibus*; there are more, over a hundred, of the French translation by Laurent de Premierfait, a professional writer and translator at the court of Charles V. Laurent had translated Cicero for the duke of Bourbon, and already tried his hand at Boccaccio in translating a Latin version of the *Decameron*. He now turned to the *De Casibus* and, at the request of the duke of Berri, did a first version in 1400, and a second much amplified version, the one used by Lydgate, in 1409. Laurent adds geographical, biographical, mythological, and other kinds of detail wherever he sees the opportunity, but the great change in the second version is that the group-chapters are expanded. Every name is now treated in detail, so that these chapters become longer than the others and all Boccaccio's carefully designed perspective is destroyed.

The process that Laurent had begun, that of inflating the *De Casibus* into a universal encyclopaedia of history and mythology, is continued by Lydgate, who amplifies, in much the same manner as Laurent, an already well-padded original. He translates, with evident approval, Laurent's defence of his practice in the Prologue:

> For a story which is nat pleynli told,
> But constreynyd undir woordes fewe,

> For lak of trouthe, wher thei be newe or old,
> Men bi report kan nat the mater shewe;
> These ookis grete be nat doun ihewe
> First at a stroke, but bi long processe,
> Nor longe stories a woord may not expresse.   (I,92–8)

Such a passage stands beside many others in Lydgate which advocate brevity as the ideal of style, and no doubt both views could be accommodated in a poetic as loosely formulated as Lydgate's. He is significantly little interested in poetic theory and is quite content, like Boccaccio and Laurent (and Chaucer's Monk), to prefix his catalogue of tragedies with the simplest and most conventional definition of their nature and purpose:

> The fall of nobles, with everi circumstaunce,
> From ther lordshippes, dreedful and unstable,
> How that thei fill to putte in remembraunce,
> Therin to shewe Fortunys variaunce,
> That othre myhte as in a merour see
> In worldly worshepe may be no surete.   (I,51–6)

He is more specific in speaking of the fall of Jugurtha:

> This may be weel callid a tragedie,
> Be discripcioun takyng auctorite;
> For tragedie, as poetes spesephie,
> Gynneth with joie, eendith with adversite:
> From hih estate men cast in low degre.   (V,3118–22)

Elsewhere Lydgate ignores even what 'Bochas' (he speaks of his author thus, though there is no evidence that he ever saw anything but Laurent's translation) provides him with. Bochas, for instance, has a long discourse on the lofty mission of poets—'Certain est que poesie est une noble science, subtille, haulte, et grandement attournee'[11]—proclaiming that their fictions are like the prophecies of the Old Testament, and thus anticipating, incidentally, Auerbach's 'figural' techniques of interpretation. He refers to his own, not over-modest ambitions as a poet, and the whole passage, like many of the incidentals in the *De Casibus*, has a Renaissance air about it. All this, whether because he didn't understand it or because he disapproved of such flights of fancy, Lydgate reduces to a few lines of commonplace, reverting to a simple moralistic view of poetry:

Ther cheeff labour is vicis to repreve
With a maner covert symylitude,
And non estate with ther langage greeve
Bi no rebukyng of termys dul and rude;
Whatever thei write, on vertu ay conclude,
Appeire no man in no maner wise:
This th'offise of poetis that be wise.   (III,3830–6)

The wisdom sounds like that of the Manciple. What Lydgate adds is the 'Chapitle on the governance of Poetis', the one in which he speaks feelingly of the advantages of having a generous patron.

Lydgate adds a long Prologue to book IV, as if he felt guilty about his omissions in book III, in which he reiterates a practical and moral view of poetry. Without writing, we should not know anything of the past; without writing, to put it even more simply, we should not know what had been written, and Virgil, Ovid, and Petrarch, amongst others, are referred to as proof. Lydgate's immediate source for this view of poetry as a sort of filing cabinet is not far to seek: it is in Guido's Prologue to the *Historia Destructionis Troiae*, one of the few accounts of poetic theory, however elementary, that Lydgate had read at all carefully. Chiefly, the Prologue is there to give Lydgate the chance to air his knowledge of Latin writers, most of which is derived from second-compilations which had precisely the same purpose.

He reverts to type in tackling the chapter on Rhetoric in book VI, concentrating on simple exposition of such things as the five parts of Rhetoric, which Laurent added, and omitting altogether the original basis of the chapter, Boccacio's vigorous polemic against the defamers of rhetoric, those who say that it is form of deception and that it is superfluous.[12] No doubt Boccaccio's invective qualified as 'termes rude'; Lydgate has instead a few additional comments on Memory which could not offend anyone. His handling of the Petrarch-Prologue to book VIII is much more lively, but ends again on a practical and moralistic note, translating Petrarch's invocation of fame as the spur to poetic ambition:

Nous hommes doncques debuons labourer et besongner, et devons esguilloner nostre engin selon toutes noz forces pour acquerir renommee qui ennoblist les hommes; affin que nous ne soyons nombrez entre les gens populaires et innobles; et affin aussi que les hommes trespassez et mors ont laboure pour nostre prouffit, aussi nous puissions prouffiter aux hommes advenir; et

affin que nostre nom soyt escript entre les noms pardurables, et que
nous acconsuivons renommee sans fin, et que les hommes voyent
que durant nostre vie mortelle nous avons travaille a la gloire de
dieu et non pas a l'exaulcement des vices.[13]

into the monastic call to 'eschew idleness':

> And for to make our names perdurable,
> And our merites to putten in memorie,
> Vices t'eschewe, in vertu to be stable,
> That laboure may of slouthe have the victorie,
> To cleyme a see in the hevenli consistorie—
> Despiht of idilnesse and foorthryng of vertu—
> Fyn of our labour be yove to Crist Jesu.   (VIII,176–82)

    With this moralistic conception of poetry at the back of his mind,
always extruding itself through the varied landscape of Bochas,[14] it is
not surprising that the most overwhelming of Lydgate's amplifications
in the *Fall* are in the form of moralisation. Of the 6600 lines of book I,
without the Prologue, over a quarter are direct moral statement.
Lydgate keeps Boccaccio's set-pieces ('Adversus Inobedientiam, or
'Contra Superbos') and Laurent's incidental additions, and himself expands and adds enormously. So we are reminded endlessly of the
inevitability of sorrow after worldly joy:

> For thilke sorwe surmountith every sorwe,
> Which next folwith aftir felicite;
> No wo mor grevous at eve nor at morwe,
> As is in deede sodeyn adversite
> Which cometh onwarli aftir prosperite,
> Nor nothyng more may hertis disavaunce
> Than of old joie newe remembraunce.[15]

of the punishment of disobedience (785) and of pride, with another
fine stanza:

> God hath a thousand handis to chastise,
> A thousand dartis of punycioun,
> A thousand bowes maad in unkouth wise,
> A thousand arblastis bent in his dongoun,
> Ordeyned echon for castigacioun;
> But where he fynt meeknesse and repentaunce,
> Mercy is maistresse of his ordynaunce   (I,1331–7)

of the transitoriness of earthly glory (1429) and the falseness of earthly fame (5104), the mutability of Fortune (2064, 3018, 3522, again and again), the inevitability of death (3788), and against these the virtues of meek obedience (953), patient poverty (6126), and cautious wisdom (4495). Such passages, as we have grown to expect, contain much of Lydgate's best writing, sonorous, evocative, and heavily figured. For once, Lydgate must have felt, he had not only an excuse but a veritable obligation to indulge his natural bent, for Gloucester had instructed him, as he tells us in the Prologue to book II (145), to add an Envoy to each chapter, offering a 'remedie' against Fortune and directed especially to kings and princes. This he does dutifully, pointing the moral (as if he had not pointed it already) in four or five stanzas, distinguished from the rest by the refrain-like last line of each stanza (occasionally he uses ballade-stanza) and by a consciously higher style.[16] These envoys often contain political comment,

> Kyngdamys devyded may no while endure,   (I,3822)

and though endlessly repetitive are often impressive in their handling of the more elaborate style, the envoys to Theseus,

> The onseur gladnesse, the joie transitorie,
> Th'unstable seurnesse, the transmutaciouns,
> The cloudi brihtnesse, the fals eclipsid glorie
> Of erthly pryncis which han possessiouns. . . .
>
>   (I,4530-3)

for instance, and to Hercules (I,5524) returning to the inspiration of the opening of the *Parlement of Foules* in their use of parallelism and chiasmus. Sometimes Lydgate must have found it difficult to combine the lessons of the group-chapters into one effective point, and here the envoys are perfunctory and mechanical (e.g. I,1814).

Noticeable again in Lydgate's moral commentary is the continual running-fire kept up against women. There is a foretaste of this in the Prologue, where Lydgate suggests that Chaucer found it difficult to think of nineteen good women (I,334). His remarks about Pasiphae are ambiguously ironic[17]: men must expect falseness from women, though they are not all false, and we should give credit to those who are true,

> And more them cherisshe because ther be so fewe.
>
>   (I,2849)

Boccaccio's attack on the deceitfulness of women (I,4719), apropos of Phaedra, is answered with heavy irony:

> He meneth of women that be born in Crete,
> Nothyng of hem that duelle in this contre.   (I,4726–7)

All the women here—'I speke of alle, I speke nat of on'—are virtuous
and patient, as their husbands can best testify. Irony is dropped for the
straightforward attack on the falseness of Dejanira (I,5503), but Lydgate
returns to the theme in the story of Orpheus, where he comments that
some husbands would have borne their wife's absence more patiently
(I,5804), and, when Orpheus declares that he will never marry again,
Lydgate twists it,

> So faire he was escapid his penaunce;
> For wedlok is a liff of most plesaunce,
> But who hath onys infernal peynys seyn,
> Will never his thankis come in the snare ageyn
> (I,5828–31)

so that the story becomes an allegory of the hell of marriage! Lydgate
usually takes his cue from Bochas in such passages, but here he is
original, and he rejects totally Laurent's explanation of the slaying of
Orpheus as being due to the anger of the women at his disclosure 'que
les femmes du pays feissent les festes et sacrifices ou temps que elles
souffrent le flux'.[18] Lydgate's explanation is that they were angry at
his discovery about marriage:

> Oon hell is dreedful, mor pereilous be tweyne.
> (I,5835)

There are further attacks on the deceitfulness of women in the story
of Delilah (I,6352), and then comes Boccaccio's famous Juvenalian
attack on women, which Lydgate translates with great vigour, especially the account of their artificial aids to beauty, adding many sharp
touches:

> Ther slakke skyn be craft abrod is streynyd,
> Lik an orenge fro the galei brouht.   (I,6567–8)

He abbreviates the examples of wicked women, and clearly takes more
pleasure in the palinode, which asserts that you can't condemn all
women because some are found to be at fault. Here he balances the
debate with some delicacy, giving us added reason to think of these
passages on women, with their humour and elementary irony, as
amongst Lydgate's happier achievements. The reason, as I have

suggested in speaking of the *Troy Book*, is that he found in the conventionalised patterns of the anti-feminist dialogue the opportunity for a degree of complexity and irony and 'suspension' in his account of human behaviour which he could rarely manage elsewhere. It has nothing to do with 'humanism', as Renoir describes it, or with respect for women as individuals, or with the 'belief that every human being has a right to be regarded as a separate entity'.[19] Renoir's tendency, throughout his book, is to look in Lydgate's poetry for *signs* of something else, usually signs of the Renaissance. One sympathises, because Lydgate's poetry is often not very interesting in itself, but it is poetry, not socio-political documentary, and it succeeds or fails as poetry. Its success here is a matter of literary technique, of balance and irony. What Lydgate actually thought of women is irrelevant: I doubt whether he thought much about them at all.

The technique clearly owes much to Chaucer: book II has an excellent envoy to widows (II,2199), which Lydgate adds to the story of Dido, in imitation of the Clerk's Envoy, advising them not to behave as foolishly as Dido:

> In on alone may be no sekirnesse.   (II,2224)

Later, in the tale of Candaules, king of Lydia, telling how he was made a 'cokold', he catches the word up—a trick he has learnt from the Manciple (*CT*, IX,205):

> Alas, I was nat avysid weel beforn,
> Oncunnyngli to speke such language;
> I sholde ha said, how that he hadde an horn,
> Or souht sum teerme with a fair visage
> T'excuse my rudnesse of this gret outrage.   (II,3361–5)

He is more independent in his account of Rhea, who becomes a vestal virgin and, as Laurent puts it, 'Neantmoins conceut et enfanta deux filz, mais len ne scet de quel pere'.[20] Lydgate, with monkish acerbity, elaborates:

> Yit natwithstandyng hir virgynal clennesse,
> She hath conceyved be natural miracle;
> Gan to encrece in hir hoolynesse,
> Whos wombe aroos, in Kynde was noon obstacle:
> Ageyn such bollyng availeth no triacle.   (II,4005–9)

Subsequent references to women veer towards outright hostility, with

little irony,[21] and on the whole tend to die out, like most other asser-
tions of independence in the translation.

Moral commentary is only one form of amplification in the *Fall*.
Lydgate adds a great deal of material, especially in the early books,
from Ovid, the Bible, and Boccaccio's *De Genealogia Deorum*, inserting,
for instance, in the story of Scylla the whole account of her murdering
her father Nisus for love of Minos (I,2480–2647), from the *Metamorphoses*. He also takes Laurent's few lines about Canace and her
incestuous love for Macareus and gives us in Canace's epistle, based on
Ovid and Gower,[22] a very effective complaint in the conventional
manner of the *Heroides*, with much original and pathetic detail, particularly of the child which she holds on her lap as she writes:

> A mouth he hath, but woordis hath he noone,
> Cannat compleyne, alas, for non outrage,
> Nor gruchith nat, but lith heer al aloone,
> Stille as a lamb, most meek of his visage.
> What herte of steel coude doon to hym damage,
> Or suffre hym deie, beholdyng the maneer
> And look benygne of his tweyne eyen cleer?   (I,6931–7)

Everyone has noticed this passage, and Gray speaks of it as having
'touched the very heart-springs of compassion'.[23] Lydgate, in fact,
always responds with immediacy of feeling to children, especially
children exposed to pain or suffering: the release of feeling is possible
because children, like animals, are innocent and helpless and make no
complex demands on compassion. It is like the *Book of the Duchess*,
where, as Lawlor puts it, 'pity is born of the Dreamer's innocence—
pity, "a naked, new-born babe".'[24] Lydgate is far more powerful than
Gower in evoking feeling for Canace and her child, but it is interesting
that he does so by concentrating exclusively on the 'complaint' as a
self-contained literary form, and makes little mention of the incest
which was the reason for the situation in the first place, and its real
context. Gower, by contrast, has a careful and reasoned discussion of
incest[25] which demonstrates a much larger concern for and understanding of the complexity of human behaviour.

Occasionally, Lydgate abbreviates what he found in Bochas, as in the
story of Atreus and Thyestes, or the account of Hercules' death, both of
which contain gory details such as he usually liked to pass over. Sometimes he makes a show of abbreviation by referring us to Chaucer's
work, on Philomela, for instance, Lucrece, Cleopatra, and Zenobia,[26]

expressing great reluctance to compete with his master—but he usually
tells the story, all the same. He also encourages his readers to turn to his
own versions of the stories of Thebes (I,3724) and Troy (I, 5937), but
again he provides a crude digest of the narratives. He could not leave
them out, because an important developing function of the *Fall* is as
an encyclopaedia, a comprehensive dictionary of universal biography.
This is not difficult in the given frame of the work, since all men must
die, and this alone is sufficient to bring them within the terms of reference of the *Fall*—indeed some of the stories are hardly relevant in any
other way. The story of Oetes, for instance, by some oversight, ends
with his restoration to kingship and prosperity—Lydgate comments
feebly

> Thus ay is sorwe medlid with gladnesse—   (I,2406)

but presumably he died in the end, and so qualified.

The encyclopaedic tendency of the *Fall* is what makes one page of
Boccaccio, 'Concursus Infoelicium', produce three in Laurent, and a
thousand dutiful lines in Lydgate,[27] with every name followed up—
Gideon, for instance, from twelve words in Boccaccio to five lines in
Laurent to 102 lines in Lydgate—and every link in the genealogical
chain fitted in (e.g. I,2003). Even when names such as those of the
Chimaera or the Minotaur are being used merely in a topos (God does
not bid us slay the Minotaur or do other mighty deeds, but only to be
humble, etc.), the need for explanation and documentation is imperious
(I,850). And when he comes to Oedipus and the slaying of the Sphinx,
which Bochas mentions briefly as a reason for Jocasta's favouring him,
he cannot resist the temptation:

> And for alle folk have nat knowlechyng
> Of this demaunde what it was in deede,
> I will reherse it heer in my writyng
> Compendiousli, that men may it reede.   (I,3368-71)

So we get the riddle and the answer, already recounted at length in the
Thebes, yet again, in sixteen stanzas, not at all 'compendiousli' (=con-
cisely). Sometimes the encyclopaedia becomes self-generating: a new
land *Citoiens* emerges from Lydgate's misunderstanding of the French
citoyens (I,3338), and his misreading of 'Aussi a la congnoissance des
hystoriens latins et par especial de moy des roys des sodomes ne est
aucune chose venue fors que. . . .' gives a ghost-king of Sodom, Moides
(I,1562).

Apart from this deliberate amplification, there is of course Lydgate's habitual verbosity, which can easily make a stanza out of a line in Laurent. An example has already been quoted.[28]

For such a massive work, and one so dependent for its significance on an external moral scheme, there is remarkably little attempt to systematise its moral teaching. The assumption is made that the misfortunes of the great provide a salutary lesson, and this for the most part is regarded as enough. 'The poet's insights into the concept of Fortune and human motivation', as Norton-Smith says, 'are inconsistent and eclectic'.[29] Sometimes the attitude is fatalistic: Fortune is a fickle and arbitrary deity who visits men with adversity regardless of their deserts. Sometimes the concept of Fortune is retributive: Fortune in this sense is only a name men give to the punishment of vice, and Lydgate develops this more philosophical, Boethian concept at length in the Prologue to book II:

> Vertu on Fortune maketh a diffiaunce,
> That Fortune hath no domynacioun
> Wher noble pryncis be governed be resoun.   (II,54–6)

He also refers to it more briefly elsewhere, as in the story of Althaea, where the mention of 'fatal purveiaunce' is qualified thus:

> For God above hath the sovereynte,
> And of Fortune the power may restreyne,
> To save and spille lik as folk disserve;
> Ageyn his will thei may nothyng ordeyne
> Of necessite, what cours that thei conserve.
>
> (I,4977–81)

He answers Messalina's complaint, that she was 'disposed' to be lecherous, in similar fashion:

> In hir excus the saide Messalyne
> Gan alegge hir constellacioun;
> But prudent clerkis pleynli determyne,
> Of the hevenly cours the disposicioun
> Is obeissaunt and soget to resoun,
> That everi man which weel governid is,
> Is nat constreyned of force to doon amys.   (VII,390–6)

There are other cases where neither concept of Fortune, fatalistic nor

retributive, is relevant, and where death, being to some extent admirable, provides no convenient moral lesson. It is in such cases—Dido,
Cato, Scipio, and a few others[30]—that Lydgate comes nearest to recognising or admiring antique virtues, though it should be made clear,
in connection with the claim that has been made for Lydgate's 'humanism', that what he is doing is to take over the eclecticism of his sources,
and that there is no independent movement, in his translation, towards
Renaissance attitudes. It is Boccaccio who provides the philosophical
variety of the work[31]—Fortune as *causa per accidens*, Fortune as divine
justice, and the half-articulate admiration for Roman attitudes—and
Lydgate simply follows where he is led. If there is any movement, it is
backward, to more conventional moral positions.

In the story of Olympias, for instance, Lydgate insists on the suppression of the potentially tragic in favour of the moral and grudges
Olympias her brave death because of her wicked life. After describing
how proudly she met her enemies, arrayed for the purpose in her
imperial robes,

> For unto tyme that she gaf up the breth,
> Was never seyen prince nor princesse
> That mor proudli took ther fatal deth   (IV,2542–4)

he turns on her with spluttering malevolence, denying any virtue to her
courage:

> Force is a vertu, bookis spesefie,
> Ageyn al vices to make resistence;
> But froward rancour and wood malencolie
> Gaff hir a spirit of feyned pacience,
> A fals pretence of hih magnificence. . . .
> Countirfet suffraunce made hir for to feyne—
> Nothyng of vertu, pleynlie to termyne,
> Nor of no manerys that be femynyne.   (IV,2549–62)

The clue to the violence of his outburst is in this last line: Olympias'
behaviour was unwomanly. Lydgate makes a similar departure from
Bochas in the story of Marius, where he persistently degrades the
nobility of his death by reminding us of his avarice in life. For all his
great virtues,

> Undir al this, ther dide his herte myne
> A werm of avarice, his worshep to declyne.
>   (VI,1315–16)

What prompted Lydgate here was the fact that Marius was of low birth, for it was one of his axioms that 'churls' should not rise to high position in the state. Lydgate is prepared to follow the authority of Bochas, even to expressing admiration for non-Christian heroes, but the torpor of his mind is stirred when some favourite moral common-place is threatened, and he shows himself in his true colours as a thoroughly conventional medieval moralist. His own awareness, when he speaks for himself, is of the life of the great man as either an exem-plum of Fortune or a saints' legend: it is towards the latter that he draws when he wishes to express unqualified admiration, as in the long and deliberate excursus on Constantine (VIII,1170), or the account of Theodosius (VIII,1911). He feels completely safe only with Christians. Even for Caesar, who was accorded a sort of secular divinity in the Middle Ages, and whose murderers were placed by Dante in the very pit of Hell, with Judas, Lydgate will make no exception. Laurent deliberately excuses himself for introducing Caesar in such woeful company, saying that he does so only to expose the wretched fate of Brutus and Cassius. Lydgate ignores this explanation, and consigns Caesar to the fate of all those who put their trust in the world:

> Princis considreth, in marcial policie
> Is nouther truste, feith nor assuraunce:
> Al stant in chaung with twynclyng of an eye.
> Up toward hevene set your attendaunce,
> The world unseur and al worldli plesaunce;
> Lordship abit nat, record on Julius
> Moordred at Roome bi Brutus Cassius.[32]

Once free of Rome, and the stoic virtues which the Christian had to admire, however grudgingly, Lydgate even returns to specifically anti-pagan comment, much as in the *Troy Book*. The account of Alexander, for instance, describes his self-deification as the origin of idolatry.[33] But there is nothing like the consistency in the development of this theme that there is in the *Troy Book*, any more than there is consistency in the response to Boccaccio's sense of the tragic nobility of the ancients. Lydgate's never-ending moral commentary, which tends to thin out as the work goes on, is mostly *ad hoc* and automatic, and reveals no grand design. The mechanical nature of his responses is exemplified in his description of Croesus' grief, to which he devotes two stanzas of amplification on the theme 'But joy always follows sorrow' (II,3634); but in the next he says that Bochas writes of his woe no more because

it was 'irrecuperable'. It is on occasions like this that the *Fall* begins
to have the appearance of a series of *membra disjecta*.

It is true that Gloucester does seem to have made an attempt to
supervise the translation, pushing Lydgate in various directions and
encouraging him to be more adventurous. We know, from the translation of Palladius *On Husbondrie*, that Gloucester took a close interest
in the works that he commissioned. The epilogue to book II of that
work describes how the translator waits in fear and trembling while
Gloucester corrects his verses, putting little crosses where revision is
needed:

> For ferd y shrynke away, no leve y take.

The epilogue to book III is similar:

> And lo, my lord in honde hath Feveryeer.
> Wul he correcte? Ey, what have y to done?
> He wul doon as a lord. . . .[34]

It is a fair supposition that the metrical precision of the Palladius-
translation is partly due to the intervention of Gloucester,[35] though the
precision is obtained at the expense of some extraordinary academic
contortions of syntax, as if the author were more used to writing Latin
than English. There are also some extremely ambitious metrical experiments in internal rhyme and *rime brisée*, culminating in the epilogue to
book XIII, which reads the same down as across.

Gloucester probably had little to do with the metre of an established
poet like Lydgate, but he did, as we have seen, suggest a major change
in asking Lydgate to provide envoys for each chapter (II,145). These
envoys, to which Lydgate may have expected Gloucester to pay particular attention, are the occasion of much of the best writing in the
Fall. It is probable too that many of the literary allusions, such as the
references to Dante and Petrarch in the prologue to book III, or the
prologue to book IV, on Poets and Writing, with its quite elaborate
accounts of Virgil, Ovid, and Petrarch, were directed at Gloucester,
and worked up from books that Gloucester provided. The interpola-
tions on good government and the body politic in book II (827), from
John of Salisbury, not a very well-known writer, at least to Lydgate,
were presumably taken from the copy of the *Policraticus* in Humphrey's
own library. Gloucester must have realised that the ageing monk
needed a little spurring on, and so he lent him books now and then
(easier than giving him money) and Lydgate wearily obliged by trans-

lating bits into the *Fall*, not seeing anything particularly gratifying in it, but glad to humour his patron. There is a particular instance: Lydgate, alluding to the story of Lucrece in book II (974), excuses himself,

> It nedith nat rehersyn the processe, (II,978)

by saying that he daren't compete with Chaucer. But then Humphrey came along with the *Declamatio* of Lucretia by Coluccio Salutati, a friend of Petrarch and famous Italian humanist, and urged Lydgate to translate it:

> But at Lucrece stynte I will a while,
> It were pite hir story for to hide. . . .
> Also my lord bad I sholde abide,
> By good avys at leiser to translate
> The doolful processe of hir pitous fate,
> Folwyng the tracis of Collucyus. (II,1002–9)

Lydgate did so, at some length, though without suppressing the earlier passage where he promised not to speak of Lucrece. And in book III, when he comes to Lucrece again, this time in her proper place in the course of events, he follows Bochas through the whole of her complaint once more—

> I folwe muste and make mencioun— (III,978)

even though, as he admits, he has done it once already. To Gloucester, it must have been like trying to stop a steamroller.[36]

Whatever structural integrity Boccaccio achieved for the *De Casibus*, little of it remains in the *Fall*. In the *De Casibus*, the rhythm of the processional is of vital importance as a dramatic linking device, just as it is in Petrarch's *Trionfi* or in the *Danse Macabre*, and Boccaccio pays careful attention to its preservation. He maintains the fiction and personal tone of the spectator, varies the pattern by allowing interruptions and arguments amongst the complainants, and keeps in our minds, with many vivid touches, the idea of a procession:

Apres le racomptement du piteux et miserable cas de Actilius, noble consul Rommain, je tournay ma plume pour briefvement escripre le cas des nobles malheureux hommes tant cytoiens comme autres plourans et faisans ung long cry qui estoient devant

moy tous nudz en une longue renge, tout ainsi comme les his-
toriens les arrengerent en leurs livres.[37]

Lydgate omits all of this, and even when he does briefly translate such
passages[38] they are submerged in the oceans of amplification. He preserves, of course, all of Boccaccio's set-piece variations, and provides
within these comparatively self-contained structures some of the most
effective writing in the *Fall*: the dispute of Fortune and Glad Poverty,
with its vivid low-style description of Poverty—

> For feer of the, childre them withdrawe,
> And many a dogge hath on thi staff i-gnawe;
>
> (III,251–2)

the dispute of Bochas and the Goddess Fortuna (VI), where Lydgate's
antithetic concept of Fortune takes on a new life from Boccaccio's
richness of invention, and where he keeps the device of having Fortune
narrate a series of stories to show her power; the strife of Caligula,
Tiberius, and Messalina (VII,320); the conversation of Bochas and
Petrarch about the responsibilities of the poet (VIII); and the very
lively argument with Brunnhilde (IX,162), who tries to tell her story
but is continually interrupted by Bochas with allegations of dishonesty.
In addition, as we have seen, Lydgate does introduce a good deal of
independent personal material, in his addresses to Gloucester, and other
innovations attributable to Gloucester's influence; and occasionally too
he can react sharply to the original, as in his retort to Bochas' slight on
the English as 'faillis et vains et de nulle valeur'[39] in the account of the
capture of John of France at Poitiers:

> His fantasie nor his oppynioun
> Stood in that caas of non auctorite;
> Ther kyng was take; ther knihtis dide flee;
> Wher was Bochas to helpe at such a neede?
> Sauf with his penne he made no man to bleede.
>
> (IX,3178–82)

But such passages amount to very little in the vast wastes of the *Fall*,
the long tracts, for instance, where he is dredging amongst the minor
descendants of Alexander. What should be well-contrived patterns of
variation and relief within a texture of continued richness are mere
islands in a sea, and for this the massive amplification of the group-
chapters and the resultant loss of perspective must be held largely
responsible.

At the same time, it must be admitted that the scheme of the *De Casibus* is not basically different from that of the *Fall*: all that Boccaccio did was to give it a more plausible dramatic frame and continuity. Boccaccio, Laurent and Lydgate all have a common belief in the validity of inorganic, encyclopaedic structures, and therefore stand in sharp contrast to Chaucer. In the *Legend of Good Women* and *Monk's Tale*, Chaucer experimented with non-narrative frames, but both are unfinished, and Chaucer clearly took little interest in them. He was probably quite happy to leave a question-mark hanging over the *Legend*, and not at all averse to the comic insinuation that there were not enough good women, when the real reason for the incompleteness of the work was that the form failed totally to engage his imagination. His technique with the *Monk's Tale* is more sophisticated: here he includes the defect of form within the meaning of the Tale by the dramatic attribution to the Monk, to whom such miscellaneous and patchwork erudition was appropriate.[40] This is not to say that he wrote the tale badly to prove his point: such a procedure would be artistically very expensive. In fact, the tale is not told badly. There is variety in the manner of narration, many vivid touches,

> Was nevere capitayn . . . strenger. . . .
> Than Oloferne, which Fortune ay kiste
> So likerously, and ladde hym up and doun,
> Til that his heed was of, er that he wiste
>
> (*CT*,VIII,2551–8)

and many hints of the swift, pregnant narrative technique of the *Pardoner's Tale* amd the exempla in the *Nun's Priest's Tale*. There is also the tale of Ugolino, which Lydgate wisely left alone but for a stanza (IX,2040). We must clearly take the *Monk's Tale* seriously, within its limits, and understand how Lydgate could take it seriously, regarding Chaucer as pre-eminently a writer of 'tragedies' (I,248). At the same time we can see how Chaucer undermined the structure by attributing the Tale to the Monk, and by having the Tale interrupted by the Knight, and how his implied criticism of the form relates to our view of the *Fall*. The *Canterbury Tales* was Chaucer's answer to the problem: Lydgate, as usual, was aware of no problem.

The *Monk's Tale*, of course, is vastly inferior to the *Fall* in power, eloquence and solemnity, but it scores by its brevity. It is the sheer size of the *Fall* to which one is forced to return, and which appals criticism. It must have appalled Lydgate too, for as the years went by he tended

17

to abridge more and more. Towards the end we even find him using
a technique of staccato rapid narration, as in the passage on King John
quoted above.[41] All nine books of the *De Casibus* are of approximately
the same length, and comparison with the number of lines in each book
of the *Fall* [42] reveals the waning of Lydgate's enthusiasm. But he keeps
up with the envoys, which contain much of his best work, like the
envoy to Women in book II (2199), or the many envoys where he
provides an eloquent descant to the prevailing theme of mutability—
on Arsinoe (IV.3445), on Mithridates and the 'sodeyn chaung of
worldli variaunce' (VI,1709), on 'Brutus Cassius' (VI,2871). Like the
splendid epilogue on Cyrus, with its echoes of the *Troilus*,

> Loo, heer th'exequies of this myhti kyng!
> Loo, heer the eende of his estat roiall!
> Ther wer no flawmys nor brondis cleer shynyng
> To brenne his bodi with fires funerall,
> Nor observaunces nor offrynges marciall,
> Nor tumbe of gold with stonys riche and fyne
> Was non ordeyned that day to make his shryne! . . .
>
> Loo, heer of Cirus the fynal aventure,
> Which of al Asie was whilom emperour!
> Now lith he abject, withoute sepulture,
> Of hih ne low he fond no bet favour.
> Loo, heer the fyn of al worldli labour,
> Namli of tirantis, which list nat God to dreede,
> But set ther lust in slauhtre, and blood to sheede!
>   (II,3921–41)

these are virtually independent poems, in which Lydgate is under no
pressure to sustain a narrative or to develop or expound ideas, but only
to amplify, out of the endless resources of his rhetoric, and the wealth
of a mind richly stored with conventional images, allusions, and illustrations, a theme of infinite familiarity and infallible power. It is in these
set contexts that the high style, with its elaborate diction and figuring,[43]
comes into its own, above all in the Envoy on Rome which closes book
II, and which, apart from one or two lapses, maintains a tone of lofty
eloquence. It is a lamentation (Where are all your great men?), but a
lamentation cut through by contempt for the pagan imperial world and
culminating in the call to abjure false gods and turn to Christ. This
Envoy, which was often separately transcribed, consists of nineteen
stanzas on three rhymes—an extraordinary technical achievement. It is

completely original, and in itself sufficient to dispel any illusions about Lydgate's 'humanism' or admiration for the classical world.

One must come to a similar conclusion about the political views expressed in the *Fall*. There is no lack of these, for Lydgate keeps in mind the purpose of providing a 'Mirror for Princes', and usually ends the envoys with a stanza addressed to them. But it cannot be maintained, as Schirmer maintains, that the expression of these opinions amounts to any sort of coherent political philosophy, except in so far as any collection of medieval commonplaces is coherent, nor that they are 'advanced', as Renoir tries to argue.[44] Occasionally he will follow Bochas in some rather unexpected pronouncement:

> Thus erthli princis, with al ther pompous fame,
> Which thoruh the world yiveþ so gret a soun,
> Of slauhtre and moordre thei tooke first þer name,
> Bi fals ravyne and extorsioun
> Clamb up so first to domynacioun.   (VI,2458–62)

This is in the account of Pompey and Caesar, and presumably refers only to pagan rulers. But where he speaks for himself, and we can identify his own voice, it is the voice of medieval tradition. The test-case is Bochas' fierce outburst against tyranny in book II, an eloquent tirade which proclaims the elective nature of the monarchic contract,[45] and the virtue of tyrannicide.[46] These views are not un-medieval in themselves, but they are expressed with an outspokenness and violence which tends to make one think they are. Lydgate recognised that they might give offence, and he omitted the whole passage, introducing in its place the interpolation from John of Salisbury on the Body Politic (II,827), with its harmless commonplaces. Elsewhere, in reference to the murder of Caesar, Lydgate introduces on his own account the generalisation,

> To moordre a prince, it is a pitous thyng,
> God of his riht wil take therof vengaunce.   (VI,2941–2)

He also tones down Bochas' attacks on the immorality of princes (III,1149). He lacks entirely Boccaccio's indignation against tyranny, which he sees as potentially disruptive, and he takes refuge in harmlessly admirable generalities about the serpent of dissension (III,1939), the dangers of false succession (III,2871), the reliance of lordship on the love of the people (III,3988), and the dangers of having 'churls' in power (VI,780). For Lydgate political views are an aspect of universal morality, and have little connection with the real world of political action. His ideas are simple and generalised. They are very similar, in fact, to those of Shakespeare in the histories and Roman plays, but it would be quite wrong to say that therefore Lydgate is a precursor of the Renaissance. The truth is rather that Shakespeare is a relic of the Middle Ages. The *Fall* was popular in the sixteenth century not because it anticipated Renaissance ideas, but because it effected a comprehensive transmission of medieval ideas to an age which was still fundamentally medieval in outlook.

At the end, one is left with something of bewilderment before the *Fall or Princes*. In itself it would seem to be, *par excellence*, the inorganic structure which Lydgate was groping after in the earlier narratives, but in achieving such a structure Lydgate exposes his own inadequacy, for there is in the *Fall* neither onward movement nor design. Yet one must assume that the long poem, even when it threatens always to revert to the encyclopaedia, has its own aesthetic. Though the theme may often sink under the weight of exempla, and though the mind is continually dragged back to the snail's pace progress of Lydgate's meaning, an aerial view reveals the lineaments of some monstrous Ozymandias-like ruin, the remains of antiquity lying strewn in apparently indiscriminate confusion, out of which emerges, from time to time, a pattern, a vast and dark perspective of human history shot through with splendour and contempt. But it is difficult to distance oneself enough from the poem to get this perspective, even in glimpses, and in the process of reading it, it is impossible. One must fall back on some sort of fragmentation of the *Fall* in order to render it intelligible, and recognise it for what it is, a non-poetic continuum in which are set a number of eloquent discourses on set themes, and particularly on the theme of mutability. It would be possible, and, indeed, given the inorganic structure of the poem, not at all improper, to compile an anthology of medieval poetry from the *Fall* which would represent it as Lydgate's most considerable achievement.

It was in this way that the *Fall* was read in its own day, and in this way that it achieved its great influence and popularity. Some thirty-four MSS. of the complete work survive, but these are mostly prestige productions of the kind that would have been admired rather than read. Its more characteristic dissemination is in the form of collections of extracts, particularly of the envoys. The poem was clearly too long for normal purposes, but parts of it were too good to miss, and scribes

were accustomed to copy into their MSS. numbers of the more quot-
able set-pieces, ranging from forty-seven items in MS. Harley 2251 to a
single envoy in several MSS. These MSS. are the 'best-sellers' of the
fifteenth century, as distinct from the prestige trade, and include familiar
Shirley texts like Ashmole 59 and Trinity R.3.20, and others, equally
familiar, like Trinity R.3.19.[47] Wynkyn de Worde continued the
tradition in the sixteenth century with his 'Proverbs of Lydgate', which
include selections from the *Fall*, two of the moralistic poems (*Look in
thy Merour* and *Consulo quisquis eris*), and two short poems of Chaucer
(*Fortune* and *Truth*).

The *Fall* was thus often regarded as a source-book more than as a
unified poem, and by its nature lent itself readily to the medieval taste
for moralistic anthologies. It was also 'used' in the way that we have
spoken of the *Temple of Glass* being 'used'. The copy of the *Monk's Tale*,
for instance, in MS. Trinity R.3.19, is padded out with extra stanzas
from the *Fall*.[48] Peter Idley's *Instructions to his Son*, a fairly elaborate
and ambitious poem in the *Disciplina Clericalis* tradition, incorporates
whole stanzas from the *Fall* into its exhortations.[49] The *Fall* was also
'useful' in a more imponderable way, as a source of consolation for those
in adversity, and not used to it. We know that Charles of Orleans asked
for a copy of the *De Casibus* when he was in prison in England—one of
those rhetorically appropriate gestures which represents the fifteenth
century at its best—and Georges Chastelain wrote *La Temple de Bocace* as
a consolation for Margaret of Anjou, the queen of the ill-fated Henry
VI.[50] The continuing relevance of Bochas and the *Fall* was recognised
in various poems which sought to bring the work up to date, such as
Lydgate's own piece on *The Sodein Fal of Princes in oure dayes*,[51] and the
poem which Robbins calls 'Examples of Mutability',[52] where the author
declares that there is no need to go to 'Bockas' for examples of the
capriciousness of Fortune and the ruin of princes, since they are readily
enough available 'here in thys lande within the xx yere'. This tradition
was carried on into the sixteenth century with extraordinary vigour,
above all in the *Mirror for Magistrates*, a poem of continuing and composite authorship to which Shakespeare was heavily indebted for much
of the mood and thinking of the history plays. The *Metrical Visions* of
George Cavendish are similar, and stylistically very close to Lydgate.
They appear in the autograph MS. of his *Life of Wolsey*, and in them
various Tudor characters—Wolsey, Anne Boleyn, Henry VIII, Surrey—
come forward to lament their lives and deaths. Cavendish's explanation
of his purpose in writing places him firmly in the *Fall* tradition:

The cause that moved me to this enterprice
Specyally was that all estates myght se
What it is to trust to Fortune's mutabylite.[53]

What Cavendish adds, like the *Mirror*, is a close application of the *Fall*
motif to contemporary politics, outspoken enough to keep the *Visions*
out of print until 1641. But the style, the manner, are exactly Lydgate's,
like this modesty-topos,

I must wright playn, colours have I none to paynt,
But termes rude ther dolours to compile:
An wofull playnt must have an wofull style   (61–3)

and may have been prompted by the 1554 print of the *Fall*. The imitation is so close as to run to the repetition of a gnomic word-play (167–
8), the lifting of a whole stanza verbatim (246–53), even a stanza whose
syntax bears comparison in bafflement with Lydgate (1133–9). But the
really remarkable thing about the *Metrical Visions* is the contrast with
the superb and assured prose of the *Life*. Medieval and Renaissance here
stand side by side, a striking testimony to the tenacity of medieval
habits of thought in an age which was already shaping itself to different
concepts and different ideals.

Notes to Chapter Eight

1 E.g. K. H. Vickers, *Humphrey Duke of Gloucester* (London 1907), esp.
chaps. IX and X; W. F. Schirmer, *Der englische Frühhumanismus* (Tübingen
1963), pp. 19–50. For a more sober account, see R. Weiss, *Humanism in
England during the 15th century* (Oxford 1957), pp. 39ff.
2 See R. Weiss, 'Humphrey Duke of Gloucester and Tito Livio Frulovisi', in
Fritz Saxl Memorial Essays, ed. D. J. Gordon (London 1957), pp. 218–27.
3 Lines 1186–95, in *The Middle-English translation of Palladius De Re Rustica*,
ed. Mark Liddell (Berlin 1896), p. 66.
4 See above, p. 44.
5 This is Hammond's account of the occasion of the Letter (*Chaucer to Surrey*,
p. 149). Norton-Smith believes the translation was finished when the Letter
was written (*op. cit.*, p. 115). But see *Fall*, III,67, quoted below.
6 *Chaucer to Surrey*, p. 174: see also her article, 'Poet and Patron in the *Fall of
Princes*', *Anglia*, XXXVIII(1920),121–36.
7 Both tables of contents are printed in Hammond, *Chaucer to Surrey*, pp.
194–7.
8 See Brusendorff, *The Chaucer Tradition*, p. 461.

9 See Seznec, *The Survival of the Pagan Gods*, pp. 220–4.

10 The *De Casibus* is conveniently available in the facsimile of the Paris edition of 1520 (*Scholars' Facsimiles and Reprints*, Gainesville, Florida 1962), ed. L. B. Hall. The references here are to pp. 25, 39. Bergen has very full quotation of both Latin and French in Part IV of his EETS edition of the *Fall*.

11 *Fall*, ed. Bergen, Part IV, p. 198.

12 *Fall*, VI,3277; cf. Bergen, *ed. cit.*, Part IV, p. 268.

13 Bergen, p. 295.

14 I shall refer to Lydgate's source thus, unless there is a special point in distinguishing Boccaccio and Laurent.

15 These fine lines (I,645–51) derive from Dante's story of Paolo and Francesca (*Inf.* V,121) via Chaucer's *Troilus* (III,1625).

16 E.g. I,967, 1380, 1814, 2150, etc.

17 E.g. I,2708, 2778, 2792, 2822, 2843.

18 Bergen, Part IV, p. 160: a rather literal-minded piece of medieval rationalisation.

19 Renoir, *The Poetry of John Lydgate*, p. 93.

20 Bergen, Part IV, p. 180.

21 E.g. III,2462, 4572; IV,2453.

22 *Fall*, I,6882–7049. Hammond prints this passage as one of her extracts from the *Fall*: see her discussion, *Chaucer to Surrey*, pp. 164–6; also Renoir, *op. cit.*, pp. 20–3.

23 'On the Poems of Lydgate', in *Works*, ed. Gosse (London 1884), I,399.

24 'The Pattern of Consolation in the *Book of the Duchess*', *Speculum*, XXXI (1956),626–48 (p. 642).

25 *Confessio Amantis*, III,151–90. Chaucer's comments, in the Introduction to the *Man of Law's Tale* (*CT*, II,80), are characteristically non-committal by virtue of their 'dramatic' form.

26 *Fall*, I,1781, II,974, VI,3620, VIII,670.

27 *Fall*, I,2171–3129. Cf. *De Casibus, ed. cit.*, p. 31; Laurent, in Bergen, p. 147.

28 See above, p. 7. Cf. I,1060, IV,3172, VI,2934, IX,1366.

29 *John Lydgate: Poems*, p. 127.

30 *Fall*, II,2171, III,1226, V,1643. See Schirmer, *John Lydgate*, p. 207.

31 As Farnham says, Boccaccio 'never draws his scattered comments upon the causes of misfortune into a definitive and consistent philosophy' (*The Medieval Heritage of Elizabethan Tragedy*, 1936, Oxford 1956, p. 102), though he does recognise some concept of character contributing to tragedy, as in Hannibal and Alcibiades (see pp. 84–116).

32 VI,2913–19. The mistake with the name is copied from Chaucer's *Monk's Tale* (*CT*, VII,2697).

33 IV,1247. Farnham considers that Lydgate adds 'a stronger taste for schematic retribution than Boccaccio or Chaucer' (*Medieval Heritage*, p. 165), especially with Julian the Apostate and Mohammed.

34 The Palladius-epilogues are printed in Hammond, *Chaucer to Surrey*, p. 206.

35 See Prologue, 109, in Hammond, p. 205.

36 See further Hammond's article, 'Lydgate and Coluccio Salutati', *Modern Philology*, XXV(1927), 49–57.

37 Bergen, Part IV, p. 231.

38 E.g. I,4852, 6739; VII,7.

39 Bergen, Part IV, p. 396.

40 See above, p. 43.

41 Cf. V,848, 2103, 2817; IX,952, 2010.

42 Viz. 7070, 4592, 5152, 4066, 3145, 3668, 1663, 3381, 3302.

43 E.g. II,4432, IV,2304.

44 Schirmer, *op. cit.*, pp. 213–14; Renoir, *op. cit.*, pp. 105–8.

45 'Les Roys et aultres princes terriens furent esleuz par consentement et ordonnance de peuple pour le garder et deffendre' (Bergen, p. 173).

46 'Il nest sacrifice a dieu tant aggreable comme est le sang du tyrant' (Bergen, p. 174). This aphorism was quoted (in the Latin) in the document prepared by the duke of Burgundy to justify his murder of the duke of Orleans in 1407 (*De Casibus*, ed. Hall, p. vii).

47 See Hammond, *Chaucer to Surrey*, p. 156; Bergen, ed. *Fall*, Part IV, pp. 105, 123; *Index of Middle English Verse*, ed. Brown and Robbins (New York 1943), p. 185, and *Supplement* (1965), p. 133.

48 See MacCracken's note in *MLN*, XXIII(1908),93.

49 E.g. six successive stanzas in book II,2344–85, are from *Fall*, I,2150–6, 6280, II,15–21, and I,3445–58. The work is edited by Charlotte d'Evelyn (Boston and London 1935).

50 *De Casibus*, ed. Hall, p. viii.

51 See above, p. 180.

52 *Historical Poems of the XIVth and XVth centuries*, p. 184.

53 Prologue, 54–6, in Hammond, *Chaucer to Surrey*, p. 371. There is a complete text of the *Visions* in the *Life of Wolsey*, ed. S. W. Singer (London 1825).

CHAPTER NINE

Lydgate's Religious Poetry

It should perhaps be made clear at the outset that this chapter is chronological neither in position nor progression. It is a convenient assumption that poets write love-songs in their youth and religious poems in their old age, and a poet, like Chaucer in his *Retraction*, would try dutifully to live up to it. But obviously it will not apply to Lydgate, who was producing religious poems of one kind or another throughout his active life. Such of them as we can date come from both the earliest (*Life of Our Lady*) and the latest (*St. Albon*) phases of Lydgate's poetic career, and even in the middle of a major translation he would make time to compose a poem like the powerful anti-Lollard *Defence of Holy Church*,[1] or *St. Edmund*. It would also be difficult to make any general statements about chronology on the basis of stylistic development, and quite mistaken, for instance, to attribute the more elaborate 'aureate' poems to a later date rather than an earlier. On the whole, it will be best to treat the religious poems as a homogeneous body of writing, by types, referring to the circumstances of composition only when there is specific evidence.

One other point should be made about the nature of our expectations in this poetry. We are accustomed, in religious poetry, to look for evidence of strong personal feeling or at least of some complex interior response to the call of faith. It is the impact of religion upon the individual consciousness that interests us. Some medieval lyrics, particularly the more passionate songs to Christ and the Virgin, may answer to these demands, and qualify as 'true' lyrics, but in doing so they will sacrifice their own truth. One or two of Lydgate's poems have a personal air about them, but this is part of the convention in which they are written, like the *Prayer in Old Age*, a penitential poem which, like the *Testament* (to be dealt with in the concluding chapter), catalogues the (unlikely) ill deeds of the poet's youth and middle age,

When lust with fors was fresh yn that sesoun   (10)

and prays for mercy. It is an exemplary prayer, not a real one, an example of the right thing to say. Another poem, *God is myn Helpere*, with its personal-sounding refrain,

Whyl God lyst helpe no man I drede,

is really better classed with the moralistic poems. It has the characteristic Fortune-contraries (41–88), and a stanza on keeping one's tongue which refers to Cato and opens with the line used elsewhere as a refrain:

Who seith the best he shal not repente.   (89)

Medieval religious poetry is all practical, and its practical purpose is always to sustain faith and aid devotion. The expression of personal religious feeling in poetry the Middle Ages would have regarded as improper, just as Dr. Johnson did. Medieval people no doubt had personal religious feelings, but they would have considered them their own and God's business, and it is significant that the outlet for them, when it is found, is in the prose of the mystics, not in the more public and vulgar medium of verse. The immediate interest of medieval religious poetry for us, therefore, is as poetry, products of literary art, not as documents of individual psychology, and their wider interest is in their profound and often complex reference to a structure of thought and belief which dominated and, in enfeebled form, still affects the Western mind. It is in this light that I shall examine Lydgate's religious poetry, which falls into six main categories: instructional works, paraphrases of hymns and psalms, prayers, poems on the Passion, Marian lyrics, and saints' lives. The bulk of it is expository and celebratory; there is comparatively little penitential or devotional writing.

A major preoccupation of the fourteenth century was the transmission to the laity in an effective manner of the basic tenets of the Christian code. 'Effective' in this case meant in the vernacular, and the development of the English sermon is accompanied by a host of manuals and treatises which expound in simple form the seven petitions of the Paternoster, the fourteen articles of the Creed, the ten commandments, the seven sacraments, the seven works of mercy, the seven virtues, and the seven deadly sins.[2] A manuscript like the Vernon MS. is itself an index to the wide currency of this kind of instruction in verse, and its authors are quite explicit about their purpose:

Lewed men be not lered in lore,
As clerkes ben in holi writ;
þauȝ men prechen hem bifore,
Hit wol not wonen in heore wit. . . .
þerfore ichave on Englisch wrouȝt.[3]

Similarly in a translation of Grosseteste's *Castel of Love*:

Ne mowe we alle Latin wite,
Ne Ebreu ne Gru þat beþ i-write,
Ne French ne þis oþer spechen
þat me mihte in world sechen. . . .
On Englisch I-chul mi resun schowen,
For him þat con not i-knowen
Nouþer French ne Latyn.[4]

These works are directed at the lower clergy, and, partly through them, at the laity, and it is to this tradition that we must refer Lydgate's simpler instructional pieces like the *15 Tokyns aforn the Doom*, another version of which appears in an addition to the translation of the *Castel of Love* already mentioned (*ed. cit.*, p. 403). Lydgate, however, is much more 'literary', and writes in ballade-stanza, as opposed to the loose four-stress couplet of the *Castel of Love*. His translation of the *Paternoster* is also in ballade, like most of the religious poems, using the Latin opening, 'Pater noster qui es in celis', as its refrain. A stanza is devoted to each of the seven petitions. Without being elaborate, the translation is careful and skilfully amplified, and is clearly not intended for ignorant lay-folk. One would associate most of these pieces with the patronage of the upper middle classes and gentry, if indeed they are not monastic exercises, perhaps written for the edification of the boys in the monastic school. Nothing could be more obvious than the connection of the *Kalendare* with the monastery. It is a calendar of saints' days, in rhyme-royal, and it was probably one of Bury's claims to distinction that it had on the premises a monk who could versify *anything*, even this, or, as we have mentioned elsewhere, the abbey's charters.

The *Exposition of the Pater Noster* is quite different, an extraordinary performance, with a stanza on *Pater*, one on *noster*, one on *qui es in celis*, and so on, to 336 lines. There are three stanzas of modesty-formulae at the beginning, with many references to the poet's advanced age, and he then goes on to speak of the four things 'longyng to prayeer'—not the four Evangelists, nor the four rivers of Paradise, nor the four spheres of

Ezekiel, nor the four elements, the four seasons, four complexions, four winds, four virtues, four wheels of Elijah's chariot. . . .

> I passe al this, grace shal my penne leede
> To speke of prayer and sevene peticiouns.   (79–80)

We hear no more of the four things that belong to prayer. The work ends with another four stanzas of modesty-topics, including an elaboration of Chaucer's familiar gleaning-image:

> Lyk as a glenere on a large lond
> Among shokkys plentyuous of auctours,
> Thouh I were besy to gadren with myn hond,
> Lyk my desire, to have founde out some flours,
> The grene was repen, russet were the colours,
> I fond no sugre in my smal lybrarye,
> Soyll dryed up of my sylver schours,
> Ferful and dul there lenger for to tarye.   (305–12)

It is difficult to think of anyone who could have been so ignorant of the Paternoster and at the same time so appreciative of Lydgate's literary pyrotechnics. It looks like a *tour de force*.

We are on safer ground with the *Virtues of the Mass*, which we are told was written for the Countess of Suffolk, that is, the former Alice Chaucer, daughter of Thomas.[5] Lydgate analyses the significance of each part of the Mass and explains its efficacy, ending with a polite envoy, 'Go lytyll tretyse'. There is an occasional literary flourish,

> And semblably, so as the morow gray
> Ys messynger of Phebus uprysyng,
> And bryngeth tydynges of the glade day,
> So the Epystyll, by processe of redyng,
> To us declareth most gracious tydyng   (233–7)

but for the most part the tone is sober. The work as it stands complete in two MSS. includes two other pieces, 'An exortacion to Prestys when they shall sey theyr Masse' and 'On Kissing at *Verbum caro factum est*', loosely linked at beginning and end. Other signs of conflation are the translation of Psalm 42, *Judica me deus*, which is inserted lines 89–144, and the prayer to the sacrament (321–92). These and other passages appear independently in some MSS. and we can conclude that Lydgate responded to his distinguished commission with some not so distinguished joinery-work. However, he knew what he was talking about, and could afford to treat the Countess as a fairly advanced pupil, unlike the author of the tail-rhyme piece in the Vernon MS., on 'How to hear Mass', who has to enliven his account with popular anecdotes and cannot even be sure that his audience of 'lewed men' know their Creed.[6]

Lydgate's paraphrases of psalms and hymns, though they have more the appearance of 'poems', are just as practical as the instructional pieces. This is not to say that they were actually used, in place of the Latin, in the service. In general, for the later Middle Ages, we can say that the only part of the service that was in the vernacular was the sermon—even that was more commonly delivered separately[7]—though in the fifteenth century we do begin to hear of short services in English, particularly the baptism and marriage services and the Office for the Dead.[8] These paraphrases are therefore intended for private use, to make the Latin of the service more meaningful, or at most to be read out in the body of the sermon. The former seems to be the function of those pieces whose occasion we know, such as the translation of Psalm 102, *Benedic anima mea*, made for the Dean of the Chapel at Windsor (Edmund Lacy), 'whyles þe kynge was at even-songe'.[9] This straightforward exercise in extended paraphrase takes a stanza for each verse, blossoming only to some obvious stimulus such as 'quoniam pulvis sumus' (105–12). The version of Psalm 53, *Deus in nomine tuo salvum me fac*, is similar, with an added ostentation at the end, where Lydgate manages to spin out the *Gloria* and the *Sicut erat* to a stanza each:

> That ys and was, withowte begynnyng,
> Thre in oo substaunce, hye god incommutable,
> Withowte ende, eternall, enduryng,
> All-myghty, ryghtwys, and mercyable,
> Gracious to all contrite, and confortable.... (65–9)

The translation of Psalm 129, *De profundis*, was made, Lydgate tells us, in his old age at the request of his abbot, William Curteys,

> At his chirche to hang it on the wal (168)

to explain why this psalm is said especially for those in purgatory. Lydgate therefore precedes his translation with an explanation of the figural interpretation of the psalm through Jonah, Daniel, Joseph, and the three children in the fire. This is interesting, but the translation is feeble.

Much freer and more elaborate is *Misericordias domini in eternum cantabo*, which takes the first verse of Psalm 88 as its theme and refrain,

> Eternally thy mercies I shal syng,

and amplifies it with delightful unexpectedness by reference to the 'song' not the 'mercies'. Lydgate speaks first of the songs he will not sing, using the 'Some talk of Alexander' topos:

> Ther be Canticulis of conquest and victorye
> That be songe at feestis marcial,
> And ther be songis of palmys transitorye,
> With corious meetrys that be poetical;
> Laureat tryumphes, proud and imperial,
> With boosty blowe in charys cleer shynyng,
> Al this left off, with voys memoryal,
> Eternally thy Mercies I shal syng.   (33–40)

Virgil, Dares, Dictys, Lucan, are gaily dismissed,

> Gret boost is maad—but as for me no fors—
> Bildyng of Ylioun in many stoory told,
> Getyng of Troye by the brasen hors,
> Of bolys, serpentys, that kept the flees of gold. . . .
>   (57–60)

The songs to remember are those of the Israelites crossing the Red Sea, or Deborah, or the three children, or Mary's *Magnificat*, and so on—a Biblical concordance to 'song'. The whole piece has a vivacity which must surely be attributed to the 'literary' nature of its inspiration, for which the Psalm provides the merest pretext.

The translations of Latin hymns are much more ambitious, more Latinate, and even further removed than the Psalms from their liturgical origin in song. No occasion is known for any of them, but they are evidently intended for (private) reading and meditation. The simplest is *Criste qui lux est et dies*, a translation in four-stress ballade of a well-known Ambrosian hymn for Quadragesima, which corresponds stanza for verse to the Latin original, and uses the first line of each verse in Latin as the last line of each stanza, a common practice in this straightforward kind of 'macaronic'. The poem has the attractive simplicity of all Lydgate's pieces in the four-stress line. *Vexilla regis prodeunt* is quite different, a lurid paraphrase of the famous Passion hymn by Venantius Fortunatus (sixth century), which quotes, or part-quotes, lines 3 and 4 of the Latin quatrains as lines 6 and 8 of the ballade-stanza, and also mixes a little Latin here and there elsewhere, e.g.

> Moriens ful hygh up in þe eyre.   (19)

The lofty tone of the translation is announced in the opening lines,

> Royal banerys unrolled of the kyng
> Towarde his batayle, in Bosra steyned reede. . . .

but not maintained. By line 4 Lydgate is resorting to 'I tooke good heede', and in the rest the impetus of the work, and sometimes its very sense, are lost in the cross-currents of allusion and aureation. This, for instance, is how he translates the Latin of verse 4:

> Impleta sunt quae concinit
> David fideli carmine,
> dicendo nationibus:
> Regnavit a ligno deus.[10]

Cf. Al thyng acomplyssched, deth and his woundes scharpe,
  With all þe misteries of olde prophesie,
  The funeral compleyntis Davit songe with his harpe,
  With wepyng tunis, notyd in Jeremie,
  Whose coote armure was lyke a bloody skye
  Dicendo nationibus,
  Recoorde Esdras and recoorde Isaye
  Regnavit a ligno deus.   (33–40)

The memorableness of the fifth line almost looks like an accident in such a context. The stanza shows Lydgate's method of expanding by allusion, and may be compared with the simplicity of the version of the hymn by Friar William Herebert in the early fourteenth century:

> Y-volvuld ys Davidþes sawe,
> þat soth was prophete of þe olde lawe,
> þat sayde: 'Men ȝe mowen y-se
> Hou godes trone ys rode tre.'[11]

Herebert did a good many such translations, evidently intending them for pulpit use, to be read out within the sermon to underline its lessons and provide variety. Herebert was skilful enough to capture the paradox of the last line, which Lydgate misses.

But there is no doubting the nature of Lydgate's ambitions, which overflow in the profusion of the *Te deum laudamus*. This psalmic hymn,[12] formerly attributed to Ambrose but later to Nicetas, bishop of Remesiana (*c.* 420),[13] was the most famous non-biblical hymn of the West, sung every day, and many translations exist in Old and Middle English. None is like Lydgate's, which takes 'Te laudat omnis spiritus' as its refrain, and sprinkles Latin and Latinate words indiscriminately in the rest of the stanza, with some heavy alliteration. The following Latin verses,

> Te gloriosus apostolorum chorus
> Te prophetarum laudabilis numerus
> Te martyrum candidatus laudat exercitus

provide this stanza in Lydgate:

> *Te chorus* glorious of apostolate,
> Memorial make, modulacioun,
> The laudable nombre of the prophetys astate
> Evir joyng gaudent in jubilacioun,
> Te letabilem laudat in laudacioun,
> *Te martirum candidatus exercitus*
> Principium polorum in al pausacioun
> *Te laudat omnis spiritus.*   (25–32)

Here, in its unloveliest form, is the 'aureation' which is so much spoken of in connection with Lydgate, and so loosely. In its strict form, the only form in which it can be usefully discussed, aureation is a comparatively rare phenomenon, found only in Lydgate, Dunbar, and a few other writers of the fifteenth century, such as the anonymous author of the five poems from MS.Add.20059 (*temp.* Henry VII) printed by Brown.[14] It consists essentially in the use of a florid Latinate diction, with the Latin barely digested into English, and is the vernacular equivalent to the taste for 'florida verborum venustas' manifested in Latin writers of the period such as Whethamstede.[15] Alliteration plays a considerable part in the aureate style, though it is alliteration derived from Latin rhetorical models (the figure *paromoeon*) rather than from native sources. In Lydgate's *Te deum*, it is concentrated in lines 5 and 7 of the stanza, and tends to die out as the poem goes on, a mark perhaps of the strain it placed on Lydgate's resources. The aureate style is commonest in religious poems, especially in those of a laudatory or celebratory nature which rely for their structure on the accumulation of recondite allusions and images. Such a structure gives a strong impetus towards Latinity in the vernacular, and the Marian hymn is thus the *locus classicus* of fifteenth-century aureation, and provides its best examples, as we shall see later. One final point to stress[16] is that aureation, though it often involves long words, is not to be identified with the use of long words. The systematic use of polysyllabic words, in Lydgate and other poets, has more to do with the influence of legal, epistolary and official language than with 'aureation' properly so called, and as much to do with French as with Latin.

The last of this group of translations is based upon a sequence, *Letabundus exultet fidelis chorus*, not upon a hymn. Sequences originated as prose texts to accompany the musical elaboration of the *Alleluia*, which later acquired, in the 'regular' sequence, a systematic rhythmical form and rhyme. The most famous of them, such as *Victimae paschali laudes* (Easter), *Veni sancti spiritus* (Pentecost) and *Dies irae, dies illa* (Mass for the Dead), exerted a profound influence upon medieval thought and imagery. The *Letabundus* was attributed to St. Bernard, like many other hymns and sequences, and was sung both at Christmas and at the festival of the Assumption. Lydgate makes reference to both occasions (15, 311). His work is not a translation, even in the loosest sense, but an extended rhapsody for which the verses of the sequence provide a series of starting-off points. The themes are diverse, but centre in joyous exultation at God's gift of himself to man—prophecies of Advent, praise of the Virgin, meditation on the Nativity,

> *Gloria in excelsis* was nat songe in veyn,
> Song of Aungellys was so delicious,
> The wyntrys nyght was nat spent in veyn
> Whoos refreyt was *pax in hominibus,*   (185–8)

and above all on the coming of the new to crown the old, the fulfilment of the 'figures':

> Somyr flours, that did in wyntir dare,
> Lowe in the roote shewyng no fresshnesse,
> Braunche, bough and tree and medewes rude and bare,
> Whan Marche approcheth, put out ther grennesse.
> And semblably prophetys ber witnesse,
> Al that they wrot was curteyned in scripture,
> Of Cristes comyng was but a lyknesse,
> The light was cloos, hyd undir figure. . . .
> Cedre and isope be joyned in the vale,

> Cristes birthe hath voyded oold figurys.
> The husk is falle, brokyn is the shale,
> The noote kernel, closyd in scripturys,
> In rejoysshyng of alle creaturys,
> Al openly shewith his swetnesse.   (209–30)

There is explanation of, commentary and meditation on each verse of
the sequence, with extended allusion to biblical texts and to familiar
literary motifs:

> Rekne in ordre alle sesouns of the yeer,
> Wynter frostys, snowes whyte and shene,
> March with his buddys at comyng in of veer,
> Fressh Aprylle, with prymerolles grene,
> Al stant on chaunge; but this hevenly queene
> Withoute appallyng conservith hire clernesse;
> Callyd *Stella celi*, this pryncesse that I meene,
> Of hevene and erthe lady and Empresse.   (153–60)

The structure of the poem depends entirely on the structure of the
sequence, moving forward deliberately from verse to verse (e.g. 144,
161). Lydgate takes up the reference to 'chorus' from the first line and
throughout addresses those who are to sing the *Letabundus*, aware both
of the chorus of 'Cristes hool Covent' (141) and of the 'querestrys
vertuous' (191) of Bury, for whose immediate benefit he was presumably writing. Unlike the two English versions of *Letabundus* printed by
Brown,[17] Lydgate's poem is not intended to be sung, but to be read
and meditated upon, so that the singers will understand fully what they
sing of. It is difficult not to be struck by the buoyancy and vigour of
individual passages in the *Letabundus*, but the sequence offers too little
control over the luxuriance of Lydgate's responses, and the rhapsodis-
ing finally runs itself into the sands: there are only eight stanzas on the
last five verses, as opposed to thirty-one on the first seven.

  The fourteen-verse Prayers are the least interesting of Lydgate's
religious poems. Some of them were written to order, like the *Devowte
Invocacioun to Saints Denys*, for the king of France, the *Invocation to
Seynte Anne*, for the countess of Stafford, and the longer *Prayer of St.
Thomas*, presumably composed at the request of the monks of the
Canterbury to be hung before the shrine of the saint (see the envoy).
In these three, Lydgate reaches after a higher style, calling, for instance,
in the *Invocation to Seynte Anne*, upon the Holy Spirit to help him,

Whos golde dewe dropes fro þy reclynatorye
Into my soule, awhaped and amaate,
Shed from aboven þy licour aureate.   (12–14)

The *Prayer to St. Thomas* demonstrates Lydgate's techniques of amplification through accumulation of lapidary and classical allusion:

Callid among martirs charboncle and ruby,
Trouthis champioun, Achaat of hih prowesse,
Sampsoun the seconde, diamaunt sturdi,
Emeraud greene, voide of doubilnesse. . . .   (57–60)

Other prayers clearly relate to more homely local needs, like the
Prayer *To St. Robert of Bury*, the child-martyr, whose chapel at Bury
was maintained by the monks, and the excellent little *Prayer to St.
Leonard*, which was evidently written for some local hospital:

O glorious Leonard! pray Jesu on thy kne
For þi servauntis resortyng to þis place.   (35–6)

The prayer *To St. Ositha* is apparently directed to the royal saint, queen
of East Anglia, martyred in the seventh century, but there is no mention
of the remarkable manner of her martyrdom, and the domestic tone of
all the references suggests that the saint in question is St. Sitha of Lucca,
patron-saint of housekeepers. The text has 'Sitha'; only the rubric of
one MS. (Harley 2255) refers to 'Ositha'. Lydgate may have confused
the two. This prayer, like those to Michael, Gabriel, Ursula, and other
saints, was probably composed for private devotion on the day of the
appropriate festival.

Lydgate wrote comparatively few poems on the Passion, and those
that he did write have little to do with the tradition of intimate,
passionate attachment to the body of Christ which plays so large a part
in medieval lyric-writing. The poems on *Cristes Passioun* and *The
Dolerous Pyte of Crystes Passioun*, and the *Prayer upon the Cross*, are
penitential rather than devotional, using the crucifix, with which at
least two of them are associated as text to picture,[18] as a stimulus to
repentance, just as the memorial of Christ's passion was used in the
moralistic poems. There is a good deal of detail of the agonies of the
Cross in these poems, but so laboriously accumulated and unimagina-
tively used as to be completely without affective power:

> Cressettys born up with many gret lanterne,
> Swerdis, stavis, scoorges inportable,
> Cryeng terryble, hydous to discerne,
> Fals accusacyouns verray innumerable,
> Knyves, pynsouns, hard hameris nat plicable,
> Craunpisshed with deth, accused of tresoun;
> And sith my deth was to the profytable,
> Man thynk among upon my passioun.
>
> *(Cristes Passioun,* 33–40)

Similarly, the address of *Child Jesus to Mary the Rose,* which most medieval poets would have seized on as an obvious opportunity for pathos, is developed, though not ineffectually, as a play upon the image of the rose.

Apart from those mentioned, and the poem on the *Fifteen Woes of Christ,* a tedious exercise, the only other poem on the Passion is *A Seying of the Nightingale,* a free improvisation on the theme of John Pecham's *Philomena.* This famous poem, of which Lydgate seems to have only the sketchiest knowledge, tells how the nightingale, before her death, flies to the tree-top and there, at the hours of divine service (Prime, Tierce, Sexte, and Nones), sings out her heart till she dies at *hora nona.* Her song thus commemorates Christ's Passion, and is also an allegory of Christ's life, of the ages of the world, and of the life of man. Pecham, a Franciscan friar who became archbishop of Canterbury (d. 1292), develops the theme with the intense devotion of Bernardine and Franciscan writing, an anguished love and pity which can only be appeased in the sharing of Christ's suffering.

Lydgate has little of this. *A Seying* opens with one of his ornamental sunset-descriptions:

> In Juygne whan Tytan was in þe Crabbes hed,
> Towardes even þe saphyre huwed sky
> Was westwarde meynt with many rowes red,
> And fowles singen in þeyre melodye
> An hevenly complyne with sugred ermonye. . . .

The bird-song fades, leaving only the nightingale,

> Whos hertely refreyde was ever 'ocy, ocy'.   (14)

The poet, like a good Chaucerian, thinks that she is singing to Venus, urging her to take vengeance ('kill, kill') on false lovers. As evening falls, þe baumy vapour of graasys gan upsmyte,   (39)

and he falls asleep, only to be awakened by an imperious messenger,

> Nought frome Cupyde but fro þe lord above. . . .
> Which to me sayde: 'Foole, what doost þou here
> Sleping alloone, gaping upon þe moone?'   (45–8)

The angel tells him to follow,

> For trust me weel, I cast þee not to lede
> No thing towardes þe gardin of þe roose.   (52–3)

The nightingale's song is interpreted as a remembrance of Christ's love and suffering, and the interpretation introduces an elaborate allusion to *Isaiah* 63:1 (133–54) and a version of the Complaint of Christ (155–231), which merges into a moralistic account of the remedies against the seven sins that the Cross provides. Further amplification is drawn from a characteristic accumulation of images for the Cross—palm of victory, key of heaven, staff of Jacob, 'hooke and snaare of þe Levyatan', harp of David, tree of Moses, 'chief chaundellabre of þe tabernacle', tree of health—before the final call to forsake the world for the 'gardeyn of parfyt paramours', where Christ the nightingale calls to man's soul, his spouse and sister.

It will readily be seen that Lydgate's poem has little to do with the *Philomena*, apart from the initial idea of a spiritual interpretation of the nightingale's song. The *Seying* is largely an anthology of familiar themes: it sprawls, picks up ideas and allusions in passing, and quite lacks the precise and pointed allegory of Pecham. But for all its motley construction, it is a remarkably effective poem, full of life and colour, and for this the 'Chaucerian' introduction and the frame of secular reference are not a little responsible. Even in this religious context, it seems, Lydgate works best when he can move into a poem along familiar Chaucerian avenues, though the juxtaposition of secular and spiritual was of course a common technique of medieval religious poetry, and is used elsewhere by Lydgate in *A Holy Medytacioun* (a poem *de contemptu mundi*), and in some of the Marian pieces. It is worth noting that the *Seying* is in rhyme-royal, which seems to be a more relaxed form for Lydgate than ballade.

There is another fifteenth-century poem on *The Nightingale* which is a direct paraphrase of the *Philomena*. It has only the briefest introduction, and the construction is careful and regular, with systematic

exposition of the allegory. It was written for the duchess of Bucking-
ham, and refers to the death of Henry, earl of Warwick (1446), and
was long attributed to Lydgate.[19] MacCracken rejected it as being too
good for Lydgate's old age, 'carefully constructed, highly artistic,
quite compact', as opposed to the *Seying*, which he calls 'digressive,
indirect and incompact'.[20] One has heard these same terms applied to
the construction of *Piers Plowman*, and they are perfectly accurate as
description of phenomena; but they mean nothing as critical judgments, unless we suppose that all poetry aspires to a logical construction. However, what MacCracken says of the *Nightingale* is valid: it is
not the kind of poem Lydgate would write, its compactness is not his,
and he would be most unlikely to show, in two poems, both a vague
and an accurate knowledge of the *Philomena*.

The Marian poems, to which we turn now, are the most important
of Lydgate's religious pieces, and represent the highest development of
his mannered art, with lavish use of stylistic artifice, elaborate aureation
and a virtually static syntax based on the invocation *Ave*. They are
totally lacking in the tenderness, intimacy, fervour, and pseudo-eroti-
cism of the Bernardine and Franciscan traditions, and concentrate on the
celebration of the mystery and splendour of the Virgin. The heaping-
up of invocation, epithet, image, and allusion is meant to overwhelm
with excess, hardly to be comprehended. The aim is not to stir to
devotion, but to make an act of worship out of the elaboration of the
artefact. The extraordinary vocabulary, the strained imagery, the
alliteration, and the hypnotic repetition of invocatory sentence-
patterns have much the same effect of assault on the sensibilities as the
flamboyant decoration of late Gothic. It is worth comparing Chaucer's
ABC or the *Invocacio ad Mariam* in the Prologue to the *Second Nun's
Tale* to see just how far Lydgate has gone beyond his master in this one
field to which he can lay claim to undisputed mastery.

The best representative of all these tendencies, and in many ways one
of the best of the poems, is the *Ballade at the Reverence of Our Lady*.
Lydgate is perfectly conscious of what he is reaching for: he begins
with a conventional-sounding Chaucerian introduction,

> A thowsand storiis kowde I mo reherse
> Of olde poetis touchynge this matere:
> How that Cupide the hertis gan to perse
> Of his servauntis, settyng tham affere,

but then turns sharply against the convention, echoing the *Troilus*:

> Lo here the fin of th'errour and the weere,
> Lo here of love the guerdoun and grevaunce
> That evyr with woo his servaunts doth avaunce. (5–7)

He promises to 'redresse' his style and begs for inspiration in his lofty task of praising the Virgin:

> O wynd of grace, now blowe into my saile,
> O auriat lycour of Clyo, for to wryte
> Mi penne enspire of that I wold endyte. (12–14)

The celebration that follows,

> O sterne of sternys with thi stremys clere,
> Sterne of the see, to shipman lyght and gyde,
> O lusty leemyng, most plesaunt to appere,
> Whos bright bemys the clowdis may not hide,
> O way of lyfe to hem þat goo or ride,
> Haven aftyr tempest surrest up to ryve,
> On me have mercy for thi joyes fyve.
>
> O rightest rewl, O rote of holynesse,
> And lightsom lyne of pite for to pleyne,
> Orignal gynnyng of grace and al goodnesse,
> And clennest condite of vertu soverayne,
> Modyr of mercy, oure troubyl to restreyne,
> Chambyr and closet clennest of chastyte,
> And namyd herberwe of þe deyte,
>
> O closid gardeyn, al void of weedes wicke,
> Cristallyn welle, of clennesse cler consigned,
> Fructif olyve, of foilys faire and thicke,
> And redolent cedyr, most derworthly ydynged,
> Remembyr of pecchouris unto thee assigned,
> Or þe wyckid fend his wrath upon us wreche,
> Lantyrn of light, be þu oure lyfis leche.
>
> Paradys of pleasaunce, gladsom to all good,
> Benygne braunchelet of the pigment-tre,
> Vinarye envermailyd, refrescher of oure food,
> Lycour aȝens langour that pallid may not be,
> Blisful bawm-blossum, bydyng in bounte,

Thi mantel of mercy on oure myschef spred,
Or woo awak us, wrappe us undyr thi weed.   (22–49)

is drawn, image by image, from the *Anticlaudianus* of Alain de Lille:

Hec est stella maris, vite via, porta salutis,
Regula justicie, limes pietatis, origo
Virtutis, venie mater thalamusque pudoris,
Ortus conclusus, fons consignatuus, oliva
Fructiferans, cedrus redolens, paradisus amenans,
Virgula pigmenti, vinaria cella, liquore
Predita celesti, nectar celeste propinans, . . .[21]

In these lines we can see the very process by which aureate vocabulary came into being, the creation of a language which John Metham referred to as Lydgate's 'halff chongyd Latyne'.[22] *Fons consignatus*, for instance, gives 'consigned', the only use of the word in Middle English; *vinaria cella* gives 'vinarye envermailyd', by far the earliest occurrence of the word *vinery*; and, a little later, *lux nubila pellens* gives, in 'þu lyght withoutyn nebule', the only use of the word *nebula* before the seventeenth century. The richness of the language is not, of course, superficial: all these images went back deep in tradition,[23] and found their origin in interpretations of the rich imagery of the Old Testament, of the *Song of Solomon* especially,

A garden inclosed is my sister, my spouse; a spring shut up, a fountain sealed   (4:12)

and of *Ecclesiasticus*:

I was exalted like a cedar in Libanus, as a cypress-tree on Mount Sion: I was exalted like a palm tree in Cades, and as a rose-plant in Jericho: as a fair olive tree in the plains.   (24:17)

Each phrase was dwelt on lovingly by the commentators, and its allegorical sense drawn out with endless ingenuity and variety. The Bible was even more of a treasure-house for figures of the Virgin birth, and in its peroration the *Ballade* explodes in a cascade of such allusions:

O precyous perle withoutyn ony pere,
Cockyl with gold dew from above i-reyned,
þu busshe unbrent, ferles set affere,
Flawmyng in fervence, not with hete peyned,
Duryng daysye with no weder steyned,

Flese undefoulyd of gentyl Gedeon,
þe fructefyng yerde, þowe, of Aron,

The myȝti arke, probatyk piscyne,
Lawghynge Aurora, and of pees olyve,
Columpne and base up-beryng from abyme,
Why nere I connyng the for to discrive?
Chesen for Joseph, whan he took to wyve,
Unknowyng hym, chyldyng be mirakyll,
And of our manly figure tabyrnakyll.   (127–40)

The bush burnt with the fire of the Holy Ghost but was not con-
sumed or touched; Gideon's fleece was wet with the dew of the Holy
Ghost—

> He cam also stylle
> þer his moder was
> As dew in Aprylle
> þat fallyt on þe gras—

whilst the threshing-floor of her virginity remained dry and inviolate;
Aaron's rod blossomed, though dry when it was put in the tabernacle.

The construction of a poem like the *Ballade* is quite arbitrary, like
that of a litany or rosary. It is at once infinitely simple and inexhaustibly
complex, and stands or falls by what it alludes to rather than by what it
says. It depends upon a community of knowledge, and depends on this
absolutely, for there can be no profit for the unprepared reader in
finding Mary referred to as 'punycall pome' and 'auryat urne'. Yet the
very outrageousness of such imagery may itself direct the reader's
attention to the fact that it means more than it says, and means it in a
special way—not in terms of a sensuous association which is apparent to
all, but in terms of intellectual and conceptual associations which have
to be learnt. It is this kind of language that medieval poetry can teach
us to need, and which we can then use to understand not only the
poetry but also the art, where 'realism' is often a cunning disguise for a
precise intellectual symbolism, as in the Merode altarpiece of Roger
Campin.[24]

The *Ballade at the Reverence of Our Lady* is the most ostentatiously
'suspended' of these aureate Marian lyrics, its point of contact with the
world of normal reality, on which it rests, being almost invisible. Like
a star, it has brightness but no apparent substance, though we are
assured of its magnitude by those who have the instruments to know.

Its truest compeer is the magnificent *Hymn to Mary* of Dunbar. Lydgate's other Marian lyrics are all alloyed in some way, their remoteness compromised. *Ave Jesse Virgula* begins as a catalogue of Marian images, using Latin phrases in the refrain-line,

> Haile, flos campi, O Ave jesse virgula,

and in the second half of line 6, to provide the rhyme, e.g.

> Haile, bussh unbrent, portula signata.   (6)

The later part of the poem is more miscellaneous, and assembles various topics in praise of the Virgin: Mary is compared to the Holy City of the Apocalypse, with lapidary interpretation of the twelve stones, and to the 'woman clothed with the sun' (*Rev.* 12:1) and crowned with twelve stars, which are interpreted as the product of the three theological and the four cardinal virtues. There is also some verbal play on an altogether lower level: *Eva* transformed to *Ave*, and acrostics on the name MARIA. These are the commonplaces of the Marian hymns in Latin.

Two other aureate poems are based on the antiphon *Ave Regina Celorum*, one of four antiphons interpolated into the Mass as a result of the influence of the cult of the Virgin (the other three are *Salve Regina*, *Regina Celi Letare*, and *Alma redemptoris mater*, sung by the Prioress's 'litel clergeoun'). The prayer *To Mary Queen of Heaven*, the first of Lydgate's two pieces, is one of the richest accumulations of Marian imagery after the *Ballade*, with some attention to grouping by association,

> Glad Aurora, kalendis of cleer day,
> Of Phebus uprist, massageer most enteer,
> Rose of Jherico, groweth noon so fressh in May,
> Gracious Lucifer, dirk morwenynges for to cleer,   (25–8)

and to patterns of parallelism and chiasmus:

> Palme of our conquest, grene olyve of our pes,
> Of hope our anker, at the havene of lyff t'aryve,
> Of feith our sheld, pavys of our encres.   (49–51)

The language is touched with Latinity, but there is no direct Latin quotation, and the refrain-line refers to the theme of devotion to the Five Joys of the Virgin. An envoy develops this theme in more direct language. The other piece, which takes its title and refrain, *Ave Regina*

Celorum, from the antiphon, is by contrast heavily aureate, with marked alliteration, and frequent quotation of Latin phrases, particularly at the end of the sixth line of the stanza. This hymn discards the *Ave* structure and reverts to discourse, though the syntax is often cryptic and obscure, in the usual manner of Lydgate's high style. The handling of allusion in this stanza.

> Hayle! gloryous lady, O rosa marina,
> Whyche hast fostryd lying in thy lappe
> Tetragramaton, that fed us with Manna,
> Of Leviathan mawgre the sleyghty trappe,
> To thys worlde a lyghte sprong ys from thy lappe,
> With virginall mylke ut castitas lilium,
> So lyst the Holygost in the hys wynges wrappe,
> Ave regina celorum! (25–32)

may be compared with the corresponding stanza in another fifteenth-century version of the antiphon, where the simplicity of language and concept echoes the miracle-plays:

> Hayle be þu! now wyrgyne clere,
> The holly gost lyȝt þe witt-in;
> Thow bare a chyld of gret powere,
> And never was fylyd witt no syne,
> Thow stod full stylle witt myld chere
> And hyme consaywyd witt mykyl wynne.
> He perssyd þi wombe as son soo clere,
> And ȝeyt þu was a cleyne wyrgyne.
> Of alle wyrgyns, þu art callyd modyre,
> þat ever bare lyfe undyre-nethe þe sone.
> I say by þe and by no nodyre,
> O mater flos virginum.[25]

These antiphons were favourite themes for Marian hymns in both Latin and English.[26] Lydgate's non-aureate version of *Regina Celi Letare*, where he uses the versicles of the antiphon as the refrain-line, and develops the theme of the *felix culpa* with freedom and skill, is matched by other fifteenth-century versions, one of extreme simplicity, in eight lines, another of extraordinary 'macaronic' elaboration:

> O dulcis diamounde, deyre damesell,
> Domina mundi, thow delykat dame,

Tronus dei, thow art to tell,
Intemerata, turtyll tame.[27]

This sort of free macaronic should be distinguished from the tradition
of aureation. Though there is a heavy admixture of Latin, the English is
mostly very homely, and it is the contrast of the two that provides the
style, not the blending of the one into the other.

Apart from the *Ave* poems, and the antiphonal hymns, the dominant
theme of Lydgate's Marian poetry is that of devotion to the Joys of the
Virgin. The number varies: *To Mary Queen of Heaven*, already mentioned, refers to five, and five are developed in the evening prayer *To
Mary Star of Jacob*, and in the translation of the favourite hymn *Gaude
virgo mater Christi*.[28] The Latin versions of the *Gaude* have extra stanzas
in some texts to give seven Joys, the more usual number, as developed
in Lydgate's *Ave Maria*. This poem combines meditation on the seven
Joys with a Latin refrain-line which uses an overlapping sequence from
the Salutation—'Ave Maria gracia plena', 'Gracia plena dominus
tecum', 'Dominus tecum benedicta tua', and so on.[29] Individual lines
as quoted do not comprise syntactical units, and do not make sense,
except of course that liturgical sequences as familiar as the *Ave Maria*
do not need to make sense on the verbal level. One is reminded of the
many poems in both Latin and English where the *Ave Maria* is employed in word-acrostics, sometimes even in multiple acrostics and
sentence-anagrams.[30] This kind of post-verbal sophistication is interesting as a further indication that the 'meaning' of much of this poetry is
not to be found in the direct reference of the language but in schemes
of number and symbol.

Prolonged meditation on the Joys of Mary resulted in their growing
in number from seven to fifteen. The most elaborate literary development of this theme was in the beautiful *Quindecim Gaudia* of John of
Howden; Lydgate's *Fyfftene Joyes of Oure Lady*, written for the countess
of Warwick,[31] is much simpler, a rosary-poem, in fact, with an *Ave* to
be said after the remembrance of each Joy. Another poem, *The Fifteen
Joys and Sorrows of Mary*, adds fifteen sorrows to correspond to the
joys, a traditional and typically medieval piece of *inventio* through
contraries. These pieces are practical aids to devotion, less 'literary'
than much of the other Marian writing, and the *Fifteen Joys and Sorrows*,
which has a pictorial connection,[32] is further linked with the group of
poems, such as the *Image of Our Lady* and *On the Image of Pity*, designed,
in a similarly practical way, to provide texts for pictures. Even in the

Ave Maria, not specifically a picture-poem, Lydgate speaks of 'we knelyng before thyne Image' (7).

What is most strikingly absent from Lydgate's Marian poetry, as we have suggested, is any intimate devotion to the person of Mary, or any affective development of the themes of joy and sorrow. There are no love-songs to the Virgin, no dialogues of mother and Christ-child, no version of the *Stabat mater*, and the one careful exercise in Marian lamentation, *Quis dabit meo capite fontem lacrimarum*, is sufficient, in its total lack of drama or emotion, to demonstrate why. It is much more characteristic of Lydgate to amplify a topic of praise, or to embroider the familiar phrases of hymn or antiphon, than to develop an organic theme. The charming *Valentine to her that excelleth all*, already mentioned in connection with Queen Katherine,[33] is his typical work, with its courtly 'turn', or the elaborately encylopaedic *Gloriosa dicta sunt de te*, written for Edmund Lacy,[34] where Psalm 87 and *Revelation* 21:19 are drawn together in celebration of Mary as the Holy City. The technique is similar to that of *Misericordias Domini in eternum cantabo*, for what Lydgate provides, essentially, is a Biblical concordance to 'city', not only the Heavenly City of St. John, but the City of Wisdom in *Ecclesiastes* (9:14) and the City of the South in *Ezekiel* (40:2), and others. There is even a place for non-Biblical cities, through an outdoing-topos:

> Auctours whylome gaf a prys to Troye. . . .
> And eeke of Roome for domynacyoun. . . .
> But al þeyre booste may nowe be layde adowne,
> So gloryous thinges beo sayde and song of þee.   (25–32)

This poem is extremely rich in allusion, and dignified in its language, but not truly 'aureate', in the sense in which the term was defined earlier. In fact, one is struck, at the end, by the very limited reference of this term to Lydgate, even in his Marian poetry. A few poems display aureation in its full extravagance, and they are certainly the most striking, but for the most part the language is only sporadically richer than is usual in Lydgate's high style. This is especially true of those poems, about a third of the total, in rhyme-royal.

The last group of religious poems with which we have to deal, the legends or saints' lives, constitute the greatest bulk of all, though it is questionable whether, with one exception, they will now sustain the greatest interest. Saints' lives begin with a simple practical purpose—to promote faith by allowing the audience to witness examples and trials of faith, and martyrdoms, beside which their own tribulations appear trivial. They were designed to be read out in church on the festival-day of the saint, in place of the usual *lectio*, and versions were collected together for this purpose into legendaries, calendars of saints' lives, such as the *South-English Legendary* of the early fourteenth century. The tone of these legends is unashamedly popular: they contain much lively colloquialism in dialogue, and a good deal of comic realism, especially in the portrayal of evil; they dwell at excruciating length upon the endless scourging, boiling, roasting, and mutilation which are the staple of the form; and they borrow freely the language and idiom of the minstrel-romances, into which they merge by imperceptible degrees.

It was Chaucer's endeavour to raise these crude pieces to the level of literary sophistication which they had long achieved in Latin and French, and, indeed, in at least two earlier but long-forgotten manifestations in English—in Old English, and in the prose lives of the Katherine-Group. His version of the life of St. Cecilia, later incorporated into the *Canterbury Tales* as the *Second Nun's Tale*, is the most straightforward product of this ambition, written in the austere high style of the *Clerk's Tale*, with an elaborate invocation to the Virgin, and lengthy etymologising of the saint's name. The form of the poem, however, despite its literary elaboration, remains essentially uncomplicated. In his later versions of saints' lives, the *Prioress's Tale* and, by an extension of the term, the *Man of Law's Tale*, Chaucer attempted, or appears to have attempted, a degree of dramatic differentiation, though it must be said that our energy in seeking out the flaws of the two narrators may be as much our basic lack of interest in the form, and a compensating desire to find 'Chaucerian' ambiguity, as anything else. The *Prioress's Tale* can probably stand as a comment on the Prioress, but the *Man of Law's Tale* is probably to be taken straight, as a superb flourish of rhetoric. The story of Constance, which had numerous popular exemplars, including the romance of *Emare*, is a saint's life in all but final martyrdom and canonisation, and Chaucer takes it through every form of rhetorical amplification, subjecting it at the same time to a continual running fire of emotional commentary, apostrophe and exclamation. The result has not endeared itself to modern taste, which would probably prefer the crude realism of the popular pieces, but there is no doubt of its influence on Chaucer's successors, or at least on Lydgate, for the others, Capgrave, Bokenham, and Bradshaw, took their cue more from Lydgate than from Chaucer.

In his saints' legends, therefore, Lydgate is attempting a literary elaboration to match and, as usual, to improve upon Chaucer's. There are greater and less degrees of elaboration: the simpler pieces seem to be the ones designed for minor occasions or commissions, such as the *Legend of St. Petronilla*, evidently written for the lepers' hospital of St. Petronilla at Bury, maintained by the monastery. The language is dignified and careful, without much contrivance, the only flourish being a spring-vignette introduced in connection with the day of the saint's martyrdom, 31st May, in order to fit the allegory of the nightingale wakeful in Christ's service:

> Take of this mater an applycacion. . . . (129)

The *Legend of St. George* was written for the London armourers, and it has already been characterised as simple in form.[35] Simple, however, is only a comparative term, and the character of Lydgate's version, refined, decorous, abstract, generalised, can best be gauged by measuring it against the raucous colloquialism and violence of the version in the *South-English Legendary*. This is how the latter describes part of the torturing:

> Wiþ kene oules þere bineþe tormentors þer stode
> And al todrowe his holy limes þat hi ronne ablode;
> Al hi todrowe is tendre vleiss, þe peces folle to gronde;
> Bernynge eoly suþþe hy nome and caste inis wonde.
> þo hi hadde him þus todrawe longe, þat ruþe it was to seo,
> Hy biþoзte him of more ssame and nome hi doun of þe treo,
> Wiþ harde scorges leide him on and wonde up oþer made;
> To þe bare bon þe scorges come, as þe oules hadde er iwade.
> þe wonden hi nome and sulte suþþe and þat salt þicke caste,
> And suþþe wiþ a clout of here hi rodde it wel vaste.[36]

The physical detail of violence, the crude visualisation of the scene ('þe peces folle to gronde'), the ransacking of imagination for new extremes of pain ('Hy biþoзte him of more ssame'), are all reminiscent of the Crucifixion scenes in the Mystery-cycles, and appeal to a similar taste. Lydgate's version, by contrast,

> þe Thyraunt þanne, of verray cruweltee,
> Bad þat he shoulde þis martir moost entier
> Naked beon hanged upon a galowe tree,
> With scowrges beet in ful felle maner,

And with brondes brennyng bright and cler,
His sides brent, were not hes peynes strong?
His entraylles opende, salt cast in among.   (169–75)

deflects the edge of suffering by the use of conventional literary phrases
and devices, and by the very syntax, where the absolute contructions of
the last two lines make the actions seem pre-ordained rather than
humanly purposed, as indeed, from a very profitable point of view,
they are. A similar point can be made in the saint's final prayer on
behalf of those who venerate him (a conventional motif), where Lydgate's abstraction and generality (232–8) contrast sharply with the
homely practicality of the *Legendary* (88–94).

The *Legend of St. Margaret*, written for lady March, is a good deal
more elaborate, though the life itself still conforms to the fairly straightforward narrative pattern of the *Second Nun's Tale*. A lengthy prologue
invokes the saint's help, offers extended explanations of her name, and
assures the reader that

> Under writyng rude of apparence
> Mater is hid of grete intellygence.
> Ful ofte falleth, in this chestys blake
> Gold and perlys and stones of gret prys
> Ben ylooke and into warde ytake. . . .
> A royal ruby in whiche ther is no lak
> May closed ben in a ful pore sak.   (6–14)

The story itself, as is usual in the more sophisticated saint's life, is conducted chiefly through speeches and prayers, with the minimum of
actual narration. The syntax of the stanza is quite complex, the language conventional and decorous, and it is again useful to compare a
popular version of the legend, such as that in the Auchinleck MS.[37]
The idiom of minstrel-romance and ballad is well illustrated in this
passage, where Olibrius speaks of his love for Margaret:

> 'Maiden Mergrete, mi leman schaltow be.
> Ichold þe for mi wiif, ȝif þou be of kin fre;
> ȝif þow be of þraldam born, y give þe gold and fe,
> þou schalt be mi leman, so long so it be.'   (89–92)

The tone is quite different in Lydgate:

> 'And of hir birthe if that she be fre,
> I wille hir have sothly to my wyfe,

> Love and cherysshe for hir grete beaute,
> And it is skyle, duryng al my lyfe,
> That atwene us ther shal be no stryfe;
> And if she be born of foreyne lyne,
> I wille hir take to my concubyne.' (134–40)

Lydgate's sense of decorum gives dignity, but it means of course that everything comes out the same. He is never ludicrous, but on the other hand he rarely conveys any sense of drama or actuality. The devil who appears to Margaret is simply a devil, 'in lykenesse of a man' (297); in the Auchinleck version he is 'a wele fouler þing', with 'honden on his knes and eiʒe on everich to'. This is ludicrous, but at least it is vividly ludicrous. Similarly, Lydgate's account of Margaret's fight with the devil totally lacks any sense of the actuality of the scene:

> By grace of God hent him by the hede
> And cast him doun, for al his felle armure,
> Under hir fete—he myghte not recure. (311–13)

The words are there, but behind the words only more words, never any sense of reality, as distinct from this:

> And þurch þe miʒt of Jhesu Crist wiþ wimpel sche him bond,
> Sche toke him bi þe temples, about sche him swong,
> Sche set hir fot in his nek, to þe erþe sche him þrong. (218–20)

It is clear that saint's life as narrative, with its continual demand, even at an elementary level, for imitation of the actual processes of life, held little interest for Lydgate, and in his more characteristic work we see him employing all his ingenuity to subdue and dislocate narrative for the sake of other artistic purposes. The best example among the shorter saints' lives is the Legend of St. Giles. This again has the elaborate prologue, with characteristically extended brevity-topics (34–42) and characteristically literal unfolding of Chaucer's modesty-topic of 'gleaning' (17–22); but the real originality of St. Giles is in the 'narrative', which is handled throughout in the second person, as something between invocation and prayer. In this way, the onward pressure of narrative is transformed into rhapsody and celebration, just as the rhythm of line in late Gothic is almost submerged in the flamboyance of decoration.

Two other poems, the Legend of St. Austin at Compton and the Legend of Dan Joos, neither of them properly speaking 'legends', illustrate the same tendency in the treatment of narrative, as does the Life of Our

19

Lady, which we shall come to later. *St. Austin*, which bears the rubric 'Offre up yowre Dymes', was clearly written for some occasion when the abbey was having difficulty collecting its tithes. It consists of a collection of Biblical texts to explain the origin of tithes, and then the exemplum to prove their necessity. The exemplum, which tells how St. Augustine conjures a ghost to tell of the pains he was in for not paying his tithes, and then conjures the priest who excommunicated him to absolve him, is a good example of the medieval delight, which Sir Thomas Browne shared, in stretching credulity:

> Oo ded man assoiled hath anothir—
> An unkouth caas merveilous t'expresse! (329–30)

The literary interest is in the ornate style and sub-aureate language, particularly in the digression on the coming of Christianity to England, where the Marian imagery of the day-star is applied to St. Augustine:

> He was Aurora whan Phebus sholde arise,
> With his briht beemys on that lond to shyne,
> Callyd day-sterre moost glorious to devise;
> Our feith was dirkid undir the Ecliptic lyne. . . .
> Til blissed Austyn, by goostly elloquence,
> Was trewe Auriga of foure gospelleeris. (89–104)

The profusion of ornament quite overwhelms the story, and so too with the *Legend of Dan Joos*, a miracle of the Virgin, where five stanzas of prologue invoke the Virgin,[38] and four stanzas of epilogue call upon lovers, like the *Troilus*, to forsake their fickle mistresses and turn to 'this lady, that can no wyse deceyve' (122). The story, of the monk whose devotion to Mary is rewarded by having five roses, inscribed 'Maria', grow from his mouth, eyes, and ears at his death, is retained, but the poem as a whole gravitates towards celebration of the Virgin, praise, prayer, invocation and rhapsody—a condition to which nearly all Lydgate's religious poetry aspires.

Despite his manifest distaste for narrative, Lydgate did embark on two major saints' legends in his later life, the first, *St. Edmund*, at the request of his own abbot in 1433, the other, *St. Albon*, for abbot Whethamstede of St. Alban's in 1439. Both are very long, far outdoing Chaucer, the former 3,693 lines, the latter 4,734 (not all Lydgate's), and both are in the nature of legend-epics, because of their length and their heroic treatment of the two national saints. It was these two works that exerted the greatest influence on other fifteenth-century verse hagiographers, not so much on Capgrave's *Life of St. Katherine*, which has its real roots in the East Anglican popular tradition of romance and saints' legends, as on Osbern Bokenham, whose *Legendys of Hooly Wummen* was begun in 1443. Bokenham was a Suffolk man, with strong Cambridge links; he may well have known Lydgate, and his patrons were drawn from circles familiar to us from the Lydgate network.[39] He pays a good deal of attention to the Chaucer-Lydgate tradition, with a thoughtful, bookish prologue, for instance, and some conventionally modest eschewing of rhetoric which does not prevent him showing off his high style from time to time. But one senses that Bokenham is most at his ease when he forgets his literary ambitions, and relaxes into the pleasantly gossiping prologues and link-passages, such as the *Prolocutorye* to the life of St. Mary Magdalene (4982–5262). The best of the lives, that of St. Elizabeth, is in a more homely style than the others, with much of the graphic detail and incident of the popular tradition: one must also admit that the life of a woman-saint who marries and dies a natural death is something of a relief after such a monstrous regiment of virgin-martyrs. If Bokenham was a reluctant Lydgatian, Henry Bradshaw was a devoted one. His *Life of St. Werburge* is on the Lydgatian model, with division into books, full apparatus of prologues and epilogues, careful amplification, and a good deal of polysyllabic Latinity. In a way, it is more ambitious than Lydgate. A work of local devotion, like *St. Edmund*, it brings into the story, in massive detail, not only Chester but the whole history of Mercia, even of England in parts, up to and beyond the Conquest, with chronicle and legend ransacked for associated and illustrative material. Bradshaw is more learned, more serious, more devout, than any of his predecessors, but his style is ponderous and graceless, a nightmare version of Lydgate's, ludicrously ill-adapted to any but the most formal of purposes. Bradshaw wrote just before 1513, and a final testimony to the long-lasting nature of Lydgate's influence may be deduced from Alexander Barclay's *Life of St. George*, written about 1515. Though it is a translation of the *Georgius* by Baptista Spagnuoli the Mantuan, one of the most popular of the Italian humanists, its deviations from the original are numerous, and mostly in the direction of the Lydgate tradition.

The *Life of St. Edmund and St. Fremund* was written at the request of abbot William Curteys, as Lydgate tells us (I,190), for Henry VI, after his successful and happy stay at Bury in 1433–4.[40] It was a work to which Lydgate would obviously devote a more than usual amount of care, both by the nature of the commission and by the fact that Edmund was his own patron-saint, and the product of his labours has some lineaments of grandeur. The source is the Latin life of St. Edmund: book I tells how Edmund came to the East Anglian throne; book II deals with Lothbrocus and his sons, Hyngwar and Ubba, Danish marauders, who are first defeated by Edmund and then, when he renounces force after seeing the carnage of battle,[41] martyr him; book III tells of Fremund, born to Offa and Bothild, sister of Edmund (like romances, saints' lives tended to generate sequels, 'son of . . .'), and of how he defeated the two Danes, slaying 40,000 with twenty-four men, and was then himself murdered. There follow some miracles of St. Edmund, such as any monastic life of its patron-saint would tend to accumulate to itself, before a final prayer for Henry VI and Envoy. Lydgate has surrounded the story with a mass of rhetorical circumstance— prayers, an interpretation of the arms of St. Edmund, elaborate prologue and envoy which provide anthologies of the modesty-topics—but this, and the miscellaneous nature of book III, should not disguise from us the surprising fact that the first two books represent one of Lydgate's most considerable narrative achievements. It is not, of course, narrative distinguished by its brevity. The opening, 'There lived in Saxony a good, god-fearing king called Alkmond', coming after 234 lines of introductory material, takes thirty-five lines of abstract cataloguing of qualities, panegyric by comparison, and moralising; and the narrative is liberally amplified with brevity-formulae and topics of excellence, with abrupt refusals to narrate followed by detailed elaboration, with gnomic comment,[42] and with the characteristic sequences of metaphorical analogies:

> Good frut ay cometh fro trees that be goode,
> From fressh hed-sprynges renne stremys cristallyne,
> In vertuous pastures holsom is the foode,
> Fro gentil blood procedith a trewe lyne,
> Tarage of trees th'applis determyne:
> So yong Edmond, pleynly to declare,
> Shewed how he kam from Alkmond and Siware.
>
> (I,347–53)

But with all this, Lydgate preserves a fluent narrative line, unclogged by imprecation and apostrophe, unlike, as we may think, the *Man of Law's Tale*. There is effective variation in the tone of voice, and in the pace of narration, charged dramatic scenes and dialogue alternating with swift background narration. The story of Lothbrocus at the beginning of book II, of his being carried off to England, accepted at court as a skilled huntsman, and then treacherously murdered, is swift, compact, even vivid:

> Aftir the grehound the knyht gan folwe a paas,
> Most secrely, and maad therof no tale.
> By whom he kam there as Lothbrocus was
> Hid under leves in a covert vale,
> His wounde bloody, his face ded and pale,
> His eyen gastlewh reversid bothe tweyne,
> His hound aside, which dide his deth compleyne.
>
> (II,218–24)

There is an economy and vigour in certain lines quite unusual for Lydgate:

> To these requestis make no rebellioun:
> For, yif thou do, thou shalt lese in this stryff
> Thy kyngdam first, thy tresour, and thy lyff.   (II,502–4)

Much of this has been learnt from Chaucer, and Lydgate has turned it to good account, like the touch of gentle humanity in Offa's parting with Edmund (I,515), but there is something more here that is not easy to find in Chaucer, what we may think of as a kind of moral conviction, an effective didacticism. It is sometimes loaded into the words of the narrative, sometimes explicit and digressive,[43] but most notable is the long description of Edmund's wise and pious rule (I,858–1116), a statement of political morality of overwhelming earnestness and Englishness, in a tradition that runs from King Alfred to Shakespeare, and to which Chaucer is irrelevant.

The *Life of St. Albon and St. Amphabell*, another double legend, was written for abbot John Whethamstede of St. Alban's. Whethamstede was a close friend of Humphrey of Gloucester, and a congenial figure in Lydgate's literary landscape, and the commission could almost have been predicted after the success of *St. Edmund* and the completion of the *Fall*. The record of payment for the work survives in the St. Alban's chronicles, a sum of £3 6s. 8d. (10 marks), whilst another MS. refers to a sum of £5 paid for writing and illumination together.[44] The work is based on familiar French and Latin sources: book I tells of Albon's training in knighthood, with a long introduction on the institution of chivalry, its observances, and some account of the arms of

Albon and Offa, and concludes with Albon's return from Rome to be
governor of Verulam; book II tells of the conversion of Albon by
Amphabell, with lengthy discourses on the Incarnation (191–295) and
the Passion (548–603), and of the martyrdom of Albon; book III, as in
St. Edmund a loose sequel, deals with the martyrdom of Amphabell,
after many conversions and many hortatory speeches displaying the
merits and benefits of declaring for Christ, and ends with a magnificent
prayer to Albon,

> O prothomartyr of Brutis Albion!

which finds a place in the equally magnificent Talbot Book of Hours.[45]
St. Albon has the heroic ambitions of *St. Edmund*, but its nationalism is
spurious, like its hero, and it reads more like an inflated version of the
orthodox type of legend than a genuine legend-epic. Though it has
loftiness and dignity, moments of fine feelings and pathos—like the
parting of Albon and Amphabell in II,751–817, Albon setting his
master on his way while he returns to face his accusers—and vivid
touches,

> Aboute the martyr they wente busylye
> Lyke wodemen upon hym gauryng,   (II,1061–2)

it is much less successful than *St. Edmund*, largely because of the great
weight of irrelevant material it is made to carry, as on knighthood, and
because of the length of the speeches in books II and III. These speeches,
though apt in themselves, are so long that all narrative progress is
clogged, and, in the tortuous sequence of martyrs converting would-be
executioners converting lookers-on, it is difficult to remember who is
converted and who is not, and harder still to care. It is a perennial
problem for Lydgate, but here one for which he is too old and too
tired to provide a solution: he finds himself committed to narrative
and can organise no satisfactory substitute.

St. *Albon* is also more pretentious than its predecessor, with more
Latinity, more classical allusion and astronomy,[46] a *Verba translatoris*
exlaiming upon the idolatry of the people, rather as in the *Clerk's
Tale* (II,1717–72), and a seasons-description of perfectly fatuous inap-
propriateness (II,856–69), introducing as it does the siege of Albon in
his house. There is also a repetitiveness so limp and so pointless as to be
noticeable even in Lydgate (II,1630, 1634); another stanza repeats the
sense of the preceding one so closely that one would have thought it
was meant to cancel it (II,1696, 1703). But there is a spurious ending in

the 1534 St. Alban's print, dealing with the suppression of heresy after the martyrdom of Amphabell, which, with its indigestible diction and chaotic metre,[47] makes Lydgate appear smooth, elegant, Chaucerian.

The *Life of Our Lady* needs no such props for our esteem. It is at once a confirmation of all that is most characteristic in Lydgate and at the same time an incomparable flowering of devotional poetry which stuns expectation. One can see how Lydgate could have come to have written it, but one could not have predicted that he was capable of it. It is certainly one of the finest pieces of religious poetry in English, and its present availability in one scarce and difficult edition[48] is a peculiar commentary on our attitudes to Lydgate. It was extremely widely read in its own day, judging from the large number of extant MSS. (forty-two, of which thirty-seven are more or less complete), more than for any other Lydgate poem except for freaks like the *Dietary*. It is not, however, an easy poem, and it does not fit the present category of 'legends' at all. Lydgate solves his narrative problem in this instance by throwing narrative overboard altogether, and the poem is less like a 'life' than an enormously prolonged Marian hymn.

There are a few references to the life of Our Lady in the Gospels, and apocryphal material dealing with her birth, childhood, the nativity and the assumption, though there is something of a lacuna for the period of Christ's life. The major events of her life were celebrated in the liturgical calendar and a great body of exegetical and homiletic material gathered around these, so that her 'life' is 'rather a discontinuous devotional progress from feast to feast, than a sequence of incidents with well-defined nexus'.[49] What has inspired Lydgate particularly, and provided the essential structure of his poem, is the *Meditationes Vitae Christi* of the pseudo-Bonaventure, a Franciscan work of the thirteenth century which is the major source of affective treatments of Christ and the Virgin in later medieval literature. Its passion and tenderness, its wealth of imagery, its whole mixture of prayer, biography, exegesis, and celebration is that of Lydgate's *Life*. Lydgate, however, despite the 5,932 lines of his poem, only gets as far as the Purification, and an explanation of Candlemas. It may have been that the apocryphal material from here to the Passion was too thin to sustain any sort of biographical treatment, or that he did not relish the prospect of the Passion. Whatever the reason, he seems to have left it a fragment, which in turn would argue against any form of patronage for the poem. It is traditionally associated with Henry V, because of a rubric in

MS.Cosin V.ii.16 at Durham (the best MS.), which states that it was compiled 'at the excitacion and styrryng of our worshipfull prince, kyng Harry the fifthe',[50] but there is no internal reference, such as Lydgate invariably makes in a major poem, to such patronage, and indeed, at the very place where one might expect such a reference, at the end of book I, he speaks of

> This first booke, compylede for thy sake.　(I,874)

Henry V may have suggested a *Life*, but not lived to see it. It is impossible, in any case, to date the poem accurately: Schick suggests 1409–11, the modern editors 1421–2, and Norton-Smith 'after 1434'. All the internal chronology and arrangements of the poem suggest that it was written for reading aloud to members of the monastic community. Especially towards the end, we can see how the material is promised and delivered for the appropriate liturgical feast.[51] The whole structure of the poem reflects the course of the liturgical year rather than any unified plan.

The *Life of Our Lady* is thus a compendium of Mariolatry rather than a life, a loosely strung series of episodes which are used as the occasion for meditation, exposition, panegyric, doctrinal exegesis and lyrical rhapsody. The account of the Nativity, for instance, in book III, is simple, tender and sensitive, with a deeply responsive sense, which we do not find elsewhere in Lydgate, of the human relationship of mother and child,[52] but it is accompanied by a full exploitation of the rich Old Testament imagery of messianic prophecy (III,680), and a lengthy treatment of the prophecies and miracles associated with the Nativity, drawn from an encyclopaedic variety of sources. There is also a Commendation of the Joy that Our Lady had in Christ's Nativity, with prolonged meditation on the suckling of the infant Jesus, which is at once touchingly homely and richly allegorical. The former quality is displayed in this passage:

> Glad mayste thou be, þat sauf hym luste to vouche,
> Withe his rounde softe lippes lyte,
> To have pleasaunce thy brestes for to touche,
> Only to souke thy blissede pappes white;
> And that hym luste so godely to delyte,
> For his playe to have so moche blisse,
> Evere among thy holy mouthe to kysse.
>
> And sodenly, with childely chere jocounde,

> Than anone thy white nek enbrace
> With his softe tendre armes rounde.
> And than at onys fallen on thy face,
> And of his eyne, fulfillede of all grace,
> A godely loke to thewarde enclyne;
> And so furthe his chekes ley by thyne,
>
> And withe his fyngres, mouthe and eyne touche;
> His smal pawmes on thy chekes layne
> His yong face betwene thy pappes couche,
> And holde hym stille, with all his besy payne,
> And grype hem faste with his handes twayne:
> For ther-in was his hevenly repaste,
> þi ȝunge sone, whan he list breke his faste. (III,1667–86)

The book ends with another Commendation of Our Lady, with much
of the familiar metaphor of apostrophe, though the best lines are not
always the most gorgeous:

> O fayre rose, O Rose of Jericho,
> That hast this day god and man also
> In Bedlem borne aȝen the gray morowe,
> The nyght to voyde of al our olde sorowe.
>
> (III,1761–4)

The Conception is similarly treated in book II, the familiar images of
sunbeams and dew (II,521, 551) blending into a passage in which the
richness of the Biblical imagery of the Conception is lavishly displayed.
There follows, however, a long defence of the doctrine of the Immacu-
late Conception, with endless lists of analogies, illustrations and proofs
of God's power, and many mechanical lines, ending with a somewhat
ingenuous reference to his

> ... ensamples, moo than two or three. ...
> Whiche, as me semyth, ought inow suffice. (II,901–3)

But there is vigour in his condemnation of those who impugn the
Virgin birth, and in his prayer that such a heretic may be bound with
Ixion in hell,

> And þat the claper of his distouned bell
> May cancre sone, I mene his fals tunge,
> Be dume for evere, and nevere to be ronge. (II,922–4)

Other major non-biographical passages include a Commendation of the name Ihesu (IV,157) and a praise of the meekness of Our Lady (V,337). The last three books of the six into which the *Life* is divided are, however, much shorter than the first three, arguing some decline in the impetus of the work, just as in the *Fall*. The riches of the first three books, by contrast, are inexhaustible. Book II opens with the debate of the Four Daughters of God, and ends with an invocation to Mary (these are scattered everywhere), preceded by a more personal passage in which he confesses his own incompetence and laments the death of Chaucer, in terms that suggest that it was a fairly recent event:

> Wherefore no wondre, tho[w] my hert pleyne
> Upon his dethe, and for sorowe blede
> For want of hym, nowe in my grete nede
> That shulde, alas, conveye and directe
> And with his supporte amende eke and corecte
>
> The wronge traces of my rude penne
> There as I erre and goo not lyne-right.
> But for that he ne may not me kenne,
> I can no more, but with all my myght,
> With all myne hert and myne inwarde sight,
> Pray for hym that liethe nowe in his cheste
> To god above, to yeve his saule goode reste.
>
> (II, 1644–55)

(The 'nowe' of line 1654 may be construed as an argument for an early date for the *Life*.) In the middle of book II, prompted by Bernard's confession of unworthiness to describe the Anunciation, there is a passage of profound self-abasement which has an intensity worlds away from the conventional formulae of the *Testament* (II,413). This devotional intensity is displayed also towards the end of book I, in a formally developed series of benedictions,

> And blisset was the paleys and the house. . . .
> And blisset was the worthy table riche. . . .
>
> (I,834, 841)

and topics of eulogy,

> O who can telle thy holy slepes softe
> With god alwaye full in thy memorye?
>
> (I,862–3)

The best writing in the *Life* is certainly in these more formal passages, and above all in the opening of book I, derived from Alexander Neckam's commentary on the *Canticles*, where the star-prologue and the flower-prologue, followed by the image of Mary's birth as the dawning of day upon the world's night, offer a richly evocative exploitation of traditional imagery. The laud of *stella maris* is especially effective, with subtle playing on the sense of 'star' and a cunning move from the conventional grief of the opening lines,

> O thoughtfull herte, plunged in distresse
> With slombre of slouthe, this long wynters nyght. . . .

which is at once the night of the day, the night of the world and the night of the soul, to a triumphant devotion as the meaning of the day-star grows brighter:

> For this of Jacob is the fayrest sterre
> That undir wawes nevere dothe declyne,
> Whose course is not undir the clyptyke lyne
> But ever yliche of beaute may be sene
> Amyddes the arke of our merydyne,
>
> And driethe up the bitter teres wete
> Of Aurora aftir the mourwen gray
> That she in wepyng dothe on floures flete
> In listy Aprill and in fresshe May;
> And causith phebus, the bright somers day,
> With his golde wayne, bournede bright and fayre,
> T'enchase the miste of our cloudy ayre;
>
> For this is the sterre that bare the bright sonne
> Which holdyth the septre of Juda in his hande,
> Whose stremes been oute of Jesse ronne
> To shede hir lyght bothe on see and lande,
> Whose gladde beamys without eclypsyng stonde
> Estwarde to us in the orient full shene,
> With light of grace to voiden all our tene.   (I,31–49)

The technical secret of this is the way in which Lydgate is prepared to disregard the stanza altogether, running on freely and avoiding the usual pressures to pad, but there is something far beyond this in the transfiguring effect of his work on traditional astronomical and seasons material, and the blending of the liturgical and the literary into a luminous rhetoric. This surely is one of the high points in English religious writing.

Notes to Chapter Nine

1 1413-14, according to Norton-Smith (*Lydgate: Poems*, p. 151), whose account of this excellent poem can be left to speak for it.

2 E.g. 'Dan Jon Gaytryge's Sermon', in *Religious Pieces in Prose and Verse* (Thornton MS.), ed. G. G. Perry (EETS,OS 26,1889), a translation of the Latin of archbishop Thoresby, which appears elsewhere as the *Lay Folks' Catechism* (ed. T. F. Simmons and H. E. Nolloth, EETS,OS 118,1901). See G. R. Owst, *Preaching in Medieval England* (Cambridge 1926), chap. VII.

3 'St. Bernard's Lamentation on the Passion', in *Minor Poems of the Vernon MS.*, Part I, ed. C. Horstmann (EETS,OS 98,1892), p. 298.

4 *Ed. cit.*, pp. 355-6.

5 See above, p. 162.

6 Line 469: in *Minor Poems of the Vernon MS.*, Part II, ed. F. J. Furnivall (EETS,OS 117,1901), p. 493.

7 Owst, *Preaching in Medieval England*, chap. IV.

8 See C. Wordsworth and H. Littlehales, *The Old Service-books of the English Church* (Antiquary's Books, London 1904), pp. 50-6.

9 See above, p. 31.

10 For this and other texts of Latin hymns referred to, see *Analecta Hymnica Medii Aevi*, ed. Dreves, etc., 55 vols. (Leipzig 1886-1922), and *Hymni Latini Medii Aevii*, ed. F. J. Mone, 3 vols. (Freiburg, 1853-5). *Vexilla regis*, Dreves, II,45.

11 *Religious Lyrics of the XIVth century*, ed. C. Brown (Oxford 1924, 2nd ed., 1952), p. 16.

12 i.e. as distinct from the Ambrosian hymn (quatrains of iambic dimeter without rhyme).

13 F. J. E. Raby, *Christian-Latin Poetry in the Middle Ages* (Oxford 1927, 2nd ed., 1953), p. 106.

14 *Religious Lyrics of the XIVth century*, nos. 12, 38, 51, 69, 117.

15 See above, p. 44.

16 It is stressed by Norton-Smith in his excellent brief account of Aureate Diction (*op. cit.*, pp. 192-5).

17 *Religious Lyrics of the XIVth century*, p. 112.

18 See above, p. 182; also Rosemary Woolf, *English Religious Lyric*, pp. 196-210.

19 As in the edition of the *Two Nightingale Poems* by O. Glauning (EETS,ES 80,1900).

20 Essay on the Lydgate canon, in *Minor Poems*, I, pp. xxxiii-iv.

21 Quoted in the notes to Norton-Smith's edition of the poem (*op. cit.*, p. 143), which contain a wealth of illustrative material.

22 *Amoryus and Cleopes*, 2194: in Metham's *Works*, ed. Hardin Craig (EETS, OS 132,1916), p. 80. See the useful note by Isabel Hyde, 'Lydgate's "Halff Chongyd Latyne": an Illustration', in *MLN*, LXX (1955),252–4.

23 There are convenient short accounts in Raby, *Christian-Latin Poetry*, pp. 365–75; and in *Medieval English Lyrics*, ed. R. T. Davies (London 1963), pp. 371–8.

24 See the articles in the *Bulletin* of the Metropolitan Museum of Art (New York), vol. XVI, no. 4 (1957).

25 *Religious Lyrics of the XVth century*, no. 24, lines 25–36.

26 E.g. in Mone, nos. 483–95; in Brown, *Religious Lyrics of the XVth century*, nos. 23–9.

27 *Religious Lyrics of the XVth century*, no. 28, lines 49–52.

28 In Mone, no. 460; another version, no. 454.

29 W. O. Wehrle (*The Macaronic Hymn Tradition in Medieval English Literature*, Washington, D.C. 1933) speaks of this as 'a new type in the macaronic tradition' (p. 139).

30 E.g. in Mone, nos. 392–403; *Religious Lyrics of the XIVth century*, ed. Brown, no. 131; *Religious Lyrics of the XVth century*, ed. Brown, no. 15.

31 See above, p. 168.

32 See above, p. 183.

33 See above, p. 164.

34 See above, p. 31.

35 See above, p. 181.

36 *St. George*, 33–42, in *The South English Legendary*, ed. Charlotte d'Evelyn and Anna J. Mill (EETS 235,1956), p. 157.

37 Printed in *Altenglische Legenden (Neue Folge)*, ed. C. Horstmann (Heilbronn 1881), pp. 225–35.

38 With again some reference to 'portreture' (22).

39 See above, p. 73.

40 See above, p. 26.

41 An influential emotive source for Lydgate's advocacy of peace.

42 For examples, see I,396, 541, 547, 711, 830.

43 For examples, see II,274, 309; I,655, 722.

44 Amundsham's *Annals of St. Albans* (ed. H. T. Riley, Rolls series, 1870–1), II,256,lxiii.

45 MS. 40–1950 (dated 1424) in the Fitzwilliam Museum, Cambridge. The first five stanzas (III,1696–1730) appear, as a later addition, on f. 135a. This Book of Hours is associated with John Talbot, earl of Shrewsbury, and with his wife, Margaret Beauchamp, daughter of the earl of Warwick. The latter commissioned Lydgate's *Guy of Warwick*, and the insertion of the

prayer is a sign of her continued interest in Lydgate's work. See the *Index of Middle English Verse, Supplement,* p. 278.

46 For examples, see I,225, 256, 500; II,765; III,457; II,844.

47 See above, p. 60.

48 That of J. Lauritis, R. Klinefelter and V. Gallagher, *Duquesne Studies, Philological Series,* 2 (Pittsburgh 1961).

49 The quotation is from the introduction (p. 5) to the edition of the *Life* by Simon Quinlan (London diss. 1957, unpublished), which I have found extremely helpful.

50 Ed. Lauritis, etc., p. 240.

51 E.g. V,456, 606; VI,204.

52 III,200. Compare the account of the Circumcision, IV,29.

CHAPTER TEN

Conclusion

Lydgate spent his last years, from about 1433 onwards, in the abbey at Bury. For some years he remained busy, completing the translation of the *Fall of Princes*, and executing various commissions, such as the *Life of St. Albon* for abbot Whethamstede. But in the 1440s the pace of production, not surprisingly, since Lydgate was now over seventy, slackened, and there are very few pieces which can be confidently ascribed to this period. Perhaps some of those, such as the *De Profundis*, in which he speaks at more than usual length about his age and infirmity, and where the verse is more than usually enfeebled, were written at this time. However, Lydgate did not lose contact entirely with the larger world, and he was asked to provide verses to accompany the street-pageants at *Queen Margaret's Entry into London*[1] in 1445. In form, these verses resemble those written for Henry VI's entry in 1432, though the pageants themselves, for which Lydgate may again have been partly responsible, are more religious, less mythological, in character. Someone clearly remembered the successes of Lydgate's laureate days, and it may have been Suffolk, who certainly knew Lydgate, particularly through his wife Alice,[2] and who was the chief architect in the arrangements for the marriage of Henry VI and Margaret of Anjou. Lydgate could have been in quite recent contact with Suffolk and the court at Windsor: Stow has preserved for us in MS.Add. 29729 a *Letter to Lydgate* by Benedict Burgh, written in the early 1440s, which is clearly an attempt by the ambitious cleric-poet to make Lydgate's acquaintance. It is a fulsome tribute to the master—

> A benedicite!
> Maister Lidgate, what man be ye. . . .
> Ye be the flowre and tresure of poise—[3]

full of praise for his learning, and interesting for the dogged imitation of Lydgate's more pretentious style. Stow adds a marginal comment:

'written by Mas Burgh in þe Prays of John Lidgate . . . boothe dwelyng at Windsor'.

On the whole, though, there is remarkably little response in these later years to the public events of the day, nothing, for instance, on the sensational trial for witchcraft of Eleanor Cobham, duchess of Gloucester, in 1441, nor on the death of Humphrey himself at Lydgate's own abbey in 1447, with all its shadowy circumstance. Both provided apt themes for commentators in the *De Casibus* tradition, and there is an *Epitaphium Ducis Gloucestrie* which was long attributed to Lydgate.[4] It is not his, however. Lydgate was very old, no longer spurred by the desire for fame or patronage, nor indeed by the need for money, which seems to have been so pressing at earlier stages in his career, for in 1439 Lydgate received the first payment of an annual grant of 10 marks from the customs at Ipswich, the grant being cancelled in the following year in favour of an identical one from the proceeds of farm-rents in Norfolk and Suffolk.[5] The records for the following years are not complete, but sufficient to make it probable that Lydgate went on receiving the annuity, a substantial sum in its day, regularly for the rest of his life. One would like to think that the grant, which came from Crown revenue, was the result of Humphrey's efforts to make some belated recognition of Lydgate's work on the *Fall*, but it is more likely that Suffolk was the instrument. His name actually appears in the record of a petition presented by Lydgate in 1441.[6] Payment of the grant ceased after the record of payment in Michaelmas (September 29th), 1449, suggesting that Lydgate died in the course of the year following. John Metham, the East Anglian poet (*mirabilis*) who has already been mentioned as an admirer of Lydgate, seems to refer to Lydgate as already dead in a tribute in *Amoryus and Cleopes*, written, he tells us, in 1449[7]:

> Eke Jon Lydgate, sumtyme monke of Byry,
> Hys bokys endytyd with termys of retoryk
> And halff chongyd Latyne, with conseytys of poetry
> And craffty imagynacionys of thingys fantastyk.[8]

This would place Lydgate's death in the last quarter of 1449.

There is one work that it seems appropriate to discuss in an account of Lydgate's last years, and that is the *Testament*, though it was not necessarily written during this period, any more than Chaucer's *Retraction* was dictated on his death-bed. The poem was popular in the fifteenth century, being extant in fourteen MSS. and one early print, and it remains one of Lydgate's best-liked poems, chiefly, one assumes, because it purports to be directly 'autobiographical'. It is in five sections, alternately ballade and rhyme-royal. The first is a meditation on the name of Jesus, ending with a prayer for his help as we draw toward death,

> Among other, I, that am falle in age,
> Gretly feblysshed of old infirmite.   (197–8)

The poet proposes to make his testament and confession, and in the second part meditates on the season of spring,

> The honysoucle, the fresshe primerolles,
> Ther leves splaye at Phebus uprysyng,
> Th'amerous foules with motytes and carolles
> Salue this sesoun every morwenyng,   (283–6)

and how, with its growth and joy, its varying sun and storms, it is an apt emblem of the wildness and uncertainty of childhood. Of his own wildness he will speak, but first he needs to pray for mercy for his misdeeds:

> I fele myn herte brotel and roynous,
> Nat purified, Jesu therin to reste;
> But as a carpentere cometh to a broken hous,
> Or an artificer repareth a reven cheste,
> So thou, Jesu, of crafty men the best,
> Repare my thought, broke with mysgovernaunce,
> Visite my soule, my herte of stele to breste,
> Graunt or I deye shryfte, hosel, repentaunce.   (551–8)

This is part III; in the fourth part he describes his wild and wanton childhood, how he hated school, and was always playing truant,

> Ran into gardeynes, apples ther I stall,
> To gadre frutes, spared nedir hegge nor wall,
> To plukke grapes in other mennes vynes
> Was more redy, than for to sey matynes . .
> Redier cheri-stones for to telle
> Than gon to chirche, or here the sacryng-belle.
>   (638–48)

There are many such lively details, an encyclopaedia, in fact, of childish indiscretions, designed to touch everyone somewhere, and the account

20

of the sins he went on committing after making his profession is similarly comprehensive. But at the age of fifteen, walking in the cloister, he came upon an image of the crucifix, with the word *Vide* upon it, which he suddenly understood,[9] and was moved to write the remembrance of Christ's passion,

> Beholde, O man! lyft up thyn eye, and see
> What mortall peyne I suffre for thi trespace. . . .   (754-5)

This forms the last section of the poem, ending, after all the Cross's pity and terror, with the comradely exhortation of the well-known last stanza:

> Tarye no lenger toward thyn herytage,
> Hast on thy weye and be of ryght good chere,
> Go eche day onward on thy pylgrymage,
> Thynke howe short tyme thou hast abyden here;
> Thy place is bygged above the sterres clere,
> Noon erthly palys wrought in so statly wyse.
> Kome on, my frend, my brother most entere!
> For the I offered my blood in sacryfice!   (890-7)

There is much in the *Testament* that is familiar, both in the implacable earnestness of tone and in the rhetorical detail, like the ornamental spring-description and the elaboration of the season's contraries (346-94). Like most of Lydgate, too, the language will not sustain a great deal of close attention, though the larger patterns are impressive, particularly the five-part structure, with its alternation of liturgical and personal styles. The modern reader will be immediately attracted to the personal passages, for their authenticity and realism, and rightly so, for they are well done, with crisp, well-chosen and unusually concrete detail, but the material is of course conventional, a hard-working conflation of the follies of youth: the purpose is exemplary, and the authenticity is that of art not nature. Having recognised this, the reader will perhaps pass on from these essentially 'easy' passages to admire the solemn and evocative rhetoric of the prayers, and particularly of Christ's address from the Cross, and the imposing consonance of the whole.

It would be pleasing to end here, but the place of honour must be occupied by a work as nearly worthless as any that Lydgate penned, an incomplete translation of the *Secreta Secretorum* which is certainly his last poem. The *Secreta* was one of the most popular and characteristic compilations of the Middle Ages, combining politico-moral instruction with much useful information, especially on medical matters. The original collection was made in Syriac in the eighth century from various sources, including Greek ones, and purported to be advice sent by Aristotle to his pupil Alexander. A translation was made into Arabic, and further translations from Arabic into Latin by John of Spain in the mid-twelfth century and by Philip of Tripoli for Guido, bishop of Valence, about 1230. All the translations add material freely, and there are many vernacular versions, including at least eight in English prose in the fifteenth century.[10] Ægidio Colonna's *De Regimine Principum* is based upon the *Secreta*, and Hoccleve uses both works in his *Regement*. The *Secreta* was still widely known in the sixteenth century.

Of the 2730 lines of the free English verse paraphrase known as the *Secrees of the Old Philisoffres*, the first 1491 are by Lydgate, the rest by the continuator, Benedict Burgh, who was asked to complete it by Henry VI. Lydgate has 735 lines of introductory material—a confused and clumsy conflation of earlier prologues, with some duplicated material[11]—followed by collections of wise laws relating to liberality in princes, an account of the elixir, further accounts of how a king should be peaceable, pious, chaste, honest, and—for the medical detail —well looked after by his physicians. There follows, without transition, description of the four seasons of the year, and appropriate moralisation of man's life. Here Lydgate broke off, responding as it were to the cue for a rhetorical gesture, for the last stanza ends with a comparison of winter with age, the inevitable cycle of the seasons with man's life:

> Deth al consumyth, which may nat be denyed.

Here, we are led to believe, the pen slipped limply from his fingers, and the aged monk slumped to the floor, or, as the rubric (perhaps by Burgh) puts it: 'Here deyed this translator and noble poete'. The gesture, the adherence to convention, is perfect, though it needed Burgh's connivance to rearrange the stanzas and make them fit.

Burgh would not have found this very difficult, since what we have in the *Secrees* is obviously fragments of a translation, perhaps done at different times, and brought together after Lydgate's death. At some points there is enormously optimistic expansion, as if the translation will go on for ever, as in the praise of Guido, bishop of Valence, which Lydgate expands from seventeen words to seventy lines (372–441), with the full apparatus of excellence-topics. At other times there is an aphoristic compression in which a whole chapter of the French original

20*

goes into one stanza.[12] Sometimes Lydgate translates the same bit over
again, while sometimes he starts (736) and restarts (792) in senile confusion. Lines 974–1029, on the elixir, have nothing at all to do with
what comes before or after: they look like an independent extract
which Burgh inserted here so that he could get the seasons-passages in
the right place. Once or twice the work comes to life briefly, when the
sap of Chaucer flows once more through Lydgate's hardened arteries,
as in the spring-description,

> So can nature prikke them in ther corage,   (1327)

or when his mind is diverted into older, familiar channels and he can
exploit again the images of duplicity (876–89) which had served him so
well for fifty years. But elsewhere individual stanzas are virtually unintelligible (813–19), syntax and metre chaotic, and rhyme, usually a
strong point with Lydgate, feeble. The advice to rulers, in which
Schirmer looks to find Lydgate's political testament, is nothing of the
sort, but a slack and incoherent sprawl of commonplaces. Only a poet
like Burgh could have had the ambition of basking in its reflected
glory, even to the extent—dog-like fidelity could go no further—of
imitating its incoherence.

There could hardly be a worse note on which to end, but perhaps
the *Secrees* will serve as a reminder that it is not wise to make extravagant claims for Lydgate as a poet—and I hope that an enthusiasm for
neglected causes will not have led me into folly. Indeed, in most of the
senses in which we ordinarily understand the word, Lydgate is not a
poet at all, for he can never, even at his best, rivet us with the uniqueness of his language, or enrich our awareness of words. But this in itself
would only argue for a broader definition of what we mean by poetry,
to include the practice of 'crafty' rhetoric, for it is essentially as a professional craftsman and rhetorician that we should see Lydgate. Here
is the value that he has for us; for, by the very bulk of his work and
the massive centralness of his position, he forces us to re-examine our
notions of medieval poetry, or poetry itself, and to modify easy assumptions about its nature. Sometimes the quality of his writing does not
make this a very valuable exercise in itself, and, having established the
nature of a tradition, one has to admit that Lydgate does not represent
it at its best. This is why it is useful to regard him as a type of the Middle
Ages, an introduction to medieval literature, presenting its themes and
methods in their basic form, without the complications of experiment,

ambiguity, or even, sometimes, of individual thought. The very mechanical nature of his processes is thus often invaluable for understanding those like Chaucer who used them more freely and independently, and every reader of medieval literature should therefore be able to *use* Lydgate in this way. It follows from this that we do great wrong to regard Lydgate as anything but typical of his age. His roots are deep in the medieval tradition, he is impregnably medieval, and there is in his work no sign of movement toward the Renaissance, except in so far as he responds fitfully to the prompting of his sources. With all this said, none of it very exciting for those who think that understanding is not enough, it should be added that at his best—and it is a rare best only in the context of his enormous output—in parts of the *Troy Book*, the *Fall of Princes*, the *Life of Our Lady*, and in some of the shorter courtly and religious pieces, his eloquence can transcend its own journeyman professionalism and, rising to its theme, can speak to us with sense and sonority across the chasm that the passage of years has opened up.

Notes to Chapter Ten

1 These verses are not printed by MacCracken in his edition of the *Minor Poems*, since they were not discovered until later (see his Introduction, p. xl). They are edited from MS.Harley 3869 by Carleton Brown in *MLR*, VII (1912),225–34. See Schirmer, *John Lydgate*, pp. 242–5.

2 See above, p. 162.

3 Lines 34–5, 39: the *Letter* is printed by Hammond, *Chaucer to Surrey*, pp. 189–90.

4 It is printed in *Historical Poems of the XIVth and XVth centuries*, ed. Robbins, p. 180.

5 'de exitibus et proficuis de alba firma et feodo vulgariter nuncupato Waytefee, in Comitatibus Norffolcie et Suffolcie', *Secrees*, ed. Steele, p. xxv. Steele translates this 'from the proceeds of the farm of Waytefee', which is ridiculous. 'Waytefee', as the context suggests, is the English translation of the technical term 'alba firma' (*blanche ferme* in French and, later, in English), meaning 'quit-rent' (quit=whyte=wayte), nominal rent paid by farm-tenants in lieu of services.

6 For all these documents, see *Secrees*, ed. Steele, pp. xxiv–xxx.

7 'the sevyn and twenty .xxvii. yere of the sext kyng Henry' (2176), i.e. 1 Sept., 1448 to 31 Aug., 1449, to be precise, but Metham is probably using the regnal dates, as was common, to refer to the calendar year 1449.

8 Lines 2192–5, in *Works*, ed. Hardin Craig, p. 80.

9 A conventional motif of spiritual autobiography and saints' lives, a metaphor

of psychological change or 'conversion', appropriate also to pictorial purposes, as in the Pisanello *St. Eustace* or the German *Conversion of St. Hubert*, both in the National Gallery, London.

10 See Schirmer, *John Lydgate*, p. 248; *Three Prose Versions of the Secreta Secretorum*, ed. R. Steele (EETS,ES 74,1898); M. Manzalaoui, 'The *Secreta Secretorum*: The mediaeval European version of "Kĭtab Sirr-ul-Aṣrar",' *Bulletin of the Faculty of Arts, Alexandria University*, vol. XV(1961), pp. 83–107 (esp. pp. 103–5).

11 'There remain', says Manzalaoui, 'signs of Lydgate's having used two Latin MS. versions, and of his bewilderment at this' (*op. cit.*, p. 96).

12 E.g. 1030, 1058, 1163.

Select Bibliography

I EDITIONS

St. Edmund and Fremund, ed. C. Horstmann, in *Altenglische Legenden* (Heilbronn 1881), pp. 376–445

St. Albon and Amphabel, ed. C. Horstmann, in *Festschrift der Realschule zu Berlin* (1882), pp. 103–95

The Temple of Glas, ed. J. Schick, EETS,ES 60 (1891). A more recent text is available in *John Lydgate: Poems*, ed. Norton-Smith (q.v.)

Lydgate and Burgh's *Secrees of old Philisoffres*, ed. R. Steele, EETS,ES 66 (1894)

Deguileville's *Pilgrimage of the Life of Man*, ed. F. J. Furnivall and Katherine B. Locock, EETS,ES 77,83,92 (1899–1904)

Two Nightingale Poems, ed. O. Glauning, EETS,ES 80 (1900). Only one is Lydgate's: a more recent text is available in *Minor Poems*, ed. MacCracken (q.v.)

Reason and Sensuality, ed. E. Sieper, EETS,ES 84,89 (1901–3)

Troy Book, ed. H. Bergen, EETS,ES 97,103,106,126 (1906–20)

Minor Poems, ed. H. N. MacCracken (Part I, Religious Poems; Part 2, Secular Poems), EETS,ES 107, OS 192 (1910, 1934)

Siege of Thebes, ed. A. Erdmann and E. Ekwall, EETS,ES 108,125 (1911, 1920)

Fall of Princes, ed. H. Bergen, EETS,ES 121–4 (1918–19)

The Dance of Death, ed. Florence Warren and Beatrice White, EETS,OS 181 (1931). Another text in Hammond (q.v.)

The Life of Our Lady, ed. J. Lauritis, R. Klinefelter, and V. Gallagher, *Duquesne Studies, Philological Series*, no. 2 (Pittsburgh 1961)

2 SELECTIONS

English Verse between Chaucer and Surrey, ed. Eleanor P. Hammond (Duke University Press, Durham, N. Carolina, 1927), pp. 77–187. With full apparatus

John Lydgate: Poems, ed. J. Norton-Smith (*Clarendon Mediaeval and Tudor Series*, Oxford 1966). With full apparatus

3 GENERAL WORKS

H. S. Bennett, *Chaucer and the Fifteenth Century* (Oxford 1947)

A. Brusendorff, *The Chaucer Tradition* (Copenhagen 1925)

W. Farnham, *The Medieval Heritage of Elizabethan Tragedy* (Oxford 1936)

D. Knowles, *The Religious Orders in England*, vol. II (Cambridge 1955)

C. S. Lewis, *The Allegory of Love* (Oxford 1936)

J. C. Mendenhall, *Aureate Terms* (University of Pennsylvania, Phil. 1919)

D. Pearsall, 'The English Chaucerians', in *Chaucer and Chaucerians*, ed. D. S. Brewer (London 1966), pp. 201–39

W. F. Schirmer, *Der englische Frühhumanismus* (Tübingen 1963)

R. Weiss, *Humanism in England during the 15th century* (2nd ed., Oxford 1957)

G. Wickham, *Early English Stages 1300–1660*, vol. I: 1300–1576 (London 1959)

Rosemary Woolf, *The English Religious Lyric in the Middle Ages* (Oxford 1968)

4 SPECIAL STUDIES, AND ARTICLES ON PARTICULAR TOPICS

R. W. Ayers, 'Medieval History, Moral Purpose, and the Structure of Lydgate's *Siege of Thebes*', *PMLA*, LXXII(1958),463–74

Eleanor P. Hammond, 'Poet and Patron in the *Fall of Princes*', *Anglia*, XXXVIII (1920),121–36

Eleanor P. Hammond, 'The 9-syllabled Pentameter line in some post Chaucerian manuscripts', *Modern Philology*, XXIII(1925–6),129–52

Eleanor P. Hammond, 'Lydgate and Coluccio Salutati', *Modern Philology*, XXV (1927),49–57

Isabel Hyde, 'Lydgate's "Halff Chongyd Latyne": an Illustration', *Modern Language Notes*, LXX(1955),252–4

C. S. Lewis, 'The Fifteenth Century Heroic Line', *Essays and Studies*, XXIV (1938),28–41

J. W. McKenna, 'Henry VI of England and the Dual Monarchy: Aspects of Royal Political Propaganda', *Journal of the Warburg and Courtauld Institutes*, XXVIII(1965),145–62

J. Norton-Smith, 'Lydgate's Changes in the *Temple of Glas*', *Medium Aevum*, XXVII(1958),166–72

J. Norton-Smith, 'Lydgate's Metaphors', *English Studies*, XLII(1961),90–3

F. Pyle, 'The Pedigree of Lydgate's Heroic Line', *Hermathena*, XXV(1937), 26–59

A. Renoir, 'The Binding Knot: three uses of one image in Lydgate's poetry', *Neophilologus*, XLI(1957),202–4

A. Renoir, 'Attitudes towards Women in Lydgate's *Siege of Thebes*', *English Studies*, XLII(1961),1–14

A. Renoir, *The Poetry of John Lydgate* (London 1967)

W. F. Schirmer, *John Lydgate: a Study in the Culture of the XVth century* (originally published in German in 1952; English translation by Ann E. Keep, London 1961)

INDEX